Border

Books by Leon Metz

Border 1989
Desert Army: Fort Bliss on the Texas Border 1988
Turning Points in El Paso Texas 1985
Fort Bliss: An Illustrated History 1981
City at the Pass 1980
The Shooters 1976
Pat Garrett: The Story of a Western Lawman 1974
Dallas Stoudenmire: El Paso Marshal 1969
John Selman: Texas Gunfighter 1966

Border

The U.S.-Mexico Line

LEON C. METZ

TCU PRESS
Fort Worth, Texas

Published by Mangan Books
6245 Snowheights, El Paso, Texas 79912

Library of Congress Cataloging-in-Publication Data

Metz, Leon Claire
        Border: the U.S.-Mexico line.

        Bibliography: p.
        Includes index.
        1. United States — Boundaries — Mexico. 2.
Mexico —
Boundaries — United States. 3. Mexico-American
Border Region — History. I. Title.
F786.M55 1989   972'.1   89-60730
ISBN 0-930208-27-7

_____

Reprinted 2008

Library of Congress Cataloging-in-Publication Data

Metz, Leon Claire.
        Border : the U.S.-Mexico line / by Leon C. Metz.
        p. cm.
        Includes bibliographical references and index.
        ISBN 978-0-87565-364-8
        1. United States--Boundaries--Mexico. 2. Mexico--
Boundaries--United   States. 3. Mexican-American
Border Region--History. I. Title.

F786.M55 2008
972'.1--dc22

                            2007043789

TCU Press
P. O. Box 298300
Fort Worth, TX 76129
817.257.7822
http://prs.tcu.edu

To order books: 1.800.826.8911

Printed in Canada

Cover painting by Russell Waterhouse

To Doc Sonnichsen
who walked the extra mile

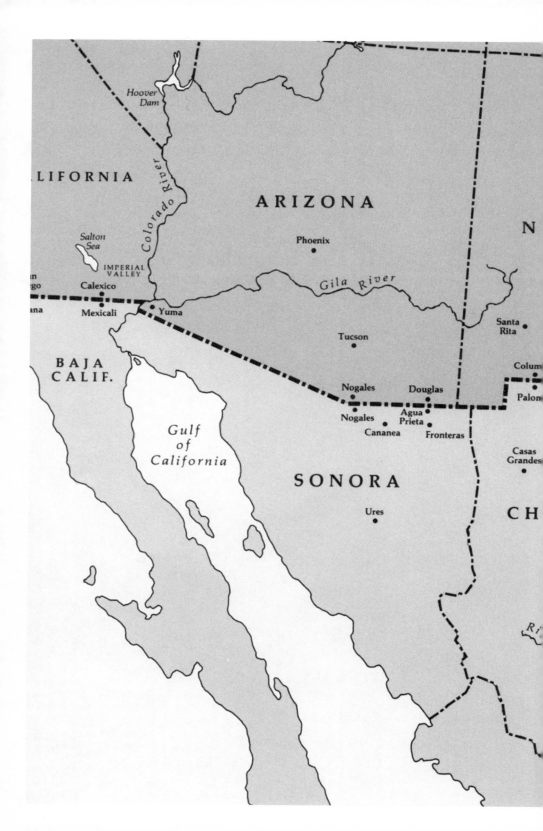

The American-Mexican border is a line
where north meets south – after a two hour wait.

*Mark Russell, at Discover El Paso
Banquet, Westin Paso del Norte Hotel.
October 30, 1986*

Official Length

The United States-Mexico border totals 1,951.36 official miles from the Gulf of Mexico to the Pacific. The Rio Grande portion consumes 1,253.69 miles. The land border from the Rio Grande to the Pacific is 697.67 miles, and that includes a brief stretch of Colorado river: 23.72 miles.

Author's Note

This is a chronicle of the Mexican border, the nearly two thousand mile international line between the United States and Mexico. It is a historical accounting described largely through the eyes and experiences of government agents, politicians, soldiers, revolutionaries, outlaws, Indians, engineers, immigrants, developers, illegal aliens, business people, and wayfarers looking for a job. What follows is essentially the untold story of lines drawn in water, sand and blood, of an intrepid, durable people, of a civilization whose ebb and flow of history is as significant as any in the world.

— LEON C. METZ

List of Maps

Contents

BOOK ONE

THE SURVEYS

Never in my whole life have I been
placed in so trying a position.

*John R. Bartlett to Secretary
of Interior Alexander H. Stuart, 1851*

1

To Establish a Border

ZACHARY TAYLOR was a great warrior, a sixty-one-year-old military tiger who defeated his enemies without rancor or bitterness. Fighting against the Shawnee leader Tecumseh during the War of 1812, he won national acclaim for his defense of Fort Harrison, Indiana. A quarter century later in 1835, he smashed the Florida Seminoles. Now his country was calling again, and what he helped accomplish would alter the world's future history. A fledgling nation would leapfrog a continent, double its territory, look out across two oceans, and establish a Mexican border so far south and west as to be almost undreamed of.

He hardly looked the part of a conqueror. He had no easy grace, was uncomfortable around academics, and if some hearty meals were giving him the beginnings of a notable paunch, he at least carried it well. Until lately his had been a muscular and stocky frame held together by a pig iron constitution. The newspapers called him "Old Rough and Ready," and the sobriquet fit like his scuffy leather boots and his slovenly, mismatched uniform. Time had now banked some of his fires. He could not straddle a horse as well as he used to, but along the Rio Grande in 1846 he was the human embodiment of Manifest Destiny. He believed in it, he fought for it, and like most Americans he had no doubt whatsoever that God had ordained it.

President James K. Polk, a shrewd, methodical and calculating man, brought Taylor out of near retirement with orders to station his forces where the new state of Texas could be defended and, incidentally, where Mexico could be attacked.

At issue was the right of Texas to be accepted by the American Union, to have the Rio Grande, and not the Nueces, acknowledged as the legitimate international border. Underlying these considerations lay additional Mexican fears. Just how far these hustling Yankees might eventually drive, and how much territory they might seize by right of possession from a Mexico struggling with enormous, complex internal problems – these were the real issues. For there was then a rowdy strain loose in American life. Men spoke with contempt about northern Mexico, as if the bronze-skinned people who lived there and spoke a funny language were not only inferior, but somehow trespassers.

Since its discovery by Europe, the struggle for North America had been one of enlarging boundaries at a neighbor's expense. Following a successful Revolutionary War, the Americans rolled across the Appalachians and pulled up at the Mississippi, an easily identified line not readily mistaken for anything other than a boundary. However, to the south, the borders were not so clear. The Spanish controlled Florida, a disputed strip extending from the present state of Florida to the Mississippi River.

Unlike the United States, which had difficulty restraining its pioneers from settling on vacant lands, the Spanish had difficulty prodding their European and Mexican populations out of the cities. The Americans were farmers who raised their own food, whereas the Mexicans were villagers who imported much of what they consumed. A dwindling population in Spain during the 17th century meant fewer peasants for North America. Those who arrived, as well as those already in Mexico, avoided the borderlands because of Comanches, Apaches, Pueblos and other Indians. They were so far from civilization that even God was forced to send tracers. The region now known as the southwestern United States in particular offered little economic opportunity.

Since the Spanish did not conquer the New World just to be mere tillers of the soil, the frontier generally moved north by acts of incorporation rather than colonization, the settlers preferring to mine precious minerals and ores rather than establish farms. Citizens lived in villages even when it meant near starvation. The countryside was abandoned to Indians, priests, a few soldiers and a scattering of *hacendados*.

Lands north of the present United States-Mexican border were forlorn and nearly uninhabitable hollow shells with random pueblos. Maps displayed the region as a desert. The land removed from Mexico by the American conquest of 1846-48 did not have as many Mexican citizens altogether as are presently enrolled at The University of Texas at El Paso (15,000 in 1989). Yet, Spain, which throughout its history had feared and hated foreigners, frequently with good reason, needed the territory as a barrier to American and European expansion. Spain spent millions maintaining forts and missions, to let the world know that a presence actually existed in this near vacuum. But flags, cannons, churches and a scattering of soldiers and priests could not substitute for Spanish-speaking colonists, people to plow and nourish the earth, to give the land a sense of cultural and ethnic continuity.

Americans took advantage of their expansionist opportunities. The slightly known, sprawling Louisiana Territory encompassed an area from the Mississippi River west to the Rocky Mountains and north to the vaguely identified Canadian border. The French under duress had ceded the region to Spain in 1762, but the Spanish could neither consolidate nor govern it. The Spaniards returned it to France in 1800 just as President Thomas Jefferson was reexamining his expansion options. He caught Napoleon short of finances, and purchased the unexplored territory for $15 million, three cents a square mile. Boundaries were obscure.

The Americans followed with an era of exploration. Lewis and Clark walked and canoed on a round trip from St. Louis to the Pacific, while Lieutenant Zebulon Montgomery Pike in 1806 allegedly sought the headwaters of the Red and Arkansas rivers, a region considered the United States-Mexican borderlands. However, the Spanish caught Pike surveying near the Rio Grande and understandably charged him with spying.

Both countries sparred over borders for the next decade, with Spain relinquishing the Floridas to the United States in 1819. This left only the Louisiana Purchase to be more precisely defined, a project Spain supported because it wanted a specific line beyond which Americans could not venture. Negotiators agreed on the Sabine River north to the

Red River, then west to the Arkansas River. The border followed the Arkansas to its headwaters in the Rocky Mountains.

Two years later, in 1821, Mexico won its independence from Spain. During the turmoil, President John Quincy Adams took advantage of Mexico's perpetual state of crisis and sent his minister, Joel Roberts Poinsett, to "establish a boundary which could be more easily defined . . . and mutually advantageous." He wanted to purchase the Mexican province of Texas.

The Mexicans outlasted Poinsett and Adams, as well as President Andrew Jackson who supported the same concept. But time favored the Americans. Texas achieved its independence from Mexico when Sam Houston's army defeated Mexican forces at San Jacinto and captured General (and President) Antonio López de Santa Anna. Santa Anna signed the Treaty of Velasco, and extended Texas boundaries to the Rio Grande. Santa Anna repudiated the treaty upon returning to Mexico, as did the Mexican Congress, doing so because the conflict was not over, and because Mexico recognized only the Nueces River as the legitimate Texas border. It flowed north of, and roughly parallel to the eastern portion of Rio Grande, its origins beginning near San Antonio and ending at the Gulf.

Manuel Eduardo de Gorostiza, the Mexican Centralist Party envoy, angrily warned Washington that a Texas incorporation into the Union might bring war. The United States therefore followed the lead of Great Britain and France in recognizing Texas as an independent nation.

Nine years later in 1845, President James K. Polk believed his government had been patient long enough. John Slidell, the United States minister to Mexico, tried negotiating with President José Joaquín de Herrera in an effort to ease the Texas annexation. Since the United States had long-standing financial claims against Mexico, Washington offered to accept the Nueces River as the Texas boundary if Mexico paid an accumulation of debts owed to the United States. If Mexico wanted released from these obligations, the United States would waive the liability *if* the Rio Grande to its source became the undisputed international border. Furthermore, Slidell was empowered to purchase New Mexico for $5 million, or offer $25 million for all lands north of a straight line drawn west of El Paso del Norte (now Ciudad Juarez) to the Pacific Coast.

President de Herrera refused Slidell an audience unless the Americans reconsidered their plans to annex Texas. The United States refused,

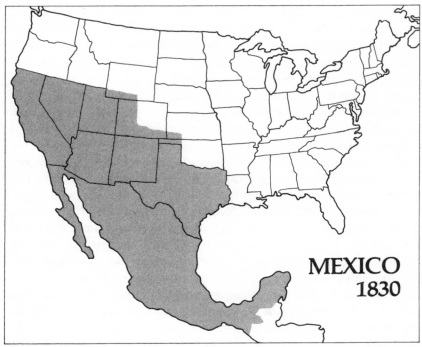

The United States and Mexico prior to Texas Independence and the Mexican War. Mexico in those days had a land mass nearly the same as the United States. At the end of the Mexican War in 1848 the Americans obtained territory (if most of Texas is counted) which today comprises all or parts of eight states. Mexico received $15 million for the annexed lands which comprised one million square miles.

and Mexico spurned the American commissioner. That rejection prepared the American conscience to acquire by force what it could not obtain by diplomatic channels.

The Union admitted Texas on December 29, 1845, and a month later General Zachary Taylor moved his army onto the disputed strip between the Nueces and the Rio Grande. On April 24, 1846, Mexico attacked with cavalry, inflicted sixteen casualties and gave President Polk an excuse for war. He would now settle the boundary question with gunpowder.

The Mexican War lasted two years. General Taylor drove south to capture Monterrey, Saltillo and Victoria. After waiting for the Mexicans to sue for peace, which they did not, he engaged General Santa

Anna in the Battle of Buena Vista when the American forces were disease-ridden, low on supplies and undermanned. Although the Americans unleashed a savage artillery bombardment, they were soon backing up, digging in and expecting to be overwhelmed. That final assault never came. Santa Anna declared himself the victor and returned to Mexico City to posture. In the meantime, with the rot of leadership extending from the top echelons to the ranks, his fighting forces disintegrated. The Mexican Army never again became a serious fighting threat.

The battle which Taylor never won, but for which he claimed victory, propelled the dour general on to the presidency of the United States.

On another front, General Stephen W. Kearny left Fort Leavenworth, Kansas, with 1,700 troops and marched southwest. After taking Santa Fe, his army continued to California and seized it too.

Forking south at Santa Fe, Colonel Alexander Doniphan and eight hundred Missouri farm boys drove toward El Paso del Norte, Chihuahua. During the Battle of Brazito, between present-day Las Cruces, New Mexico and El Paso, Texas, he routed a strong Mexican contingent. A couple of days after Christmas 1846, his army quietly occupied El Paso del Norte. Three months later he marched 240 miles south of the Rio Grande and captured Chihuahua City. Northern Mexico collapsed.[1]

Farther south, General Winfield Scott, a Polk political appointee, landed an army at Veracruz, fought to the portals of Mexico City and waited for the arrival of Nicholas P. Trist, chief clerk of the United States Department of State. Trist spoke fluent Spanish and had spent eight years as American consul in Havana. As a well-known man about Washington, he had married Thomas Jefferson's granddaughter and served briefly as Andrew Jackson's private secretary. While he possessed a genteel background with moderate expansionist views, he also had fragile feelings. He wrote letters about everything, could be long-winded to the point of distraction, and his tactlessness was surpassed only by his arrogance.

Trist negotiated with Santa Anna, whose strong point was an instinct for self-preservation. Santa Anna tendered the Nueces River as the Texas boundary, and also offered the northern portion of California beginning immediately after San Francisco. When these "concessions" reached Polk, the president blustered that Mexican obstinacy was compelling him to continue fighting.

Scott crunched inside the capital, and Santa Anna fled to Queretaro after ordering Manuel de la Peña, president of the Mexican Supreme Court, to take charge of the country. De la Peña did his duty, his first directive relieving Santa Anna of command.

Mexico's new leaders wanted an immediate treaty. The country wavered on anarchy. Powerful elements in Washington and Mexico called for American annexation of the entire nation. Mexico needed to meet the invaders' ultimatums and be rid of the occupying forces.

At the instigation of resident British and French diplomats, Trist and Mexican authorities met on February 2, 1848, in the village of Guadalupe Hidalgo, now inside Mexico City. A peace treaty followed, and ratifications were exchanged in Mexico on May 30. The Americans proclaimed it on July 4.

In less than one hundred years, the United States had expanded from a sliver of colonies hugging the Atlantic coast to a colossus with shores washed by two oceans. By treaty terms the Americans obtained Mexican territory (if most of Texas is counted) which today comprises all or parts of eight states. The land mass included roughly one-third of Mexico's entire country, a region nearly equal in size to the United States from the eastern seaboard to the Mississippi. No event, except for the Civil War, imparted to the country such development, wealth and change. Those states comprised one million square miles, and they included the future oil fields of Texas, the gold fields of California, and the incredibly diverse prairie, mineral, tourism and agricultural resources of the Southwest. Out of the war came American presidents and political shifts that the country might otherwise have missed, and it set the tone for the uneasy relations we still share with our southern neighbor. Mexico received $15 million for the annexed lands, and the United States assumed liability for claims held by American citizens against Mexico. Trist also bargained for Lower California but failed.

According to the Treaty of Guadalupe Hidalgo, the Rio Grande would form the United States-Mexico boundary from the Gulf to slightly north of El Paso del Norte. At that point, the border would extend west overland to a few miles south of the southernmost tip of the San Diego harbor. To define these frontiers, a boundary commissioner and a surveyor from each country would meet in San Diego within a year to survey and mark the international line from the Pacific to the Gulf of Mexico. Their compromises would become part of the treaty, and commissioner agreements would bind both nations.

The diplomats did not foresee faulty maps, niggardly politicians, hostile Indians, fluctuating rivers, dry water holes, towering mountains, awesome deserts, hordes of immigrants, impossible supply problems and argumentative, self-important commissioners. Reputations would be destroyed, diplomatic exchanges would irritate the two countries, the civilian and military members of the United States commission would quibble and obstruct each other, and partisan politics would lead to sectional strife. The Treaty of Guadalupe Hidalgo was an interesting case of sign now and worry later.[2]

A Commissioner Falls

THE MEXICAN BORDER had been defined on paper but now it had to be surveyed and marked. Considering the significance of the task, neither side should have economized on talent or money. As it turned out, Mexico sent men with strong engineering backgrounds but provided few expenses. The Americans were better off financially, but the officials chose politicians rather than technical men as commissioners.

Ambrose B. Sevier, Arkansas senator and chairman of the Foreign Relations Committee, was the initial Washington selection for American boundary commissioner. He died before the Senate confirmed him.

President Polk then turned to John B. Weller, a stocky, clean-shaven politician with an iron jaw, deep-set eyes and an orator's voice. After returning from the Mexican War, and failing to become governor of Ohio, Weller accepted the position of boundary commissioner on January 16, 1849. Andrew Belcher Gray signed on as surveyor, and Major William Emory was chief astronomer and head of the Topographical Scientific Corps.

Surveyor Andrew Gray was a twenty-nine-year-old Virginian who had assisted with the Republic of Texas-United States boundary surveys,

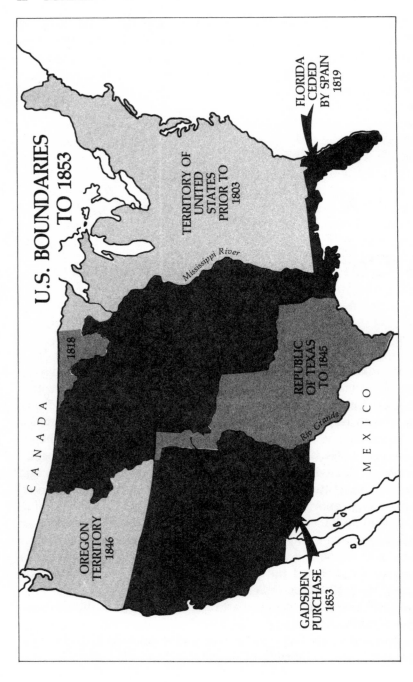

U.S. BOUNDARIES TO 1853

CANADA

OREGON TERRITORY 1846

1818

TERRITORY OF UNITED STATES PRIOR TO 1803

Mississippi River

FLORIDA CEDED BY SPAIN 1819

REPUBLIC OF TEXAS TO 1845

Rio Grande

GADSDEN PURCHASE 1853

MEXICO

the Mississippi River delta survey and the Keweenaw Peninsula of Michigan survey. He had ridden with the Texas Rangers. Gray had interests (as did practically everyone with the commission) in seeing a transcontinental railroad across the American Southwest, and he would be remembered as a controversial member of a very contentious group of boundary men.

Next in line, and the American team's most knowledgeable and experienced figure, was Major William Hemsley Emory, better known as "Bold Emory" to his 1831 classmates at West Point. Emory later admitted that Polk offered him the post of boundary commissioner, but wanted his resignation from the army. Emory refused and settled for being Weller's assistant.[1] As a brilliant mathematician, he held several positions during the boundary surveys such as chief astronomer and commander of the military escort. He had entered the topographical engineers as a young lieutenant in 1838, and from 1839 to 1842 had engineered harbor improvements along the Delaware River. After two years of similar tasks near Washington, D.C., Emory became principal assistant on the northeastern boundary survey between the United States and Canada. The British commissioner commended him for his winter accomplishments in the mountains separating the drainages of the St. Lawrence and the Atlantic seaboard. Emory also distinguished himself in the Mexican War, having gone to California with Kearny's Army of the West. Out of those frontier exposures came *Notes of A Military Reconnaissance.*[2]

Since boundary surveying required an expertise found in abundance only in the Army (West Point was primarily an engineering school), Emory picked his assistants from the military. These included lieutenants Amiel Weeks Whipple of Portsmouth, New Hampshire, and Edmund L. F. Hardcastle of Maryland.

Secretary of State James Buchanan cautioned Weller twice about his "highly responsible position," saying the actions and agreements of both commissioners would be as legally binding as original language inserted into the Hidalgo treaty. Weller's conduct should be characterized by "prudence, firmness and a conciliatory spirit." Buchanan said "the President would be gratified" if the commissioner took time to determine the feasibility of a road, a canal or a railroad near the border. However, Buchanan cautioned that the $50,000 appropriated by Congress was "limited to the expenses of running and marking the boundary." There would be no extra funds for additional tasks, nor would there be more monies if and when the allocation ran out. Weller was to keep precise records.[3]

While the government expected a dollar's worth of results for every fifty cents spent, the State Department promised that commissioner and surveyor salaries would either be set by Congress or "fixed by the President before departure."[4] But Congress did not adequately respond, nor could Polk, nor would the incoming Taylor. The new secretary of state, John M. Clayton, informed Weller that "compensation for your services as commissioner and for those of Mr. Gray as surveyor, cannot be lawfully paid" until Congress decides what the sum is supposed to be and appropriates the money. Meanwhile, Weller had completed his arrangements, withdrew $33,000 for expenses, and sailed for California by way of Panama during the first part of February 1849. Weller's appointment infuriated the Whig Party which like a political lemming was already marching to national suicide on the eve of its greatest triumph. The party elected war hero General Zachary Taylor as President, and denounced Weller as a "midnight appointee." It railed that the position should have remained vacant until March 4 when Taylor assumed office, and delegates denounced Weller's prompt departure as an attempt to get beyond recall by the incoming administration.

Emory crated his heavier instruments, placed them in care of Lieutenant Hardcastle and shipped them around Cape Horn. He and 105 soldiers, plus a large contingent of civilian employees, disembarked at Panama, crossed the isthmus and planned to catch a ship for California, normally a quicker procedure than traveling around South America.

All hopes for arriving in San Diego prior to May 30, 1849, the treaty deadline for beginning the survey, went astray when the commissioner's party collided in Panama with four thousand impatient forty-niners struggling to reach California. Weller fretted about the delay from March until May, writing indignant letters to United States Consul William Nelson. Weller's nagging irritated Nelson, and the consul finally located a berth on the *Panama*, now rounding the tip of South America with the commission equipment.

When Weller sailed from Panama, he left part of his work force behind due to insufficient room on ship. Lieutenant Whipple complained about rations, pay and shipping costs, details for which Weller promised to assign a quartermaster but neglected to do so. Whipple's smoldering letters criticized Nelson until the consul obtained a ship's berth for Whipple on the *Oregon*, and happily watched him depart.[5]

Commissioner Weller, plus Gray and Emory arrived in San Diego on June 1. Emory noted that the village had not changed since Kearny's occupation in 1846.

Three hundred years earlier, Juan Rodríquez Cabrillo, a Portuguese navigator and conquistador, explored San Diego Bay. He left his bones on a nearby island. For the next two centuries, priests of the Franciscan, Jesuit and Dominican orders established Indian missions throughout Baja (Lower) California. While explorers and even the renowned Father Kino, frequently visited San Diego, it remained for Father Junípero Serra on July 16, 1769, to raise a Cross and intone the first High Mass. Serra was a short, chubby, balding, fifty-six-year-old Franciscan who practiced personal flagellation, burned his flesh with torches and struck himself with stones. Serra established the first mission in the bay area, and upon that foundation the settlement of San Diego began.[6]

Yankee ships plied the coast for hides, but cow-killing never flourished until secularization reached California in 1834. The mission system crumbled, its financial structure looted of land, goods and money by the central government.

To support the dwindling Indian population, the mission fathers encouraged hide sales. *Vaqueros* flushed cattle from the thickets into corrals where riders turned death into a dangerous sport. Swinging machetes and leaning low in the saddle, they galloped past the steer, severing its spine with a single swipe of the blade. *Peladores* (skinners) stripped the hide, usually discarding the stringy beef. After soaking the hide in sea water, they stretched and staked it, then scraped off the fat — the toughest, dirtiest work of all. This common sight caused American sailors to dub the scrapers, "Greasers." What started as an apt description eventually became a derogatory reference for dark-skinned Mexicans.

While the golden age of hide trading had declined by 1849, the commission party had plenty to observe. R. P. Effinger, a surveyor, described a California rancho to his Lancaster, Ohio relatives as about the size of an Ohio county. Small amounts of wheat, corn, onions, pumpkins and occasionally pears and peaches flourished there. The countryside abounded in cattle and horses. Colorful rancheros dressed in broad-brimmed hats and tight-fitting clothes with silver buttons. On average they each possessed between 5,000 and 6,000 steers, plus 600 horses. "To see a Californian ride," Effinger wrote, "you would think he is a part of the horse. He never jolts."

But if Effinger spoke admirably of the *vaqueros* and *rancheros* (to say nothing of the ladies, whom he described as alluring), the Ohioan had few kind words for Mexican peons, considering them "the most deceitful, treacherous set of beings in the world." He once wrote, "I fear they would never make good American citizens" because their morals and religion are "heathenish."

Effinger cared even less for Indians. He considered them too lazy to work and too cowardly to fight, an inferior people possessing only "enough cunning to steal what will barely sustain them."

Effinger strolled through the empty missions (vacated earlier because of government-enforced secularization) and examined the wine cellars, the chicken and pigeon houses, the beehives and the gardens with untended peas, peaches, apricots, grapes and figs. As he paced the cavernous, rock-walled rooms, the echo of his footsteps reminded him of a place once "lively and boisterous with the mirth of pot-bellied, red-faced, jolly old priests." The surveyor suspected the priests had accomplished all this prosperity by enslaving the Indians. "Hundreds of these savages were constantly employed about the missions without receiving one cent in compensation," he wrote.[7]

San Diego was "nothing more or less than an Indian village composed of adobe huts" with four hundred inhabitants. The port was four miles west. Natives and Mexicans had stripped the timber. Firewood had to be packed in from six miles away. Most houses had dirt floors.

The Americans camped at Punta de los Muertos (Dead Men's Point), later called New Town. Major Emory placed his observatory on a knoll south of San Diego, naming it Camp Riley in honor of the California commanding officer. Since the Mexican contingent had not arrived, Weller explained to Washington that he intended to proceed "as if the meeting had taken place within the time limit prescribed by the treaty."[8]

A month later, Mexican Boundary Commissioner General Pedro García Conde arrived on the English frigate *Caroline* with an escort of 140 troops. While traveling from Mexico City to the Pacific, his coach had overturned at San Juan de los Lagos, Jalisco. When he finally arrived at the coast, gold seekers on their way to Sacramento had already deprived his party of a ship's berth. Ultimately, the *Caroline* brought them sick and shaken forty-one days later to the San Diego shore.

As a forty-three-year-old native of Arizpe, Sonora, the commissioner had been captain of engineers and had drawn the first geographical map of Chihuahua. Before moving up to brigadier general and then secretary of war, García Conde directed the Military College in Mexico City and supervised the National Palace reconstruction. The president tapped him as boundary commissioner while he served in the National Senate.

Comandante (Major) José Salazar Ylarregui introduced himself as the Mexican commission surveyor. He too was born in Sonora, an intelligent man of twenty-six and an accomplished engineer. His notes and records would document the Mexican boundary efforts.[9]

Captain Francisco Jiménez, first-class engineer, was the most knowledgeable member of the Mexican team, although he remained one of the least known. He made all arrangements, checked and verified the survey figures, consulted with the Americans and received little credit. United States historians suspect that he wrote what Salazar signed.

Other key figures were Martínez de Chavero, also a first-class engineer, Agustín García Conde, the commissioner's brother, and Ricardo Ramírez, a second-class engineer. Felipe de Iturbide, son of the executed Mexican emperor, was translator and interpreter. To the east, Colonel José María Carrasco, a tough Indian fighter, was hauling supplies and bringing one hundred Sonoran cavalrymen across the desert.[10]

Effinger described Pedro García Conde as "a fine looking man" who "in dignity and grace I do not know his equal." As for the civilian officers, Effinger considered them "intelligent and genteel, far ahead in all of the refined rules of etiquette and politeness to the rough-looking specimens of the American characters comprising Colonel Weller's party."

However, Effinger said nothing pleasant about the ordinary Mexican trooper. "The consumption of pork would go entirely out of use," he wrote of the 140 man escort, "if hogs were as filthy as those Mexican soldiers." He characterized the officers as "little better than the men," commenting that García Conde had assured the Americans that in Mexico his soldiers were "not permitted to go into good society. In California there would be no deviation from the rule."[11]

After being welcomed on shipboard by Lieutenant Cave J. Couts, commander of Company A of the 1st Dragoons, the Mexican commissioner paid a courtesy call at Weller's residence. Weller invited Mexican participation in the July 4 celebrations, and García Conde graciously consented.

A company of dragoons led the parade, closely followed by García Conde, Weller, Emory and other distinguished members of both commissions as well as the leading ladies and gentlemen of the region. Infantry of both nations brought up the rear, followed by a long column of Yuma Indians, the males in breechcloth and war paint. Late that afternoon, the Americans barbecued an ox and six sheep for the Yumas. Effinger dryly remarked that the way those Indians drank and "tore up the ground was a sin to Moses."

After Weller read the Declaration of Independence in English and Spanish, the distinguished guests partied. Effinger wrote his mother that she "could judge by the [party's] magnificence when I tell you it cost five hundred dollars." Practically everyone drank to excess, and the handsome Iturbide who "resembled a Mexican only in his actions," boasted he could "whip a half-dozen Americans." As several challengers arose, García Conde seized Iturbide by the throat and furiously choked him.[12]

On July 6, 1849, the surveys began.

Profound currents were moving in the United States that summer of 1849, and a few gradually fused into a great tide sweeping everything before it. That phenomenon was the California gold rush.

Effinger said these hordes turned California into a country "without law, order or gospel." The wayfarers had "neither the fear of man nor God before them." He estimated three thousand gold seekers passed through San Diego in just a few months, and "while the heart sickens at . . . their distress and suffering, [it] finally grows cold and callous. I have known cases of persons worn out by hunger and fatigue being deserted by their companions, and [who] would ask in vain to those passing by for a drink of water or a morsel of food." Taken as a class, "a more selfish, more cowardly bunch of scamps never immigrated to a country," he said.[13]

When the boundary commissioners arrived in San Diego they anticipated cheap, plentiful labor. What they found was a population migrating to San Francisco to work in the gold fields. San Diego carpenters demanded $10 per day. Common laborers earned $150 a month. Between eight and ten military enlisted men deserted each month. More might have disappeared had not General William Tecumseh Sherman permitted soldiers during their free time to be employed by the boundary commission "at a rate of pay equal to that paid civilians."

Dissension divided military officers. Brevet Major Justus McKinstry, quartermaster for the boundary commission escort, borrowed several hundred dollars from Lieutenant Cave J. Couts to cover gambling losses of government funds. He never repaid it.

Military authorities filed charges against McKinstry for "playing cards while he was supposed to be on duty," and for conduct unbecoming an officer. A delighted Couts and Lieutenant George F. Evans told the editor of a San Luis Rey newspaper, *El Coyote*, that "the notorious Major McKinstry will be court-martialed on the usual charges." The article enraged McKinstry. He cornered Evans in the San Diego Square and beat him so savagely that Evans begged for mercy. A charge of assault followed.

At the trial, allegations emerged that McKinstry lived too well for an ordinary officer. Hints circulated of embezzled quartermaster funds appropriated for boundary commission work. In his defense, McKinstry accused Couts of employing dragoons to kill him, and offering early discharges as pay. Hugh Owens, one of the alleged hired assassins, denied the story but did admit that "Couts wanted me to whip a nigger and a Spaniard who worked for McKinstry."[14]

Couts in his *Journal* referred to "the dirty and cowardly J. McKinstry" as "slandering a young lady who would not permit the free use of his vulgar tongue in her presence." Emory in his private papers mentioned an unnamed girl, saying McKinstry had "trifled, quibbled and lied," and that the dispute among Evans, Couts and McKinstry had its foundations within "the most honorable families in [this] country."

The court found McKinstry guilty, handing down a severe reprimand and suspension in rank for three months. He and Evans were transferred under arrest to Washington, D.C. on additional unspecified charges, although the Army released them when no one appeared to testify.

As petty jealousies and gargantuan egos clashed, Couts and Whipple argued over their relative importance to the boundary project. Weller complained that he had to pamper Emory, everyone disliked the haughty Gray, and Colonel J. J. Abert, chief of the United States Topographical Engineers in Washington, ordered Emory to "try and get along with Gray by using common sense." He also chastised Emory for requesting an additional brevet (temporary, non-paid promotion) for past services, reminding him that one brevet was enough, and asking, "Why do you want another?"[15]

Finally, the United States and Mexico got down to defining an initial point (a point of reference) on the Pacific coast one league south of the San Diego harbor, and another initial point at the confluence of the Gila and Colorado rivers. Next they would connect these points with a straight line and mark it. The task sounded easy, and Washington never understood why it took so long and cost so much.

Disagreements began at the Pacific. No standard distance or reference defined a marine league, so the commissioners compromised on 5,564.6 meters (slightly more than three miles). Of greater importance was where to begin measuring. The treaty called for one marine league south "of the southernmost point" of the harbor, but nobody agreed on what constituted the southernmost point. Since the tides rolled restlessly back and forth across a flat plain, an exact "shore" line was impossible to verify.

Emory and Salazar selected a site where each considered the shoreline, and disagreed by 3,500 feet. Weller and García Conde split the difference. To eliminate future difficulties, Gray surveyed the harbor.[16] Then, after measuring south one marine league, and erecting International Boundary Marker No. 1, the commissions sealed English and Spanish statements inside a bottle and buried it beneath the monument (initial point) on the shores of the Pacific. Then we "drank a toast with prudence and moderation," Salazar wryly wrote.[17]

Whipple and Couts left San Diego for the junction of the Gila and Colorado rivers on September 11, 1849, to establish an opposite initial point so that a line could be drawn and marked between International Boundary Marker No. 1 and the Gila-Colorado confluence. Both men left written records, Couts his *Journal* and Whipple his *Report*. The *Journal* bulges with stories of weary forty-niners. With their roosters, their old yellow dogs, and little else except hope and a rusted musket, they set out for California from the East. Now they were collapsing along the trail, ragged, starving and exhausted. To assist the forty-niners, Couts provided army rations, which were food packages containing three pounds of flour and two-and-one-fourth pounds of pork. Emory responded by sending Couts 1,260 additional rations, and readying a pack train of two thousand more. A maximum of ten rations would be issued to women and children in absolute want, and to seriously ill men.[18]

Otherwise, the tall, ramrod Couts was a man quick to find fault. He considered Whipple a weakling, a "Washington City dandy with white kid gloves." If you "take away his books, he's not worth a tinker's damn for anything under God's heaven," he wrote. "I now doubt his capacity for determining . . . the mouth of the Gila."[19]

Whipple showed more reserve than his fellow officer. The pages of his *Report* abounded with descriptions of the country. Indians (mostly Quechans) fascinated him, and he devoted more space to them than he did to the survey. For a weakling with white kid gloves, Whipple acted almost unconcerned about the difficult tasks, and never mentioned any significant feats performed or any great problems encountered. He complained once that his instrument boxes had cracked due to wood shrinkage.

By eastern standards neither river has ever inspired much poetry. The Gila was brackish and shallow, whereas the Colorado was wider, of reddish color but more swift and perhaps twelve feet deep in places. While Whipple located the exact center of the confluence, where the Gila intersected the Colorado, Couts established Camp Calhoun (later Camp Yuma) on the east bank of the Colorado River, and built a ferry at the Yuma Crossing. (The town of Yuma was not yet organized, and the crossing, as well as the camp, was named for the Yuma Indians.) When Couts left for San Diego, he handed the ferry over to Mexican friends, who in turn sold it to Dr. Abel B. Lincoln, a forty-niner who collected gold for hauling passengers on a raft across the Colorado. However, the unconscionable rates attracted bounty hunter John Clanton, who became a partner. The enterprise went out of business on April 21, 1851, when Yumas bashed both men in the head and threw their bodies into a fire.[20]

Meanwhile, Whipple built an observatory atop a rise he dubbed Capitol Hill, and after several astronomical readings, he asked Salazar in San Diego to confirm his findings. Unfortunately, while Mexican responsibilities were broad, its means were limited. Sore-back mules and damaged equipment barely survived a hazardous journey laced with unseasonable rains. Salazar complained that García Conde should examine the readings, and when the commissioner refused, Salazar protested in writing before leaving. His report called the Capitol Hill station well selected, noting that the sightings were not only accurate but slightly favorable to Mexico.[21]

A straight line from International Boundary Marker No. 1 to the Colorado–Gila confluence remained to be surveyed and marked. However, the Gila pushed the Colorado slightly northwest, driving it into a "hook" pattern before it adjusted and continued south toward the Gulf of California. The international boundary therefore left the junction, cut across the hook and the Colorado again before stretching out toward the Pacific.

General García Conde suggested that the short wedge of land south of the Colorado, which belonged to the United States, be swapped for equal property south of San Diego. Weller refused, arguing that unequivocal language in the treaty denied the commissioners that authority.[22]

One hundred and forty-eight miles separated the initial point on the Pacific from the initial point at the Gila and Colorado confluence. Emory groaned that the countryside rose "in steps from the sea, [creating a land] devoid of water, and covered with spined vegetation" until the altitude reached five or six thousand feet. "For about thirty miles more, the country is occupied by a succession of parallel ridges striking the boundary nearly at right angles, and separated by deep and sometimes impassable chasms. It then falls abruptly to near the

Since the Colorado flowed north to south, and the Gila east to west, the Gila collision jarred the Colorado into a hook pattern, giving the United States a tiny slice of land on the south bank of the Colorado. The "hook" on this map has been exaggerated for emphasis.

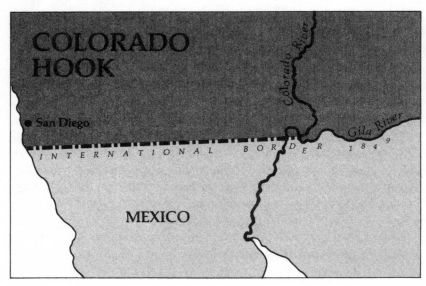

level of the sea. The remainder of the line stretches across a desert of shifting sand . . . destitute . . . of both water and vegetation, rendering it impossible to mark the boundary in the usual manner. . . ."[23]

In a country so poorly suited for geodetic operations, Emory sent Captain Hardcastle to reconnoiter the high country. Hardcastle identified several elevated boundary positions, and hastened the surveys at night with gunpowder flashes.

In the meantime, Gray left San Diego on October 11, 1849, to confirm Whipple's calculations at the Gila. Along the way he encountered a straggling party led by Colonel Collier, the collector of customs for the Port of San Francisco. Since the group was obviously lost, and weak from fruitless wandering, they prevailed upon Gray to lead them through the mountain passes to the coast. When the surveyor reappeared in San Diego, and explained his unexpected reappearance, Weller growled that "your reasons for returning without making a personal examination at the mouth of the Gila River (for which your expedition was started) are far from being satisfactory to my mind."[24]

Gray justified his delay by claiming discovery of a shorter route to the Gila. However, when he traced it on a map, Commissioner Weller impatiently described the trail as already well-known but little used. "You are a liar," Gray screamed. The white-faced Weller struck Gray across the jaw, only to have the surveyor draw a pistol and shoot Weller in the thigh. The wound wasn't serious, and as both men were intoxicated, they hushed-up the incident.[25]

Weller's position as commissioner grew tenuous. In a job needing profound understanding of Mexican culture, an ability to speak the Spanish language, the talents of a practical and canny politician, and the enormous skill of an administrator, Weller had hardly a trace. And Washington still smarted because Weller had accepted the job in the first place. On the pretense that Weller had overspent his funds, Secretary of State John Clayton shut off voucher payments without informing Weller. Major Emory ordered the army quartermaster to furnish supplies and transportation. Emory pressed enlisted men into commission service, and paid each soldier an extra two dollars a day.

On June 20, 1849, Clayton offered the position of boundary commissioner to John Charles Frémont, formerly a dashing lieutenant in the topographical engineers. Frémont had trekked across vast portions of the far West, and while the precise value of his explorations were open to question, he had the newspaper reputation as a "Pathfinder."

Along with the letter to Frémont was a dismissal for Weller, the note to be delivered when and if Frémont accepted the job.[26]

Frémont and a group of volunteers had led the *Bear Flag Rebellion* against Mexico in 1846, capturing Los Angeles, which was essentially California in those days. When General Stephen Watts Kearny occupied California shortly thereafter, Frémont refused to recognize him as supreme commander. Kearny court-martialed Frémont, finding him guilty on three counts. Frémont now considered the office of boundary commissioner a repudiation of his 1847 trial. "I regarded that [boundary] commission," Frémont wrote, "as a disavowal on the part of the President of the proceedings recently held against me. Respect for the President . . . did not . . . permit me to decline, so I accordingly accepted the commission, with the intention . . . shortly afterwards to resign."[27]

Frémont planned to campaign for the United States Senate from California, and having a background as a boundary commissioner would enhance his political profile. He informed Washington of his acceptance without supplying a specific date. However, he did not hand Weller the dismissal letter, giving an impression that he wanted Weller to continue the boundary work while Frémont retained the title.

While most historical accounts describe Weller as having no knowledge of being replaced, commission letters seem to refute this. Even Frémont's 1856 biographer conceded it was "well understood by both that whether he accepted or not, Mr. Weller would not be retained."[28]

Frémont resigned without ever visiting the field. To his credit, he helped Weller cash a government draft of $10,000 in San Francisco, money which kept the boundary surveys active. However, Washington disavowed the vouchers, and California bankers seized Weller's property.[29]

By now the boundary commission had been transferred in Washington from the State Department to the recently created Interior Department. On December 19, 1849, Secretary of Interior Thomas E. Ewing, a bitter political enemy of Weller from Ohio, dismissed Weller. California's freshman Senator William McKendree Gwin promptly accused Secretary of State Clayton of attempting to "butcher this official incumbent."[30]

Ewing charged Weller with failing to provide a list of employees, of not itemizing salaries and not submitting vouchers for the $33,000 congressional limit on spending. Later accusations said Weller had deliberately delayed leaving Panama, had been extravagant, and that his commission reeked with internal dissension.[31]

In a technical sense, a few of these charges were correct. Weller did not furnish a list of employees or their salaries because the California situation was so chaotic due to gold discoveries that most civilians deserted. His vouchers for the $33,000 arrived in Washington only a few days behind schedule, a commendable promptness considering the mails. He had not been extravagant but had pinched pennies because of unexpected delays in Panama and soaring costs in California. True, he had not started work when anticipated, but this was partially due to the late arrival of the Mexican commissioner. Command problems plagued him, but except for being shot by Gray, and compared to what was to come, the Weller administration was a model of good order. Finally, Weller had not overspent his budget, but still had $6,000. And while a government two thousand miles away moralized and complained about money, it had never established the rate of Weller's salary, had never paid him a cent other than expenses, and never would.

Weller angrily wrote Ewing of how "fortunate" it was that the government had recalled him when the boundary was nearly complete between the Pacific and the Colorado-Gila junction; otherwise it might have cost Washington another $50,000 to finish. And how "unfortunate" it was for him (Weller) because he might have entered a profitable business instead of making himself "liable to suits for protested drafts."[32]

Weller relinquished his commission records to Major Emory and left the boundary service. After borrowing $900 from Effinger, which he never repaid, he moved to San Francisco and became an attorney. On January 28, 1851, Californians sent him to the United States Senate as a Union Democrat. He replaced Frémont, who was a Whig, and he became a harsh critic of the subsequent boundary commission.

Ironically, the commission's temporary directorship fell upon Emory who was unsuccessfully attempting to resign. Frémont's tentative appointment infuriated Emory, especially since Emory had testified against Frémont at the court-martial. Emory believed Frémont had incorporated into his map of 1848 the whole fruit of Emory's reconnaissance of the Southwest. Emory called recent events an "outrage inflicted on the commission by withholding funds, and attempting to place at its head persons [Frémont] avowedly hostile." Rancorously he

General Zachary Taylor recognized early in the Mexican War that while the United States sought territorial expansion, this was primarily a war of political objectives. Gradual military pressure was a means to an end. (U.S. Military Academy Archives)

PRESIDENT JAMES J. POLK
(National Archives)

JOHN R. WELLER
(San Diego Historical Society)

AMIEL W. WHIPPLE
(San Diego Historical Society)

JOHN CHARLES FRÉMONT

CAVE JOHNSON COUTS
(San Diego Historical Society)

ALEX. H. H. STUART
(Library of Congress)

reviled the way Frémont held the commission in abeyance for months. The boundary commissioner position "was open to the highest bidder to the everlasting disgust and dissatisfaction of every scientific man on the work," he said. On September 15 he asked Secretary of State Clayton to release him from the commission.[33]

Clayton handed the request to Secretary of War George Crawford, who turned it down because "it might start a precedent." When President Taylor upheld Crawford's decision, friends of Emory prevailed upon the secretary to retain Emory as director only until the Pacific to the Gila-Colorado survey had been completed and marked. Emory considered this satisfactory, and he reorganized the commission.

Captain Hardcastle and Francisco Jiménez would survey a line between the Pacific and the Gila-Colorado confluence and install seven markers. The two initial points would be of marble, the intermediate monuments of iron. The government appropriated an additional $144,000 to complete the task, most of it earmarked for mules and supplies.

Hardcastle arrived at the river intersection on April 10, 1850, erected a monument and surveyed west by using front and rear sightings to maintain a straight line. Soon he encountered Ricardo Ramírez, second-class engineer and assistant to Jiménez, who had been delayed because intense San Diego rains had created mud so deep that the mules bogged down. Furthermore, Mexican Commissioner García Conde had left the surveyors unprotected by inexplicably permitting the soldiers to "amuse themselves with the pleasures of California."

Ramírez and Hardcastle formulated two surveying steps in the 148 mile Pacific-Confluence line. They surveyed west from the Colorado to the New River-Immigrant Trail junction, erected a marker, then returned to San Diego and worked east. However, the two lines did not mesh. The Pacific survey east ended 1,864 feet south of the western survey. The officials returned to their slide rules and agreed that the San Diego east measurements were the most accurate. The terminal of the western line was moved south 1,864 feet. The United States picked up a thin wedge of land one-third of a mile wide at its broadest point.[34]

While Hardcastle and Ramírez installed the intermediate markers, the commissioners adjourned and ordered a November 1850 meeting at El Paso del Norte in northern Chihuahua. High prices and chronic labor shortages made surveying untenable in California. Of more significance, at El Paso del Norte an initial point on the Rio Grande (where the boundary left the river for the Pacific) would allow surveys to start in two directions, downstream toward the Gulf of Mexico as well as west from the Rio Grande toward the headwaters of the Gila.

Even so, the adjournment lacked majority agreement. Gray and Salazar claimed the treaty made no provisions for disruptions in surveying. García Conde and Emory overruled them. Gray vowed to remain in Califoria until relieved by his government. Salazar complained of "great sacrifices . . . to maintain harmony," and said he "could not be blamed for anything."[35]

When the two camps separated, Whipple took the instruments by sea to Indianola, Texas, and overland to El Paso del Norte. García Conde and José Salazar traveled by ship to Guaymas, Sonora, then by coach to Mexico City, and north again to El Paso del Norte. Emory went to Washington, made his official report and was reassigned.

The next phase of the survey would center at El Paso, Texas. Gray would be sulking in California. On hand would be a different United States commissioner, and difficulties sufficient to plague both countries for over a century.

A Boundary Too Far North

THE NEXT SURVEY THRUST would begin at El Paso, Texas, in mid-continent. Since surveyors could mark both the land and river (Rio Grande) borders at the same time, a new crew of contentious individuals would be be gathered together.

John Russell Bartlett would leave a strong imprint on border history. He was an imposing man, slender and yet muscular, an intellectual who leaned forward when expressing determined views. The hands were strong, the fingers square, the eyes deep-set and quizzical, the forehead high and almost dome-shaped, the hair light and wispy, resisting a tendency toward baldness. He had sloping shoulders, a straight, prominent nose and the masculine, physically attractive appearance of a man used to having his way. He would be neither easily intimidated or tricked, and he would bring to the American Boundary Commission some very obvious political, scientific and artistic talents.[1]

He was born in Providence, Rhode Island in 1805, but grew up in Canada. In 1836 he opened a New York bookstore, and through it became acquainted with scholars and government leaders. Albert Gallatin, Jefferson's secretary of the treasury, frequently dropped in, as did John L. Stephens, who conducted the first scholarly exploration of the Mayan ruins in the Yucatan. Other patrons included critic Henry

Tuckerman and author Edgar Allan Poe, the latter complaining because Bartlett's coffee kept him awake and forced him to write.[2]

Bartlett belonged to the Franklin Society, the Rhode Island Historical Society, and the Providence Athenaeum. He wrote the *Progress of Ethnology* in 1847, the *Dictionary of Americanisms* one year later, and the *Reminiscences of Albert Gallatin* shortly after that. Scientific and historical journals sought his articles, and Brown University recognized his scholarly achievements with an honorary Master of Arts in 1848. Yet, for all these successes, satisfaction eluded him. Book royalties and a business could not adequately support a wife and four children. He sought a ministry in a Scandinavian country, but was offered the position of American boundary commissioner on the Mexican border.

Major Folliot Lally, a Whig by political choice and an engineer by profession, contested Bartlett's appointment. Lally had been breveted for gallantry at Cerro Gordo, Mexico, and enjoyed the popularity of a war hero. Bartlett had not served, and indeed had opposed the conflict. However, Lally faded for lack of political clout, and on June 29, 1850, President Zachary Taylor, ten days before his death, appointed the forty-five-year-old Bartlett as commissioner.

Nearly three hundred applicants sought work with the boundary commission, most of them farm boys anxious to break the monotony of their lives. Politicians paid off debts by recommending relatives and friends. Rhode Island's Senator John H. Clarke talked Bartlett into accepting one of the senator's sons, Edward Clarke. Bartlett hired nearly one hundred people, and said another fifty would be employed in Texas.

The commissioner and surveyor would each be paid $3,000 annually. Five others, including the commissioner's brother, George, in charge of stores and warehouses, had salaries of $1,500.

Carpenters, laborers, cooks and mechanics formed the work core. Dr. Thomas Webb was Bartlett's personal physician and companion, as well as commission secretary and surgeon. Andrew Gray, the surveyor, was still in California. He, along with Lieutenant Amiel Whipple, the dependable astronomer, was carried over from the previous boundary expedition. John C. Cremony, hunter, scout, trapper and interpreter, tagged along, as did Lieutenant Isaac G. Strain, a navy man assigned to boating chores on what the government confidently believed would be navigable rivers. Finally, Lieutenant Colonel John McClellan was Major Emory's replacement.

While Bartlett awaited a more comfortable ship, the *Galveston* sailed for Indianola, Texas, on August 3. To save money, the government quartered twenty-six laborers on the boiler deck and fed them tubs of boiled meat. Strain and several companions went ashore when the ship docked at Key West, Florida, and a brawl started upon their return. Strain and Clement Young, a chain-bearer and station-marker, fought, and Strain ordered Young thrown overboard. McClellan prevented it.[3]

When the *Galveston* docked at Indianola, and Bartlett arrived shortly afterwards, the commission started for San Antonio, the primary stop on its way to El Paso. Near Victoria, Lieutenant Strain formed the engineers into make-believe cavalry, and the mechanics and laborers into "riflemen." Since "soldiers" needed uniforms, George Bartlett sold them blue-flannel shirts, dark pantaloons and broad-brimmed white hats. Everybody signed for a musket, and learned to shoot with tolerable accuracy. Commissioner Bartlett said the troops made "a very respectable appearance." Of course, Bartlett's quartermaster brother deducted charges from the salaries.[4]

The procession left Victoria in September, heading west toward San Antonio — the next stop on its way to El Paso, six hundred miles farther west. Only on Sundays did the caravan pause. Bartlett preached from under a tree and everyone sang hymns, the commissioner believing the rough teamsters and laborers appreciated his Christian services.

Near Goliad a teamster named Green destroyed a private fence for firewood, and the owner drove him off with a knife. So Green returned and killed the farmer with a revolver. A horrified Bartlett ordered Green's arrest, apologized to the bereaved family and provided $100 for funeral expenses. After promising to surrender Green to San Antonio authorities, Bartlett imprisoned him in a tent. Late that night Green lifted the flap and escaped.[5]

One week later, John Tenant, a commission butcher, and Robert Turner, a teamster, quarreled over beef. Tenant tossed aside his pocket knife, and put up his fists. Turner fatally stabbed him. The murderer fled on horseback but pursuers caught him, brandished revolvers and forced his surrender. A San Antonio judge assessed a fifteen year sentence.

The commission left San Antonio immediately after the trial, with Bartlett and other members driving ahead. Bartlett's train contained forty men, thirty-nine mules, six wagons, an ambulance and Bartlett's own Rockaway carriage with folding bed and curtained windows. By the commissioner's own account, the Rockaway bristled with fire-power: double-barreled shotguns, rifles and revolvers. The driver boasted that thirty-seven rounds could be fired without reloading.[6]

Under murky skies in mid-October, Bartlett moved through Mormon settlements of tiny houses with squared logs and rifle slots. Fredericksburg was populated with five hundred Germans, few of whom spoke English.

On the 24th, two Lipan Indian guides, Chipota and Chiquita, spent a night near the commissioner. Chipota tapped on the carriage window the next morning, awakening Bartlett and chattering, "Mucho frio. Poco de viskey." (It is very cold. How about some whiskey.) When Bartlett handed them a steaming cup of coffee, the Indians disgustedly stomped away, leaving the Americans to find their own trail. As the commission struggled along, water, forage and corn supplies ran low. Several migrating ducks were shot, and these birds provided the only food for days.

A two-day snowstorm buried the travelers in early November, and Bartlett sent riders for help to the Post Opposite El Paso, a frontier army garrison eventually to become Fort Bliss. His letter to Major Jefferson Van Horne described a series of northers, animals "reduced by fatigue," and a weary caravan short on rations and strength. "We need mules, bread, pork, sugar and coffee, sufficient rations for five days," he wrote.[7]

When the storm lifted, the commission caravan continued under threatening skies until several mules collapsed. This time Bartlett's carriage plunged on ahead. He struggled past Guadalupe Peak, the highest point in Texas, and onto the barren salt flats where Bartlett encountered a stalled wagon train. Benjamin Franklin Coons[8], the owner, and Frederick Augustus Percy[9], the wagonmaster, had been stranded almost two months while awaiting water from El Paso, eighty miles west.

Bartlett consumed a meal, then ordered his driver to whip the horses toward the Hueco Mountains, the final obstacle to El Paso. A few hours later the trail disappeared in the snow, and the horses and carriage had to be lowered by rope over a precipice. At this point, his requested military escort brought him to El Paso, better known as Franklin. Bartlett arrived on November 13, two weeks ahead of the Mexican commissioner. General García Conde was in Chihuahua City, 240 miles south.

The remainder of Bartlett's 140 men straggled in, their presence adding serious economic burdens to the estimated six thousand people in the El Paso valley. Not since Doniphan's army invaded Chihuahua in 1846 had prices so soared. Flour went to $32 a barrel, whiskey from $2 to $8 a gallon, corn to $3 a bushel. To counter inflation and find suitable winter quarters, Bartlett scattered assistants, wagons and mules up and down the valley. The majority went to Socorro, fifteen miles southeast of El Paso. McClellan, Whipple and the surveyors worked in the Mexican presidio ruins of San Elizario, five miles farther. However, Whipple later shifted his observatory to Frontera, a half-dozen miles north of El Paso. Bartlett occasionally lived at the military post, but spent most of his time at the adobe, hacienda-style home of James Magoffin, a Chihuahua trader.

In the meantime, Lieutenant Strain and Colonel McClellan had bickered across Texas. Each suspected the other of undermining his authority, and each was correct. A disgusted Bartlett asked Secretary of Interior Alexander H. Stuart to assign Strain four iron boats and send him to "survey the headwaters of the Gulf of California and the Rio Colorado to the mouth of the Gila." Instead, Stuart ordered Strain back to Washington. The lieutenant believed McClellan had arranged his dismissal, and he filed charges against the colonel for "drunkenness and conduct unbecoming an officer and a gentleman."[10]

As for McClellan, he shared an adobe hut in San Elizario with Lieutenant Whipple and Captain S. D. Dobbins, a hunter and guide hired by McClellan in San Antonio. Dobbins and Uel B. Wakeman, wagonmaster of the ox train, quarreled over cards, and Dobbins shot Wakeman in the thigh and calf, allegedly in self-defense. Wakeman died in misery ten days later, complaining that "the doctor has no instruments to work me with." An inquest acquitted Dobbins, but he brooded over the death, and two weeks later committed suicide in his San Elizario quarters.[11]

During this period, McClellan and Lieutenant Whipple secretly audited a work box belonging to A. DeVaudricourt, an eccentric French artist and chief topographical draftsman. When DeVaudricourt learned of it, he demanded that Bartlett punish Whipple and McClellan for burglary. The commissioner ignored him and told McClellan to return any items taken. The colonel considered the request an accusation of theft and a threat to relieve him. He demanded a list of charges and a court-martial.

Bartlett asked Washington to recall McClellan for "intemperate habits," and Secretary Stuart suggested that the colonel be returned "in such a manner as to wound as little as possible the high-toned and gentlemanly corps of which he is a member." The commissioner therefore suggested that McClellan resign for health reasons. When the colonel disdainfully refused, Bartlett dismissed him on December 16.[12]

McClellan departed for Washington where he leveled charges against Bartlett: incompetence, mismanagement, fraud, conduct unworthy of a commissioner, unpardonable neglect, and conduct calculated to destroy all discipline in the commission. He accused George F. Bartlett of hauling private goods to the Southwest at government expense, and selling them at enormous profits, and he said quartermaster James Myer had defrauded the United States with Bartlett's knowledge and consent.[13]

Stuart ignored the charges against Bartlett but recalled Myer and Bartlett's brother. Later the secretary said George Bartlett was "able to furnish satisfactory explanations for his conduct," but "his near relationship to the Commissioner gave grounds for injurious suspicions."[14]

Additional boundary problems further delayed the border surveys. Twenty-six commission members in San Elizario signed a petition on January 6, 1851, asserting they were "not properly provided with food necessary for comfortable subsistence; and that the provisions . . . are insufficient in quantity and inferior in quality." The rice would be "condemned by a board of inquiry," the pork and flour already were "condemned by the military post," no bacon, saleratus (baking soda), or hard bread has ever been issued, and the beef "should not be eaten by man regardful of his life or health."[15]

Bartlett replied that these items supplied his own table as well as officers at the post. The flour was excellent, he said, but everyone should understand that the food had been coming overland "from the coast during the entire summer, and was exposed to the intense heat of the plains."

If Bartlett dismissed this complaint easily, he found it tougher to disregard the fifty or so teamsters he had dismissed from government service in El Paso. They drifted to Socorro and engaged in rowdyism. Commission employees reported ruffians "parading in the streets . . . with firearms in hand, killing and intimidating." They slashed A. Von Steinwehr, a draftsman, across the face, and shot his associate, Charles Gates, in the leg.

At a Socorro dance, drunken teamsters fired shots into the wall. When Edward Clarke, the Rhode Island senator's son, and now the commission assistant quartermaster, interfered, they stabbed him nine times.[16]

Since the village *alcalde*, according to Bartlett, was a sickly imbecile, the community asked Captain Johns of the military detachment at San Elizario, to restore order. Johns called the trouble "a civilian matter." Therefore, the citizens deputized themselves and searched every house in Socorro until they had captured and filed murder charges against former teamster Marcus Butler, former teamster and Englishman, John Wade, and William Craig, a Scotsman and former commission cook. The posse also searched for Alexander Young, the leader, but he had escaped.

Justice of the Peace Alex Berthold swore in a jury of Mexican-Americans and boundary employees. Bartlett described the trial in his journal:

There sat the judge, with a pistol lying on the table beside him; the clerks and attorneys wore revolvers at their sides; and the jurors were either armed with similar weapons, or carried with them the unerring rifle. The members of the commission and citizens, who were either guarding the prisoners or protecting the court, carried by their sides a revolver, a rifle, or a fowling-piece, thus presenting a scene more characteristic of feudal times than of the nineteenth century. The fair but sunburned complexion of the American portion of the jury, with their weapons resting against their shoulders, and pipes in their mouths, presented a striking contrast to the swarthy features of the Mexicans, muffled in checkered serapes, holding their broad-brimmed glazed hats in their hands, the delicate cigarritos in their lips. The reckless, unconcerned appearance of the prisoners, whose unshaven faces and disheveled hair gave them an appearance of Italian bandits rather than American and Englishmen; the grave and determined bearing of the bench; the varied costume and expression of the spectators and members of the commission, clad in serapes, blankets or overcoats, with their different weapons, and generally with long beards, made altogether one of the most remarkable groups ever to grace a courtroom.[17]

A verdict of guilty followed a two day trial. Butler wept loudly, begging for mercy because of his twenty-one years. Nobody responded. Instead, ropes slid over a cottonwood limb in the mission plaza, and all three outlaws were hanged.

The town placed a reward of $400 on the head of Alexander Young, and a few weeks later someone collected. Young was hanged from the same tree limb. Unlike the others, he made his peace with God.

John R. Bartlett wrote few descriptions of the El Paso Southwest, adopting the bromide that if you've seen one desert, you've seen them all. The Franklin Mountains (which he called the "El Paso Mountains," and which most maps referred to as the White Mountains or the Organs), received scarcely a mention in spite of their craggy precipices forming the region's most outstanding landmark, the southern tip of the Rockies. [18]

He also paid little attention to the Rio Grande as a river, noting that after spilling out of the nearby gorge, it entered wide curves and capriciously overflowed, jumped channels and sometimes eddied almost to a stop. Small lagoons formed, nourishing dense thickets called *bosques*.

El Paso del Norte (eventually Ciudad Juarez), with two or three thousand residents, lay on the southwest bank. Founded in 1659, it was the largest and most prosperous community in the area, although Bartlett called it a mud village with desperately poor people. The Piro Indians had existed at nearby Senecú for almost two centuries since the 1680 Pueblo Revolt in northern New Mexico. Because of disease and assimilation, only about eighty remained, and these rarely spoke their native language. Within another generation, Bartlett estimated, they would vanish. He was right.

Back in 1827, Ponce de León, an El Paso del Norte businessman, established a small ranch in what is now downtown El Paso. After Alexander Doniphan and his Missouri Farm Boys conquered the area in late 1846, Benjamin Franklin Coons, a Missouri trader and (some say) confidence man, leased Ponce's rancho and named it after himself, Franklin. The California gold rush and the Butterfield Overland Mail turned Franklin into a small community. It became home in 1849 to the Post Opposite El Paso, today's Fort Bliss.

Two nearby ranches included the Hugh Stephenson place near present-day Concordia Cemetery, and Magoffinsville, two miles east of Franklin. No one ever envisioned the metropolis of today's El Paso encompassing them all.

Even by 1850 standards, the town had come a long way. After the Mexican War, the federal government had attached it to New Mexico. However, in 1850, the residents relinquished their New Mexico heritage and joined Texas. In 1859, Franklin changed its name to El Paso.[19]

Twelve miles southeast of El Paso on a heavily-thicketed island twenty miles long and three miles wide, squatted the Indian mission communities of Ysleta and Socorro. These church-oriented villages began in 1680, a result of the Pueblo Revolt near Santa Fe.

San Elizario was five miles southeast of Socorro, a Spanish presidio (fort) dating back to the 1780s. In 1850, San Elizario became the first seat of El Paso County.[20]

Two miles northwest of El Paso, at the Rio Grande ford, the aristocratic Simeon Hart had taken advantage of a waterfall and makeshift dam to build a rambling hacienda and gristmill. He sold flour for twelve and one-half cents a pound. The dam raised the water level to eight feet, and diverted the river into *acequias* (irrigation ditches), one being the *Acequia Madre*, a fifteen-foot-wide Mexican canal with numerous feeders. These ditches supported grapes, fruit and agriculture.

At the north end of the three-mile gash through the mountains, Frank White's rancho doubled as a custom house called *Frontera* (the Border or Frontier). The commission built an astronomical observatory there, a building destroyed by Apaches after the surveyors moved on.

Chihuahua City was 240 miles south of El Paso; Fort Fillmore 40 miles north; Albuquerque nearly 300 miles north; Santa Fe 350 miles north; Tucson 325 miles west; and San Antonio, Austin and Fort Worth, 600 miles east.

The Treaty of Guadalupe Hidalgo never precisely defined where the Mexican border would leave the Rio Grande and strike out toward the Pacific. It described the international line as following the Rio Grande from the Gulf until it reached "the southern boundary of New Mexico . . . which runs north of a town called Paso." Paragraph 2, Article 3, said, "the southern and western limits of New Mexico . . . are those laid down on the map entitled 'Map of the United Mexican States' and constructed according to the best authorities. Revised edition. Published at New York in 1847 by John Disturnell."

The Disturnell map may have been "constructed according to the best authorities," but its origin and background suggest negligence and fraud. H. S. Tanner, an American publisher, printed a "Map of North America" in 1822, and followed it in 1825 with a "Map of Mexico," the latter assembled by using the southwestern portion of his 1822 map, enlarging the scale, adding notes and orienting it to new meridians. At least two editions were printed within twenty-five years.

In 1828 the New York firm of White, Gallagher & White plagiarized the 1826 Tanner map, and it in turn was plagiarized by John Disturnell, a salesman and producer of guide books. He too circulated numerous editions. In fact, Disturnell's seventh edition was attached to the United States copy of the Treaty, and the twelfth edition to the Mexican copy. Both versions bore .the 1847 date, the differences being so slight that diplomats probably never realized they were negotiating with two different maps.[21]

Boundary officials were in a quandary, for the map was the authority by treaty for making decisions and measurements, but it was inaccurate. The international line should leave the Rio Grande and go west at the New Mexico border, eight miles north of El Paso. However, El Paso on the map and El Paso on the earth were in two different locations. Disturnell placed El Paso at 32° 15' north latitude and 104° 38' west longitude, in other words thirty-four miles north and one hundred miles east of its true position. So should the border be eight miles north of El Paso's actual location, or eight miles north of where *the map* identified El Paso as being?

The treaty determined the southern New Mexico border as extending west three degrees from the Rio Grande before turning northwest toward the headwaters of the Gila. But once again, was that three degrees west of where the Rio Grande existed on the ground, or where it existed on the map? If it began at the river's true location, the Americans would get an additional strip twenty-five miles wide and fifty miles long. Both ambiguities left the problems without a solution except through commissioner negotiations. Their decisions would be binding.

General Pedro García Conde arrived on December 1, 1850[22], and insisted upon sticking with Disturnell, pretending El Paso was thirty-four miles north of its actual location. The initial point would be eight miles beyond that. García Conde refused to compromise, so Bartlett suggested an exchange of statements regarding their official position.[23]

Meanwhile, Bartlett asked Lieutenant Whipple for an independent opinion. The treaty contained no references to latitude and longitude, Whipple said. In his judgment, the commissioners had confused the map's "irregularly waving lines" as boundaries usually marked by natural features such as mountains or streams, or specific lines and curves, all easily understood. The Disturnell map had those "waving lines," but the lieutenant interpreted them as only approximate boundaries. The border should be within that "portion of territory equal, as nearly as possible, to that within the waving lines." The initial point should be eight miles north of El Paso's actual position, and the line should extend three degrees west from the Rio Grande's actual position, before turning northwest toward the Gila headwaters. That "appears to me as strict a construction of the treaty as is practical to mark upon the ground."[24]

A week later, on December 20, General García Conde handed Bartlett a wandering, repetitious statement, vague verbiage containing few references to the subject. Any position other than his own would risk "destroying the boundary system of New Mexico [with old Mexico]," he claimed, a remarkable evaluation since the boundary he understood as in danger of imminent destruction had not yet been scrupulously defined.[25]

In the end, the commissioners compromised. Bartlett agreed to an initial point forty-two (34 plus 8) miles north of El Paso's location on the ground, explaining to Washington that he was "strictly confined to a particular map." García Conde conceded the three degrees west of the Rio Grande's actual location, which meant that the United States acquired southern New Mexico's Santa Rita copper mines.

The international line went west for 175.28 miles along roughly the same path as today's Interstate 10. Then the border turned northwest for fifty miles and intersected the Gila headwaters.

To his credit, Bartlett made the right decision. For a New England book dealer who would soon be damned as an incompetent product of the political spoils system, he showed uncommon political sagacity. In this give-and-take situation, Bartlett relinquished the largest chunk of land, but forced Mexico to be generous too. Had United States railroad companies not complained that Bartlett's blundering had cost the nation a rail route, his efforts might have gone down in history as a sharp piece of bargaining.

In his elation about settling the initial point controversy, Bartlett confused Whipple's tactful disagreement as assenting to the compromise. "Now that my original position and claim has been fully accepted by the Mexican commission," he crowed to his young assistant, "I shall take great pleasure in placing [your statement] on file with the records of the joint commission" to demonstrate that "your opinion fully coincided with mine."[26]

Bartlett promoted Whipple temporarily to chief astronomer, a replacement for Colonel McClellan, and ordered him to establish an initial point marking the precise location where the boundary forked, going downstream along the Rio Grande and west overland toward the Pacific. The point would be forty-two miles north of El Paso.

Whipple and José Salazar took 434 astronomical observations before precisely identifying the site. They marked it as slightly north of today's Mesilla, New Mexico.

Additional complications arose. With dedication ceremonies scheduled for April 24, 1851, the initial point could not legally be ratified unless *both* surveyors signed the agreement, and Andrew B. Gray, the official American surveyor, had not been seen since the California adjournment. No one knew when Gray would make an appearance, if ever, and Bartlett complained to Secretary Stuart.

The commissioner also deplored his lack of manpower. A. DeVaudricourt, the last of three draftsmen, had resigned. Washington had recalled McClellan and Lieutenant Strain. Hardcastle was still installing boundary markers in California.

Washington sympathized with Bartlett's lack of high-level staff, but urged him to continue as best he could since inactivity was costing the government $110 a day. So Bartlett appointed Lieutenant Whipple as *ad interim* chief surveyor in Gray's absence. Whipple signed the initial point agreement, and Mexican lancers in splendid uniforms escorted commissioners and civil authorities to the dedication ceremonies. A statement in Spanish and English certified that "the two commissions do establish this point on the right bank of the Rio Bravo or Rio del Norte, in 32° 22' north latitude . . . as the point where it strikes the southern boundary of New Mexico." An adjoining page included the names of boundary employees and witnesses. Someone sealed a fragment of the Washington Monument, plus a message, in a container and deposited it beneath the marker.[27]

Back in California, Andrew B. Gray had not been idle in advancing his private interests. After the 1849 boundary adjournment, Gray talked merchant and investor William H. Davis into financially supporting a southern California seaport known sometimes as Gray Town, but historically as New Town. San Diego was too far from the bay, and unless New Town was built, the future belonged to La Playa, where Boston firms were erecting hide-drying barns. Davis and Gray

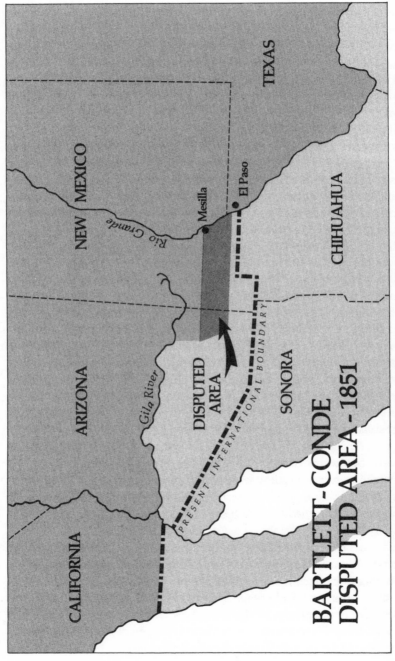

BARTLETT-CONDE
DISPUTED AREA - 1851

The southern portion of this strip is today's international boundary. As it turned out, this area was unnecessary for the construction of a railroad. However, had it not been for the dispute, the United States would never have sought the Gadsden Purchase. Such communities as Tucson, Mesilla, Douglas and Yuma would not now belong to the United States.

suspected that San Diego and New Town, if properly promoted, could become *the* important commercial center south of San Francisco.

The investors purchased land alongside the bay and constructed a wharf. They slipped stock shares to quartermaster Lieutenant Thomas D. Johns, and he installed an Army depot. The partners donated land for a government fort, and the "Post of San Diego" started, later known as San Diego Barracks.

However, New Town failed even as a dream. Heavy boats collapsed the wharf. The village jutted into the ocean, but had not a drop of water to drink. Wood had to be hauled long distances. Vegetables refused to grow. The government denied a post office, and when Gray traveled to Washington to complain, he found the Capital unwilling to discuss his California project when he was supposed to be in El Paso attending to boundary business. An anguished but still optimistic Gray wrote Davis that their municipal vision would eventually become a "flourishing and beautiful town." Then he sailed for Texas, reaching El Paso on July 19, 1851.[28]

Three commission members, including Gray's new assistant, Charles Radziminski, arrived at the same time. The others were Lieutenant Colonel James D. Graham, principal astronomer and chief of the Scientific Corps (McClellan's replacement), and Lieutenant Ambrose E. Burnside of forthcoming Civil War fame. Burnside was the military quartermaster.[29]

Graham stayed in El Paso, and Gray hurried to meet Bartlett at the Santa Rita copper mines in rugged country near present-day Silver City, New Mexico. Bartlett asked Gray to examine the past proceedings, sign the papers and commence surveying the Gila River. In the meantime, Lieutenant Whipple stepped aside as *ad interim* surveyor and astronomer.

When Gray realized Bartlett had accepted a boundary forty-two miles north of El Paso when it might have been eight, he refused to certify the compromise. Instead, he dismissed Whipple's signature as illegal, and warned Bartlett that "the final decision of this line may be changed for the want of confirmation and agreement by your colleague."[30]

Three alternatives now faced the commissioner: Gray could change his mind and drop the matter; the Department of Interior could drop it for him; or the location of the initial point could be renegotiated. As Bartlett did not see any likelihood of the first or third possibilities, he opted for the second and sent Secretary Stuart a strong plea for support.

Bartlett said he had relinquished an area only twenty-five or thirty miles long and thirty-four miles wide, and he considered this a minor concession. The region was "a strip without water, wood or grass, where not one acre can ever be cultivated, where no military post can be sustained, and which can never be inhabited." The most important part was the Mesilla Valley, worth fifty cents to one dollar an acre. He called Mesilla a "stick and mud" community of two thousand persons. The residents formerly lived in Doña Ana (ten miles north), but because of American abuse, had migrated across the border and built new homes. (The same pattern occurred when Ysleta, Socorro and San Elizario residents created Guadalupe and San Ignacio on the south bank of the Rio Grande. At Laredo, the residents crossed the Rio Grande and founded Nuevo Laredo.) If Mesilla became a part of the United States, the population would simply pick up and move south again. On a positive note, the commissioner emphasized United States ownership of the Santa Rita copper mines, calling them an American advantage "completely unforeseen and unexpected by Mexico."[31]

Bartlett wrote like a man fearful of being overruled, and arguing like he had to win his case all over again. Since the United States had obtained valuable mineral property, and since the treaty urged and recognized compromises between the commissioners, Bartlett asked, "Where is the conciliatory spirit . . . spoken of by Mr. Secretary Buchanan in his instructions [to Commissioner Weller]?" Buchanan insisted that we "take no advantage of the Mexican government, but maintain our just rights under the treaty." If the "line should fall one mile or one hundred miles north of El Paso, it will conform to the treaty." Anyone believing otherwise has "sinister motives."

Gray and Bartlett were amiable while awaiting a sign from the gods in Washington, so friendly that they cooperated in a jurisdictional dispute against Colonel Graham. "Never in my whole life have I been placed in so trying a position," Bartlett sighed.[32]

Lieutenant Colonel James D. Graham, a fifty-four-year-old Virginian with thirty-two years experience in the Army, had served with Major Stephen H. Long's expedition to the Rocky Mountains, worked as an astronomer with Gray during the Texas-United States boundary survey, and had supervised the resurveying of the Mason-Dixon Line. Following McClellan's dismissal from the commission, the Interior Department appointed Graham as principal astronomer and chief of the Scientific Corps. However, nobody ever defined the titles and duties.

JAMES D. GRAHAM
(National Archives)

PEDRO GARCIA CONDE
(San Diego Historical Society)

WILLIAM H. EMORY
(National Archives)

JOSÉ SALAZAR ILARREGUI
(Benson Latin American Collection,
U.T. Austin)

John R. Bartlett, the most
controversial of many
boundary commissioners,
was a man of enormous
literary talents. His two-
volume memoirs regard-
ing the American
Southwest and northern
Mexico constitute a
significant contribution
to America's heritage.
(Library of Congress)

ANDREW B. GRAY
(San Diego Historical Society)

JOHN C. CREMONY
(Arizona Historical Society, Tucson)

Furthermore, Graham had an obsession about rank and importance which made Bartlett and Gray appear as relatively modest men. Graham judged his status equal or superior to everyone except Bartlett. He would supervise the surveys and assign the work load. Gray would be a Boundary Commission spear carrier keeping a pen handy for signing documents submitted by Graham and approved by Bartlett.

Graham had no sooner reached El Paso than he ordered Whipple off the surveying line for consultations. He notified Bartlett that within a few days we "will be cheerfully united. . . ." However, he again postponed their meeting until all employees had "presented their work for my inspection."[33]

The second letter of postponement antagonized Bartlett because Graham wrote it in pencil. The commissioner felt slighted and never forgave the colonel.

Meanwhile, a choking General Pedro García Conde complained that Lieutenant Whipple had left the boundary line without explanation. "The increased expenses I am incurring in this desert," wrote the Mexican commissioner, "and the loss of time could lead to serious consequences. I am telling you how I feel and I am reporting it to my government."[34]

Bartlett apologized. The harassed and thoroughly disgusted commissioner then ordered Graham to quit examining papers and report to Santa Rita.

Graham arrived with information to "greatly expedite the future progress of the survey." He envisioned the entire border as divided and subdivided into eastern and western divisions. A work force would "cut a line 20 feet wide through the forests of southern and western New Mexico . . . to place the iron markers." The colonel would organize and direct activities. All he asked was recognition by his official title.

On August 4, Bartlett introduced Graham to commission and military authorities as "colonel and principal astronomer." Two days later Graham wrote a hysterical letter to Bartlett demanding to know why he had not been acknowledged as *head* of the Scientific Corps.

Bartlett explained that Graham was not "head" of the *topographic* Scientific Corps. "Topographic" was an easily understood term. Without that qualifier, Graham could "take over every officer and assistant in the commission from Mr. Gray . . . downwards."[35]

Graham responded that Gray was Graham's superior *unless* Gray sought to direct the day-to-day surveying details. That was Graham's job. If Gray did assume those mundane particulars, he would have to submit to Graham's supervision.[36]

Bartlett referred to a letter by Secretary Stuart stating, "The duty of the chief astronomer is to determine the initial and intermediate astronomical points, while that of the surveyor is to run the boundary line between such points, each acting under the direction of the commissioner, their common supervisor. . . ."[37]

A stunned Graham demanded a copy, a request Bartlett denied. Graham then halted all boundary work, his action supported by lieutenants Burnside and Whipple. Burnside even left for Washington with secret messages from Graham to the Secretary of Interior.

To strengthen his position, Graham hit where the commissioner was vulnerable: the initial point compromise near Mesilla. "With that question I do not intervene as its decisions belong to the joint commission," the colonel wrote Stuart. Then, after admitting the subject was none of his business, he damned the commissioner for five and one-half paragraphs as a scoundrel giving away territory belonging to the United States. "I allude to the circumstances sir to show . . . how important it is that I not surrender into the hands of Mr. Bartlett," he said.[38]

He also blasted Bartlett to Colonel J. J. Abert, commander of the Topographic Corps. Graham said he had been "kept actively employed for 32 years in the corps without any rest," and swore he would not permit his reputation "to be tarnished by being responsible for the work of incompetent people. . . ."[39]

García Conde again complained about the interminable stalling. On September 12, 1851, Stuart reassigned Major William Emory to the border as a replacement for Graham.

Stuart also accused Gray of dawdling and pouting in California, snapping that the Mexican and American commissions had other things to do than sit around awaiting Gray's arrival. Gray was to cease delaying the surveys, and to "remove the obstacle [to the initial point agreement] . . . by affixing your signature to the requisite papers."[40]

After mailing the letter, Stuart had second thoughts and decided to dismiss Gray along with Graham. New orders dated November 4, 1851, reached Emory in Texas. He would replace both Gray and Graham, and sign all the documents. Bartlett, of course, had not been informed about anything.[41]

Seeing Inez Home

COMMUNICATIONS took weeks between New Mexico and Washington, and while awaiting government decisions regarding the initial point, Bartlett examined the borderlands in detail. Sonora especially tweaked his curiosity, and he was determined to explore it. So in mid-May, 1851, Bartlett pulled a commission wagon train from Santa Rita, and took it south for a firsthand observation of Mexico.

Along the way, some commission business would be done, of course. Bartlett planned to follow Cooke's Road to the Gila River, and determine if surveying equipment could be shipped across it. Lieutenant Colonel Philip St. George Cooke had laid out the trail in 1846 as the rugged Mormon Battalion marched with the "Army of the West" toward California. As roads go, it was a rough, narrow washboard between Santa Fe and San Diego, but it linked the West Coast to the American Union.

Bartlett did little more than cross the wagon road on his journey south into Sonora, his initial destination being Fronteras. A desolate community of crumbling adobe buildings greeted him, the people jostling around to trade, gawk and gossip. The Mexicans assumed the Americans to be wealthy because they carried such a varied assortment of iron cooking utensils.

General José Carrasco, who provided a military escort for the Mexican Boundary Commission in California, had been preparing to ride out of Fronteras on an expedition against Apaches when Bartlett and his entourage unexpectedly arrived. Carrasco delayed his foray for a few days in order to entertain his guests, and that delay gave Bartlett an opportunity to evaluate the Mexican militia.

Four hundred soldiers (three companies of infantry and one of cavalry) lined up for Bartlett's inspection, and the commissioner described them in his journal as wearing loose-fitting white cotton trousers and shirts. Broad-brimmed sombreros (some of straw) covered their heads. The soldiers were either barefoot, or wore rawhide sandals laced with leather thongs. Even the officers looked ragged and tattered. In terms of food, each combatant carried six days rations (one ration being a half-pound of dried jerky, two pounds of wheat, and a half-pound of brown sugar). A blanket, an earthen cup, a sheath knife, a musket and forty rounds of ammunition rounded out the supplies and armament.[1]

Bartlett considered Carrasco well-read and articulate, grounded in science and literature, a soldier who lived on the northern frontier because he had the gritty soul of a relentless fighter. Carrasco talked knowingly of politics and war, but he growled angrily of how the neighboring state of Chihuahua had signed a peace treaty with the Apaches. This meant that Chihuahua need not fear the dreaded marauders. Meantime the Apaches soaked Sonora in blood, hauling back Sonoran booty and captives to Chihuahua for trade. In revenge, Carrasco had raided Janos, Chihuahua, forty miles north of Casas Grandes, killing twenty warriors and capturing sixty women and children, all of whom he sold into slavery. This strike demolished the peace treaty, the furious Apaches growling that if Chihuahua could not protect them, they might as well pillage both states instead of one.

Carrasco had prepared Monterrey's defenses during the Mexican War, and knew the power of American cannon. He also showed a surprising knowledge of American officers, commenting that he respected General Winfield Scott, but hoped the Whig ticket would not nominate him for president. Scott should be given three or four million dollars and retired to Great Britain or France as minister, Carrasco grunted.[2]

When the visit ended, Carrasco marched away to new adventures while the commissioner had trouble getting out of town. Fronteras wasn't the most romantic nest in Mexico, but it beat cold camps on the desert. Bartlett planned to depart on Sunday, and had promised his men additional pay, but the mechanics refused to labor on the Sabbath. The commissioner grumbled that he had never known his teamsters so spiritually inclined, especially since they drank so much mescal.

From Fronteras, Bartlett traveled to Bacoachi, a Sonoran village "degraded and filthy," its adobe buildings crumbling. The church had no roof. People lived in terror of Apaches, an apprehension so destructive of self respect that the residents could not even improve their defensive positions. The town squatted on a sun-scoured desert plateau, the inhabitants preferring the security of the high mesa to the more comfortable, but dangerous, luxury of greenery and coolness along the Sonora River, a mile away.

In Bacoachi, Bartlett encountered the *Quien Sabe* (Who knows?) syndrome. When asked questions, the people replied, *Quien Sabe*, a response infuriating to Bartlett. To him, it marked a paralyzed society unable to define its needs, unwilling to care for itself.

The commission paused in Bacoachi long enough to catch its breath, then hurried to Arizpe, formerly the capital of Sonora, where Bartlett wrote with relief of the intelligent classes. The *pueblo* retained a semblance of past glories in its bold architecture, the walls higher than anything seen thus far in the Southwest or Mexico. Several buildings were of stone, capped with brick and ornaments sufficient to impress a visitor. At one time Arizpe had five thousand people, but because of civil discords and Apache encroachments the figure had been reduced to fifteen hundred. It "was indeed melancholy to walk through deserted streets and see dilapidated tenements, neglected courts, closed stores," Bartlett wrote. For three days the Americans relaxed, enjoying the courteous manners of the aristocracy and tolerating the curiosity and grossness of the masses. The crowds never understood why these foreigners had not come to trade. Throngs swarmed around the tents, fascinated by the Anglo habit of tooth-brushing, and puzzled by the consumption of Seidlitz powder, a pioneer laxative.

Because fifteen cases of scurvy threatened his employees, Bartlett now returned to Santa Rita, New Mexico, treating the sick along the way with citric acid, vinegar, pickles and dried apples. All things considered, Santa Rita looked good when the tired caravan arrived on June 17, 1851.[3]

The little valley of Santa Rita was over six thousand feet above sea level, and the Mogollon Mountains, the Mimbres and the Black Range refracted the sun's rays, twisting the rocky bluffs into oblique shadows and colors. These same mountains held copper, and Don Francisco Manuel Elguea, a Chihuahua merchant and delegate to the Spanish court, had discovered it in 1804. During the next decade an estimated two hundred mule trains with six million pounds of copper ore streamed thirteen hundred miles each year to the smelter in Mexico City.[4]

The mines sank into disuse after Mexican independence in 1821, and while historians generally blame their demise on hostile Apaches (certainly a factor), they actually died from a lack of market. Santa Rita languished until the 1880s when it restarted, and the site gradually became the largest open-pit copper mine in the world.

During Bartlett's time, the Apaches at Santa Rita were at peace with the United States. Mangas Coloradas, the Mimbres Apache warlord, operated with a hundred nearby warriors. Colonel Lewis S. Craig, commander of the 3rd Infantry boundary escort of eighty-five soldiers, gave Mangas a field officers coat with epaulettes. In his half-uniform (Apaches did not generally wear trousers), Mangus strutted around the clearing. Of course, since Indians were a democratic people, Mangas lost the uniform while gambling. Then another Indian strutted.[5]

Although the Apaches were peaceful, the commission always escorted them from the compound prior to darkness. On June 27, John Cremony, the guide, investigated a campfire along the creek, suspected Indians, but instead of finding Apaches, he encountered Comancheros. "Comanchero" referred to anyone trading with Indians, especially Comanche Indians. During the late 1700s, Comancheros were mostly Mexicans or Pueblo Indians. After the Civil War, the word "Comanchero" acquired an evil connotation due to cattle rustling, whiskey selling and gunrunning. Americans considered Comancheros filthy, ignorant and bedraggled, oddities rather than dangerous, and their trade was restricted through licensing. Pueblo Indian Comancheros received free permits. Mexicans and Americans needed testimonials, plus a list of tribes they planned to contact. They agreed not to deal in weapons, and paid a fee of ten dollars.

Comancheros regularly purchased captives and if the prisoner was an Indian child, it was frequently sold as a slave to Mexican *hacendados* or mine owners. However, if the captives were Mexican children, they were often swapped for trade items or held for ransom.

In the United States, trading in captives was illegal, and these Comancheros in Santa Rita were caught in the act. A young Mexican girl rode with them, and Bartlett sent Craig to enforce the 11th Article of the

Treaty of Guadalupe Hidalgo forbidding the slavery, purchasing or selling of Mexican citizens. He ordered the Comancheros arrested and the
girl released. Craig promptly shackled Peter Blacklaws and José Faustin
Valdez of Santa Fe, and Pedro Archeveque of Algodones. Blacklaws
claimed to be a trader, although he had no license, whereas Valdez and
Archeveque said they were laborers.[6]

Blacklaws admitted acquiring the girl from the Pinal Indians, but
could not get his story straight as to whether he had outfitted his expedition for the express purpose of buying her, or whether she had
been an incidental purchase. The commissioner regrettably had no
authority to punish the Comancheros, only to take charge of their cap-
tive, Inez Gonzáles. He released the Comancheros with a warning that
a delay in leaving would have serious consequences. In less than twenty minutes, the traders vanished.[7]

Inez Gonzáles was fifteen years old, attractive and mature. She explained that the Pinal Apaches, who lived in the Pinaleños Mountains,
had attacked a caravan near Santa Cruz, Sonora, and had taken her,
two female companions, and a young boy into captivity. Comancheros purchased the other three and hustled them north. The Pinals
worked Inez in the fields until her recent sale. She had not been raped.

Bartlett had barely assigned living quarters to the girl when a more
ominous incident occurred. As John Cremony lay reading in his tent,
two naked Mexican boys dashed in and dived beneath his cot. The
youths had escaped from the Mimbres Apaches.

"Are there any Indians around?" Cremony shouted to his black
slave.

"Not yet," came the reply. "But there is a bunch of them headed this
way."

The interpreter jammed on his boots, buttoned his trousers, grabbed
two revolvers, and yelled for a carbine and shotgun. With the two
Mexican boys clinging closer than the sweat oozing down his back-
bone, Cremony started toward the commission compound. Within
thirty feet the Apaches had him surrounded and were demanding the
boys. Cocking his six-shooters and, standing back-to-back with his
slave, Cremony bluffed his way for another two hundred yards. By
this time several soldiers had arrived. Bartlett came on the run too, and
Cremony turned the boys over to him with an explanation.

Saverro Aredia was about thirteen as near as he could guess, and
was the older of the two. The Apaches stole him from Bacoachi six

months earlier. José Trinfan was ten or twelve, and he came from Fronteras. He had been a prisoner nearly all of his life.

The Apaches looked physically capable of retaking the boys. However, since Mangas Coloradas was missing, Bartlett convinced the Indians to hesitate. Then while everyone waited for Mangas, Bartlett quietly dispatched the boys to the camp of General García Conde.

When Mangas arrived, Bartlett warned the huge Indian that Article 11 of the Treaty of Guadalupe Hidalgo obligated him to return Mexican captives to their homelands. Mangas Coloradas countered that he had a right to enslave Mexicans, that he and they were still locked in warfare, and that he could not understand how the Americans could be so friendly with a people who were enemies a short time earlier. The United States ought to be assisting his efforts, not hindering them.

Discussions dragged on until the Apaches accepted payment in trade items plus $250.[8] The significance was not that Americans had prevailed, or that Mangas Coloradas had settled for dry goods and money. The action clearly demonstrated that the United States would take seriously its treaty obligations. Mexico, which lost everything and gained nothing from the late war, now saw returns trickling in. For Bartlett had done more than just free several captives; he had recognized the legal and moral responsibility of a large and powerful nation toward a smaller and weaker one. The border could be more than just a line between two cultures, it could be a place where friends meet.

The Bartlett-García Conde Compromise of a few months earlier, where the western boundary had left the Rio Grande forty-two miles north of El Paso rather than eight, was delaying the surveys. Until Washington made its decision, it made little sense to work west toward the Gila headwaters. Some of the Rio Grande could be surveyed, of course, but with most of the commission in Santa Rita, over a hundred miles northwest of El Paso, disruptions and delays lasting weeks would occur if employees left the line and shuffled back to Texas. Anyway, Apaches had stolen half the livestock, so the major equipment could not be moved. While the Americans awaited additional work animals, John R. Bartlett decided to see Miss Inez home to Santa Cruz, Sonora, about eighty miles. He would also visit General García Conde.

The commissioner's party headed southwest out of Santa Rita on August 27, 1851, with Inez on the gentlest mule. Seventy men made up the caravan, including Gray who wished to explain his "Compromise" opposition to García Conde, and Graham who wanted to discuss with García Conde the abuses and humiliations he had suffered by not being recognized by his proper title. He also did not want important decisions made without his knowledge.

For days Bartlett followed García Conde from one water hole to another, and finally caught the Mexican Commissioner at a sulfurous spring. Gray argued his position, but never changed García Conde's mind. The Mexican commissioner adamantly said, "the initial point has been determined and cannot be reversed." In the meantime, the commission agreed to finish surveying the Gila and portions of the Rio Grande. Gray and Whipple would supervise operations from the Gila to the Colorado junction, and then proceed to San Diego. Graham and Salazar would survey the Rio Grande from El Paso to the Gulf. Bartlett would go to the Gila after returning from Santa Cruz.[9]

The American commissioner struck out for Santa Cruz on September 9, as unrelenting rains turned the desert into a quagmire. Wagons sank to their hubs. The weather improved near the Chiricahua Mountains where Bartlett learned that Graham, instead of heading toward El Paso, had been following and was running short of provisions. Bartlett reluctantly shared his commission supplies.

Days later the commission straggled into Santa Cruz for a joyful reunion of Inez Gonzáles with her family. Mother, uncles, aunts, stepfather, brothers and sisters screamed and wrapped her in frenzied embraces. Bartlett said even the teamsters had "big tears . . . on weather-beaten faces."[10]

With the girl's release now behind him, Bartlett turned to the perplexing actions of Graham. On one occasion Graham approached Bartlett's tent for water, and encountered Dr. Webb, who raised his voice and censured the colonel for consuming too many supplies. Webb yelled that the colonel should not be in Sonora but on the Rio Grande. "Do not get excited or in a passion," Graham snapped back.

The doctor screamed that he was not excited, that he was not in a passion, that he always talked this way. He accused Graham of commissary negligence.

Colonel Graham swore profanely, then snickered at Webb for using "baby talk." He accused the doctor of "blackguarding" him. Choking, Webb responded, "You have taken advantage of me. I cannot compete with anyone who swears or drinks."

"Is that so?" replied the scarlet-faced colonel. Graham censured Webb for removing several gallons of whiskey from Lieutenant Green. "You must drink as much as anyone," Graham snickered.

"If you had opened your ears, you would have heard me say it was for the preservation of reptiles and insects," Webb shouted. At this point, Bartlett separated them, and Graham stormed out. In his own quarters he fumed, decided he had been insulted, and sent a crisp note to the doctor demanding satisfaction "according to the rules of honor."

"After a night of calm repose," Webb responded that he was declining to "take the field . . . and blow one another's brains out. . . ." The incident thus passed without any apologies. Graham departed for El Paso.[11]

After describing Santa Cruz as a sewer of thieves, Bartlett headed for Ures, the capital of Sonora. The road was but a footpath, and the water holes polluted. Most of the commission became sick, Bartlett collapsing with backache, fever, chills and intestinal disorders. He struggled into Ures, rented a small room and rested. John Cremony and artist Henry Pratt were ill too, but less critically than Bartlett. Dr. Webb diagnosed typhoid in all cases.

Bartlett spent two months recovering while José Carrasco died of cholera and García Conde of typhoid. The Mexican commissioner had fallen ill in Santa Cruz, but recovered after six weeks in bed. He moved to Arizpe, his birthplace, where he suffered a relapse and died on December 19 in the same house where he had been born forty-seven years earlier.[12]

As Bartlett slowly recovered, the commission's diminishing financial status demanded his time. The commission had no money, and no one in Ures could cash its vouchers. Bartlett considered returning to Santa Rita, but doubted he could survive the trip.

Bartlett dispatched Pratt, Cremony, Webb and others toward the Gila to intercept Gray, while he himself took a carriage to Guaymas and caught a ship to San Diego, arriving on February 9, 1852. Gray and Whipple greeted him. They had surveyed the Gila to within sixty miles of the Colorado, then shut down operations due to supply shortages. While coming west, an assistant surveyor, Tom Harper, drowned while bathing in the Colorado.

Webb and the others straggled in a week later. They had avoided the Gila, marching straight for San Diego while exhaustedly discarding bedding, books, records and clothing.[13]

Half of the American Boundary Commission was now stranded in San Diego. Payrolls had to be met, new equipment had to be purchased, two-thirds of the boundary had not yet been surveyed, and the American commission was on the wrong side of the continent from where the work needed doing.

Like Weller before him, Bartlett had no money, and San Francisco was the only place to cash vouchers. He made a hurried trip on the *Sea Bird*, and obtained financing. Upon returning to San Diego, however, he learned that Gray and Graham had been replaced by Major William A. Emory. John Cremony suspected the boundary commission was dissolving, so he resigned as guide and was replaced by mountain man Antoine Leroux.

Lieutenant Whipple wanted to be released too, and he asked Secretary Stuart for permission to return home by way of China so that he might make "extensive studies of magnetic observations around the earth." Stuart apparently was not ready for all that knowledge, and he ordered Whipple to join Emory in El Paso.[14]

As for Emory, he left Washington in the fall of 1851, a man destiny had called to bring order out of the boundary chaos. He was an efficient officer, staid when compared to Graham, as picturesque as a mesquite bush, afflicted with self-importance. The *New Orleans Picayune* described Emory as assisting with the survey, and the young officer flew into a rage. He demanded a retraction, saying "It is a belittling matter to be sent out there as an assistant."[15]

He arrived in El Paso on November 25, 1851, and described the surveys as having "more complications than expected." He said the commission "comprised a large party, half with Colonel Graham at this place, and the other half with Mr. Bartlett God-knows-where, the whole numbering one hundred and upwards, no money, no credit, subdivided among themselves and the bitterest feelings between the different parties." Emory accused Bartlett of not only spending all the appropriations, but most of the anticipated money, too.[16]

Although ordered to join the commissioner in the field, Emory growled that "no one knew where the commissioner was." Bartlett, he said, was "doing nothing but playing the game of Kilkenny cats," and agreed with Lieutenant E. L. F. Hardcastle, who wrote from Washington, that new appropriations would be wasted unless the government recalled Bartlett. As for the remaining survey work, Emory and interim Mexican commissioner José Salazar agreed to finish the Rio

Grande, then concentrate on southern New Mexico. Emory figured four months would be sufficient for the entire project.[17]

El Paso was too wild anyway, and Emory wanted a firmer disciplinary hold on civilians and soldiers. Already a near riot in Pioneer Plaza had caused Emory to jail Lieutenant O. H. Tillinghast on unspecified charges. A hint of what happened came when Tillinghast from solitary confinement asked if his arrest stemmed from "playful conversations with Mrs. Wilkins."[18]

As Emory organized his work, finances and low morale dogged him. Employees demanded back pay, and Emory wrote, "I was obliged to put down a riot . . . at the risk of being shot by an insubordinate fellow insane from the effects of intoxicating mescal." M. V. Hipple, supervisor of a surveying party, was down to his last three pencils, and had no money for more. Creditors pressed for payment of boundary supplies, and in despair Emory wrote the chief clerk of the Department of Interior, saying, "God knows how the thing has happened, but unless relief is afforded I stand a chance of seeing the inside of a Texas jail." In April 1852, he asked Secretary Stuart for an additional $35,000, advising him that to discontinue the boundary work for want of finances would mean greater expenses at a later date.[19]

The situation eased with authorization from Stuart to draw funds against the department. A San Antonio-bound train had $5,000 in coin, so Emory exchanged a government draft for it. Cash enabled him to pay the employees.

Major Salazar, the acting Mexican commissioner, appeared on August 1 with survey maps of the initial point at Mesilla, New Mexico. Emory had avoided acknowledging the initial point because he lacked faith in Bartlett's judgment. Yet, by refusing to sign, he risked being recalled as Gray had been. Therefore, Emory signed, stipulating that he was merely "confirming a boundary line agreed on by the two commissioners, April 20, 1851."[20]

Turning to the downstream Rio Grande surveys, where several channels existed, Emory and Salazar recognized the deepest one as the international boundary. Ysleta and Socorro had been established in 1680, San Elizario about 1781, all of them on the south bank. But that main channel of over a century ago had become the *Rio Viejo del Brazito* (old arm of the river) in 1852. Now, the communities were on the north bank and in the United States.

The Rio Grande enters the rugged Mariscal Canyon of the Texas Big Bend. Note horseman in foreground. (Clifford B. Casey Coll., Archives of the Big Bend, Alpine, Texas)

Next, Emory and Salazar hoped to map the rugged Rio Grande country between Presidio and the Pecos River. However, as the weeks passed, Salazar fell behind since he was more hampered financially than his American counterpart. Emory moved ahead, assigning Tyler Wickham Chandler, son of a Whig congressman, to survey the canyons of the Rio Grande. Lieutenant Duff C. Green and a thirty-five man military escort went with him. They entered the Big Bend of the Rio Grande at the Bofecillos Mountains, crossed to the Mexican side for easier traveling, and obtained a clear view of the Chisos Mountains in Texas. Chandler named the most prominent peak, Mount Emory. After losing nearly eighty mules in the dense thickets, Green circled farther south while Chandler and a small party floated down the Rio Grande on skiffs. The river repeatedly swamped the boats, destroying provisions and forcing Chandler to scale cliffs. Green figured that either the river or the Comanche or Lipan Indians had killed Chandler.

The remaining Big Bend surveys were just as discouraging. The rapids in Santa Elena Canyon were too fierce. In Mariscal Canyon, the surveyors lost a craft carrying clothes and provisions, and in Temple and Reagan canyons, most of the boats capsized. The boundary men went without food for three days. Shoes split on the sharp rocks, and blood occasionally stained the stones. "I . . . expect (God willing) to report to you with my notes in about eighteen days," Chandler wrote Emory. On November 24, he and his ragged party, barefoot, destitute and bruised, stumbled into Fort Duncan, near Eagle Pass.[21]

By now, Emory had again reached the end of his financial tether. His additional funds were nearly expended, employees had quit, and broken and destroyed equipment could neither be repaired or supplemented. The Seminole chief, Wild Cat, operating out of Mexico, repeatedly threatened Emory's surveying parties. To make matters even more dangerous, his route cut the Comanche War Trail where it entered Mexico. Emory asked Colonel D. S. Miles of Fort Fillmore, New Mexico, for advice. "If you are not furnished a safe and suitable escort," Miles told him, "I would sit down, report the fact and await further instructions from the War Department. You cannot be blamed for preserving the lives of your men, but you might be if any get massacred."[22]

Emory considered these words good guidance. He would continue downstream, avoid Indian encounters by momentarily ignoring the incomplete Big Bend surveys, and await instructions from Washington.

5

Where Egos Collide

Across the continent Bartlett prepared to leave San Diego. By now he knew of Emory's arrival, and the dismissal of Gray and Graham. He also knew his travels and expenditures had created national controversy. In addition, because the initial point on the Rio Grande was drawn forty-two miles north of El Paso, the Whigs were being derided as a party of land give-aways.

Anticipating a forthcoming conflict between himself and politicians opposed to the present administration, Bartlett published a full-page explanation of his actions in the *San Diego Herald*. His defense was also a counterattack on McClellan, Graham and Emory. He accused the first two of blocking every constructive act, and the latter for seeking "paramount honors for himself."[1]

On May 28, 1852, Bartlett's caravan of thirty-five civilians and fifteen soldiers left San Diego for El Paso. Four days later, two soldiers, Corporal William Hays and Private John Condon deserted from Fort Yuma and headed on foot for California. Searchers led by Lieutenant Thomas W. Sweeney couldn't find them, but they did warn Colonel Lewis S. Craig, in command of Bartlett's military escort, of possible trouble should the deserters be confronted.

As often happened, Bartlett was out ahead of his escort on the evening of June 2, when Craig encountered the deserters near Alamo Mucho, roughly eight miles from present-day El Centro, California. The colonel paused to talk, assuring the soldiers that he understood the unpleasantness of life in the primitive, remote border furnace of Fort Yuma. If they would return to Yuma, he promised to try transferring them to his command.

Both deserters ignored the offer. Craig watched them disappear, discussed options with sergeants Quin and James Bales, then decided to talk again. After trailing them for five miles, Craig dismounted from his mule, leaving his revolver and sword hanging on the saddle. As the deserters hesitated and listened to Craig's reasoning, the colonel's mule wandered off. Craig shouted for Sergeant Quin to retrieve it. The deserters panicked, chased Quin off, wounded Sergeant Bales, and shot Craig down, killing him instantly.

Quin frantically rode into Bartlett's camp, and within minutes a relief party led by Lieutenant Whipple was riding hard. They found Craig's body and buried it at Alamo Mucho.

The government reinterred the remains in San Diego and named Fort Craig, New Mexico, in the colonel's memory. As for the murderers, the Army offered its usual $30 reward for each deserter, and then tacked on an additional $100. Less than two weeks later, on June 13, a band of California Indians purchased the deserters' weapons and took the men prisoner. A court-martial followed in San Diego. The condemned rode to the public gallows on January 31, 1853, while dressed in shrouds and sitting on their own coffins. Before dying, they advised others not to imitate their wicked ways.[2]

Bartlett's boundary commission continued east across the muddy Colorado to where Whipple and a small crew had surveyed the final sixty miles of Mexican border along the Gila River. The task took a month in the 120° heat. Mexico and the United States now had a common boundary from the Gila headwaters to the Pacific Ocean.

In Tubac, with its "dilapidated buildings, . . . and an equally ruinous church," Bartlett again encountered the beauteous Inez González, the young woman upon whom he had lavished so much time, expense and attention. She now lived in sin with Captain Gómez, commander of the small Mexican garrison. Such licentious behavior nearly shattered Bartlett's puritan sensibilities, and he prevailed upon the captain to per-

The organ pipe cactus grows only in south central Arizona and Mexico, areas crossed by Commissioner Bartlett on many occasions. (National Park Service)

mit an interview with Miss González. No doubt he suspected that if given an opportunity, she would once again return to Santa Cruz. He was wrong. If being the mistress of Gómez was not the best of all possible worlds, it was surely the best since being returned to Mexico by the Americans.

Bartlett asked the village priest to intercede, but the padre shook his head. Bartlett thereupon wrote the governor of Sonora, requesting his influence in terminating the relationship. In the end, Bartlett's pleas came to nothing, and John C. Cremony, who later wrote his memoirs, is the source of what happened to Inez. Cremony said Miss González had two sons by Captain Gómez, and "he subsequently made amends by marrying her." He died shortly afterwards, and in the fall of 1862, she married the *alcalde* of Santa Cruz and bore him two children, a boy and a girl. Inez now needed medical attention, which she apparently found. Two years later, Cremony heard from her again, this time the news being more cheerful. In good health, she was the respected wife of the most influential man in the village, and "was universally esteemed for her many excellent qualities."[3]

The footsore John R. Bartlett entered El Paso on August 17, 1852, a year almost to the week after he abandoned Santa Rita to return the beauteous Inez González to her Sonoran home. Bartlett had traveled over two thousand miles, spent the appropriations and had less than one-third of the entire border surveyed. Now, he ordered Whipple to finish the line west from the initial point on the Rio Grande to the headwaters of the Gila. With that underway, he asked Lieutenant Duff Green for an escort to Eagle Pass, Texas, so that he could join Emory. Green refused, and suggested military assistance from Fort Fillmore, near Mesilla.

Instead, Bartlett prevailed upon Mexican Colonel Emilio Langberg, in El Paso del Norte for a visit, to provide an escort to Chihuahua City. The gracious colonel had no objections, but ten days later as the caravan rumbled past the decaying pueblo of Carrizal, forty mounted Apaches stormed from an *arroyo* and attempted to break the line of wagons. Fortunately, the Apaches had no firearms, and just as fortunately the caravan did. Nevertheless, the Mexicans and Americans hesitated to shoot because of the time needed to reload. The defenders pointed their weapons whenever the warriors rode close, and that successfully warned the attackers off.

The marauders captured ten mules and a horse. One Apache was shot, and one herdsman died from a lance thrust. So ended the only known Indian fight ever engaged in by a United States boundary commissioner.

Fellow travelers buried the luckless victim, and the caravan plodded to Chihuahua City, the largest town encountered by Bartlett since arriving in the American Southwest and Mexico. The village lay cupped in a mountain basin, its twelve thousand residents working in silver mines, business houses and haciendas. Although the cream of northern Mexico's society lived here, Bartlett was pleased when General Angel Trías and American Consul Bennet Riddells placed commission wagons behind walled enclosures. At least we were "free from the annoyance of the lazy, pilfering class which hover about town, and by whom a train and party like ours would be considered fair game," Bartlett wrote.[4]

Trías treated the Americans to a huge reception with quadrilles, waltzes and polkas. "One would imagine," Bartlett said, "the most fashionable hair dressers and dress makers had been employed," and that "Steward had a branch of his great New York establishment here, from which the gorgeous silks and satins and elegant muslins displayed in such profusion had been procured." However, the ladies soured Bartlett by smoking *cigarritos* between dances, a practice he at least agreed was "not accompanied by the filthy practice of spitting."[5]

Bartlett left Chihuahua City on November 1, and swinging southeast through Monterrey, the commissioner re-entered Texas at Rio Grande City, where he met Emory. They conferred on Christmas Day, 1852.

As might be expected, their discussions concerned money and the legality of the initial point north of El Paso. By then Congress had passed a supplemental boundary appropriations bill of $120,000, but it could not be spent until the administration renounced the initial point agreement. In the meantime, Franklin Pierce had defeated Winfield Scott for the presidency, and Bartlett no longer had a Whig power base. Changes would obviously be made in the boundary commission regardless of the surveying controversies.

Bartlett and Emory lacked sufficient funds to complete the Rio Grande surveys. Equipment was auctioned in San Antonio, the money satisfying employees for back wages. Disgustedly, Bartlett called the situation "a sad dilemma for a large body of men to be placed in by an act of Congress." He and Emory headed for Washington, and arrived on February 1, 1853.[6]

In a time for patience, California's new senator, the dark-eyed, former boundary commissioner, John Weller was not a patient man. Since his dismissal as boundary commissioner almost two years earlier, he had brooded about the injustice, and the more he nursed his humiliation, the deeper sank the heavy lines in his ruddy face. Now he would have his revenge. He would strike back at Secretary of Interior Ewing and the Whigs by destroying the credibility of a man he had never met, a man who, because of circumstances and politics, had taken Weller's place on the boundary commission.

Jealousy poisoned any charity in the little senator, for he had waited a long time to criticize all boundary commission acts other than his own. Before Bartlett had even left Texas, Weller stood on the Senate floor and ticked off a long list of Bartlett shortcomings: untidy, misdirected, discouraging, too expensive, blundering. He demanded that Secretary Stuart turn over to a Senate committee all papers relating to the boundary surveys.[7]

Weller based his denunciations on the accusations of Colonel John McClellan, the former chief astronomer dismissed by Bartlett for excessive drinking and incompatibility. The rambling, almost hysterical charges by McClellan had been ignored by Secretary Stuart, who believed the attacks were "referred under circumstances and sustained by such testimony," that they did not justify any investigation. Weller denounced the State Department excuses, and in a tedious speech he defended his own conduct as commissioner and indicted that of Bartlett. Angrily he insisted upon a full investigation by the Foreign Relations Committee and its eccentric chairman James M. Mason, a Democrat and a strong expansionist from Virginia.[8]

Over in the House, Texas Congressman Volney E. Howard, castigated the Bartlett-García Conde compromise regarding the Rio Grande initial point, and scolded the still absent Bartlett for destroying the possibility of a southern railroad route. Howard wanted Stuart reprimanded for protecting Bartlett, and for dismissing Gray, Graham and McClellan.[9]

Senator Thomas Jefferson Rusk, Democrat from Texas and the choice of many delegates for the 1856 presidential nomination, believed the Treaty of Guadalupe Hidalgo, because of the compromise, "had been departed from — palatably and clearly departed from — to the damage of the United States and in favor of Mexico." Rusk thundered that he would never vote another dollar of boundary appropriations without assurances "that the Treaty of Guadalupe Hidalgo, and not the negotiations between commissioners" would decide the initial point on the Rio Grande.

Senator John Clarke, the millionaire whiskey distiller whose son had been slain in Socorro, Texas, an act leading to the four hangings in front of the Socorro Mission, defended the administration and Bartlett. He questioned the unfairness of condemning Bartlett while the commissioner was still in the field, and before anyone had heard his side of the dispute.

But Congress was of no mind to wait. Judging by past wanderings, Bartlett might yet dawdle for months in Mexico or the American Southwest. So Washington politicians and most of the nation's newspapers flailed away, accusing Bartlett of bargaining away several thousand square miles of United States territory, yielding to Mexico the only feasible route for a transcontinental railroad.

The criticisms had a point. By the 1850s the national desire for an all-weather link between East and West was not necessarily the lustful yearnings of a few power-mad individuals. A steel ribbon between the two continental extremes was deemed imperative.

However, from the national uproar one might judge the southern route as the only one under consideration when in fact additional corridors were being contemplated. The shortest and most direct was from Missouri across the South Pass of the Rockies, and on to San Francisco. Other possibilities involved passes in the Rockies west of Albuquerque, New Mexico, although these were unproven by the Army Corps of Topographical Engineers. But until surveys demonstrated the feasibility of other routes, the Mesilla Strip, as the Compromise in question was often referred to, offered the only certain coast to coast connection.

The Foreign Relations Committee completed its investigation on August 20, 1852, and censured Secretary Stuart for defending Bartlett's "illegal acts." Chairman Mason, who imagined Northern plots everywhere, and who dressed in homespun clothing as a protest against Northern spinning mills, considered the Mesilla Strip more than worthless desert. A railroad across the Strip would tie the South economically to the West. Mason believed Bartlett had foolishly thrown it away, and he demanded that Mexico "give it back" because its loss was "a departure from the treaty." The Senate, or at least the Foreign Relations Committee, had spoken.[10]

If President Fillmore accepted the committee findings, he would have to censure Bartlett and declare the initial point agreement null and void. But if the president upheld his commissioner, the Senate would continue its freeze on boundary appropriations, and the surveys could not be completed within the foreseeable future.

Fillmore asked Stuart for an appraisal of the initial point controversy, and the secretary offered two options. He could declare Bartlett's appointment of Lieutenant Whipple as surveyor to be illegal, and therefore Whipple's signature on the agreement would be invalid. This would automatically void the Bartlett-García Conde compromise. Or Fillmore could simply repudiate the Compromise by denying Bartlett's authority to establish the initial point forty-two miles north of El Paso. The president considered his possibilities, and concluded that Bartlett had indeed acted improperly and illegally. Stuart notified the Mexican minister that New Mexico's southern boundary would have to be renegotiated.[11]

Meanwhile, Fillmore could not get Whig support for another term. The party chose the Mexican War hero Winfield Scott to oppose the unknown Democrat, Franklin Pierce. Scott might have won if the Whigs had not been branded as blunderers, participants in land giveaways. In the political overhaul that followed, President Pierce appointed Robert McClelland as secretary of the interior. Bartlett was out of a job even though, once back in Washington, he struggled to save his reputation from further inroads. In a political free-for-all, he and Gray took turns denouncing each other. A writer named "Vindex," generally assumed to be Emory, wrote newspaper letters describing the former commissioner as having "befogged brains."[12]

The *New York Herald*, one of Bartlett's few supporters, wrote editorials denying the United States had lost land because of the Bartlett-García Conde agreement. It referred to a map in the Chihuahua City governor's mansion which placed New Mexico's southern boundary as forty-two miles north of El Paso. According to this map, the Santa Rita mines rightfully belonged to Mexico, but Bartlett had skillfully negotiated them for the United States.[13]

Gradually the national controversy faded and in March 1853, the ex-commissioner asked the government to publish his memoirs. The Senate did not wish another furor, so it tabled the request. Bartlett therefore took his manuscript to Appleton and Company in New York. The publisher printed the two-volume work in 1854, included ninety-four woodcuts and sixteen lithographs, and added the artistic creations of Seth Eastman and Oscar Bessau. John Russell Bartlett's *Personal Narrative of Explorations and Incidents in Texas, New Mexico, California, Sonora and Chihuahua, 1850-1853*, is a classic of frontier history and literature.

Bartlett later wrote *The Literature of the Rebellion*, and *Memoirs of Rhode Island Officers in the Service of the Country During the Civil War*. He became secretary of state for Rhode Island, and served with the International Prison Congress in London. The commissioner lived to be eighty-one, dying of a heart attack in 1886. He never again visited the American Southwest.

BOOK
TWO

THE BORDER
ESTABLISHED

This is a [Mexican] Government of
plunder and necessity; we can rely on no
other influence but an appeal to both.

James Gadsden to Secretary of State
W. L. Marcy, October 18, 1853

Bad Roads and Flags of Contention

WHILE POLITICIANS BICKERED in Congress, and Bartlett and Emory were busily defending their records, other events moved the Mexican border toward conflict. In a sense it all started two decades earlier as Texas shifted into the status of a republic after being part of Mexico.

Texas had claimed the Rio Grande to its source as the republic's western boundary. Since the Rio Grande extended past Albuquerque and Santa Fe, New Mexico, and into present-day Colorado, this territory belonged to Texas, at least by Texas reasoning. However, in far-off El Paso del Norte and Santa Fe, the two towns largely affected, citizens ignored the Texas events taking place six hundred miles to the east. Few believed that Texas would ever seriously affect their lives. Most had always resided in Chihuahua or New Mexico, and the notion of themselves as Texans was preposterous. Nevertheless, Texas still annexed them, at least on paper.

So while this paper Texas was an enormous territory, the republic controlled only the lands north of the Nueces River and from the Gulf Coast west to Austin and San Antonio. The region between the Nueces and the Rio Grande, called the Nueces Strip, remained disputed between Texas and Mexico. However, the subsequent Mexican War allowed Texas to occupy the Nueces Strip. This left only the western territories to argue about.

To place the western territory of Texas in perspective, make it easier to govern, as well as to solidify its legal claim, Texas created on paper the immense county of Santa Fe. It included what is now West Texas (El Paso, the Panhandle and the Big Bend), New Mexico to the Rio Grande, the Oklahoma Panhandle and a sizeable chunk of Colorado, Wyoming and Kansas.

However, while Mexico had relinquished the land, the United States controlled it and refused to recognize Texas jurisdiction. Santa Fe County simply did not exist in Washington's eyes. Although boundaries were vague and yet to be sorted out, property west of the Pecos River belonged to the Territory of New Mexico.

The government created its own road from San Antonio to El Paso in February 1848 when Lieutenant Henry Chase Whiting carved a southern route through what is now Uvalde and Del Rio. Not to be outdone, Texas responded a month later. Robert S. Neighbors, a courageous Texas Indian agent, and Texas Ranger John Salmon Ford, opened a road from Austin, through Fredericksburg, to El Paso. Both trails carried forty-niners to California. In August alone, over four thousand immigrants refitted at El Paso for the grueling dash west.[1]

Primitive wagon roads from El Paso to California ran parallel to the international boundary, and were the nation's only year-round, overland route to the Pacific. They were twisting, dry, remote, generally uninhabited, plagued by marauding Indians. Yet, the wheels of a restless country left their ruts of empire in these sands of forsaken monotony, and by a quirk of history and geography, these southern highways gave the United States unforeseen leverage against Mexico. Americans would come to dominate the border because of a continuous east-west motion. More movement meant more villages, more people, more industry and business, and better communications and supply. Mexico could not counteract because its isolated border towns were merely terminal points of north-south arterials. Unlike the Americans, the Mexicans had few reasons to be traveling east and west along the international line.

Texas Governor George T. Wood notified President Polk in 1848 of his state's intention to organize (and occupy) Santa Fe County, and he requested that American troops not interfere. Of course, Washington did interfere, as there were uneasy national questions about Texas jurisdiction. Texas responded by splitting Santa Fe County into Presidio, El Paso, Worth and Santa Fe counties, and vowed to organize them one at a time.[2]

Presidio and El Paso counties comprised roughly what is far West Texas today. An exception is that El Paso County included a part of present New Mexico to the tiny village of Doña Ana, fifty miles north of El Paso, and alongside the Rio Grande. Otherwise, Worth County occupied the lower part of New Mexico, and Santa Fe County held everything else.

Texas assigned Robert Simpson Neighbors to organize counties out of the disputed region, and he concentrated on El Paso because Presidio County had too many Indians and not enough settlers. El Paso elections took place on March 4, 1850, and 760 residents voted to transfer their region out of New Mexico and into Texas. That evening several rousing balls occurred in the precincts, especially Doña Ana. El Paso had relinquished its New Mexico connection and voted to join Texas for two reasons: the influence of Anglo residents with cultural ties to the South, especially Texas, and economic advantages. Most of the commerce went east and west, and not north toward Santa Fe.

Federal officials thwarted Neighbors in the potential counties of Worth and Santa Fe. Newspapers refused to print stories of how advantageous it would be if New Mexico joined Texas. Northern New Mexico was composed of Hispanic elements, plus Anglos from the northern United States, settlers not ordinarily sympathetic to Texas and Southern claims.

Federal Judge Joab C. Houghton led the anti-Texas campaign, and threatened Neighbors with jail for attempting to organize the territory. In disgust, Neighbors returned to Austin and reported to Governor Peter Hansbrough Bell that Houghton, "a bitter, unprincipled and vindictive Whig," was not only corrupt, but feared change. Neighbors accused the judge of controlling the Mexican population, and threatening to incite the Pueblo Indians in order to keep himself in power.[3]

Houghton's efforts to prevent annexation brought accusations of interference in Texas' internal affairs, and Texas residents called upon Bell to put down the "insurrection." Neighbors suggested an army of three thousand. Bell called for two regiments of mounted troops, and offered military commissions to anyone raising volunteer forces. The legislators voted to retain Texas integrity "at all hazards and to the last extremity."[4]

By now President Zachary Taylor had died, and Millard Fillmore moved decisively to avert misunderstandings about his position on the Texas controversy. He admonished Texas by saying New Mexico had been "conquered and severed from the Republic of Mexico by American arms," and no state government could be established until boundaries had been clarified. He warned that any attempt by Texas to enforce its jurisdiction in New Mexico would be resisted by United States troops. Fillmore sent an additional 750 soldiers to New Mexico just to drive home the point.[5]

The Texas-New Mexico controversy also involved slavery and sectional disputes. With the exception of the South, most of the nation opposed New Mexico's annexation. If New Mexico became a part of Texas, it would amount to an extension of slavery. If New Mexico could resist Texas encroachment and align itself with the North, slavery would probably never enter the territory. However, since Washington considered conciliation the mood of the day, Senator Henry Clay authored the "Compromise of 1850." Texas would relinquish its trans-Pecos claim in exchange for $10 million.

Texas refused the offer, and Senator James A. Pearce of Maryland compromised the compromise by suggesting that the westernmost point of Texas be extended to El Paso, offering Texas the far western boundaries it has today. His plan retained the $10 million payment, a sum equaling the Texas national debt as a republic.[6]

As events shifted from the specter of Americans threatening to fire on other Americans, squabbles beset the border neighbors of Chihuahua and New Mexico. In October 1852, Mexico approved the *Jalisco* or *Guadalajara Plan* calling for a return of the presidency of General Antonio López de Santa Anna, the nation's hope as well as its curse. Santa Anna's ascension would cost Mexico a free press and concentrate legislative and executive powers within himself.

Since the new President feared revolution, he forbade private ownership of firearms, a decree throwing the residents of Chihuahua on the mercy of Apaches. Mexico promised regular soldiers for defense, but the lancers were too few and too poorly trained and armed.

In January 1852, José Cordero, a wealthy businessman and leader of the Liberal Party, became governor of Chihuahua and immediately issued proclamations empowering the people to arm themselves against Indians. The governor criticized the ineffectiveness of the local garrison, suggesting to Mexico City that military monies might be better spent by employing scalp hunters.

When the federal bureaucracy refused to finance scalp hunters, and denied Cordero's authority to arm the *Chihuahuenses*, the governor considered paying scalp hunters from his own tremendous wealth. Furthermore, he reorganized the Chihuahua military.

These statements and actions caused General Robles Pezuela, the minister of war, to question the governor's allegiance. Cordero responded with a cold challenge, saying "I beg his excellency to make a formal charge against me so that all the nation will know whether or not the governor of Chihuahua is a factionalist and guilty of an unbelievable lie." Pezuela hesitated to press charges he could not prove, so he encouraged the ambitions of Angel Trías, a former Chihuahua governor, and an equally wealthy man. Two days before Christmas 1852, Trías overthrew Cordero in a bloodless coup.[7]

Trías sent Colonel Emilio Langberg,[8] a Mexican military officer of Swiss extraction, to imprison and properly reindoctrinate the civil authorities of El Paso del Norte. Langberg swept through the border village, jailing the mayor, the customs agent, and Don Alejo García Conde, brother of the late boundary commissioner. Ramón Ortiz,[9] the local priest, and several citizens escaped to the American bank of the Rio Grande and sought the protection of Colonel Dixon Miles, commanding officer at Fort Fillmore. (El Paso's Fort Bliss had been vacated in an economy move.) Miles warned Americans to observe neutrality, and asserted that his soldiers would forcibly halt any attempt by United States citizens to interfere.[10]

In New Mexico, the ineffective John C. Calhoun, territorial governor, was doing what most ineffective governors do, which was nothing. He believed himself to be dying, and he was, so he devoted little time to the Indian problems, the border problems, the economic, political and military problems. Most of his energy went into construction of a suitable coffin, one built to specifications and kept in constant readiness. In mid 1852 he started his last trip to Washington, D.C., and he included the casket in his entourage. When approaching Independence, Missouri, he finally made use of his eternal home.

President Fillmore appointed William Carr Lane as Calhoun's replacement. The handsome, athletic Lane had studied medicine, fought in the Indian Wars against Tecumseh, and would have joined Latin America's Simón Bolívar had not his wife objected. He was a former mayor of St. Louis, and Millard Fillmore thought Lane the perfect answer to the neglected affairs of New Mexico.

Lane entered Santa Fe in September 1852, and his first obstacle was Colonel Edwin Vose Sumner, military commander and acting governor in Calhoun's absence. Sumner was a capable officer but had lamentable tendencies to undercut any authority other than his own. In a fit of pique, Sumner removed the American flag which had flown over the city plaza since the triumphant entry of Kearny in 1846. He reprimanded Colonel Horace Brooks for giving Governor Lane an extravagant welcome replete with cannon salutes and spirited tunes by the army band. He suggested to Washington that only the military should govern New Mexico, otherwise Santa Fe might as well be turned over to the Mexicans who would make "a pronunciamento every month or two."[11]

Lane requested a flag, any flag, and Sumner refused, saying he could not release government property to civilians. Later when Sumner blocked five hundred New Mexico volunteers from fighting the Navajos, Lane challenged him to a duel. Sumner refused.[12]

Both antagonists practiced a policy of self-interest. Lane was an ambitious governor who believed reputations were made by creating and then solving issues. Sumner agreed with Secretary of State Charles Conrad and General William Tecumseh Sherman. Conrad said the expense of protecting New Mexico came to over half of the territory's economic value. He urged that settlers be paid a fair price for their property, and be transferred to "more favorable regions." Sherman suggested to the House of Representatives that the entire territory be returned to Mexico.[13]

As for the Mesilla Strip, the Rio Grande border compromise between commissioners Bartlett and García Conde, strident voices called for American possession, and Richard T. Weightman, New Mexico's voteless delegate in Washington, openly urged Governor Lane to occupy it. The opportunity appealed to Lane because he was a romantic, a man whose background rang with all sorts of causes. He was not a soldier, but he loved the art of command, and if conceit and ambition led him to make foolish moves, such is the nature of those who are dream-smitten. And because he was a romantic, he took himself seriously — the greatest mistake of all.

Meanwhile, the *Chihuahuenses* resented American discussions and arguments regarding land the United States did not own, but acted as if it did. To demonstrate Chihuahua's effective control over the Mesilla Strip, Governor Angel Trías confiscated all Anglo property in Mesilla. However, instead of intimidating New Mexicans, the action merely hardened their stand for military intervention. The issue now became a prisoner of emotion and unreason, factors useless to judge by the standards of sensible men.[14]

Lane wrote his wife in February 1853, saying he planned to inspect southern New Mexico, and cautioning her not to be surprised if he took possession of the disputed strip. "Do not fear," he chatted easily, "that your husband will go filibustering in his old age; but be assured that if duty calls upon me to occupy and protect this country, provisionally, until the line [international border] shall be definitely established, I will do it."15

In the American village of Doña Ana on March 13, Lane issued a seven-point proclamation, terminating the rambling statement in this manner:

I, William Carr Lane, governor of the Territory of New Mexico (upon my own official responsibility and without orders from the cabinet in Washington) do hereby, in behalf of the United States, retake possession of the said disputed territory to be held provisionally by the United States until the question of the boundary shall be determined by the United States and the Mexican republic.16

In spite of these threats, Lane carefully stepped around the Mesilla Strip and continued south to El Paso where Hugh Stephenson, the white-haired, barrel-chested, square-jawed Chihuahua trader invited him to his hacienda. From the doorstep Lane tried to rally Texas volunteers to his cause, and expressed disappointment when only a few responded. The majority preferred to await a United States commitment.

In Chihuahua City, Governor Angel Trías wrote his own manifesto, one reasserting Mexican rights to the Mesilla Strip. It had been so for centuries, he thundered, and Commissioner Bartlett had affirmed it. Trías vowed to defend Mexican honor, and he led eight hundred fighting men toward El Paso del Norte.

As Mexican forces approached the border, Trías softened his belligerent attitude and appointed long-time political allies, Antonio Jáquez and Luís Zuloaga, to negotiate with Lane. The Chihuahua *Periódico Oficial* published the Trías and Lane positions, as well as a copy of letters exchanged. The discussions proceeded in mild terms, with Trías appearing in print as the more moderate and flexible.17

Governor Lane believed the United States would support his declaration of redefining the border. But when the government ignored his actions, Lane said Washington's silence "did not in the least invalidate the act."

Lane called upon Sumner and Miles to occupy Mesilla, and they frostily rebuffed him. The governor then reminded Miles that "the army was subordinate . . . to the civil authorities," and snorted that "some 350 U.S. troops . . . are unemployed and within five miles of the scene of the action; [yet they] fold their arms in frigid tranquility and thereby sustain the enemies of their country."[18]

As days passed and passions cooled, the United States minister in Mexico, Alfred Conkling, advised Governor Lane to "recede from his position as gracefully as possible."[19] Lane's support had now thoroughly eroded. The military had rebuffed him. Even Trías realized Lane had been beaten by his own superiors, and with the governor of New Mexico sitting in humiliating attendance, Trías threw a fourteen-hour victory fandango in El Paso del Norte. Late that summer, Lane resigned as governor, and waged an unsuccessful campaign for a New Mexico congressional seat.

President Franklin Pierce appointed David Meriwether as the next governor of New Mexico, and gave him explicit instructions not to aggravate the Mesilla Strip difficulties. The times required new ideas and different men. Pierce had a different approach for solving the Mesilla Strip question, so he recalled Conkling and appointed James Gadsden to replace him as the United States minister in Mexico.

Sell the Land,
or We Will Take It

JAMES GADSDEN hardly seemed suitable to negotiate the famed Gadsden Purchase, or the Treaty of Mesilla, as it was known in Mexico. During the Mexican War he had opposed the confiscation of Mexican territory, and sneered at Polk's war aims. While he never disputed the need for continental expansion, he saw no valid excuse for imposing it with gunpowder and bayonet.

Yet, his rabid convictions about Southern nationalism had made him a prominent figure. Slavery and State's Rights were God-given privileges that politicians had no business regulating. Northern abolitionists were the nation's greatest curse, and he believed the tax-gathering, monopolistic interests of the North should be countered by a pro-slavery alliance between the South and West. Such a partnership would need railroad connections, so Gadsden encouraged those Americans advocating acquisition of the Mesilla Strip.

Like many active and respected men, Gadsden served during the War of 1812 and the Florida Campaign of 1817-1818. He and Andrew Jackson became friends, and Gadsden rose in the diplomatic ranks. President James Monroe made him commissioner of the Seminole Indians, and he negotiated the Treaty of Fort Moultrie, Florida. In 1824 Monroe appointed him to the first Legislative Council of the Florida

Territory. Nevertheless, in spite of varied political experiences, Gadsden repeatedly stumbled while building a political career in Florida.

Discouraged, he went to South Carolina as president of the Louisiana, Charleston, and Cincinnati Railroad. Its 136 miles of track were meager even by standards of those days, but a more ambitious company might arise if the Mesilla Strip were acquired. A railroad from California through New Mexico and Texas might choose the Louisiana, Charleston and Cincinnati as its eastern and southern terminus.

Even so, Gadsden's name would scarcely be a historical ink blot had it not been for President Pierce and Secretary of War Jefferson Davis. Pierce had deep respect for the abilities and opinions of Davis, a lean Kentuckian whose physical appearance bore a similarity to Abraham Lincoln, then an obscure Illinois politician. Davis upgraded the United States Army, introduced an improved system of infantry tactics, and purchased modern weapons. He arranged the Southwest camel experiment to see if camels could replace horses, and although the idea never had a chance, it revealed Davis as an imaginative, innovative man.

Davis wanted a trans-continental railroad built across the Mesilla Strip, and that would require the purchase of sufficient land to avoid the Rocky Mountain barrier. So Davis prevailed upon Pierce to appoint Gadsden as minister to Mexico. Although the government refused to nominate Andrew B. Gray as Gadsden's personal adviser, Gray made an independent survey in 1853 for the Texas Western Railroad, and sent a report to Gadsden.[1]

Secretary of State William L. Marcy also wanted the United States released from Article XI in the Treaty of Guadalupe Hidalgo because Washington realized it could never prevent Indian marauders from crossing the border into Mexico. So long as the obligation lasted, it made the United States liable for damages.

Minister Gadsden traveled to Mexico and met with President Santa Anna on August 17, 1853, outlining the American concept of geographical predetermination, asserting the United States' need for sufficient and protective boundaries. He suggested Mexico sell her surplus, underpopulated regions and accept natural borders with mountain and desert outlines. The United States would pay a fair price.

The United States had money and wanted land; Santa Anna had land and wanted money. Since the Americans could afford to be generous, Santa Anna considered his opportunities. The Mexican treasury resembled the Chihuahua desert. Debts were unpaid, taxes were crushing, political corruption rampant. Filibusters crossed the border with monotonous regularity, and rebellion constantly fermented. Santa Anna needed cash, he needed it quickly, and the Americans were the only ones offering. "This is a government of plunder and necessity," Gadsden wrote to Marcy. "We can rely on no other influence than an appeal to both."[2]

A special messenger left Washington on October 22 with instructions regarding proposed boundary lines. Congress would pay $50 million for large portions of northern Coahuila, Chihuahua, Sonora, and all of Lower California. "It would be a permanent boundary, guarded and defended at much less expense than any other," President Pierce said. A second proposal of $35 million excluded Lower California. The line extended a little farther north in all of the mentioned Mexican states. A third offer of $30 million included Lower California and a line further north still, and a final suggestion of $20 million held the line but dropped the request for Lower California. Should none of the offers be accepted, Gadsden was to settle for enough land to build a railroad. If Mexico hesitated, Gadsden was to warn Santa Anna that the necessary territory might be taken by force.[3]

A panicked Santa Anna called for support from Europe. Spain responded by signing a vague treaty of defense, and France came through with equally meaningless gestures. Great Britain expressed no confidence in the dictator and refused any pledges.

In the meantime, Mexico could lose portions of its northern frontier and not get any money at all. New Mexico's Governor Lane blustered and threatened to overrun Mesilla. American filibusters, who were soldiers of fortune interested in conquering a piece of Hispanic America and creating an independent republic, also rampaged along the border.

Over in Lower California the American filibuster and newspaper-styled "Grey-eyed Man of Destiny," William Walker, had invaded the province with less than fifty adventurers and knocked that outpost to its knees. Although Walker could not hold his prize, his initial success demonstrated weaknesses in the Mexican government's ability to protect its territory. That same conquest also vividly demonstrated how close the Americans were to walking off with Lower California. Gadsden told the Charleston, South Carolina, *Daily Courier* that, "I could probably have obtained Lower California had not the insane [Walker] expedition caused Santa Anna to set his face against it." Actually, it likely cost the United States even more, as Santa Anna insisted upon a land bridge connecting Lower California with the Mexican

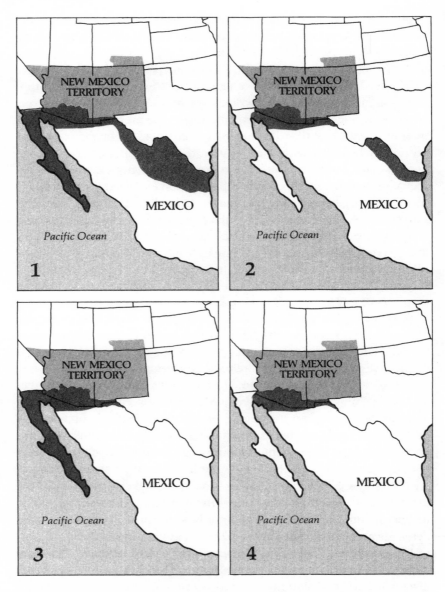

James Gadsden's four proposals for Mexican territory. (1) Offer $50 million. (2) $35 million. (3) $30 million. (4) $20 million. In the end, the Americans offered $15 million for substantially what is proposal 4. Congress reduced it to $10 million. Mexico then lopped off those areas that are presently south of the Mexican border.

union. Thus the present boundary angles northwest from near Nogales to the Colorado River, and deprives the United States of a seaport on the Gulf of California.

These violent forays by American opportunists plus a lack of support and confidence by foreign governments, undermined the negotiating strength of Santa Anna. In the end it is not surprising that he gave in to the Americans, but that he resisted giving more. Gadsden secured an area several times larger than the Mesilla Strip, a region shaped like an inverted triangle with its apex near Nogales. The east end was anchored three miles north of El Paso and terminated six hundred miles west at a point six miles north of the Gulf of California. On December 30, 1853, Gadsden and Mexican officials inked a "Treaty of Boundary and Cession of Territory," the Gadsden Purchase. The United States would pay Mexico $15 million, and assume all claims against the Mexican government by American citizens.

The United States had gained "sufficient land for a railroad," and Article XI of the Treaty of Guadalupe Hidalgo was abrogated. While the United States would aid Mexico in suppressing Indian attacks originating north of the border, it would not reimburse that ravaged country for damages. Both nations could navigate the Colorado north from the Gulf of California. Mexican land grants, religious preferences and traditions (but not laws) would be respected.[4]

All parties agreed to keep treaty details secret until ratification, but in early 1854 the news leaked and the document was in trouble. The *New York Herald* suspected Jefferson Davis' sly hand in the wording, and on January 20 the editor predicted the eventual addition of slave states. Several northern newspapers believed the purchase might eventually lead to the creation of a Mexican and Southern confederation.

The *New York Times* supported the treaty, as did the *Washington Union* and the *Savannah Republican*. Negotiations and acquisitions were far cheaper than armed conflicts, they said.[5]

Pierce's cabinet split over the proposed treaty, and the president himself expressed disappointment for not getting additional territory. He considered rejecting the treaty outright without even submitting it to the Senate. Only his secretaries, Marcy and Davis, plus the entreaties of Senator Thomas Rusk of Texas, persuaded him to accept it.

As for treaty timing, it could not have been worse. The emotion-charged Kansas-Nebraska bill had the country's attention, and the heated arguments involved slavery more than the mere admission of additional territories to the Union. The Gadsden Purchase injected new slavery issues into political debates, and legislators who were frustrated with the Kansas-Nebraska Act took out their anger on the Mexican treaty. Pierce growled that senators would have the responsibility for war, and just when it appeared the Purchase could not survive, William C. Dawson, a Whig and former Georgia judge, and James C. "Lean Jimmy" Jones of Tennessee, amended the document. They reduced the purchase price from $15 million to $10 million, and the Senate accepted it.[6]

Santa Anna criticized the United States for lopping one-third off the price, and he reduced the land size by nine thousand square miles. Juan Nepomunceno Almonte, the Mexican minister to Washington, suggested that the land reduction take place by shifting the western end of the Arizona border to twenty miles south of Yuma. That would get the boundary away from the tidal bore (where the ocean tide sometimes collided with such force against the Colorado channel, that the river current was pushed backwards), and establish the line at a point along the river where a bridge could safely be constructed. Reluctantly Santa Anna signed, lamely muttering that Mexico had done far better by this sale than with the Treaty of Guadalupe Hidalgo.[7]

The purchase embraced 29,640 square miles, of which 27,305 (24 percent) comprised today's southern Arizona. The remainder went to New Mexico, including the Mesilla Strip. The Rio Grande's new initial point, where the boundary left the river and struck west toward the Pacific, was three miles north of El Paso at 31° 47'. The boundary moved west for one hundred miles, then south to 31° 20', west again to the intersection of the 111th meridian, then west to the Colorado River 23.72 miles south of its confluence with the Gila. From there it followed the middle of the stream north to the already established boundary extending to the Pacific.

The Gadsden Purchase went for ratification to the House of Representatives, and unexpectedly stumbled into the formidable Thomas Hart Benton of Missouri. As a leading advocate of westward expansion, a man who fought so stubbornly for gold and silver currency that his colleagues nicknamed him "Old Bullion," the hawk-faced Benton favored an agricultural expansion into the West and the government sale of cheap land. He dreamed of a transcontinental linkup across the Midwest, not the South. Benton denounced the treaty as another Southern scheme to obtain slave soil, and accused Pierce of failing to

WILLIAM CARR LANE
(McNitt Coll., State Records Center
& Archives, Santa Fe)

JAMES GADSDEN
(Arizona Historical Society, Tucson)

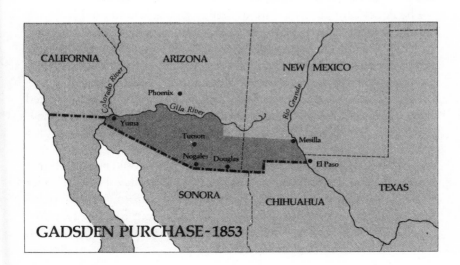

consult the House during negotiations. However, the House listened respectfully to his arguments, then approved the funds on June 29, 1854.

Two days later Juan N. Almonte, the distinguished silver-haired Mexican minister to Washington, called for the money. He received a check for $7 million, and a promise that the remaining $3 million would be paid when boundary surveys were complete.

The blighted regime of Santa Anna blew the $7 million in three months. In the meantime, Chihuahua's Governor Angel Trías refused to hand Mesilla over to the Americans even though it now belonged to the United States. Rumors said Trías would reinforce the village with additional troops, a threat upsetting Colonel Dixon Miles, now post commander of Fort Webster near Santa Rita. Miles threatened to march south and lob a few artillery rounds into El Paso del Norte.

New Mexico's Governor David Meriwether ordered Miles to keep quiet while he hurried to Fort Bliss, Texas, and invited Trías across the border for a series of conferences. The talks went so well that Trías dropped his hostility and offered to surrender the town. At the approach of a United States column, he would lower the Mexican flag and abandon Mesilla.

The Trías guarantee shocked Fort Bliss officers, who warned Meriwether that should American forces enter the Mesilla Strip, the Mexicans might declare war. Meriwether scoffed, and at noon on November 16, 1854, he and a detachment of soldiers occupied Mesilla. Trías pulled down the Mexican banner and departed.

The Americans cheered, ran up their own flag and saluted with two ground-shaking rounds of artillery. A military band played "Hail Columbia," "Yankee Doodle," and other patriotic tunes. Meriwether gave a brief address welcoming Mexican residents to American citizenship, promising protection from the Apaches and fairness in the courts.[8]

In spite of the Trías concession, Santa Anna claimed the United States had no right to Mesilla until Mexico received *all* of its money. Washington dismissed the flag-raising ceremony as a meaningless gesture.[9]

As matters stood, even the balance of payments could not save Santa Anna. At issue in Mexico wasn't the amount of money, but that Santa Anna had sold portions of the motherland. Within months the president had been forced into exile, and did not return for twenty years. On July 20, 1876, Santa Anna, "The Napoleon of Mexico," "The Man Who Was Mexico," died in Mexico City, poor, friendless and alone.

A Complete Line at Last

MAJOR WILLIAM HEMSLEY EMORY had nearly all the qualities necessary for success and greatness. His salty language and glistening red whiskers added emphasis to his nickname, "Bold Emory," a tag reputedly given in his youth when he shipped blooded Maryland horses to Kentucky. Emory rather liked the moniker. All prominent leaders had them, the tags implying a certain folksiness and making the wearer appear as one of the boys, which of course he was not. Emory had a propensity for haughtiness and was more of an aristocrat than Bartlett. He took care even to marry well, a decided asset for military advancement.

Men who did not like him, and this included practically everybody, admitted his brilliance. Yet his exploits, which rivaled Frémont's, never caught the public eye, probably because he did not have Frémont's charisma. Editors consistently ignored his accomplishments, even sneering at the landmarks named in his honor, such as Emory Pass in southern New Mexico and Emory Peak in the Big Bend of Texas, saying the public would next hear of Emory toads and other such objects.

Nevertheless, Emory was a man for tough assignments. Congress agreed to release sufficient money for the unfinished portion of the Rio Grande surveys, and on March 6, 1853, President Fillmore appointed Robert Blair Campbell as commissioner and William Emory as surveyor and chief astronomer. Campbell, a sixty-three-year-old South

Carolinian, had served as congressman as well as United States consul in Havana. He now resided in San Antonio.

Unlike Bartlett, Campbell possessed no extensive ambitions. He did not travel in Mexico, and he showed no literary interest. If Emory would handle the labor, assign the crews and make the decisions, Campbell would remain discreetly out of sight, sign the necessary documents and authenticate the surveys. It bothered him not at all to delegate authority, and his relationship with Emory seems to have been cordial, if not spontaneous and enjoyable. For his part, Emory paid little attention to his superior, and left the impression in reports, letters and journals that Campbell hardly existed.[1]

According to treaty terms the commission would survey the Rio Grande trench three miles into the Gulf, the territorial limits, and the trench would thereafter be the underwater international boundary. For this task, Emory utilized survey ships already mapping the Gulf Coast. His crews would make the soundings and perform the astronomical and topographical calculations.

As the surveys proceeded upriver from the Gulf, Emory encountered thousands of wild horses. Their numbers awed him, although he was unimpressed by their physical condition. "I never saw a good one," he said. "Most were heavy on the forehead, cat-hammered and knock-kneed."

Indians were a similar nuisance and just as unattractive. The white man had two choices, as Emory saw it: either exterminate or ignore the natives. Indians lived only "to kill the defenseless and to avoid collision with a superior or equal force," he wrote, and "no amount of forbearance or kindness could eradicate or essentially modify their predominant savage element of character."

Mexicans did not fare much better, although Emory drew a distinction between those of full Spanish blood and mixed blood. The Spaniards impressed him and he marveled at the ruins of their churches and presidios. But their glory had faded because of careless intermarriage with Indians. The mixing of races has created a "decline and retrograde march" of an entire civilization, he stated.[2]

Meanwhile, surveying parties along the Rio Grande had encountered filibusters. José María Carbajal, Texas-Mexican born, supported by the Mexican liberal party, denounced the central Mexican government and tried to establish a republic along the Rio Grande. Texas and Louisiana encouraged him, hoping Carbajal would return fugitive slaves and reduce the tariffs.

Americans joined his ragged but optimistic forces. The best known were John S. "Rip" Ford, a Texas Ranger, and Robert Chatham Wheat, a tall, Virginia attorney. Wheat was a war-lover, riding with William Walker in Nicaragua, with General Juan Alvarez during his rise from a *guerrillero* to the presidency of Mexico, and with Giuseppe Garibaldi in Italy. Finally he rode to his death at Gaines' Mill during the United States Civil War.

Unfortunately for Carbajal he had everything except Wheat's killer instinct. American mercenaries deserted because of his suspect leadership and because of stringent United States laws regarding filibustering. Emory hired many of these intemperate and irresponsible men with no scruples about dashing across the international line and helping themselves to a steer. Such activities attracted the Mexican Army, and both sides repeatedly taunted the other. Emory arranged for American soldiers to protect his employees.[3]

Meanwhile, eleven islands dotted one hundred miles of the river between its mouth and Rio Grande City. National ownership had to be determined even though most islands were patches of marshy thickets lightly regarded by either country. An example involved a stretch of the lower Rio Grande near Roma, Texas, which had three channels and two islands. Since the deepest channel (a "thalweg" in surveying terms), lay between the islands and Mexico, these islands belonged to the United States.

When Emory reached the Big Bend country where the Chandler Expedition had failed, he assigned Lieutenant Nathaniel Michler to complete the assignment. As the young officer entered Langtry Canyon, he placed two skiffs and a flatboat in the water. Within seconds the current slammed them against a chain of cliffs. Boulders split the channel into chutes of foaming, tumultuous water. The skiffs slid safely through, but the flatboat careened off the walls and splintered on a rock. Two Mexican crew members dived overboard, attached lines and towed the craft onto a sand bar. After repairs, the boat continued.[4]

Michler walked and boated 125 miles in completing the Big Bend surveys. In doing so, his skiff capsized one evening in relatively quiet water. Thomas Walter Jones, an assistant surveyor, drowned.

As the surveys neared completion, yellow fever infected the commission. Emory and Felipe Iturbide (a Mexican translator since the García Conde days in San Diego), caught it. Iturbide did not recover.[5]

After finishing the Rio Grande surveys, Emory left for Washington to write his final report and draw his maps. Meanwhile, the United States and Mexico ratified the Treaty of Mesilla (Gadsden Purchase), and on August 4, 1854, President Pierce named Emory as a combination boundary commissioner and surveyor. He and José Salazar, now the Mexican boundary commissioner, replacing the deceased García Conde, met in December and shared the fireside comforts of James Magoffin's hacienda in El Paso. They shaped plans for a new initial point, moving it downstream on the Rio Grande from forty-two miles north of El Paso to only three, and near the outcroppings of *Cerro de Muleros* (Muleskinner Mountain or Hill), now Mt. Cristo Rey. Astronomers marked the site of 31° 47' on January 9, 1855, and three weeks later on the 31st, several documents were sealed and buried five feet beneath a pyramid-shaped marker.[6]

As surveying parties fanned out across southern New Mexico, Emory praised Salazar to Secretary of State Marcy as a "person eminently qualified to perform his duties." But Emory cautioned that due to disturbed and revolutionary conditions inside Mexico, Salazar operated with "means wholly insufficient," and because of that, he rarely left El Paso del Norte. The Mexican commissioner could not get adequate money, mules, wagons, equipment or supplies. Mexican employees went unpaid. The initial point on the Rio Grande (Boundary Marker No. 1) was the only monument site surveyed by both parties, as Salazar simply accepted Emory's word for the accuracy of the others.

Emory suggested that $100,000 of the $3 million still due Mexico be earmarked for the Mexican Boundary Commission. The idea appealed to the United States but it had no support south of the border. With the central government near collapse, Santa Anna refused to allocate one peso to the boundary commission.

However, the recommendation embarrassed Mexico, and a furious Santa Anna railed not because his commission had no funds, but because such a paucity of materials had become common knowledge not only to the Americans, but to Santa Anna's political opposition as well. Salazar was recalled and briefly jailed. The reindoctrination taught him proper discretion about shortages you do not discuss, especially with foreigners. Salazar recognized his errors in judgment, and after returning to the border, he still lacked financial resources, but he no longer complained about them.[7]

DAVID MERIWETHER
(McNitt Coll., State Records Center
& Archives, Santa Fe)

ANGEL TRÍAS
(Benson Latin American Collection,
U.T. Austin)

If early boundary men had a view of the Big Bend from the air, they might have given up all hopes of surveying it. (IBWC)

While Salazar languished in jail, Mexican Minister Juan Almonte requested a portion of the $3 million for "boundary expenses." A suspicious Washington agreed to pay it, but Acting Secretary of State W. Hunter instructed Secretary of Treasury James Guthrie to be certain those monies were advanced "for the object of which it is intended." So Hunter hesitated to release the funds, proposing to send the money to Emory, who would dole out the cash according to Salazar's needs. Mexico refused, so the Americans reluctantly released some money to Mexico through diplomatic channels.[8]

While the two nations discussed finances, Emory sent Lieutenant Michler to survey the Colorado River boundary south of the Gila junction. The task was almost impossible. Parties just a few yards apart vanished in the brush-covered bottomlands. Michler frequently moved his crews to the high mesas and cut lines of sight through the thickets to the river. Triangulation then computed a boundary line down the middle of the stream.

Due to heavy rains, the Gila and Colorado rose rapidly. Floods flushed out snakes and insects. In places the Colorado spread to five miles in width. Fatigued, bedraggled engineers fashioned rafts and floated out equipment and supplies. Not until April 1, 1855, did the Colorado retreat sufficiently for the surveyors to chart the channel. Meanwhile, Captain Francisco Jiménez, first engineer of the Mexican commission, who possessed rank and authority equivalent to Michler, arrived with his Mexican crew. He had started from Guaymas, Sonora, with forty soldiers. But upon reaching the Colorado River, due to the arduous trip, his escort had dwindled to twenty, the deserters vanishing with most of the horses and equipment. Michler's slime-covered assistants had already surveyed the initial point on the Colorado, but Jiménez had an obligation (and orders) to do the same. The work took ten days and agreements were signed on April 20. Both parties then marked an azimuth or straight line from the initial point to the 111th meridian at 31° 20' north latitude, where Emory was waiting.[9]

The border stretched taut across the most desolate country in North America. Mules starved. Wagons bogged down in sand and broke apart in ancient lava flows. Temperatures soared to 120°, water holes dried. Instruments scorched the fingers. Michler exhaustedly wrote that not even birds crossed that portion of the desert. A servant (slave) died of thirst while searching for water. Nevertheless, by mid-October the surveys were complete, Jiménez doggedly doing his share, surveying by spit and prayer, the suffering of his crew surpassing that even of Michler's. The United States and Mexico finally had a complete, uncontested boundary from ocean to ocean. President Pierce proclaimed it so on June 2, 1856.[10]

Meanwhile, Emory and Salazar left the border, having accomplished all they could in the field. Their paths never crossed again.

The Mexican commissioner moved to Chihuahua City in 1857 as a deputy in the National Constitutional Congress. After the French invasion of Mexico during the early 1860s, he supported the Europeans as one of 250 Mexican conservatives voting to abolish the republic. José Salazar helped declare Mexico an empire, thus inviting Maximilian to take the throne "at the request of the people." In gratitude, the emperor appointed Salazar as the Imperial Commissar to Yucatan. When the Mexicans expelled the French in 1867, Salazar adroitly survived the upheaval. Three years later he founded the "Scientific School of Trinidad" in Mexico City, and died there in 1892 at age sixty-nine.[11]

Emory returned to Washington and cautioned Secretary of Interior Robert McClelland against releasing any more of the $3 million to Mexico until the paperwork had been completed and approved. "This is required by the [Gadsden] treaty," he said, "and if the three million is paid before it is due, we will have nothing in hand to coerce the Mexican government and commission."[12]

Secretary McClelland had reservations too, but due to the near bankruptcy of Mexico, the United States had already paid Mexico approximately half of the $3 million. Some of the cash may have assisted the surveys, but Mexico used most of it to support a faltering regime.

Instead of asking for the balance, Mexico demanded the entire $3 million, insisting that since Santa Anna and his government had been disgraced, and were out of power, all financial dealings with them had been illegal. United States officials responded that it had negotiated with governments, not individuals, and its agreements had been in good faith. Mexico continued to quibble, but seeing the futility, accepted the remainder of the money on February 7, 1856.

While the two nations bickered, Emory finished his first volume of a *Report on the United States and Mexican Boundary Survey*. Ten thousand copies were printed and distributed at government expense in 1857. The *Report* contained items so dull they appeared to have been written by a committee. The narrative lacked interpretation, readability and organization. It never matched the verve of his *Notes of A*

Military Reconnaissance, nor did it compare in grace, style and romanticism with Bartlett's *Narrative*. The *Report* needed a brutal editor to eliminate the repetitions, and to dissuade Emory from using his book to settle old feuds, particularly those with Bartlett.

The strength of the *Report* lies in its scientific and cartographic value, its numerous sketches (some in color), and its reams of tabulations and astronomical observations. His "Map of the United States and Their Territories Between the Mississippi and the Pacific Ocean and Part of Mexico," was for a time the most reliable guide available. However, Lieutenant G. K. Warren of the Topographic Corps assigned to the Pacific Railroad Surveys drew a more detailed map. It eclipsed Emory's efforts and became the standard by which regional maps were judged.

This left Emory with his fifty-four sectional maps of the Rio Grande. Nobody thought them valuable, but they have since become the only reference available regarding the nature, size, curves, position and resources of the river border during the critical 1850s. These maps remain the determinates for the exact, original international boundary.

As for volume two of Emory's memoirs, Congress forced him to settle for a publication of three thousand copies. This book dealt with botanical and zoological reports, and most of the copies went to universities and libraries. The small printing irked Emory, and he called the publishing industry nothing but "trashy swindles got up for the benefit of authors and private printers."[13]

Thus Emory, the most efficient American boundary commissioner ever to serve during those hectic and controversial years, resumed his career in the military. Although a Southerner by birth and cultural inclination, he refused a Confederate rank of major general during the Civil War. Instead he took charge of all Union forts in Indian Territory (Oklahoma), withdrawing to Fort Leavenworth with his entire command after being convinced that his forces could not survive in a sea of insurrectionists. He participated in the defense of Washington, and rose to full colonel during the Manassas and Virginia campaigns. His brilliant tactics at Hanover Court House earned him four brevets (non-permanent, non-paid promotions), when he separated the wings of a Confederate army, captured numerous prisoners and destroyed several railroad bridges between Hanover Junction and the Chickahominy. War's end found him a major general in charge of volunteers in the Department of West Virginia. Bold Emory died in 1887 at Washington.

Teeth of Iron

WITHIN THIRTY YEARS of the mid-1850 land boundary surveys, the Mexican border had attracted a scattered assortment of forts, settlers (mostly ranchers), miners and businessmen, the latter drawn partly by the prospect of international trade and military contracts. A few modest villages showed promise of expansion, and over a period of time a need had grown to better distinguish the border. Markers were miles apart, and oftentimes missing or crumbling. Customs agents argued about jurisdiction; ranchers quarreled over water holes; and miners disputed ownership of mineral rights. Federal authorities in the United States and Mexico foresaw unending litigation unless the boundary was more clearly defined.

A survey would determine the border communities, identify the monuments, record their condition and make a determination of how many more might be needed. Delegates from the United States and Mexico met in Washington on July 29, 1882, and specific recommendations emerged. A preliminary reconnaissance by military officers of both nations within six months would reconnoiter the border from El Paso to the Pacific.

Secretary of War Robert Lincoln hand-picked Lieutenant Thomas W. Symons to lead the American inspection team. The thirty-four-year-old New Yorker had graduated at the head of his West Point class in 1874, and had become a second lieutenant in the Corps of Engineers. He surveyed the Columbia River, and worked with the Mississippi River Commission until Lincoln tapped him for the Mexican border assignment on June 15, 1883.[1]

Secretary of State Frederick T. Frelinghuysen instructed Symons to cooperate with Mexican General Ignacio Revueltas in El Paso del Norte. The two men would assist each other where necessary, but their studies would be separate. Frelinghuysen cautioned Symons to avoid hostile Indians, and gave him $750 in expense money.

Symons arrived on July 1 to a far different El Paso, Texas, than the one experienced by either Emory or Bartlett. Five major railroads had transformed the town from an isolated village of five or six hundred to several thousand souls, most of them lost. Miners, promoters, developers, preachers, gunmen, Indians, prostitutes, businessmen, confidence men, Mexicans and Chinese swarmed everywhere. Sweating horses and rickety wagons competed for space in the cluttered, caliche streets. Saloon patrons bellied up to the rough wooden bars, paid their nickel for a tin cup of rye whiskey or moderately cold beer, and spiked the drink with pepper, tabasco or tomato juice. When mental and physical exhaustion overcame them, and it was late enough, most saloons charged only a modest nickel or dime to sleep on the wooden benches or floor. Otherwise, customers walked to the Central Hotel or the Parker House and paid fifty cents for a night's lodging.[2]

City marshal Dallas Stoudenmire and his successors James Gillett and Frank Manning shook down the just and the unjust. Prisoners who could not pay court fines (of which the lawmen took one-third), were placed in a cramped, dingy jail where drunks, murderers and madmen shared a common bedlam.

Tents lined the thoroughfares, particularly San Antonio Street, and sanitariums in the foothills treated consumptives by laying them outside in the high and dry atmosphere. Undertakers transferred the losers to Concordia or Evergreen Cemetery. Those with money were interred in wooden coffins. The majority went with blankets.

City fathers assigned the prostitutes to specific areas of town, the regions having a variety of colorful names: Tenderloin, District, Reservation, Zone, or Zone of Toleration. The girls were "fined" ten dollars a month, a form of licensing, and a police officer collected. The fines paid police department salaries and kept the streets in good repair.[3]

El Paso's modest number of churches campaigned for a safe community with schools, parks and businesses. The *Lone Star, El Paso Morning Times* and the *El Paso Herald* (today's *Herald-Post*), plus a couple of Spanish language newspapers published all the news that was fit to print and much that wasn't. The State National Bank had just begun its rise as the leading financial institution. The town had a volunteer fire department and an acceptable police force. Residents bragged of a forthcoming water treatment plant and even an electric streetcar. Several physicians practiced medicine.

Symons crossed to the bustling village of El Paso del Norte on July 3, 1883, and conferred with General Revueltas. They agreed to inspect the border separately until reaching the Colorado River where they would compare notes, exchange information and travel together to San Diego. Revueltas promised to assign Symons two soldiers as representatives of the Mexican government since the Americans would occasionally drop south of the international line and technically be in violation of Mexican sovereignty. However, as Symons left El Paso, Revueltas said the Mexican escort was unready for travel and would catch up. It never did.[4]

Symons left Deming, New Mexico on July 12, seething because the egocentric and slightly mad General Ranald Mackenzie, commander of the New Mexico Military District, had not furnished adequate pack transport and cavalry escort. Instead, Symons got infantry and wagons unsuitable for desert conditions. With Chief of Scouts Frank Bennett, two Mescalero Apache scouts, and interpreter C. A. Mahoney, the column passed Palomas Lake, fed by underground seepage from the Mimbres River. The lieutenant found boundary marker No. 7 in a damaged condition and noted it in his journal. Symons also mentioned, but did not explain, the resignation of two teamsters, both of whom he replaced with soldiers. At nearby Ojo del Perro, Symons wrote of a Mexican customhouse three miles inside United States territory. The Mexican bureaucracy had mistaken a pile of stones for a boundary marker, and had been illegally collecting duties from American citizens for two decades.

Violent desert thunderstorms dogged the small group, washing out trails and raising the humidity to almost intolerable levels. Broad arroyos turned into muddy creeks. Symons expressed amazement when he lost no men or animals due to lightning strikes on iron instruments and equipment.

The surveyors straggled into a small silver mining village in the Tres Hermanas Mountains where Symons said the need of "an accurate definition of the boundary line is severely felt here. At present the prospectors . . . [are uncertain] if their claims are in New Mexico or old Mexico."

Near San Luis Pass in the Animas Mountains, Symons found springs, excellent forage, and abundant trees and wild game. He also found a valley victimized by "the land monopoly schemes of certain unscrupulous capitalists." An English firm was "quietly obtaining control of . . . the best land in the Middle Gila," he said, a takeover made possible by bribing phony settlers to homestead the water holes, and then selling out to the British. On a map the English had only a modest scattering of sites, a deceptive view because by owning the water holes, the English controlled the entire range.

Within the week, Symons reached Fort Huachuca, Arizona, a military post sealing Apache plunder trails into and out of Mexico. Here the two Apache scouts quit because their ancient enemies, the Papagos and Yumas would kill them. Symons shipped them home by rail to Fort Selden, New Mexico, and employed four Yumas from the San Carlos Reservation. He used the same opportunity to dismiss C. C. Young, better known as "Texas Charlie," who had been hired in El Paso as a guide and laborer. According to the Symons journal, Texas Charlie was "a most despicable fraud."

The reconnaissance team now numbered twenty-three men and forty-seven horses. The monument surveys went on.

In Nogales, two towns by the same name straddling the boundary, Symons mentioned huge American and Mexican customhouses servicing the Sonora-Arizona trade. A small garrison of irregular Mexican troops watched for Indians and smugglers. Most had never been issued modern weapons, and they fought Indians with a strong lance, while protecting themselves with a leather shield. Rawhide sandals covered their feet. Paydays were infrequent, and the soldiers stayed constantly in debt to company commanders. Symons now made one of the first known references to illegal aliens. "The regular soldiers of Mexico, who are nearly all conscripted," he wrote, "have an unquenchable desire to sever their bonds of military servitude and decamp across the line whenever an opportunity occurs."

In fact, desertions became so frequent that the Mexican government enlisted Sonorans for a period of five months. As an incentive to work and not flee to the United States, each soldier received a lump sum of $125 (125 pesos) upon discharge.

After leaving Nogales, the reconnaissance meandered from town to town and from ranch to ranch, following the trails whichever way they went . . . as few of them led from one marker to another. Symons often wandered several miles north or south of the line to acquire supplies and information, and to refresh his men and animals. The side trips broke the monotony and were in effect the shortest distance between two points.

On one occasion the patrol swung south to an immense hacienda and customhouse of an *hacendado* identified only as Señor Lucero. His adobe home, built in the typical Mexican fashion of a square building surrounding an enclosed plaza, had a circular, fortified *torreon* (guard tower) on each corner. Gun ports protected two sides of the house. The hacienda was a government outpost intercepting contraband which, in the modern age, would be known as "Levi's." Cotton Levi Strauss overalls, manufactured in San Francisco, sold for a dollar a pair in Arizona. In Mexico, with a $1.62 duty imposed, the cost rose to nearly three dollars. The difference in price led to lucrative smuggling operations, although overalls were but one item slipped surreptitiously across the boundary. The penalty for smuggling was not death or prison, but induction into the Mexican Army.

As the bearded Americans, powdered with gray dust and weary from weeks of riding, filed along the narrow trail leading to the customhouse, guards mistook them for smugglers. Symons submitted to arrest, and he and his men were escorted to the hacienda where Señor Lucero apologized.

After relaxing for a day, the Americans slid aching bodies back into saddles and streamed west into the most turbulent weather imaginable. When it cleared, the caravan passed *temporals* (temporary Indian villages), with *charcos* and *presas*, natural and artificial depressions which held varying amounts of run-off water. Papagos and Yaquis planted corn in these depressions, and when the water evaporated and the mud hardened, the Indians pulled down their makeshift homes and departed.

When at last the riders struck the Colorado River, they rode to Fort Yuma, an abandoned military supply depot. Thirty years earlier, the town of Yuma thrived as a desert distribution center for trade between

El Paso and San Diego, and between Sonora and the southwestern United States. In 1852 the paddle-wheeled steamship *Uncle Sam* navigated the Colorado to the Gila. Other steamers such as the *General Jesup, Colorado, Explorer, Cocopath* and *Mojave* traveled even further upstream. All roads, like spokes of a wagon wheel, pointed toward the commercial hub of Yuma. However, this wagon trade underwent a recession when the Southern Pacific arrived in 1877. Business faltered, people moved on, buildings crumbled. Yuma decayed. Symons seemed almost overtaken by what these ruins implied. He wrote of a former Yuma, "crowded day and night with innumerable freight wagons and stages. Now its glories are departing, the corrals and diverging wagon roads deserted. Yuma is just a way-station for the railroad."

The party crossed the Colorado at Hanlon's Ferry where laborers towed a craft several hundred yards upstream. Then everybody struggled aboard and the flatboat, secured by a rope from the opposite bank, drifted diagonally across the river to where another group of workers dragged it onto the landing. The transfer of men and equipment took six trips and three hours. "The heat experienced throughout the crossing eclipsed anything we had endured on the reconnaissance," Symons wrote.

After a short march they reached the New River, now no river at all since it depended upon high tides in the Gulf of Lower California or floods in the Rio Colorado for its water. Here the road deteriorated further. Night marches became the rule. At Coyote Hole an advance squad found water, "sulfurous, salty and bad smelling, but still most welcome." Now the reconnaissance team faced the final mountainous barrier to the Pacific. Symons ordered the water barrels unloaded, and the mules and horses fed the last kernels of grain. He sent the wagons back to Yuma.

Symons followed the New River slough south to the international boundary to take advantage of meager moisture and grass. From that point the travelers climbed one mountain range after another until one morning they encountered cattle and "an abundant supply of the most delicious water." He and his exhausted riders drank their fill, turned their horses into corrals and went immediately to sleep, having been constantly in the saddle for the last twenty-seven hours.

On the following day they reached Campo, a tiny settlement near the headwaters of the Tecate River, then dry. Campo had stores, a post office, a blacksmith shop. A stage ran three times a week to San Diego, and a telegraph wire connected the two.

The Gaskell brothers were the town's most prosperous citizens, and they owned a store about a half-mile south of Campo. On various occasions, Mexican officials forced the firm to pay taxes, insisting the business lay in Mexico. Symons promised to inform United States authorities.

The long journey from El Paso was now almost over, and the reconnaissance party traveled through beautiful canyons to the Tia Juana River. They reached the Pacific on September 18, and the next day stood beside marble Marker No. 1, now chipped and defaced. Symons recommended a heavy iron fence to protect it.

Symons discharged his civilians, and reassigned his soldiers to San Diego Barracks. The men "endured the hardships and severe labor of the trip willingly and cheerfully," he wrote in his journal.

As for General Revueltas, he never left El Paso del Norte. The Americans made the border inspection alone. In his journal, Symons accused the officer of violating agreements, but Revueltas was a general and Symons a mere lieutenant. Revueltas probably regarded any joint effort between himself and Symons as demeaning. Many American generals would have thought likewise. The difference is that United States officers would have swallowed their pride and gone.

Altogether the reconnaissance had traveled 1,252 miles in sixty-eight days, and charted fifty-two marker sites. A few were in good condition, several were missing, and many were severely damaged. Symons suggested that markers be placed two miles apart except in uninhabited country. He recommended construction of three-fifths-of-an-inch of iron to deflect bullets from bored cowboys.

The reconnaissance expedition had now ended and the United States and Mexico were to implement the findings by more clearly defining the boundary. But nothing happened for nearly six years. On February 18, 1889, delegates met to reaffirm their convention of 1882, to discuss clarifying the international line. On November 18, 1891, the United States and Mexico re-created boundary commissions to assume the project.

A flurry of activity jarred the old Mexican customshouse in Juarez on the morning of November 17, 1891. Official carriages paused in front, discharging Mexican bureaucrats with dispatch cases and portfolios. These dignitaries scurried up the stone steps and disappeared through the big double doors, carrying blasts of chilly air into the Victorian-style building. Promptly at ten o'clock a train of carriages from the American side discharged its quota of officials, some in United States Army uniforms, some in formal dress, most in business suits and overcoats. Lieutenant Colonel John Whitney Barlow, engineer-in-chief (commissioner) of the American Boundary Commission, shook hands with his Mexican counterpart, the distinguished Jacobo Blanco. These two wise and amiable gentlemen were charged with implementing border agreements, relocating and repairing the existing land markers, and erecting more than two hundred additional iron teeth to further identify the line.

The brooding border situation had occupied a low priority since the 1850s. So preparations had creaked forward even as secretaries in both capitals itemized the latest complaints and outrages.

Passions flared easily along the border, and men who had never learned to endure wrongs with patience were oftentimes convinced that great injustices had been done them by the international line. An example occurred in the twin villages of Nogales on the Arizona-Sonora boundary.

The mistress of Colonel Francisco Arvizu, commander of twenty-five Mexican irregulars, fled to the American side in early March 1887, and spurned the colonel's pleas to return. Since only an unguarded boundary separated them, Arvizu sent a man named Rincón, one of her former lovers, to lure her down to the boundary where a squad of soldiers would kidnap and whisk her back to Mexico.

The woman rejected Rincón's affections, however, and asked two American law officers, known only as Constable Littlejohn and Deputy Sheriff Sheedy, to protect her. They escorted Rincón to the border where Lieutenant Benjamín Gutiérrez, a subordinate of the colonel, thought Rincón was being arrested instead of deported. Gutiérrez stepped from the shadows, confronted Littlejohn with a revolver and demanded Rincón's release. The constable convincingly argued that no arrests had been made, so Gutiérrez holstered his weapon. Thereupon Littlejohn charged the lieutenant with threatening a peace officer. As they started toward the jail, another Mexican soldier intervened. Shooting commenced, and the soldier died from his wounds. The lieutenant escaped to Mexico.

The shooting caused consternation among Americans, many of whom believed the Mexican Army would now invade Nogales, Arizona and murder everyone. They telegraphed William C. Endicott, the secretary of war, and demanded military protection. Endicott consulted with General Oliver O. Howard, commander of the Division of the Pacific, and General Nelson Miles, commander of the Department of Arizona. They sent Captain H. W. Lawson with a detachment of 4th Cavalry to secure Nogales. Lawson viewed the crisis level-headedly, reported all was quiet, and said good citizens on both sides of the border regretted the incident. He called the episode political, and doubted his presence was needed.

The United States insisted that Gutiérrez be returned to Arizona for trial. Mexico refused. President Porfirio Díaz, and Governor Lorenzo Torres of Sonora, vowed not only to catch and severely punish Lieutenant Gutiérrez, who had now deserted, but to make a harsh example of Arvizu as well.

To Díaz, the rights and wrongs were unimportant. With revolutionary turmoil rising throughout his unhappy country, he needed to demonstrate effective control of the army, and thereby prove that he could insure domestic tranquility. Arvizu and Gutiérrez gave him that opportunity, and the two officers were swiftly captured and sentenced to be shot. Such a harsh verdict surprised the Americans, and they petitioned Díaz for a reduction of penalty. Since the president had now made his point, and done so in front of an observing United States, he graciously agreed. The death sentences were commuted to twenty years in prison.[5]

But while boundaries could frustrate love affairs and might even lead to long incarcerations, at least in these instances men knew within a few feet the exact location of the border. Outside of town, that boundary was not so easily defined. Monuments usually had miles of desert and mountains separating them, and the international line was vague and uncertain.

George James Roskruge, of Arizona ranching interests, in December 1886, started surveying the southern boundary of Pima County, which was also the Mexican border. He had barely commenced when Fernando Ortiz, a Mexican customs agent, charged him with violating Mexican sovereignty. Roskruge believed he was still a half-mile inside the United States, and he demanded that United States Marshal H. D. Underwood protect him. Underwood overreacted and jailed the Mexican. An international incident threatened, but both countries had the good sense to dismiss the affair and await accurate border surveys. As it turned out, the Americans were correct, but they nevertheless apologized for Underwood's conduct.[6]

Meanwhile, incoming President Benjamin Harrison never provided the exceptional leadership necessary for great statesmanship. But he instituted a broad program of revamping American thinking regarding its southern neighbor. While he largely owed his few successes to the strong and brilliant James G. Blaine, the secretary of state, Harrison set the direction and policy for his administration. Even though the American people limited him to one term, his accomplishments were respectable: six states entered the Union, the nation developed a two-ocean navy, and he pushed through Congress the Sherman Antitrust Act outlawing industrial monopolies. Harrison deplored national violence toward blacks when such a position took courage and won no votes; and he strongly favored a fair and equitable treatment for Indians. The Southwest smiled when he endorsed the Sherman Silver Purchase Act, then frowned during the silver financial panic of 1893. During his term he devoted attention to Latin America, vigorously pushing for establishment of the Pan American Union, a forerunner of the Organization of American States.

Harrison chose the religious, beardless and soft-spoken Lieutenant Colonel John Whitney Barlow as engineer-in-chief of the American Boundary Commission. Today Barlow and his predecessor William Emory are generally included among the commissioners, and technically they had the title. However, both were military men and neither resigned to serve on the boundary. No one cared about this discrepancy in Emory's case. Barlow ran into all kinds of trouble.

The President granted Barlow and his two assistants — David Du B. Gaillard, a lieutenant in the Corps of Engineers, and A. T. Mossman of the Coast and Geodetic Survey — the sum of $10 per diem. Records provide no hint if Gaillard or Mossman accepted the money, but Barlow did because R. S. Souler, United States comptroller, challenged his right to it. Comptrollers had clout in those days, for Souler claimed the United States Boundary Commission did not legally exist because it had not been created by Congress. Nor had Barlow's name been confirmed by the senate. The three administrators had been *assigned* to the border. They did not vacate their military positions, and they were still recognized as army officers, receiving the pay and allowances of such. By statute they could not legally be given additional funds, and so Barlow owed the government $14,400 when he finished his boundary service. Barlow complained to Secretary of State Walter Q. Gresham, and Gresham presumably resolved the matter.[7]

Barlow never used the title of commissioner in his official correspondence. He signed with name and military rank, following with "Engineer-in-Chief, U. S. Boundary Commission."

A native New Yorker, Barlow was born in 1838, graduated from West Point in 1861, and participated in the Battle of Bull Run. He fought in the Peninsular Campaign, marched with the Army of the Potomac, and rode with Sherman into Atlanta. Altogether he won three brevets in the artillery and engineers. He was chief of the Yellowstone Geological Survey in 1871, and Yellowstone became the first United States national park. After completing his boundary service, he rose to full colonel, then brigadier general and chief of engineers. While in retirement he visited Jerusalem, dying there in 1902. He was buried in Arlington National Cemetery.

Jacobo Blanco was his Mexican counterpart, a man with connections in the capital since his brother, General Miguel Blanco, was minister of war for President Benito Juárez. The Mexican commissioner had established the frontier between Mexico and Guatemala, and had explored the Mexican Sierra Madre as well as Baja California. Blanco was a unique personality, mild and gentle of manner, a handsomely bearded scholar who kept the United States-Mexican survey going when Barlow broke his arm and left the field for several months. It is an indication of his character and ability, and of the great respect afforded him by the Americans, that he officially translated for both commissions.

The first joint meeting created the International Boundary Commission with instructions to resurvey the line, locate and rebuild the old monuments, and install additional markers. The commissioners would correct any maps, obey all treaties and verify the Emory astronomical measurements.

In late February, 1892, Barlow left El Paso on the first portion of his survey, the *El Paso Times* remarking that the commission would spend $100,000 at the Pass as well as make the community a base for supplies. The Mexican and American parties expected to work alongside each other, but the Barlow people were so much better equipped and organized that they quickly outdistanced the Mexicans. So the two commissioners ran the line independently and compared findings at convenient times and places.[8]

New monuments were procured in El Paso and paid for by the Americans (fifty percent to be reimbursed by Mexico) at a price of $150 each. Inscriptions on the original Emory-Salazar markers were preserved where possible. Refurbishings carried the bilingual notations (English on the north face; Spanish on the south): "Repaired by the Boundary Commission created by treaties of 1882-1889." A penalty notice in two languages said: "The destruction or displacement of this monument is a misdemeanor, punishable by the United States or Mexico."[9]

An eighteen-cubic-foot-slab of concrete anchored the new monuments, the iron column being six feet high, twelve inches square at the base, and pyramidal at the top. Plaques in English and Spanish read: "Boundary of the United States [or Mexico], treaty of 1853, re-established by the treaties of 1882-1889."

Barlow purchased several $50 Mexican mules, and over one hundred barrels of Eagle Cement at $3.50 a barrel. Although the cement weight caused massive transportation headaches, cement was nothing compared to the amount of water needed to mix the concrete and keep the men and animals supplied. In hot weather each employee consumed an average of seven quarts a day, and the laborers even more. Mules drank close to twenty gallons, and Barlow said "the failure of a water wagon to arrive on time would have resulted in a water famine that would have been disastrous."[10]

Half the laborers deserted near Yuma. The teamsters continued operating only because the commissioner promised an increase in wages every thirty days if their performance remained satisfactory.

Military patrols constantly passed, the soldiers futilely searching for the Apache Kid, a former Indian policeman who had slain his guard while being escorted to the Yuma Territorial Prison. Now he had a reward of $5,000 on his head, money which no one on the commission had any aspirations to collect. Tales of his brutality chilled the employees. They went armed, stayed in groups, and upon sighting any distant unrecognizable figure, ducked behind defensive works and prepared to fight.

Now and then friendly Indians briefly mingled, Barlow observing that the Yumas of the Lower Colorado were fond of games and "like all savages delight in painting their faces." He described the females as generally fat and unattractive, unlike the Papagos (a tribe living along the border) whose women were "far above average in good looks."

Papagos were essentially of the Pueblo culture. That they gleaned a living from this desperate land speaks volumes for their durability. (Arizona Historical Society, Tucson)

Early Yuma, Arizona. To exist in such a frontier harshness, one had to appreciate the sun and the earth. (Arizona Historical Society, Tucson)

Barlow respected the Papagos, considering them intelligent and peacefully disposed toward the United States and Mexico. These Indians spent their days in anticipation of Montezuma, a Messiah who would right wrongs, make the desert bloom and raise the Papagos higher than all other tribes. Their homes always faced east so that when Montezuma came striding across the mountains with the rising sun, he would find all doors open to him.

As Barlow continued west he encountered jagged peaks and ridges of granite, barren of moisture and profusely covered with yucca, ocotillo, creosote brush, dead cottonwoods and beavertail cactus. No deviations from the original boundary line was permitted, so the surveyors scaled the steep precipices, blasted off the sharp edges, hoisted equipment and monuments with ropes and ladders, bolted the markers to solid rock, and then carefully descended the mountain and trudged to the next ridge.

Somewhere along the line Barlow broke his arm. He never explained how it happened, but his journals describe a flood-swollen arroyo near Fort Huachuca, Arizona. Two mules stumbled and went under, and the wagon flipped and splintered on a boulder. Barlow fell into the torrent but with the aid of a Mexican bystander, he struggled ashore. While Barlow did not mention any problems with his arm, shortly after the incident he spent several months in Nashville, Tennessee, where he recuperated.

While the commissioners had anticipated occasional misfortunes and complex problems, they did not anticipate John T. Brickwood, who owned a saloon in Nogales, Arizona. John was born in Fayette County, Illinois, in 1849. By 1867, he worked in the mines of Georgetown and Central City, Colorado. Three years later he settled in Prescott, Arizona, freighting supplies for the Army and dabbling in mining claims. He moved to Tucson, then Harshaw, then Tombstone, and by 1882, Nogales, Arizona, a ramshackle village of one frame house, one adobe building and a dozen tents. Two years later he married Guadalupe Canes of Guaymas, Sonora.

Nogales straddled the Don Pedro Camou Land Grant. A ranch called "Los Nogales de Elías" (the Walnuts of Elías) was named after groves of walnut trees. Nothing existed there when Emory passed through in October 1855 and installed a pyramid stone designated as Monument 26. After that, however, developers had conceived the area as a strategic link between the Gulf of Lower California and the American South-

JACABO BLANCO
(Mexican Boundary Commission)

JOHN W. BARLOW
(U.S. Military Academy Archives)

THOMAS W. SYMONS
(U.S. Military Academy Archives)

JOHN T. BRICKWOOD
(Pimeria Alta Historical
Society, Nogales)

west. The Sonora Railway Company laid line from Guaymas to Hermosillo in the fall of 1881. By 1882 the iron rails had reached the border at Nogales and hooked up with the Santa Fe Railroad operating as the New Mexico and Arizona Railroad Company.

An international trading center, a pole-and-mud village on the north side of the boundary was dubbed "Line City." Hispanics called it "Villa Riva," and Jacob Isaacson, a postmaster, immodestly delegated it "Isaacson." However, since "Nogales" was already on the railroad maps, Nogales stuck.

Unlike Nogales, Sonora, which created a fifty-foot vacant space between itself and the border, Nogales Arizona snuggled against the line. Open space on the Sonora side became International Street, although it was not "international" at all since Mexico owned every foot of it.

The stocky Brickwood purchased a portion of the Don Pedro Camou Land Grant on January 7, 1884, and constructed a one-story, wood-frame saloon and gambling house sixty by forty feet. He lined the interior with pine and redwood, and installed an ice chest. A saucy lady winked from a painting over the bar, and many a nickel entered Brickwood's pockets for drinks hoisted in the young woman's honor. An eight-foot-wide cellar lay underneath; a cistern and warehouse were out back. Along the fifty-foot saloon frontage which was flush with the boundary, Brickwood poured a concrete porch covered with redwood boards. A cigar box hung on the outside, south wall. Cigars were purchased inside the saloon in American territory, but taken from the case outside the door in Mexican territory, thus avoiding taxes. Brickwood, who served as mayor from 1906 to 1910, claimed an average net of $500 a month from the saloon and swore the business had a total value of $14,950.[11]

Boundary Marker No. 26 sprawled grotesquely on the Brickwood porch, a pile of jumbled stones supporting the wall and infuriating Commissioner Barlow. "The grasping and overreaching action of the United States settlers," he wrote, "results in many inconveniences to the customs officials and peace officers, who, in order to patrol the important [International] Street must rely for permission to do so upon the kindness and courtesy of the Mexican officials." The system encouraged fraud, he claimed, and noted that not only were duties avoided on cigars, but Mexicans drank in Brickwood's saloon and avoided liquor taxes in their own country. The commissioner foresaw the same conditions approaching in Columbus, New Mexico, and he recommended the Department of State create a fifty-foot reservation along the entire American side of the line.[12]

Several other Arizona residents also fronted on International Street. Joseph DeLusignan owned a home, plus smaller dwellings. Edward Gaynor allegedly used a bakery for smuggling; Theodore Gebler operated a grocery; Arthur L. Peck opened a restaurant and lodging house; Thomas D. Casanega had fences, trees and shrubbery; Joseph H. Berger claimed a twenty-six-room hotel; and Leander W. Mix rented a four-room house.[13]

J. L. Hathaway, United States customs inspector in Nogales, explained law enforcement quandaries when American businessmen fronted on the international line:

> The buildings along International Street are built with their southern walls on or a little over the line, so that doors and windows open into Mexico. Between the buildings are fences, adobe and stone walls with gates and doors, through and over which contraband goods pass, and it is necessary for the inspectors to step across the line into Mexico before they are able to see them cross; and when they are seen, a trip through Mexico is the nearest way to catch them. When chase is given, it is a scramble over fences and through back yards where the inspector gets lost and bewildered while the smuggler is on to the dodges and gets away.[14]

Barlow could do nothing except tear down a portion of Brickwood's saloon wall, repair the marker, redesignate it as No. 122, and continue the survey west. On June 25, 1897, President William McKinley authorized a sixty-foot wide, two-mile-long boundary reservation on the American side through Nogales. Brickwood and the others were now trespassers, and from Washington a terse wire to United States Marshal William M. Griffith, ordered him to "remove squatters from the Nogales Strip."[15]

Deputy Marshal Hunter dispossessed the "squatters" on November 21, 1898. All of the buildings, fences, trees, walls and outhouses underwent a wrecking sledge except for Berger's twenty-six room hotel. The government found only seven rooms in violation, so these were sawed off.

Brickwood and most of the violators retained attorneys, insisting that by purchasing portions of the Camou grant, they had the authority to build anywhere they wished, even up to the international line. However, in the Supreme Court decision of *Ainsa vs the United States*,

Brickwood Saloon with replaced Boundary Marker 122. (Rochlin Archives)

Monument 122. (Pimeria Alta Historical Society, Nogales)

International Street in Nogales. By 1917 the street had been widened. The
Brickwood Saloon was but a memory. A fence marked the border. U.S. troops
guard American property during Mexican Revolution. (Pimeria Alta Historical
Society, Nogales)

the judges found that the grant had never been perfected in Mexico, the
site being general and never precisely identified by metes and bounds.
So if Camou had not possessed a valid title in Mexico, then Brickwood
and his friends could not possess one in the United States. The court
dismissed Brickwood and the others in 1912, saying "the claim here is
neither a legal nor an equitable one against the United States and payment [of claims, if any] rests in the bounty of Congress."[16]

Senator Carl Hayden of Arizona took up the cause and sponsored
Senate Bill 15. Brickwood had already died, but on January 4, 1939,
Congress awarded compensation to him of $3,750. Gaynor received
$4,250, Gebler $1,200, Peck $2,350, Casanega $500, Lusignan $3,250,
Berger $1,800 and Mix, $1,450.[17]

Meanwhile, the two commissioners moved on toward California,
pausing at the Tia Juana River where past floods had buried the
marker beneath several feet of sand. While Barlow and Blanco had no
authority to change any locations, on their own they established a new
site approximately 1,200 feet east of the former one, and on higher
ground.

This left only Boundary Monument No. 1 south of San Diego and overlooking the Pacific. The commissioners redesignated it as No. 258. (Since the surveyors had worked from the Rio Grande east, and did not know how many monuments would be installed, it made more sense to redesignate the marker at El Paso as "International Boundary Monument No. 1", and begin the numbering from that point. The monument on the Pacific thus became the last one instead of the first.)

Americans sent the San Diego monument to the firm of Simpson & Pirnie, who repolished the sides and re-engraved the letters. During installation ceremonies, a parchment message in a copper tube was buried in the concrete foundation beneath the monument. To discourage further vandalism, an iron picket fence protected the site.

Barlow and Blanco had now increased the monuments from Emory's 52 to 258. In the years since, another eighteen have been installed. Because of confusion, time and expense in changing numbers every time a new monument is added, both nations retain the original numbers but add letters. For instance, the Southern Pacific near El Paso runs alongside much of the Mexican border, but the railroad unknowingly placed a small strip of maintenance road in Mexico, doing so in the vicinity of Boundary Monument No. 2. No one discovered the error until the 1960s. The tracks were then re-routed, and to identify the line more precisely, there are now Boundary Monuments 2-A, 2-B and 2-C.[18]

As of the late 1980s, there are a total of 276 teeth (eighteen of them bearing letters in addition to numbers) of iron and granite reaching from the Rio Grande to the West Coast, the intervals varying from 0.14 to 4.91 miles. There will not likely be additional monuments in spite of confusion still occasionally surfacing over the boundary's true location. The United States and Mexico hesitated to continue installing large, expensive pillars, so they agreed in 1975 to consider all 276 sites as "monuments." Everything else is a "marker." Markers are smaller, of concrete and lettered "United States" on the north face and "Mexico" on the south.[19]

Out in California, the boundary surveys were ending in June 1894 with angry words. The *San Francisco Examiner* quoted Barlow as critical of the Mexican survey team. He also unwisely said Salazar and Emory had incorrectly surveyed the border during the early 1850s, and Mexico had lost land.

Barlow profusely apologized to Blanco, claiming he had been mis-
quoted, that newspaper articles "in our country are generally written
. . . without regard for accuracy." He admitted saying the United
States had gained territory by virtue of incorrect earlier surveys but
denied boasting of it.[20]

Actually, Emory and Salazar had performed commendably in the
early years considering their equipment and obstacles. Telescopes and
sextants bounced around for weeks in wagon beds. Instruments had to
function in all temperatures and climatic conditions. Barlow and Blanco had come along forty years later, and had surveyed much more
precisely because of better equipment and modern transportation.
They also had the telegraph. The longitude at Monument No. 40,
where parallel 31° 47' intersected with the meridian, was determined
by the use of a temporary field telegraph erected by Brigadier General
Adolphus W. Greely, chief signal officer of the United States Army.
He connected it to the Western Union line at Separ, New Mexico, on
the Southern Pacific Railroad. While military operators exchanged
signals for ten nights, the astronomers observed the same stars and
made calculations.

Anyway, the two commissioners lacked authority to make adjustments in the 1850s boundary. To realign the border would have set a
precedent permitting constant readjustment. Today's boundary would
never be tomorrow's boundary as each new advance in surveying
techniques (such as by the use of satellites), would continuously shift
the border by inches. Neither Mexico nor the United States would ever
again be certain of the exact line. Diplomats drafting the Treaty of
Guadalupe Hidalgo foresaw the endless possibilities of litigation, and
wisely provided that once the boundary had been agreed upon by the
respective 1850s commissioners, it would never change regardless of
how inaccurate it might later prove to be.

As for who gained and who lost, Monument No. 1 at El Paso is approximately fifty feet south of parallel 31° 47', which means the
Americans are richer by fifty-feet of land. Other monuments shift back
and forth, sometimes too far north, sometimes too far south. The 31°
47' parallel is supposed to extend one hundred miles before forking
south to the 31° 20' parallel. Instead the line goes but ninety-nine miles,
a one mile strip gain for the United States. However, that is slightly off-
set by the line stopping barely short of 31° 20', thus enabling Mexico to
pick up a little property. The boundary then follows the parallel west

4.5 miles past the Sonora Azimuth where it is supposed to stop, and from that point strikes the Colorado River twenty-three miles south of the confluence of the Gila rather than twenty miles as it was supposed to. That too represented a small gain for the Americans.[21]

While these win-loss statistics were based on thin strips here and there, not individually significant, it altogether amounted to 320 square miles. Mexico, therefore proposed a new convention to redefine the border.[22]

The United States declined for reasons already stated, especially because of the unending litigation. If the boundary moved but a fraction here and there, the owners could file suit against either government, and who could tell how much their land value would increase or decrease by virtue of such claims. Mexico quietly agreed, and neither country became excited about the newspaper articles and revelations. What might have turned into an international squabble, didn't. Far larger problems were troubling the mutual borderlands of the United States and Mexico.

BOOK THREE

RIFLES
TO THE BORDER

I shall remain in Mexico with my rangers
. . . and will cross back at my own
discretion. Give my compliments to the
secretary of war and tell him and the
United States soldiers to go to hell.

Leander H. McNelly to Captain James F.
Randlett, November 19, 1875

10

Filibusters and Slavers

HISTORY BOOKS have names for private armies imposing their will on small, usually fragmented societies. They have been called legions, Hessians, pirates, freebooters, vikings, conquistadors, mercenaries. In 18th and 19th century Mexico, they were filibusters.

Spaniards coined the term, although Mexico used it in reference to Texans, Europeans or Americans who swept across the borders of Latin America. With Mexico preoccupied with its revolt against Spain (1810-1821), groups in England and the United States sent adventurers through the port of New Orleans into Spanish Texas. The Gutiérrez-Magee filibusters led by former United States Army Lieutenant William Augustus Magee and José Bernardo Gutiérrez, a mercurial Mexican, occupied San Antonio for two years. Other freebooters, such as the visionary Dr. James Long, often cooperated with the pirate Jean Laffitte in raiding the east coast of Texas.

Rank and file filibusters sought their own rewards: land, money, adventure, women, power. The leaders had grandiose visions of kingdoms. As a general rule, Mexican military strength existed only in the interior, and boundary areas were relatively lawless, poorly defended, ineptly and corruptly governed. Should the *filibustero* bite off a territorial chunk, hold it for a decent length of time and declare it a separate republic, there were certain economic and political opportunities and advantages. If successful, the filibusters would consolidate and apply to the United States for statehood. If tough Mexican opposition appeared, the filibusters could melt north across the border and either disband or regroup.[1]

Filibuster leaders were rarely ordinary riffraff. William Walker was a physician, an attorney and a newspaper editor. Henry Crabb was a lawyer, also a newspaper editor, a California state senator and an aspirant to the United States Senate.

Their followers, especially those striking the western portion of Mexico, were oftentimes disappointed forty-niners who found no gold in California, but did find riot and lawlessness, lean-to-shanties, scurvy and a citizenry unrestrained by family, government or religion. The forty-niners had come west for riches, and not acquiring any in California, had shrugged their shoulders and gone searching for El Dorado along the Mexican border regions of Baja California and Sonora.

Filibusters shared a degree of fatalism tempered with a sense of invincibility. Few had any religious tenets, yet they were wonderfully adept at finding Biblical motivations for their crusades. "In God We Trust" represented more than just the lining of an American coin. Yankees were firmly convinced that the Almighty supported their objectives. William Gilpin of Colorado said the American people were destined "to subdue the continent — to rush over this vast field to the Pacific Ocean . . . to regenerate superannuated nations . . . to cause a stagnant people to be reborn . . . to shed new and resplendent glory upon mankind."[2]

Horace Bell of California expressed the same feelings:

. . . first, that the earth is the Lord's, and the fullness thereof, and we are the Lord's people; second, that all Spanish-American governments are worthless, and should be reconstructed, . . . that the people of Lower California and Sonora are, or should be, dissatisfied with Mexican rule, and are, or should be, ripe for rebellion, and if not in terror of the Mexican central despotism would cry out for American aid to shake off their galling chains . . . and cry for help from the generous filibuster.[3]

John Louis O'Sullivan, a New York lawyer and diplomat, as well as editor of the *United States Magazine and Democratic Review*, is generally credited with coining the phrase "Manifest Destiny," claiming the United States should govern not only from ocean to ocean, but all of North America. "The Mexican race now see in the fate of the aborigines of the north their own inevitable destiny," he wrote. "They must amalgamate and be lost to the superior vigor of the Anglo-Saxon race, or they must inevitably perish."[4]

A financially weak Mexico could not adequately protect its borders, and it repeatedly asked the United States to prevent filibustering expeditions. Washington responded with the Neutrality Act of 1818, a law forbidding Americans from invading their neighbor. However, sympathetic juries failed to convict, and even the court frequently found it impossible to remain neutral. Judge Ogden Hoffman of the United States District Court in California said, following the acquittal of William Walker, that "From my heart, I sympathized with the accused . . . [and] I . . . admire the spirited men who have gone forth upon these expeditions to upbuild, as they claim, the broken-down altars and rekindle the extinguished fires of liberty in Mexico. . . ."[5]

From across the border, *El Siglo XIX*, a Mexico City newspaper, claimed the "turbulent water of the Rio Grande" is not a hindrance to the "audacious marauders of the opposite bank." *El Universal* declared if the Americans occupied Sonora, they would be reinforced so quickly that the Mexican Army could never dislodge them.[6]

Mexico obviously needed a barrier to the filibuster, and since the Rio Grande and the Sonoran desert did not provide adequate restraint, and since the Mexican military had neither the arms nor the training for such protection, one answer was additional colonization of the frontier, to remove vacuums attractive to foreigners by placing nationals in them. Such colonists would hopefully be Mexican citizens, but if insufficient numbers volunteered, then Europeans would be invited.

Still, if Mexico could see with a tolerable clarity what needed to be done, its leaders were forever squabbling about the methods. In 1848, President José Joaquin de Herrera recommended dividing the frontier into three sections: the Eastern, consisting of Tamaulipas and Coahuila; the Middle, which would be Chihuahua; and the Western, composed of Sonora and Baja California. The government would place eighteen colonies alongside the international boundary. Each male would be a civilian settler and soldier. He would discharge his military obligations in six years and receive free land near the post for cultivation. Regional Indians would be bribed to remain peaceful.[7]

Because of Mexican delays and internal dissension, the money and leadership never materialized. Two years later, in 1850, Mariano

Paredes, a Sonoran legislator, warned the Chamber of Deputies that the United States was poised to annex Sonora, and only a rapid implementation of civilian colonies could prevent it. He recommended 177 acres of irrigable land (more for cattle raising) for each family, more European participation, and a duty free port at Guaymas. Such a harbor would entice trade, and the additional business possibilities would attract settlers.[8]

The Paredes approach failed for substantially the same reasons as Herrera's.

Juan N. Almonte, an aging former boundary surveyor, advocated proposal number three. He recommended settlements of Germans and Belgians along the border, describing those people as "more industrious than Mexicans." The Mexican government should contribute five hundred pesos for transportation, and sell land at $1.50 an acre. Foreigners would be released from taxes and military service for five years.[9]

Had Mexico adopted any of these basically sound plans and stocked its borderlands with colonies of foreign and domestic settlers, the United States might never have pressured it into the Gadsden Purchase, as that huge area of several thousand square miles had less people than a half-dozen square blocks of Mexico City. So while the arguments of what to do and accusations of whom to blame continued unabated in the capital, raiding flourished without mercy along the border.

Many filibusters were Mexicans themselves, examples being Antonio Canales, an attorney, and his military friend, Colonel Antonio Zapata. They sought a territory dubbed the "Republic of the Rio Grande," and from late summer of 1839 through the fall of 1840, the Republic had its encouraging and its dismaying moments. Some grandiose schemes envisioned a strip of northern Mexico being ripped off from ocean to ocean. However, Canales identified Nuevo Laredo as his capital, which suggests territory more manageable. Since he needed better trained troops than Mexican irregulars, he retained Texas colonels Reuben Ross and S. W. Jordan to conquer his republic. Ross and Jordan commanded 180 volunteers, promising each man $25 a month, a half-league of land, and a share of the booty.

While the Texans seemed quite capable of winning battles, Canales seemed quite incapable of consolidating the victories. He postured and wrote proclamations, which made him feel important but added little to the cause. Canales devised a flag, wrote a constitution, appointed a president, and named himself commander in chief of the army and secretary of war, doing this before he even had a recognized country. He also distrusted the two Americans, perhaps suspecting an eventual double-cross. In short, he played friends and enemies against one another, and the Republic of the Rio Grande ended in late 1840 when Jordan's forces shot their way out of a trap suspected to have been set by Canales at Saltillo. The army retired to Texas, leaving Canales to ponder what might have been.[10]

Over to the west, William Walker was North America's most famous and successful filibuster. The slight Tennessean conquered Baja California in 1852 with fifty men. After imprisoning the La Paz authorities, he avoided Mexican reinforcements by sailing north to Ensenada. Walker occupied Santo Tomas and San Vicente, annexed Sonora (on paper) and forced what Mexicans he could find to take a loyalty oath. He and thirty-three survivors crossed the United States border at Tijuana. American officials arrested him for violating the Neutrality Act.

Even while Walker was being arrested, a rumor swept Mexico that he planned another invasion. To counteract the anticipated assault, President Santa Anna recruited French volunteers from San Francisco, and placed them under the command of Count Gaston Raoul Raoussett de Boulbon, a French national jealous of Walker's growing reputation. In April 1854, Raoussett brought 350 men to Guaymas, Sonora, and planned to use that port as a base to overthrow Baja California. To his dismay only a few Europeans joined him, and a firing squad executed the count against an adobe wall. So ended the French filibustering experiment.

By now, Walker's luck wasn't running any better. After being acquitted of filibustering, he overran Nicaragua in 1855 and temporarily installed himself as president. Five years later he tried the same tactic in Honduras and died while standing blindfolded against a wall.

Henry A. Crabb, a bearded, dark-eyed aristocrat, was the last American filibuster of note to threaten Mexico. In 1856 he settled briefly in Sonora where he met Ignacio Pesqueira, the intelligent *caudillo* (military ruler), federalist, Mason and anti-cleric whose spokesmen urged Crabb to settle colonists in Sonora. A year later when the "Arizona Colonization Company" of between sixty and seventy filibusters approached, Governor Pesqueira called for armed resistance. Crabb crossed the border on April 1 and killed several Mexicans during a skirmish. A few miles down the road, the filibusters entered Caborca where they drove Mexican resistance inside a church but were unable to demolish the door and get inside. As the battle continued, Mexican reinforcements arrived, and soon the filibusters were on the defensive, taking refuge inside a thatch-roofed building which the Mexicans set ablaze. Crabb tried to extinguish the fire with dynamite, but killed and wounded several comrades in the process. Reluctantly Crabb surrendered, his army receiving assurances of prisoner of war treatment. The survivors submitted to being bound, and early the next morning were marched dejectedly in small groups to the unkempt cemetery and executed. Crabb's head was preserved in a keg of mescal.[11]

Trade issues, as well as slavery, also led to filibustering, and Texans in particular resented the *Zona Libre*, or free zone whereby imported goods (usually from Europe) could be dispensed along the Mexican side of the border without paying a tariff. Until the *Zona Libre*, most Texas bordertowns had enjoyed an economic advantage over their neighbor, but the Zone shifted the windfall, and Texans resented it. They longed for the good old days when American merchants, backed by General Taylor's bayonets, sold whatever they wished south of the Rio Grande. Since then, Americans believed great wrongs had been done them by stiff Mexican duties. Texans sought a champion on horseback to redress grievances by force, and José María Carvajal said he could ride.

The Texas born and Virginia educated Carvajal declared for the Plan of La Loba, formulated in the Tamaulipas town by the same name in September 1851. The scheme called for a return of Texas slaves and the establishment of free border trade. Since most of Carvajal's financial support came from his mentor, General Antonio Canales, and from wealthy and influential Brownsville businessmen, in some circles what followed became known as the "Merchants' War."

American adventurers joined Carvajal in carving a perceived "Republic of the Sierra Madre," a snappy name for substantially the same territory as the "Republic of the Rio Grande." Captain John S. Ford and numerous former Texas Rangers signed on, the number of participating Americans estimated at two to four hundred. The filibusters captured bordertown Camargo, Tamaulipas, after a day's fighting. Next came the siege of Matamoros, which the ex-rangers conquered but could not hold because of Carvajal's failure to send support. So after eleven days of attacking and sacking without consolidating and occupying, the Texans went home. Ford still had confidence in Carvajal

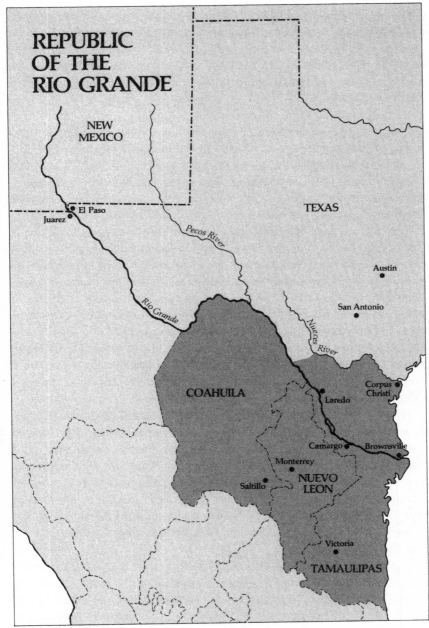

REPUBLIC
OF THE
RIO GRANDE

NEW
MEXICO

Juarez

El Paso

TEXAS

Pecos River

Rio Grande

Austin

San Antonio

Nueces River

COAHUILA

Laredo

Corpus
Christi

Camargo

Brownsville

Monterrey

Saltillo

NUEVO
LEON

Victoria

TAMAULIPAS

The "Republic of the Rio Grande" was a flashy name, proving only that it was easier to create a country on paper than it was to conquer and govern it.

even though the general was losing power and influence everywhere else. Mexicans in particular rarely trusted any Hispanic who was *muy agringado* (too Americanized). Meanwhile, the Mexican central government reduced its tariffs, which made the Brownsville merchants happy and less inclined to support Carvajal. The Republic of the Sierra Madre collapsed.[12]

Mexico's plantation peonage came as close to slavery as any system in the world, but the government closed its eyes to its own evil and took a moralistic attitude toward nations who practiced it openly. While Mexico's 1824 constitution did not specifically abolish slavery, a federal act of the same year freed slaves who entered Mexico, most of them fleeing across the border from the United States.

The Mexican province of Texas, however, required an adjustment in thinking since one out of every five persons in Stephen F. Austin's colony was a slave. To make slavery legal, while giving the appearance of making it illegal, required political expediency plus the illusion of motion akin to picking up both feet and putting them down in the same place. In a remarkably adroit bit of maneuvering, the Mexican congress acknowledged the need for slave labor, and at the same time, condemned the practice. To abolish slavery in the province of Texas might diminish the Anglo immigration that Mexico so desperately needed. So slavery continued in Texas, although blacks escaping to other parts of Mexico were declared free.[13]

After the Texas annexation into the United States, the issue of slaves seeking freedom in Mexico became an international topic. Texas wanted Washington to request a Treaty of Amity, Commerce, and Navigation, with a clause guaranteeing the return of fugitive slaves. The Mexican Senate initially approved, considering slavery as a legitimate institution of a neighboring country. Such a treaty should give the United States less cause for intervening in Mexican affairs. However, the Mexican Chamber of Deputies sharply disapproved, and the clause died.

The border issue of slavery continued to fester. Hundreds of blacks sought sanctuary in Mexico after the Mexican War, generally fleeing through the Piedras Negras gateway across from Eagle Pass, Texas. The village had become a freedom symbol by the early 1850s when several hundred Seminole Indians and Negroes migrated from Indian Territory to Colonia de Guerrero and San Fernando de Rosas, both near the Rio Grande. Mexico provided a small grant of land to each refugee in return for occasional military service. Ironically, when given an opportunity to settle in the interior, most blacks refused. Although they ran a greater risk of being abducted by Americans and removed from Mexican soil, their grasp of English gave them a trade and business advantage along the border that the average Mexican did not possess.[14]

As auction prices in Texas soared to $1,500 for a healthy black male and $1,200 for a female, the monetary incentives attracted border ruffians who slipped across the line and kidnapped former slaves, returning them to previous owners for a fee. Sometimes the slavers bribed Mexican officials to look the other way, and sometimes they just snatched the victims and shot their way out of the country. Even quasi-and-regular American military forces in pursuit of Indians across the border were not above grabbing a slave or two on the way home. Texas Ranger Captain James Hughes Callahan led an expedition of 115 men across the Rio Grande in October 1855, supposedly seeking marauding Indians. After snatching several former slaves, he clashed with a Mexican garrison and retreated into Piedras Negras where Rio Grande floods delayed his departure across the river. As a diversionary tactic, he burned the town. Such clumsy and brutal leadership cost the United States $50,000 in claims.[15]

As the nation headed toward a divisive Civil War, with abolitionists seemingly everywhere in Texas and slaves either running for the North or heading for the border, parts of Texas underwent a period of black hysteria. A series of incendiary fires in Dallas and Henderson, plus rumors of water wells laced with strychnine, convinced officials and citizens that abolitionists were fomenting a revolt. The *Houston Telegraph* described a plot to burn Waxahachie. Two white abolitionists had already been hanged, and twenty Negroes awaited execution, according to a report.[16]

The *State Gazette* published rumors saying Dallas "was destined to be burned, the [white] people to be poisoned or slaughtered, and their property to be distributed among the victorious blacks." On July 24 a mob removed blacks named "Sam, Cato, and Patrick" from jail and lynched them. The *State Gazette* quoted one prisoner as saying two white men promised to take him to Mexico after he burned Georgetown.[17]

The *Bastrop Advertiser* said:

The woods around Bastrop seem to be alive with runaway slaves. Not less than six bucks have been confined to our county jail within the past week or ten days. Some of them hailed from a long ways off, and declared their intention was to enter Mexican territory, where they expected to be free.[18]

The *Colorado Citizen* suspected as much too:

Last week a plot was discovered . . . [near] Lyons . . . among the negroes to organize themselves into a body of about two hundred, go to meet another band at La Grange, and thence proceed to Mexico. The leaders have been arrested.[19]

Over in Louisiana, New Orleans newspapers looked calmly at the Texas "uprisings," then wrote the most outlandish editorials of all. The *Daily Picayune* reported on August 19, 1860:

We see no evidence . . . among the negroes for permanent insurrection. . . . There are no specifications given, even surmised, that [they] . . . had any serious plan for setting themselves at liberty, or . . . escaping from the punishment of those crimes. The purposes of the conspiracy were mere wanton mischief — murder and arson — without any definite idea about what the actors were to gain. Doubtless the uppermost idea was of unrestrained riot, the luxury of unbounded license, and the immediate gratification of every animal appetite, the orgies of idleness, gluttony, and lust.

In the meantime, as more Negroes crossed the border, Mexico offered freedom and sympathy, but insisted upon "Letters of Citizenship." Since the blacks had none, they gathered at the American consul's office in Matamoros, and "asked for papers." Minister Gadsden angrily instructed consular officers to refuse all requests:

. . . Africans who are flocking in numbers from the United States to Mexico . . . are not recognized as Citizens at home; and cannot claim abroad what would be denied them in the states. . . . [20]

Gadsden referred to the Negroes as a "degraded class of low plunderers," and applied pressure against Mexico for a fugitive slave extradition clause. Mexico adamantly refused. When John Forsyth, who replaced Gadsden as minister to Mexico, tried to satisfy Texas slave interests by purchasing additional portions of Mexico along the border, suspecting that might stop the slave exodus, or bring those living along the international line back into United States jurisdiction, Mexico again said no.

11

Blue and Gray
at the Border

WITHIN WEEKS after the presidential election of Abraham Lincoln in 1860, South Carolina seceded from the Union. Most Southern states swiftly followed, forming the Confederate States of America. Texas joined the Confederacy in March 1861. New Mexico (which included Arizona) and California remained with the Union. One month and ten days following the Texas decision, however, the South fired on Fort Sumter. A great war had begun although few anticipated just how ruthlessly Lincoln would deny this attempted disintegration of the Union.

In Texas, much of the fighting took place along the Rio Grande frontier, a region of vast cattle ranches and a predominantly Hispanic population. The five largest *Tejano* border counties (Cameron, Hidalgo, Starr, Zapata and Webb), voted overwhelmingly for secession, although how many Hispanics voted is open to question. While an estimated ten thousand Hispanics served both the Blue and Gray (at least half in New Mexico), their participation is only now being evaluated by scholars.

Adrian J. Vidal, for instance, was born in Monterrey, Mexico. His mother had married Mifflin Kenedy, a wealthy partner of Richard King, the Texas cattle baron. Vidal enlisted as a private in Captain

James Duff's company of Partisan Rangers at San Antonio in 1862, and rose to captain in the Confederacy when he captured a Federal gunboat. For reasons known only to himself, however, Vidal deserted and enlisted in the Union Army at Brownsville. It commissioned him captain, and put him in charge of "Vidal's Independent Partisan Rangers." This force scouted the Texas brush country, frequently slashing into Mexico. But Vidal could neither speak, write nor understand English, and the bureaucratic paperwork set his teeth on edge. He requested a discharge, and was declared a deserter when he left a few days before the certificate reached him. After returning to Mexico, Vidal joined the *Juaristas*, but was captured and executed by the French in 1865. As historian Jerry Don Thompson expressed it, "The young captain had served both the blue and the gray, deserted from both armies, joined a third and was shot by a fourth."[1]

By late 1863, the Union had blockaded the seaport of Brownsville. Lieutenant Benjamin F. McIntyre of Company A, 19th Iowa Infantry, and his fellow soldiers had crossed the Gulf of Mexico in crowded, leaky vessels and bumped ashore near the muddy mouth of the Rio Grande on November 2. The seasick veterans trudged through lagoons and patches of chaparral and coarse grass. Abandoned shacks dotted the skyline, their grass roofs and walls reinforced with boards, boxes and whatever the tide washed in. Only the rutted, clay roads with their streaks of white fluff provided evidence of straining cotton wagons having once passed this way.

Brownsville did not impress McIntyre, perhaps because Fort Brown (for whom the town was named) had been destroyed by panicky, retreating Confederates, and the resultant flames had burned portions of the village. The churches looked as if God had forsaken South Texas. The population existed in ramshackle houses with dirt floors and sugar cane walls. McIntyre wryly suggested the descriptive name of "Dogtown" for the village. Mongrels prowled the littered streets and if the Union Army did little else in Brownsville, it executed hundreds of these stray canines.[2]

Brownsville and Matamoros were side by side thirty miles from the Gulf and separated by the Rio Grande. Matamoros was organized in 1826 to relieve the congestion at Veracruz, although Brownsville was not a seaport. Shipping exited from the satellite port of Bagdad. When the Union occupied Brownsville in April 1863, Matamoros became an

Matamoros, Mexico, as seen by Union artillerymen, was a cotton staging area for the South that cannon could not dominate. (Arnulfo Oliveira Memorial Library, Brownsville)

Brownsville, Texas, during the 1860s had the appearance of a typical Southern community. (Arnulfo Oliveira Memorial Library, Brownsville)

extension of the Confederacy because Texas cotton was smuggled through it. One correspondent described it like this:

Matamoros is to the rebellion west of the Mississippi what New York is to the United States — its great commercial and financial center, feeding and clothing the rebellion, arming and equipping, furnishing the materials for war and a specie basis for circulation that has almost displaced confederate paper. . . . [3]

The roads across Texas teemed with cotton caravans heading for the border and Matamoros. Ships carried the cargo from Bagdad to textile mills in England, France, Cuba, New Orleans and New York. In a war filled with ironies, few are more incredible than Texas borderland cotton keeping the Northern industries humming. Those northern plants manufactured munitions that were then exchanged for more cotton. Each side provided the other with portions of the necessary materials to continue fighting.[4]

But the cotton trade was even more complex than that. When the French invaded Mexico in 1863, driving President Benito Juárez to El Paso del Norte, cotton shipped from the seaport of Bagdad was taxed, the money used to purchase weapons for the *Juaristas*. France, of course, threatened to occupy Matamoros and seal off the cotton trade, so the United States invaded South Texas to confiscate the cotton before it reached Mexico. However, the Union occupation forced cotton farmers to cross the Rio Grande boundary farther west, making the shipping of cotton to Matamoros more inconvenient, expensive and time consuming, but not materially reducing the flow.[5]

Lieutenant McIntyre visited Matamoros and found the village built on high ground one mile south of the Rio Grande. Like Brownsville, it had no gas works, no water works, no graded streets. It did have a larger population. A massive cathedral fronted on the Plaza de Armas, a square surrounded by an iron fence. Orange trees grew in the narrow streets. The lieutenant's words depicted a town of more inspiring proportions than Brownsville, and yet he returned to Texas with the brief journal disclosure that his own country was best.

Union officials in Brownsville forced a loyalty oath on the residents, and most of the Hispanic population complied. However, a few Texans were recalcitrant. George Dye, a former mayor, swore allegiance, but his wife and daughter expressed contempt for the oath. An exasperated military finally hustled the females into exile across the border.[6]

With so many residents professing loyalty to the United States, it followed that the Union would recruit additional soldiers. Negroes formed what McIntyre called the "Corps d' Afrique." These men whose ignorance was nearly absolute due to a lifetime in the plantation fields, treasured their role in freedom's fighting army. McIntyre tried to be fair, but he obviously did not want his prejudices disturbed. In his judgment, the common white soldier took pride in his rifle, while the Corps d' Afrique took pride only in its picks and shovels. The Corps swept the streets and cleaned the buildings. It handled work "which of necessity must have been performed by soldiers had we not had negroes with us," McIntyre dryly said.

Hundreds of Mexican nationals also enlisted, their concern for freedom's call being more pragmatic than idealistic. French invaders of Mexico had placed Emperor Ferdinand Maximilian in the capital and sent President Benito Juárez reeling toward northern Mexico. With French boots striding toward Matamoros, and the region in political and military chaos, the indecisive Governor Manuel Ruiz of Tamaulipas was ordered executed by Lieutenant Governor Romolo Villa and Mexican General José María Cobos. During the coup, Juan Cortina, a conspirator and sometime-bandit, sometime-general, and always an opportunist, entered the fray against everybody. He managed to execute Villa and Cobos. Ruiz fled into Texas and organized an army of eight hundred for a counterattack on Matamoros. In a furious, decisive battle, Ruiz fell back across the border, leaving his followers to be chopped up by Cortina's machete-swinging militiamen.

Scores of Mexican refugees, fleeing Cortina *and* the French, swam the Rio Grande into Texas, and accepted asylum from Union officers. Since many had no source of livelihood, they signed on for a hitch in the United States Army. The Lower Rio Grande Valley was now partially composed of wistful exiles looking both ways across the border toward home.

The Union used its Mexicans primarily as irregulars, guerrillas who waged hit and run attacks. A group attacked Laredo in March 1864, burning several hundred bales of cotton ready for shipment south.

Yet, for a variety of reasons, these same Union soldiers of Hispanic descent had an indifference to discipline. Part of the reasons were that prejudice was as rampant with the Federal forces as with the South. The Mexicans were rarely paid, and rarely equipped. Desertions occurred in droves, and harsh punishments were extracted. Private Pedro

García left his post without permission, and a court martial sentenced him to death by firing squad. On execution day a company of soldiers slowly tramped toward the cemetery while a band played the dead march. García and a priest rode in a cart with the condemned man's coffin. The procession halted at an open grave where García, appearing stout, middle aged and (temporarily) in the best of health, spoke briefly to his confessor, removed his shoes, stuffed his trouser leggings inside his socks, and sat upright on one end of his open casket. At the command of fire, several bullets knocked him backwards into the coffin. Two officers stepped forward and shot him through the head. As he lay in the open grave, the entire regiment marched past and gazed upon "the doom of a deserter." The Army had made its point.

But while the Union struggled to maintain discipline at Brownsville, the Confederates rebuilt their forces upstream along the border. Hawk-nosed Colonel John S. Ford commanded the Rio Grande Military District, and assigned considerable authority to Colonel Santos Benavides, the highest ranking Mexican-American to serve the South. Benavides took command of Fort McIntosh near Laredo.[7]

Although Rio Grande counties had solidly voted for the South, not all Hispanics believed their views had been taken into consideration. Zapata County rebelled against the rebellers. Antonio Ochoa, a thirty-nine-year-old ranchero seized control of his district, issued a *pronunciamiento* against the Confederacy, and rode with about eighty men to Clareno, a tiny ranch overlooking the Rio Grande. Confederates attacked them there, and drove them across the river where they teamed up with the bandit and politician, Juan Cortina. This reinforced band of irregulars now moved upstream on the Mexican side, and on May 19, 1861, crossed into Texas and struck a ranch as well as the village of Carrizo. When Confederate reinforcements led by Santos Benavides arrived from Laredo, they caught Cortina and Ochoa sacking Carrizo. Over a dozen partisans died before the others escaped back into Mexico.[8]

Meanwhile, Colonel Ford moved southeast toward Brownsville with the "Cavalry of the West," a motley army of old men, young boys and a variety of rangy characters. As Ford advanced, the Union retreated toward the coast, leaving only a token force on Brazos Island. Such a departure threw Brownsville into turmoil. Most Mexican residents had taken a loyalty oath to the United States. If they remained on the north bank, they ran the risk of Confederate vengeance.

French troops were about as effective in Matamoros as the Union Army was in Brownsville. Not much was accomplished, and in the end both armies left in frustration. (Arnulfo Oliveira Memorial Library, Brownsville)

If they fled south, they might be slain by their own countrymen or by the French who were momentarily expected in Matamoros.

McIntyre expressed pity for these border refugees and blamed his government for their plight. "Now they are being rewarded for their loyalty," he said. "Poor deluded half civilized creatures," he wrote in his diary, "they are in a dilemma and half crazed with fear." In their panic they chose Mexico as the lesser of two perversities. Tearing down their cane and stick *jacales* (huts), they floated their possessions across the Rio Grande. "A Mexican leaves nothing behind," McIntyre said.

The same could not be said for the Union Army as it withdrew in July 1864. Soldiers scattered overcoats and blankets along their line of march to the sea. Troopers collapsed of heat prostration and ambulances ran full with unconscious bodies. When at last the regiment reached the ship, it boarded at night. In the darkness and confusion, a soldier fell overboard and floated a half-mile out to sea. As a small boat pulled alongside his outstretched fingers, he sank.

Except for the battle of Palmito Hill in mid May 1865, fought after the Civil War had ended (and lost by the Federals who had advanced out of Brazos Island), the Union excursion on the Lower Rio Grande border had ended. Money, time and opportunity had been squandered. The Union Army had moved into South Texas with expectations of helping bring the war to a quick end. It had accomplished only a minor disruption. The brief occupation of Brownsville had brought neither peace nor understanding.

Prior to the Civil War, in the El Paso del Norte — El Paso region, the two populations had intermingled and intermarried. They were neighbors in the literal sense. Isolation ordinarily added up to compatibility.

El Paso, Texas was a village of sand-covered caliche streets even though they petered out in a block or two. An *acequia madre* meandered lazily past the *plazita* at the north end of El Paso Street. Several large ash and cottonwood trees furnished shade for fruit and vegetable vendors as well as strollers, sitters and lovers. An armed sentinel pretended to protect the village, but everybody knew his duty was to chase skinny-dippers out of the ditch, the town's primary source of drinking water.

The unit of exchange was the peso or Mexican Ounce, the latter a gold coin worth about sixteen dollars. Spanish was the language of commerce, and maids frequently went south to work. The town had no bank, and Fort Bliss sold the only greenbacks. If an El Paso merchant ran out of supplies, he could borrow from a storekeeper in El Paso del Norte. Men did not kill each other the way books and movies would eventually portray them; and the most unpardonable sin along the ante-bellum border was to refuse the loan of a horse or buggy.

El Paso County had three thousand residents, of which 144 were Anglos. Only Anson, Emmett and William Wallace Mills openly supported the Union, doing so with vociferous gusto. Slavery seldom figured in local arguments and discussions. Except for two slaves owned by Simeon Hart, gristmill operator and local aristocrat, blacks were as rare around El Paso as intellectuals. The disputes involved states' rights. Why should the North interfere in the internal affairs of Texas? Why should the North deny Texas the right to secede?

Back in Richmond, Virginia, Confederate President Jefferson Davis discussed the border's future with Major Henry H. Sibley, an ailing alcoholic and former commander of Fort Union, New Mexico. Davis believed the boundary at the Pass of the North should play a significant role in the forthcoming struggle. El Paso could link the South and

West, provide a critical border hookup with Mexico, and act as the junction of a transcontinental railroad. Davis gave Sibley authority to take and hold it.

Sibley already had things going his way. General David Emanuel Twiggs, in poor health and close to retirement, surrendered his Department of Texas to the state commissioners, those representatives of the Austin government who would sign for the Union posts. Such orders astonished Colonel Isaac Van Duzer Reeve, the Fort Bliss commander. Reeve was to turn equipment, property and supplies over to James Magoffin, and march his troops to San Antonio where they would surrender and be paroled. However, Reeve had another option. He could link up with Federal forces at Fort Fillmore, forty miles north, as New Mexico was considered Union territory. Anson and W. W. Mills urged him to do this, but Reeve, not the Army's most decisive officer, hesitated because he lacked specific instructions from Washington. Anson volunteered to approach Secretary of War Simon Cameron, but in the confused state of Potomac politics he received no answer. Anson Mills then joined the Army and served without distinction in the Tennessee theater of operations. As for Reeve, he went to San Antonio.

With military conditions collapsing at the border gateway, W. W. Mills hurried north to bolster Major Isaac Lynde, the vacillating commander at Fort Fillmore. Conditions had almost broken Lynde's nerve. The secessionist flag flew openly in the Mesilla plaza, and the *Mesilla Times* demanded an end to Union occupation. Many of Lynde's 750 men threatened to "go south" and join the three-hundred-man force approaching El Paso from central Texas under Colonel John R. Baylor, an egocentric, flamboyant, former Comanche Indian fighter.

Mills urged Lynde to seize El Paso, and keep Baylor out on the prairie, forcing either his surrender or retreat. But Lynde sat paralyzed while Baylor and his men rode unmolested into the Pass. Mills therefore became an exile across the border in El Paso del Norte, watching in fury as his former friends, Hart, Magoffin and others supplied the Confederacy. Hart even paid acting-sheriff Albrecht Kuhn $100 to kidnap Mills off the El Paso del Norte streets. The abductors whisked Mills to the Fort Bliss stockade where Baylor treated him kindly but kept open his option for hanging him as a spy. Baylor needed Mills in custody while Texas feinted Lynde out of position. When Baylor moved against Fort Fillmore, he captured it easily. He chased Lynde east across the Organ Mountains and accepted his humiliating surrender at San Agustin Springs. Baylor subsequently gave Mills the freedom of the post, knowing he would escape. Mills did. He rode north to join Colonel Edward Richard Sprigg Canby, a determined Union fighter who commanded the Department of New Mexico.[9]

As Baylor mopped up, he not only created the Territory of Arizona, he proclaimed himself governor of it. (The Territory comprised roughly the southern portion of today's New Mexico and Arizona.) Baylor's capital was Mesilla.

Forty miles away in El Paso, however, Sibley had become a general, and had officially assumed command of Confederate operations in the West. In spite of his faults (mostly liquor), Sibley recognized the value, and the dangers, of the international boundary. In particular he envisioned a land corridor of Confederate territory along the border from El Paso to the Pacific. Of course, he would have to deal with Canby in New Mexico first, but in the meantime he dispatched Colonel James Reily of the 4th Regiment of the Texas Mounted Volunteers to negotiate with Governor Luis Terrazas in Chihuahua City. Sibley wanted to know if Mexico would permit Union troops to cross its soil for an attack on Texas. He also wanted an unlimited right to pursue marauding Apaches into Mexico.[10]

At the Chihuahua capital, Terrazas treated Reily cordially, even refunding customs duties for supplies. The governor had no intelligence regarding a possible United States invasion corridor through Mexico, and doubted such permission would be granted. He also did not consider the Indian menace so threatening that Confederates should slash across the border at will.[11]

Sibley now sent his forces north along the Rio Grande for a showdown with Canby. However, after capturing Albuquerque and Santa Fe, the Confederacy crested at the Battle of Glorieta Pass. Sibley did not exactly lose the engagement, but he absorbed enough of a beating to believe he did. With much of his wagon train destroyed, his supplies burned, Sibley's army stumbled back toward El Paso.

Sibley's broken remnants found no relief at the Pass. His soldiers had made the common mistake of confusing Mexican hospitality with weakness. Supplies had always been scarce, and neither Baylor nor Sibley had exerted much discipline. Irregulars had foraged back and forth, trampling gardens near the Pass, pulling onions, eating the peaches, playing ball with the melons and drinking the wine. Blankets disappeared from beds along with occasional wives and daughters. So

JOHN ROBERT BAYLOR
(Arizona Historical Society, Tucson)

JAMES H. CARLETON
(McNitt Coll., State Records Center
and Archives, Santa Fe)

HENRY H. SIBLEY
(U.S. Military Academy Archives)

EDWARD R. S. CANBY
(U.S. Military Academy Archives)

when Sibley's starving army trudged back into the El Paso Southwest, many wheat fields and adobe buildings became contested areas. Soldiers and Hispanics died in furious, now forgotten scraps.[12]

The cold-eyed General James H. Carleton and his California Column moved in behind the retreating Texans. These volunteers had not participated in the recent fighting, having just crossed the New Mexico territory from California and winning a skirmish in Tucson. They raised the Union flag in El Paso on August 20, 1862.

While the war had not really touched El Paso in terms of fighting or destruction, except that Fort Bliss at Magoffinsville was reduced to shambles, the conflict nevertheless depopulated the town. Hart closed his mill and transferred his library and household belongings to El Paso del Norte before fleeing to San Antonio. Saloon keeper Ben Dowell and Chihuahua trader James Magoffin did likewise. Other southern sympathizers moved into El Paso del Norte and watched in frustration as the Union Army took command of the north bank.

W. W. Mills returned to El Paso in triumph, his mind teeming with political opportunities. Eventually he wrote *Forty Years in El Paso*, insuring that he would have the last word on every controversy. His creation was an inspired, if at times awkwardly phrased account containing inaccuracies as well as astute observations and ringing hatreds — a mine of information regarding early El Paso, a book as remarkable for its silences as for its observations. For awhile, he considered campaigning for Congress, and did support a legislative concept of a Territory of Montezuma, whereby West Texas would be attached to the southern half of New Mexico and Arizona. El Paso and Mesilla would be the territorial trade centers. The plan failed enactment because the legislators ran out of time and adjourned, so Mills settled for collector of customs in El Paso.[13]

But if El Paso had few people, it also had rumors of a planned rebel counterattack. Carleton, who replaced Canby in Santa Fe, left Fort Bliss in the inexperienced hands of Major William McMullen, a young officer with a quick temper, an active imagination and a deep suspicion of Mexicans. The rumor mill whispered that Baylor planned a new assault by slipping an army up the south bank of the Rio Grande. This militia would have the support and guidance of spies and Southern exiles living in El Paso del Norte. To blunt this anticipated invasion, McMullen stationed two squads of soldiers to intercept the border highway in Mexico, across the Rio Grande from San Elizario. Union

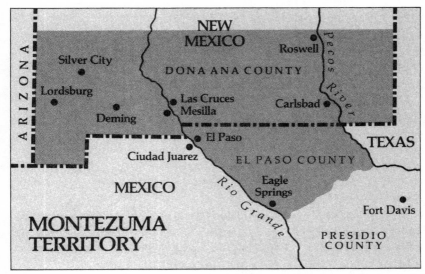

Had this territory or state come into being, El Paso would have become the capital and leading city. New Mexico, Arizona and Texas would have been far different.

troopers summarily arrested travelers unable to account for their presence. His actions brought a protest from José María Uranga, the *jefe politico* of the Rio Grande District. Uranga's carefully worded letter gave the major an opportunity to gracefully back down. "There is no doubt," the *jefe* wrote, that such actions have been taken "without your knowledge." The note argued firmly that "international rights have been violated and treaties existing between the two countries have been broken."

While McMullen did not fully comprehend what he had done, he did have the capacity to be indignant:

I have to say that it does not astonish me that you are surprised to hear of such a proceeding on my part; when I take into consideration the injustices practiced by the Mexican authorities in permitting the *avowed* enemies of the United States government to establish an outpost in the town of El Paso [Mexico], from which to send out Mexican and Indian spies to learn the strength and movement of the US troops in New Mexico and Texas. . . .

I assure you I entertain the most friendly regards for Mexico . . . yet my sense of duty to my Government will not permit Mexican soil to shield our enemies when protected by Mexican authority in violation of international obligations.[14]

Four days later Uranga patiently replied, saying any person had a right of asylum in Mexico. Unionists had taken advantage of it, and now the Confederacy was doing the same. So long as its laws were obeyed, Mexico would not force anyone to leave. As for McMullen's acknowledgment of sending soldiers into Mexico, Uranga asked, ". . . are you not confessing that you have violated international obligations?" McMullen paused. His rashness could create political repercussions, so he covered his backside and dispatched his version of events to General Joseph R. West, his commanding officer. The major mentioned hordes of rebels in El Paso del Norte, and closed with the plea: "Hoping the genl. may consider my action justified under the circumstances."

West replied, "You did perfectly right and your straightforward letter to the prefect will be too much for Mexican diplomacy." And so the matter ended with no political ramifications but more importantly, no further invasions of a sovereign territory.[15]

Officially Tucson, like Mesilla, operated as a part of the North; unofficially, like Mesilla, it had compassion for the South. Slaves were rare. The Mexicans condemned slavery unilaterally, suspecting that anyone who owned a black man was only a step away from owning a brown one. Most Anglos did not have slaves either, nor did they believe in the practice. However, they supported states' rights to such a degree that Union military officers considered them "traitors of the deepest dye . . . mostly outlaws . . . who were early sympathizers with secessionists."[16]

When Captain Sherod Hunter and his company of Texas Mounted Rifles occupied Tucson in February 1862, the soldiers found a friendly reception. Only a few Unionists, such as Peter Brady, fled to Sonora. The goateed Brady with the iron hair and an iron constitution had fought in the Mexican War, had been a forty-niner, had worked with A. B. Gray during the 1853 railroad survey from Indianola to San Diego, and had been Emory's official interpreter during the Gadsden Purchase surveys.[17]

Brady became a spy who moved around Sonora, obtaining information regarding Hunter's activities. His reports went to Colonel (later general) James H. Carleton and his 1,500 man California Column, snaking east parallel to the border, heading toward Tucson, Mesilla and El Paso. Brady kept watch also on James Reily who, unable to convince Chihuahua Governor Terrazas to support the Confederate cause, had forked off from Hunter's command and disappeared into Sonora for a conference with Governor Ignacio Pesqueira. Reily had the assistance of J. T. Pickett, friend of the governor and a spy-negotiator for the South who traveled the entire length and breadth of Mexico, especially along the border. Because of Pickett, Pesqueira considered countermanding a recent government agreement to permit Northern troops to land at Guaymas and invade Texas or New Mexico. (Never seriously planned, anyway.) However, the governor's hesitation and vacillation ended when an American gunboat near Guaymas congratulated him for having the good judgment to ignore Confederate requests.[18]

When Carleton arrived in the old presidio city of Tucson, he decreed that Unionists could come home, but Confederates would have to take a loyalty oath. That brought Carleton into conflict with Sylvester Mowry, who considered himself neutral. The handsome, articulate Mowry wore tailored clothes, selecting only the most soft and elegant cloth, and was a dandy in manners along a frontier noted for its rough and unwashed characters. Folks would remember his cultured bearing as well as the glossy, neatly trimmed beard, twinkling eyes and black wavy hair. In the early 1850s, Mowry led a struggle for statehood or territorial status of the Gadsden Purchase lands, property Colonel Baylor referred to as the Territory of Arizona.[19] When the dreams of statehood faded, Mowry purchased the Patagonia Mine north of Nogales. He called it the Mowry Silver Mine and turned it into a prosperous operation. However, he wasn't exactly a father figure to the employees, and one disgruntled laborer accused Mowry of selling percussion caps to Captain Hunter, as well as placing a cannon near the mine, claiming he could defeat any Union force sent against him. So on June 13, 1862, the Army arrested Mowry and charged him with having Southern sympathies. A court sentenced him to four months imprisonment. The government seized his mine, returned it after his release, then seized it again and auctioned it by authority of the Confiscation Act. Mowry sued Carleton for over a million dollars. The case never went to court, and eventually the government returned the mine, although it never again earned large profits for Mowry.[20]

The Civil War ended with Southern soldiers on both sides of the Mexican border. Human fragments from a dispirited and beaten army clotted the roads, preying on each other. Confederate generals John B.

Magruder, J. E. Slaughter and Jo Shelby crossed the international line and tried selling their services to the French emperor.[21]

Washington now had power to awe the French, and it dispatched fifty-two thousand troops to the Lower Rio Grande Valley under the command of Major General Philip H. Sheridan. Sheridan's major contribution, other than keeping the French nervous with invasion threats, was in stacking arms where Mexican generals could find them.

Upstream at El Paso del Norte, the Mexican hopes rallied. Napoleon's invasion and the capture of Mexico City had sent President Benito Juárez fleeing north in a small black carriage. Behind him, French legions stacked their rifles in Chihuahua City, declining to risk an incident with the Americans at Fort Bliss, Texas.

Thus the weak and reeling Mexican federation continued to survive, helped along by a strong American presence. General Carleton "condemned" a large quantity of arms and ammunition, and donated it to the Mexican Army. Juárez forces dragged several cannon to the high ground southeast of El Paso del Norte where their firepower dominated the approaches from Chihuahua City.

Carleton also offered asylum to Juárez and his officers: "You must believe that in your reverses you have our deepest sympathy," he wrote. The general expressed confidence that Juárez would soon regain Mexico City where "neither foreign influences nor foreign bayonets can coerce or distract you from the free discharge of your duty."

The president thanked Carleton but declined even to visit the United States since "I am resolved never to leave the soil of Mexico during its occupation by foreign invaders." Unstated, however, were deeper fears. Mexican aristocrats and bishops opposed him and supported the French because Juárez had so reduced their wealth and influence. For Juárez to have accepted refuge in the United States might have been interpreted as an abdication of office. And so El Paso del Norte, the largest village along the Mexican-United States border, became the provisional capital of Mexico.

Such a capital had to act like one, and this meant rounds of social affairs. Fort Bliss decked itself out for a great reception, but rose to the occasion when the president explained why he could not attend. If Juárez could not come to El Paso, then El Paso would go to him. Juan Zubirán, collector of Customs at El Paso del Norte, and Rafael Velarde, a merchant, held grand balls in their Mexican homes. W. W. Mills, along with Consul Henry J. Cuniffe "visited the president very often,"

Benito Juárez is revered as one of Mexico's great patriots. His memory is perpetuated by a great border city which bears his name. (Author's Collection)

IGNACIO PESQUIERA
(Arizona Historical Society, Tucson)

HENRY SEWARD
(Library of Congress)

and photos reveal them playing cards. I. S. Bartlett, assistant customs collector under Mills, was greatly taken by Juárez, and his description defines how Americans still think of him:

I saw before me a descendant of the Aztec race, of pure lineage, a short, solidly built, thick-set man, probably a little over five feet in height with a face strongly bronzed, handsome dark eyes, high cheek bones, a strong, prominent nose, and black hair cut close. His expression of countenance was winning and serene. His manner was that of a cultivated gentleman and scholar, easy and dignified. His conversation lacked the fluency and vehemence characteristic of the Spanish. His voice was low and pleasant and he frequently paused as if weighing the import of his words.

His dress was that of a "citizen" president and from an American point of view, faultless. He wore coat and trousers of black broadcloth, a white vest, standing collar, black neck tie, kid gloves and highly polished boots. His dress fitted his sturdy, compact figure to a nicety and was worn with the grace of a finished cosmopolitan.[22]

Juárez showed an easy familiarity with United States history, and on one occasion, the president asked everyone to remain seated while he ordered wine. After the Americans proposed toasts to the Republic of Mexico, Juárez responded by proposing one to "the brave men who established liberty and union in the United States."

And in living along the border, a region where the central Mexican government ordinarily had little influence, he did more to identify himself with the Mexican people than he might have done had the French not intervened. Juárez and these *mestizos* of the desert borderlands came to know and to understand each other, and the Mexicans grew to love this somber man who dressed unpretentiously in dark clothes. They identified with his agony: a wife in New York where an infant son lay dying, a nation under his leadership struggling not to advance but just to survive. "My brain is so overwhelmed I can hardly write these lines," he wrote his son-in-law in what must have been the quiet understatement of the age.[23]

Over in the United States, most Americans supported armed intervention to drive France out of Mexico. Presidents Lincoln and Andrew Johnson pitched the negotiating responsibilities to Secretary of State Henry Seward. Repeatedly Seward struggled not only against the French but against politicians in his own party who advocated military power as the solution. Grant and Sheridan wanted George Armstrong

Custer to take command of Mexican cavalry. More than any other person, Seward wheedled, cajoled and threatened the French into withdrawing. They did, leaving Maximilian to a firing squad.[24]

In gratitude, El Paso del Norte changed its name to Ciudad Juarez (City of Juárez), in September 1888. The citizens built a heroic statue of Benito Juárez which still stands in the central park. Later, they erected a statue to Abraham Lincoln, a symbol of friendship and hands-across-the-border, a reminder of a common brotherhood in the days when the people of El Paso and El Paso del Norte had only themselves to fall back upon.

12

Cowhides and Rangers

THE NAMES Thomas P. Robb, F. Mead and Richard H. Savage are not ones even regional historians easily recall. By themselves they are footnotes to an era, men selected to become the 1872 investigative commissioners to Texas. President Ulysses S. Grant responded to a joint congressional resolution defining their mission: to uncover the factual story behind the wholesale cattle rustling along the Mexican border in the Nueces Strip of the Lower Rio Grande Valley.

For three hundred miles the Strip protruded like a green peninsula westward across Texas from the Gulf. One hundred and fifty miles of prairie separated the Nueces River from the Rio Grande to the south. Under Spain, the Strip had been part of Nuevo Santander, and under Mexico a portion of Tamaulipas and Coahuila. Both nations referred to it as *El Desierto Muerto* (the Desert of Death). Coarse grass grew waist high away from the Gulf and its alluvial, sedimentary deposits. Sand hills and barren areas of white saline deposits were common. In the infrequent watercourses, wind-twisted clumps of live oak were of little use for anything except firewood and holding the ground together. Across this relatively flat and sandy area moved immense herds of mustangs and wild cattle. In days past, the region had been allocated to wealthy *hacendados*. Comanches regarded the Nueces

Strip as their special hunting and killing ground. American outlaws, Mexican *ladrones* (bandits), and Indian marauders, all fought and traded inside the Strip.

Following the Texas war for independence, Texas and Mexico each claimed ownership of the Strip (Texas claiming the Rio Grande as the border, and Mexico conceding only the Nueces), although neither exercised total control. The dispute periodically flamed and abated, awaiting final settlement by the Treaty of Guadalupe Hidalgo.

The Rio Grande had miles of tortuous curves filled with semi-tropical thickets choked with vines and cactus. Gnarled mesquite trees three feet in diameter lined the river. Longhorns took refuge in the brush, becoming as mean and as fierce as their thorn-infested world.

After the Civil War, herds of rangy cattle grazed the entire length and breadth of the Nueces Strip. With a rope, saddle, horse and ample courage, the Texans dragged protesting longhorns from the thick underbrush and stamped on their brands with hot, smoking irons. Gradually, huge cattle empires evolved, and in spite of yearly trail drives to Kansas, the steer population remained stable until the early 1870s, when the herds diminished.

An assumption pointed to Mexican rustlers. Mexico was the only place a Texas rancher could not investigate his losses.

The 1872 commissioners arrived in Texas to research the cattle thefts, to determine why the herds were vanishing, and to determine where they were going. The commissioners little anticipated that on September 6, 1872, while steaming up the Rio Grande, they would encounter a daylight rustling operation. Naked *vaqueros* guided lead steers through the water, out of Texas and into Mexico. Wooden poles discouraged animals from changing direction. Several grim riflemen squatting on the Mexican bank made certain that no one interfered. From that time on, the commissioners rarely discounted Texas testimony regarding the nature and extent of the thefts. They concluded that Mexican factional disputes, the French invasion and governmental business interference had created a stagnant Mexican economy which nearly depleted Mexican herds. Since the Mexicans could not purchase cattle due to a dearth of finances, they rustled livestock from Texas.[1]

Texas cattlemen had an estimated seven dollar investment in every steer, and the cattle usually sold for ten to fifteen dollars on the American market. Those same cattle in Mexico sold for between one to six dollars, but since Mexican rustlers got them for nothing in Texas, the thieves had no overhead unless they were caught in the act. At that point the rustlers were totaled.

In Mexico, the stolen cattle neither supplemented, nor built, Mexican herds. Nor were they rustled for meat, as meat was a by-product and cheap. "No article in southwest commerce had more value and importance than dry and wet hides," the commissioners' report stated. Each hide sold for approximately $4.50 to American shoe markets, and thousands were stacked in Matamoros awaiting boat transportation to New York or Europe. When insufficient ships were in port, hides entered the United States through Texas custom houses for shipment to the East Coast. In the Lower Rio Grande Valley district of Brazos Santiago, 272,256 hides were inspected between 1866 and 1872; and in the district of Corpus Christi, 158,688 hides came through during the same period. Commission investigations claimed twenty-five percent had Texas brands, and another twenty-five percent had mutilated, unreadable brands. The commissioners concluded that if such numbers entered Texas through legitimate channels, an even greater number of Texas hides must be leaving Mexico through Matamoros and Bagdad.[2]

Texas Adjutant General William Steele described the rustlers as "Mexican-Mexicans," and not "Mexican-Americans." Mexican nationals crossed the border and worked as herders for a few weeks. Then they were paid and they disappeared. Within a few days, a raid occurred.

Major General Alexander McDowell McCook, commanding officer at Fort Brown at Brownsville, believed the system of stock-stealing could lead "to a predatory war on either side of the river."[3]

To a large extent, violence and rustling had their origins in the *Zona Libre* (Free Zone). For almost a decade after the Mexican War, the United States had relatively low border import duties. Goods in Texas sold for half as much as in Tamaulipas. Then Mexican President Ignacio Comonfort abolished the constitution and dissolved Congress in 1857. Mexican states reasserted their sovereignty. Tamaulipas Governor Ramón Guerra established the *Zona Libre* in 1858 along the northeastern border with Texas. Foreign goods entered these areas duty free. Although not intended to hamper American prosperity, but to rejuvenate the Mexican side of the frontier, the zone's practical effect impoverished Texas. Materials could now be purchased cheaper in Mexico, so Mexicans rarely crossed the border to shop. Since Mexican rustlers did not pay duty on livestock slipped into Mexico, the *Zona Libre* actually encouraged rustling. Numerous Texas merchants transferred their businesses across the border where they could buy and sell for less, and Texas border towns languished.[4]

In drawing their conclusions, the American Commissioners called the Mexican border authorities "effete and corrupt," and described their inactions as a significant cause of rustling. They criticized the *Zona Libre* as an unwise system "of legislation regulating the commerce" in Mexico. Until Mexico changed its laws, the commissioners would "recommend the employment of a sufficient force of cavalry to enforce [the law] and protect life and property on the Rio Grande." It suggested "a regiment of volunteers."[5]

Texas Rangers had been around since 1823 when Stephen F. Austin called for "ranging" companies to protect settlements from Indians. During the next few decades, Texas Rangers usually concentrated on Comanches and Kiowas. During the Mexican War they had notorious reputations for summary executions of Mexican partisans. Following the Civil War period of reconstruction, State Police replaced rangers until the intrepid John B. Jones organized the Frontier Battalion, a forerunner of the modern Texas Rangers. The Battalion suppressed Indians, and made life hazardous for Texas and Mexican outlaws.

Following the Frontier Battalion, ex-theological student Leander H. McNelly organized a ranger company to stifle border outlawry. The ailing Bible reader saw little practical sense in taking prisoners. During his brief career, he destroyed several Texas gangs, slowed the Sutton-Taylor feud in DeWitt County, and did his best to put the murderous King Fisher of Nueces Strip fame either in jail or the graveyard. The colorful Fisher was often suspected of rustling horses and cattle out of Mexico, and although McNelly arrested him on several occasions, none of the indictments resulted in a conviction.

McNelly had successful methods for extracting information from Mexican rustlers. Ranger Jesús "Old Cayuse" Sandoval hoisted suspected cattle thieves up and down a few times by means of a rope around the neck. When the suspect told all he knew, the unfortunate fellow often underwent one more hoist.[6]

One such interrogation revealed a forthcoming cattle raid near Brownsville in 1871. McNelly and forty-eight rangers reached the site just in time to intercept the thieves. During a thunderous gun battle, fifteen rustlers were slain and 265 beeves belonging to the King Ranch were recovered. On the following day, McNelly stacked dead bodies in the Brownsville plaza, where residents identified them as riders associated with Juan Cortina.[7]

The overzealous McNelly wasn't satisfied with attacking Mexican outlaws in Texas, however. He longed to strike them in Mexico too. Since the Navy had sent the *Rio Bravo* gunboat to patrol the Rio Grande, halting rustling and smuggling wherever it might be found, the ranger had an idea. On board were Lieutenant Commander DeWitt C. Kells, seven officers, forty-five men, four howitzers and a thirty-pound rifle gun. McNelly wanted to destroy an outlaw stronghold known as Las Cuevas Ranch, so he and Kells allegedly planned to provoke the Mexicans into firing on the *Rio Bravo*. A retaliatory attack would strike Las Cuevas, but the plan fell through when Thomas Wilson, United States consul at Matamoros, informed the State Department. Washington promply recalled Kells and dispatched a new commander for the *Rio Bravo*.[8]

McNelly bided his time until Sandoval had information of renewed rustling near Las Cuevas. This time Captain James F. Randlett of the 8th United States Cavalry fought a skirmish with *vaqueros* struggling to free steers from the Texas mud. The battle broke off at nightfall when McNelly and twenty-nine rangers arrived.

Early on the morning of November 19, 1875, as the rustlers and cattle had now disappeared, the rangers forded the international boundary and rode toward Las Cuevas. At first light, they killed twelve residents at the wrong ranch, a half-mile short of the true destination. Undeterred, the rangers continued until encountering a larger than expected Mexican force at Las Cuevas. The lawmen immediately fell back to the river, but the water level had risen and the rangers were unable to recross. McNelly settled back to await military assistance from Texas, but Randlett had orders not to intervene. When the captain demanded McNelly's return to Texas soil, McNelly scribbled the following message:

I shall remain in Mexico with my rangers . . . and will cross back at my own discretion. Give my compliments to the secretary of war and tell him and the United States soldiers to go to hell.[9]

In the end, McNelly was the consummate bluffer. While he knew American soldiers would not save him, he kept the Mexicans wondering. Juan Flores, their leader, had been slain, and his death left the outlaws confused and demoralized. So when McNelly demanded that the rustlers surrender the livestock or risk having the American army called down on them, the outlaws capitulated. The rangers not only returned safely to Texas, they took seventy-five head of livestock with them.[10]

That McNelly's brashness was effective, few questioned. He was an unusual, brave, dedicated individual whose methods were as brutal as they were decisive. Had tuberculosis not killed him in 1877, there is no telling what this ferocious fighter might have accomplished.

In the short time left him, McNelly appeared in Washington before a congressional committee in January 1876. Since Mexican officials "lived solely on the profits of these enormous stealings of cattle," he testified, and the cattle thefts were "extraordinary and beyond belief," he insisted that American military forces be permitted to cross the border when in hot pursuit of rustlers.

McNelly described three types of Mexican armed forces along the Rio Grande: regulars, irregulars and *rurales* (police). The rurales carried Spencer Rifles and had reputations as fearsome fighters. The irregulars were indifferently armed, a sort of inept national guard. The regulars, most of whom were from the Mexican interior, were "a miserable set of starved wretches who had to be kept locked . . . in barracks." Their uniforms consisted only of a cap, and they were "shamefully naked."[11]

A week later General Edward Otho Cresap Ord, commanding the Military Department of Texas, took the stand. He and McNelly agreed on the awesome extent of cattle rustling, and on the ineffectiveness of Mexican authorities. General Ord sneered at Mexican troops, saying the soldiers had been recruited as sailors formerly were shanghaied in England, "by a sort of press gang system." While the general had three thousand troops in his department, most were either opening roads and building telegraph lines, or battling Apaches, Comanches and Kickapoos in the western part of Texas. Only about four hundred, which included three hundred cavalry, were available for the Lower Rio Grande Valley. Ord testified that "when the colored troops went out, the Mexicans avoided them and, in some instances, attacked them." The general gave orders that "no patrols or small parties should be sent out from posts except under the command of a white officer," and mentioned that he was transferring Negroes from the valley to the high plains and replacing them with white soldiers. He never explained what caused such caustic relations between blacks and Mexicans, but he alluded to them three different times.[12]

EDWARD O. C. ORD
(U.S. Military Academy Archives)

GENERAL ALEX McCOOK
(U.S. Army Military History Institute)

Ord had but two permanent posts along the Lower Rio Grande open for duty: Ringgold Barracks and Fort Brown. When asked why the Army did not scatter patrols along the river, stationing them a few miles apart, Ord argued that sickness due to the bad water would make them ineffective. Furthermore, the border often curved three miles in order to go one mile in a straight line, thus requiring so many soldiers along the Rio Grande as to be prohibitive. Besides, Ord did not like defensive warfare. If the raids were to be stopped, he needed permission to pursue the rustlers into Mexico, punish them and return the stolen property to its owners.

Meanwhile, Mexico had not suffered idly the American charges of corruption and sole responsibility for outlaw raids in the Lower Rio Grande Valley. It appointed its own investigative commissioners: Ignacio Galindo, Antonio García Carrillo and Agustín Siliceo. They made two reports. Both were signed in Monterrey and dated May 15 and December 7, 1873.[13]

When translated and printed in English, the reports comprised 443 pages. The committee spent months visiting remote towns along the

Rio Grande, interviewing witnesses and examining documents. However, unlike their American counterparts, they did not keep, or at least did not print, verbatim records of the testimony, nor did they publish any direct transcripts with the exception of various American newspaper and journal articles, plus selected comments by United States commissioners, all of which supported the Mexican point of view.

While the report admitted partial Mexican blame for the outlawry, it stoutly defended Mexico. The investigation "proves that the complaints of the Texans are groundless, inasmuch as the cattle stealing done among them is not the work of any residents in the adjoining country, but of Indians belonging to the United States, and their own outlaws disguised as Indians," it said. It identified American rustlers, most of whom were Hispanic. It argued persuasively for the patriotism and decency of Juan Cortina, vigorously justified the *Zona Libre*, and denounced Richard King of the King Ranch and Adolphus Glavecke, a deputy sheriff of Brownsville, as hindrances to border tranquility.[14]

The report accused soldiers of the American "Confederate War" (Civil War) of ravaging the Rio Grande country. Finally, the commissioners devoted nearly half their comments to the evaluation of border Indian troubles, pointing out that Mexico, throughout its history, had been the victim of these savage onslaughts, not the perpetrator.

The Mexicans called for tighter border security because the "old and modern history of Texas, filled with calumnies, outrages, invasions, and ambitions against Mexico, is a lesson which should . . . [demand] all the energy of the Mexican government." The United States and Mexico should "put an end to the restless spirit of the floating population of Texas, which . . . is ever dreaming of revolutionary enterprises inconsistent with the maintenance of peace and harmony between the two nations."[15]

Each country had now denounced the other for its miseries. And still the violence continued.

13

Marauders, Soldiers and Salt

JOHN W. FOSTER, the temperamental minister to Mexico, recognized during the 1870s that peace along the boundary "was essential to the cordial relations between the two countries."[1]

Yet, for nearly seventy-five years after the Treaty of Guadalupe Hidalgo there existed no harmony because the borderlands fundamentally remained outside the effective control of the two governments. Both nations had priorities, and their mutual border was not one of them. With each step away from Mexico City the central authority became increasingly feeble. With each stride away from Washington, interest faded in 'the international line, a concern stretched thin by distance and lack of a large voting population. For three quarters of a century, the border underwent destructive upheavals. No particular border area from the coastal plains of Brownsville and Matamoros to the high desert country of El Paso and on to San Diego had a monopoly on turbulence. To the Indian the border was a scene of last stands; to the American and Mexican, it was an opportunity to evade the law.

In spite of its youth, however, the border possessed its legends. One was Juan Nepomuceno Cortina, a terror to Texans, a savior to Mexicans. Most narratives claim he was born in Texas. His mother ranched on portions of the Espíritu Santo Grant upon which Brownsville was established. She accepted American citizenship after the Mexican War, and raised several sons and daughters, all taking advantage of good educations, with the exception of Juan. He associated with restless men who swung wide loops.

Cortina came to historical notice on a hot July morning in 1859. According to oral tradition, he had paused for coffee in Brownsville when he observed City Marshal Robert Shears striking an intoxicated Mexican. Cortina intervened, a struggle started and Cortina shot Shears in the shoulder. The prisoner and Cortina escaped, and as warrants went out for their arrest, a hundred or so Cortina riders occupied Brownsville on the night of September 3.

Specifically Cortina had come to kill Adolphus Glavecke, the "squinting sheriff" (actually a deputy) who had migrated from Germany in 1836 and married a relative of Cortina. He and Cortina once shared a cattle rustling partnership; Cortina rustled and Glavecke fenced. For unknown reasons they bitterly parted. On this particular morning in Brownsville, Glavecke avoided Cortina, so the outlaw's marauders murdered the jailer, a constable, a youth named Neal and two unidentified Mexicans defending their friends. Cortina's Mexican raiders opened the jail, released the prisoners, and for a short time possessed Fort Brown (abandoned by the American Army), even hoisting a Mexican flag over it.[2]

José Carvajal, former filibuster but now a general for President Benito Juárez, conferred with Manuel Treviño, the Mexican consul in Brownsville, and they prevailed upon Cortina to leave town. He did, but one of his desperado friends, Tomás Cabrera, remained behind and was captured by local residents, locked in jail, then removed and lynched by a citizen's committee. Cortina now vowed to burn Brownsville, and he might have done so had terrified residents not appealed to General Carvajal. The general sent elements of the Mexican Army to protect the American village, an unparalleled and little-known event in border relations.

In a struggle which history has dubbed the "Cortina War," the wily chieftain trounced and sent running a force of Texas Rangers ineptly led by Captain William G. Tobin, a former city marshal in San Antonio. It was not until December 5 that Major Samuel Peter Heintzelman and portions of the 2nd Cavalry, the 1st Infantry, and the 1st Artillery (122 soldiers altogether) restored order and cleared the river road. Famed Texas Ranger Rip Ford, and fifty-two other rangers joined him, fighters with more spirit than Tobin's vagabonds. The rangers and soldiers pursued Cortina upstream, and drove the outlaws across the border near Rio Grande City. The bandit had now become enough of a Mexican folk hero to be immortalized by an obscure troubadour who wrote *El General Cortina*. The song is played with a *corrido* strum (one-two-three, one-two-three) on the guitar at a moderate tempo and with a fairly free delivery.

> *Ese general Cortinas*
> *es libre y muy soberano,*
> *han subido sus honores*
> *porque salvó a un mexicano*

"The famed General Cortinas is quite sovereign and free, the honor due him is greater, for he saved a Mexican's life."

> *Viva el general Cortinas*
> *que de su prisión salió*
> *vino a ver a sus amigos*
> *que en Tamaulipas dejó.*

"Long live General Cortinas, who has come out of prison; he came to visit his friends that he had left in Tamaulipas."

> *Los americanos hacían huelga,*
> *borracheras en las cantinas,*
> *de gusto que había muerto*
> *ese general Cortinas.*

"The Americans made merry, they got drunk in the saloons, out of joy over the death of the famed General Cortina."[3]

In spite of Cortina's popularity among Hispanic people, his raids into Texas gradually ceased. Lieutenant Colonel Robert E. Lee arrived on the boundary. Lee had that polite, cultured, unflinching manner too serious to be ignored. He passed the word that either the raids stop or northern Mexico would risk occupation by the United States Army. The threat worked, and the Mexican government coaxed Cortina into the interior. He returned as a general and even governor of Tamaulipas, a crafty politician and strategist, but one who never again invaded American territory.[4]

For sheer audacity, few outlaw attacks equaled the Corpus Christi raid of May 1875. Texas residents professed to see the evil hand of Juan Cortina behind it, but that was never proven.

One hundred and fifty raiders split into four bands, three of which ran afoul of the United States Army and were forced back across the Rio Grande after reaching San Diego, Texas, eighty miles north of the border. The fourth slipped through under the leadership of Alberto Garza, an ordinary outlaw. Some estimates place the number of his men at thirty, but other guesses say half that. They halted in Oso on the outskirts of Corpus Christi, where they detained and robbed travelers. However, one victim escaped and fled screaming into Corpus Christi.

Residents of Corpus Christi, believing they were invaded by a huge force of Mexican outlaws, crowded aboard two steamers anchored in the bay, and sailed three miles out to sea where the boats floundered in rough water. Passengers were more in danger of drowning than robbery.[5]

Back in Oso, Garza assumed a posse would arrive any moment. He released the women, and herded male hostages toward Nuecestown. Along the way, Garza ransacked the store of George Franks, added him to the captives, and killed an aged Hispanic employee. At Nuecestown they attacked the post office, and were rebuffed by postmaster Thomas Noakes who wounded the first bandit through the door. The raiders thereupon murdered an employee and burned the building.

By now, a Corpus Christi posse had ridden out in spiritless pursuit. Only John Swanks, a merchant, wanted a fight, and he cursed the posse for its lack of enthusiasm. When the lawmen caught up with the outlaws, Swanks charged, hoping his friends would follow. They didn't, and a ball knocked Swanks from the saddle, killing him instantly.

Since the Mexicans were already retreating toward the border, the posse contented itself with taking into custody and lynching the wounded man shot by Noakes and abandoned by his comrades. Otherwise, the bandits withdrew unmolested, recrossing the Rio Grande and submitting to arrest by Mexican officials, who immediately released them. The United States made futile demands for extradition.[6]

Indians were a third source of outlawry. From the 1850s to the early 1890s, they struck both sides of the border, making raids and retreating home. Home in Texas usually consisted of obscure hideouts on the

RANALD S. MACKENZIE
(National Archives)

JUAN CORTINA
(Texas State Library and Archives,
Austin)

Seminole Military Scouts along the Texas Border. (Institute of Texan
Cultures, San Antonio)

plains. Indians in Mexico, however, frequently lived in their own towns, which Americans considered sanctuaries.

If Mexico could not stifle the raids of Indians operating from its soil, the United States would. In May 1873, the 4th Cavalry and a detachment of Seminole-Negro scouts crossed the Rio Grande into Coahuila. In the lead rode Colonel Ranald Mackenzie. He had not come to plead or parlay or threaten. The Kickapoos had raided Texas for years, and now retribution was at hand. Mackenzie would lay waste their villages.

The eccentric officer, already showing the mental stress that would eventually force his retirement and early death in an insane asylum, would nevertheless have a brilliant military career. Seven times the government breveted him for gallantry during the Civil War, and he would go from this particular strike to lead the famous Red River Campaign of 1874-75, totally destroying the Kiowa and Comanche marauders, handing Mexico its first relief from these Indians.[7]

The Kickapoos were not native to Mexico, but had migrated from as far away as Kansas. They detested Americans and happily abandoned the United States when Mexico lured them with land grants to the border. In return, the Kickapoos defended the area from Texas Indians.

Once in Mexico, the Kickapoos launched cattle raids north of the Rio Grande, striking as far inland as San Antonio. Texans accused Mexican officials of instigating the assaults, and said the authorities were not only protecting the Indians but paying them for the rustled livestock.[8]

Mexico denied United States permission to cross the border in pursuit, but it did invite the American Bureau of Indian Affairs to encourage a Kickapoo exodús to a reservation in Oklahoma (Indian) Territory. When that failed, the Army sent Mackenzie to exert stronger persuasion, and the colonel met with Secretary of War William W. Belknap and General William Tecumseh Sherman at Fort Clark, Texas. Sherman allegedly called for a "campaign of annihilation, obliteration and complete destruction" of the Kickapoos, making it obvious the border should be no barrier to the American military and no refuge to the Indians. When Mackenzie requested written instructions, Sherman reportedly pounded the table and shouted, "Damn the orders! With us behind you . . . you can rest assured of the fullest support."[9]

On the night of May 16, Mackenzie and several columns of men rode out of Fort Clark, reaching the Rio Grande the next day. After dark they crossed at El Moral Ford, and headed for three villages near

Nacimiento, Coahuila, nearly seventy miles inside Mexico. After a day and two nights in the saddle, traveling in a series of walk, trot, gallop marches, the nearly exhausted troopers forded the Rio Sabinas and shortly reached the first Kickapoo village. They lined up and charged.

Scouts had informed Mackenzie that the warriors were gone, and any resistance would come primarily from women, children and old men. Mackenzie thundered unmolested through the Kickapoo huts and wickiups on the morning of May 18. Waves of troopers rolled in, fired their rifles, peeled off to the right and rode to the end of the column where they reloaded and moved forward again. Nineteen Indians died in the assault. Forty were taken prisoner. Three soldiers had wounds, one of whom died on the return trek. Leaving the village obscured in smoke and flame, the 4th Cavalry ignored the other Indian towns and headed toward the border before pursuit could organize and overtake them.

Indian children, three to a horse, repeatedly fell asleep from weariness and toppled onto the sand. Bleary-eyed soldiers on the move for nearly sixty hours, lashed their prisoners to the saddle and kept the column moving. In spite of rumors and scares, the unit recrossed the border without incident.

Compared to other Indian battles, the Kickapoo raid is hardly worth mentioning. While one cannot help but admire the audacity, durability and toughness of Mackenzie's fighters, the fact remains that a surprise attack on women and children hardly qualifies as a military feat worthy of inclusion in any pantheon of heroes.

On the surface the assault was a failure since it had eliminated practically no warriors. Yet it was successful for reasons soon apparent. The strike shattered Kickapoo invincibility against retaliation from across the boundary. Indian supplies were destroyed, leaving the Kickapoos nearly destitute. Finally, many Indian relatives were now hostages in the United States. The males could either join their families by surrendering and coming to live on a reservation in Oklahoma, or relinquish all hope of ever seeing them again. (A similar tactic would be used a few years later against Geronimo in Arizona.)

Mexico did not seem sympathetic to the Indian plight. Although it denied that Kickapoos were responsible for rustling in Texas, the Mexican central government no longer seemed to believe it. The Kickapoos were also costing more than Mexico wanted to pay, for as long as they remained south of the border, guilty or not, their presence would draw the American Army down upon everybody. So after perfunctory complaints to Washington, Mexican authorities encouraged a Kickapoo exodus north. Over three hundred Indians resettled in the United States, and the American Army escorted them to the reservation. As for those Kickapoos remaining in Mexico, they scaled down their forays, and never again became a serious border menace.[10]

Two additional military faces along the border were Lieutenant Colonel William Rufus Shafter, a profane, egocentric, physically prepossessing man, and First Lieutenant John Lapham Bullis, a spare, short, beet-faced soldier with a bristling mustache. Shafter won the Medal of Honor during the Civil War, and in 1898 would lead expeditionary forces successfully against Santiago de Cuba. The fame of Bullis rests on the odd assortment of scouts he supervised: the Seminole-Negroes. With some exceptions they dressed like Indians (even to an occasional buffalo horn war bonnet), looked like Africans, talked like Mexicans, and worshipped like Southern Baptists.[11]

Many of the Negroes were former slaves, or descendants of slaves, who had fled to Florida. There they intermarried with the Seminoles and went into exile when the United States crushed the tribe, banishing it to Oklahoma Territory. By the late 1840s and early 1850s, many had fled into Mexico and settled along the border. However, by 1870, most had returned to Texas. The Army hired them as scouts for six months at a time, and paid them the same as privates. They worked as guides.

The Army frequently had fifty scouts on duty, and most were stationed at Fort Clark near Brackettville. Throughout the decade from 1870 to 1881, none suffered a serious wound. Sixteen participated in the Mackenzie raid of 1873, one capturing an aged chief and marrying his daughter.

These scouts were especially loyal to Bullis, and had saved his life during a foray into Mexico south of Eagle Pass, Texas. Though Comanches unhorsed the lieutenant, three scouts charged in and rescued him. Each scout earned a Medal of Honor for heroism.

Bullis and Shafter often lunged two hundred unauthorized miles south of the border.[12] Mexicans resented this, and they especially despised Seminole-Negroes who led the way. These scouts had formerly accepted Mexican friendship, even citizenship, so when two were captured during assaults into Mexico, the country accused them of treason and implied that firing squads might set some examples.

Shafter considered the prisoners to be Americans, not Mexicans, and he demanded their release from the Piedras Negras jail. When the doors did not promptly open, General Ord ordered Shafter to protect United States citizens. He left the methods unstated, so at dawn on April 3, 1877, Piedras Negras awoke to an occupation by three companies of United States cavalry and two of infantry. The American Army bivouacked in the plaza, seized the jail, and to Shafter's fury, found the occupants had been transferred to Saltillo. Shafter returned to Texas. Meanwhile, one of the prisoners escaped, and the other was later released.[13]

Although in this instance, the Seminole-Negro scouts seemed appreciated, when the need for their services ended, Washington dismissed them with barely a word of gratitude. The government even evicted families of scouts from the Fort Clark reservation.

While history has been remarkably diligent in recording American armed excursions across the border, it has generally downplayed the Mexican penetrations with exception of the cattle raids. Though they never equaled American attacks either in number or ferocity, they could be just as slashing and just as cruel and devastating.

One such event occurred at Rio Grande City, the seat of Starr County, Texas, on August 12, 1877. The tiny town had a modest jail, and its two most notable prisoners were cattle thief Rodolfo Espronceda and multi-murderer Segundo Garza, both Mexican nationals.

Although Garza had not yet been sentenced, his execution seemed certain, so much so that he coaxed his brother into gathering a group of Mexican nationals for a midnight rescue. Unfortunately, the jailer and his wife appeared. He was shot and she was slashed with a machete. County Attorney Noah Cox stumbled from sleep to his second story balcony overlooking the jail. He was wounded.

The prisoners fled, Garza's leg irons placing serious limitations upon his speed. He could not straddle a horse, and wagons were unavailable. Therefore, his friends placed him on a strip of cowhide, dragging him through the chaparral and across the river into Mexico. He arrived scratched, bruised and nearly drowned, but alive. Behind him, Major William Redwood Price and twenty-five soldiers from Ringgold Barracks reached the banks, but Garza had vanished. Price hesitated to cross the Rio Grande and risk an ambush in the thickets.

Governor Richard Bennett Hubbard wired President Rutherford B. Hayes for assistance. Secretary of State William M. Everts assured Hubbard that Mexican President Porfirio Díaz would return the criminals to Texas jurisdiction according to the Extradition Treaty of 1861. The wheels of Mexican justice now started to creak without actually beginning to turn. Tamaulipas Governor Servando Canales bitterly resented the Díaz commitment, although he reluctantly arrested Espronceda and two of his liberators.

Canales argued that the Extradition Treaty had no jurisdiction. The last sentence in Article VI, stated, "Neither of the contracting parties shall be bound to deliver up its own citizens under the stipulations of this treaty." Nevertheless, Díaz had pledged himself to do just that, risking the displeasure of his own countrymen because he needed diplomatic recognition by the United States. Since this was one way to demonstrate Mexican responsibility, the president ordered 1,500 soldiers to board the steamship *City of Merida* to enforce his edict, and only the partial capitulation of Canales stopped their passage. Díaz and Canales reached a compromise. Espronceda was merely an illiterate cattle thief, so Canales turned him and his two accomplices over to Texas authorities. Garza went free. Mexican newspapers warned Díaz that further extraditions of Mexican nationals would not be tolerated.[14]

Farther west along the Rio Grande, Colonel George L. Andrews had just completed an exhausting eighty-mile ride on December 11, 1876, coming from Fort Davis south to Spencer's Rancho (Presidio, Texas). Through field glasses Andrews could identify the twin spires of the Mexican cathedral, the customhouse and a few of the one thousand inhabitants across the Rio Grande in Presidio del Norte (Ojinaga), Mexico. A narrow, rutted road led toward the Rio Conchos and the Sierra Madre.

The forty-two cavalrymen wondered what Andrews would do regarding the hundred or so armed men in Mexico across the Rio Grande and a half-mile away. A lancer asked for a parley on an island. Andrews refused, warning the Mexican soldiers to evacuate women and children because at noon he planned to bombard the town.

Andrews hoped this promise of force and determination would free kidnap victim Henry Muller, a naturalized American of German descent who owned the Bank of Chihuahua in Chihuahua City. Muller represented a new breed of immigrant to Mexico. Eventually such men as he would acquire a third of the nation's land and financial assets. He and others would invest in mining, lumber, real estate, construction and ranching. They created enormous baronies and assimilated into the upper and middle ranks of Mexican society.

However, border politics were always perilous. Chihuahua had supported President Benito Juárez, and with his death the state shifted support to Sebastián Lerdo de Tejada. Lerdo was exiled by Díaz as the borderlands approached another of its flash points. Mariano Samaniego became governor of Chihuahua, and the political warhorse Angel Trías fled to the rugged mountains near Presidio del Norte.

In such uncertain times, contenders for Mexican power leveled "forced loans" to meet expenses. Along the border it was not uncommon for whoever legally or illegally held the gun, to "borrow" from towns and ranches. Though the loan was "forced," it wasn't "stealing" to the "borrower," as the recipient always claimed honest intentions of repaying it. Of course, when the men in authority were driven out or overthrown, others just as desperate replaced them, and the "forced loan" procedures started all over again. Although Trías was technically a fugitive, most *Chihuahuenses* anticipated his return to power, a fact making forced loans for him fairly easy to acquire. According to Louis H. Scott, United States consul in Chihuahua City, Trías obtained a forced loan of $56,000 from foreign businessmen. It made the average Mexican happy to see the rich pay, and foreigners had few outlets to complain. The American-owned Santa Eulalia Silver Mining Company was the wealthiest corporation, so it kicked in $21,000.[15]

While these forced loans temporarily satisfied Trías, they were insufficient to support his small insurgent army. To raise additional funds, General José Delgado, a Trías partisan, kidnapped Muller in November of 1876 when he and four visitors, including the German consul in Chihuahua, were inspecting a mine near Presidio del Norte. The outlaws released the others, but demanded $3,500 for Muller.

Governor Samaniego wrote the commanding officer at Fort Davis complaining that Muller had been captured by "horse thieves." The governor also asked Mose Kelly, a merchant, tax collector, notary public and ladies' man at Spencer's Rancho near American Presidio to use his influence and do what he could.[16] Samaniego told Kelly that if his (Kelly's) efforts failed, he should "call on the United States to cross over [the border] and give those bandits a good thrashing."[17]

In the meantime, Samaniego dispatched General Fermín Fierro to capture Trías and his men. Their forces met in the Battle of Cuchillo Parado, where Fierro was slain, his equipment captured, and his soldiers either dispersed or inducted into the Trías army.

As for Colonel Andrews, he half-heartedly lobbed two three-inch shells and one round of solid shot across the border. Insurgents and non-combatants scattered for cover. While the brief bombardment seems not to have had any physical or damaging effect, something apparently came out of it which the reports did not mention. Angel Trías fell into the custody of Andrews, which could mean that American soldiers dashed across the river and kidnapped him. Andrews decided to hold him pending the release of Muller.

This odd affair now became even stranger. Trías "escaped" within a few hours. Two days later Muller crossed the border to Spencer's Rancho, barely pausing as he hurried to El Paso, and hence south to his bank in Chihuahua. Upon his arrival, he withdrew $3,500 and sent it to Trías, who returned in triumph to Chihuahua City within a week. Although Trías presumably extracted more forced loans, he took no more hostages.[18]

While American illegal crossings into Mexico caused innumerable diplomatic squabbles, an opposite series of events created problems and turmoil too. Mexican revolutionists invariably campaigned along the border. When their battles failed, the insurgents fled north across the international line to escape capture, death, or induction into the army. The Americans did not want them, could not indefinitely feed, guard and board them, but could not in good conscience force their return to Mexico either. Revolutionaries on American soil were therefore arrested and their weapons confiscated. The Army extracted promises from them not to re-enter Mexico and continue fighting. Then the officials usually paroled the prisoners without supervision.

The policy caused political consternation on both sides of the border. An example was Pedro "Winkler" Valdez, whom the Mexican Army chased into Texas. Valdez surrendered at Fort Clark. Officials paroled him, and warned him to stay in San Antonio. However, Valdez re-entered Mexico immediatly with an armed band. A Colonel García just as promptly smashed Valdez back into Texas on June 10, 1877. In an attempt to permanently end the conflict, García illegally crossed the international line and overtook the revolutionists between the Pecos and Devils River. Only thirty-nine insurgents survived the battle, and those scampered back to Fort Clark for asylum. An exasperated Lieutenant General Phil Sheridan telegraphed Washington, asking, "What shall be done with these prisoners? I doubt they are worth the rations we will be obliged to issue them." The War Department as usual recommended parole, and that's what happened on July 2.[19]

An angry President Porfirio Díaz criticized the United States for its policies. Border tranquility could not be assured, he complained, unless insurgents were released to the Mexican federal government. Díaz said the American policy of paroling prisoners actually led to additional bloodshed because few parolees refrained from further guerrilla attacks against Mexico.

Still, the Americans were doing the best they could consistent with trying to please both sides. When insurgent General Mariano Escobedo, a former military leader for President Juárez visited Rio Grande City in July 1877, Major William Redwood Price, commander of Ringgold Barracks, grew suspicious of Escobedo's interest in the steamer *Ackley*. Price boarded the *Ackley* and confiscated eight cases of Remington breech-loading rifles not registered on the ship's manifest, but ordered by Escobedo. He arrested the general and fourteen of his officers, all of them in full dress uniform, including sabers, and hauled them before United States Commissioner J. C. Eiret. The commissioner charged them with violation of the neutrality laws, and placed them on parole. In August, the Army again arrested Escobedo as he prepared for a Mexican raid. Although aggravated and frustrated, the United States was doing what it could to keep the revolutionaries off balance, and still keep them alive.[20]

Essentially the same kind of border restlessness continued in West Texas. German immigrant Ernst Kohlberg described the border town of El Paso as "nearly the end of the world and the last of creation." If I had known then "what I know now, I would never have come here," he wrote. These words expressed the disgruntlement of an eighteen-year-old boy who had bonded himself to work for a year at no pay (except for room and board) in exchange for passage from Europe to the Mexican border.

The Kohlberg letters to Germany provide a tangible inside view of El Paso, Texas during the early 1870s. His accounts describe the various classes as mixing well. Everybody freely crossed the international boundary for social and business purposes. Not everyone spoke English, but they did speak Spanish, since it was the language of culture and commerce. El Paso was a tiny American village, the people usually working in the neighboring Mexican community of El Paso del Norte.

Kohlberg blamed most troubles on politics, saying it "furnishes the excuse for revolution in Mexico." The "real purpose [of politics] . . . is robbery and the enrichment of new elements," he said.[21]

Díaz strengthened El Paso del Norte in March 1887 with one hundred cavalrymen. I have "never seen so many cutthroats together at one time," Kohlberg recalled. He complained that the two-day stay of these soldiers cost each El Paso del Norte businessman $160 in forced loans. "The money will not be lost if no other party gets control," he wrote, but "if another crowd gets the upper hand they will declare the levying of the tax as illegal and make us pay again."[22]

Well, they paid again. Colonel Paulino Z. Machorro brought the 2d Regiment of Mexican Infantry into El Paso del Norte on May 28, 1887, and declared himself a revolutionary for Lerdo. He then jailed fifteen city officials including Mayor José Mesa and Collector of Customs Rafael Varios. Machorro appointed businessman and former vice consul to El Paso, Guadalupe Miranda, as the new mayor. He further collected a series of forced loans to meet the expenses of his rebellion.

With the final forced loan, Machorro went too far. He not only assessed the businessmen, but he also levied a cent-and-a-half "loan" from the poor. Peons would submit patiently to practically any indignity, but not to direct taxation. By June 8, two hundred and fifty *vaqueros* and farmers carrying muskets and lances surrounded the town. Forty Pueblo Indians, nominally used as scouts and trackers against Apaches, joined the uprising. Machorro looked upon this rabble, chuckled and marched his men out to disperse them. Instead, he himself was dispersed, the bodies of his soldiers littering the hills and streets. Those who survived, including Machorro, nearly drowned while fording the Rio Grande into the protection of El Paso. The Texans accepted the refugees, although the Americans also feared for their own security. Citizens organized "committees for safety and defense," and wired General Ord for military protection since nearby Fort Bliss had been abandoned during an economy move.[23]

As it turned out, the Mexican farmers faded back to their homes. Machorro and what men he had left were released by the United States on parole. They drifted east and blended into other revolutionary units operating throughout the Lower Rio Grande Valley.

Few events along the Mexican boundary had a greater impact on border life than the El Paso Salt War. For centuries Southwesterners and Mexicans had gathered salt from the shallow lake beds beneath the shadow of Guadalupe Peak in far west Texas, ninety miles east of El Paso. Ox carts from El Paso, San Elizario, Socorro and Ysleta groaned along the narrow desert trail, avoiding Apaches and returning two weeks later with dirty piles of salt. Nobody got rich, but the salt sold for a few coppers, sufficient to provide a subsistence living.

By 1868 the trade had attracted Americans with political and economic clout, most of whom lived in El Paso and formed a "Salt Ring." Prominent names were W. W. Mills, collector of customs, Albert J. Fountain, state senator, Ben Dowell, saloon owner, civic leader and soon to be the first El Paso mayor, Benjamin Franklin Williams, an attorney, Gaylord Judd Clarke, district judge, Luis Cardis, an Italian representing the Mexican political and economic interests, and Father Antonio Borrajo, the pale, stoop-shouldered priest at San Elizario. Father Borrajo was a complex individual with hate and love locked inside a dual personality. Intellectually he acknowledged the American presence in the Southwest. Emotionally he never would.

The Ring filed claims on the public lands containing salt and charged a fee for every bushel. Cardis and Borrajo advised their Mexican followers to pay the money. Then Borrajo and Cardis quietly accepted their cut.

The Ring disintegrated when State Senator Fountain and W. W. Mills split over politics. Fountain organized an anti-Salt Ring. Shortly afterwards, Fountain and attorney Ben Williams confronted each other in the Dowell Saloon. After exchanging accusations about ancestry, Fountain began beating Williams with a walking stick, while Williams pulled a derringer and put a couple of little, round holes in Fountain. Fountain stumbled home to bleed and to get his rifle, on the way explaining events to District Judge Clarke and State Police Captain Albert French. Meanwhile, Williams had reached his residence and was still there when Clarke and French hammered on the door. Williams slipped out through a window, confronted Clarke and killed him with a shotgun. The attorney was then slain by French and Fountain, the latter now approaching with his rifle.

Fountain's political career in Texas dimmed, so he moved to nearby Mesilla, New Mexico. Meanwhile, the Salt Ring more or less dissolved, the pieces falling to newcomer Charles Howard a few years later.

Digging salt on the salt flats near El Paso. (Harry Ransom Humanities
Research Center, U.T. Austin)

Howard had guts as well as arrogance, and was a man who earned his
living as a democratic party leader, an attorney and district judge.
Howard filed on the salt beds in the name of his father-in-law, and
negotiated an understanding with Borrajo and Cardis. But for whatever reason, the friendship between Howard and his allies decomposed.
Howard called Cardis "a liar, a coward, a mischief maker, and a med-
dler," and the pudgy, impeccably dressed Cardis had some equally
unflattering remarks for Howard. The judge terminated the feud by
killing Cardis with a shotgun.

Time passed with Howard tightening his legal grip on the salt beds.
However, the Hispanics refused to pay, and vowed they would mine
the salt anyway. A group of Texas Rangers were organized in El Paso,
most of the rangers being New Mexico outlaws and drifters. On
December 12, 1877, they and Howard foolishly rode into San Elizario,
scene of the salt rebellion, intending to jail the Mexican leaders or extract a fee for each bushel of salt. They encountered an angry mob,
and the outnumbered rangers took cover for three days in an adobe
building. The Mexicans demanded Howard as a condition for lifting

the siege. Howard complied. "I will go," he told the rangers. "They will kill me but it is the only way I can save your lives." He shook hands all around, handed someone his money and papers, said "Goodbye, boys," and stepped into the street.

Lieutenant John B. Tays, a well-meaning but slow-thinkng ranger commander, went with him. He talked with Chico Barela, an Ysleta farmer and spokesman for the mob, and received assurances that all bloodshed including Howard's would be avoided if the rangers surrendered. The peace officers therefore gave up, handed over their weapons and submitted to incarceration. From across the border where Father Borrajo had been transferred by the Church, he allegedly said, "Shoot the gringos and I will absolve you."

If Borrajo actually said that, his advice contributed to the forthcoming murders. Enraged Hispanics led Howard to a vacant lot where a ragged volley knocked him to the ground. Horse-thief Jesús Telles tried to dispatch him with a machete, but missed and whacked off two of his own toes. As Telles hobbled off, several of his neighbors finished the chopping job on Howard. Two Anglo friends of Howard also underwent a sloppy execution, and all three bodies were tossed into a well. The exhausted peace officers were sent back to El Paso, forever bearing the stigma as the only Texas Rangers in history to surrender.

Now that everyone involved on both sides of the border had disgraced themselves, a posse of Anglo ruffians rode through the El Paso valley, adding rape to several crimes of murder.

The Army restored order, and a four-man congressional committee assembled in El Paso and took reams of testimony. It agreed that a deplorable incident had taken place, and recommended the re-establishment of Fort Bliss. A grand jury returned six indictments, and Governor Richard Hubbard offered rewards. However, the wanted men had fled to Mexico. Thus ended the El Paso Salt War, the bloodiest and most brutal such conflict in border history.[24]

General William Steele, adjutant general of Texas, told a congressional committee about the dual nationality many Mexicans enjoyed along the border. About ninety percent fell into that classification, and while most were law-abiding, the remainder created a sticky citizenship dilemma for police officers and courts. Along the border, everybody crossed with little more than a wave of the hand. Few needed papers, or personal recommendations about character and background, or proof of job or income. Few ever filed an application to become an American citizen, primarily because they rarely thought of themselves as anything except Mexicans. Children born in the United States became citizens practically without the parents even realizing it.

Many borderlanders charged with crimes disappeared across the border, in one direction or another, without fear of extradition, for while the United States and Mexico had treaty commitments, as a practical matter each seldom returned its own nationals. An American fleeing Mexico and a Mexican fleeing Texas were often treated as prodigals returning home.

Southwestern history overflows with examples of how the system operated along the international line. The Mexican Army without American permission occasionally swept Ysleta, Socorro and San Elizario looking for deserters. When found, officers beat the wayward troops while hustling them back into Mexico. On the other hand, it was not unusual for Texas lawmen to seize criminal suspects in Mexico. An example of the latter had its genesis in the upper Rio Grande community of Socorro, New Mexico, on Christmas Eve, 1880. A. M. Conklin, irascible, outspoken editor of the *Socorro Sun*, antagonized Eunofrio Baca by demanding that he and his brother, Abram, remove their muddy boots from a lady's shawl lying on a bench in the Socorro Methodist Church. A scuffle took place, and when Conklin left the church, the Bacas murdered him outside the door.[25]

The killing ignited a racial incident with Anglos beating Mexicans in the streets, and the Army restoring order. The Bacas fled south as rewards of $500 were posted. One circular reached the headquarters of Company A, Frontier Battalion of the Texas Rangers at Ysleta, Texas, and it intrigued Sergeant James B. Gillett. The young Gillett had recently married Helen, the fifteen-year-old daughter of his commanding officer, Captain George W. Baylor. She was a pretty girl who liked to read but cared little for housework. Nevertheless, the Gilletts had two children, one child died in infancy, another would renounce the Gillett name and become Harper B. Lee, a bullfighter of note in Mexico. Since Helen had a weakness for life's better things, to provide her with them, the curly-headed ranger watched for fugitives with prices on their heads. In particular, Gillett placed the Ysleta home of County Judge José Baca under surveillance, suspecting that the judge and the accused might be relatives. Within days Gillett earned his first $500 by arresting Abram Baca as he squatted on the judge's front porch.

Eunofrio Baca surfaced in April 1881 as a store clerk in Zaragoza, Mexico, across the Rio Grande from Ysleta. Gillett gave him sufficient time to feel safe, then he and Ranger George Lloyd slipped across the river, caught Baca unaware, laid a six-shooter alongside his ear, and as a female customer fainted, ordered him to step lively. The two rangers, with Baca manacled between, barely beat a posse of angry Mexicans to the border. Gillett took Baca to Socorro, New Mexico, turned him over to the vigilantes, and collected his reward. Vigilantes lynched the outlaw.[26]

Mexico vigorously protested the Gillett invasion and the kidnapping of Baca. Washington put pressure on Texas Governor Oran M. Roberts, who asked for Gillett's resignation. The ranger became an El Paso deputy city marshal during the flamboyant reign of gunman-killer Dallas Stoudenmire. When the municipal council forced Stoudenmire's resignation as city marshal in 1882, Gillett accepted the position and served diligently for two years until he cracked his revolver across the head of a businessman and was forced to resign. Gillett had other problems too, for Helen charged him with adultery and divorced him. He thereafter moved to Marfa, Texas, busied himself with ranching interests, and organized a series of religious cowboy camp meetings.[27]

14

The Order of June 1, 1877

THE UNITED STATES had substantially reached the watershed of its covetous policy toward Mexico by the end of the Civil War, and a doctrine toward its neighbor could be summed up in three short clauses: It wanted Mexico to establish internal order, it wanted favorable trade terms, and it wanted peace along the border.[1]

None of these were possible without a stable Mexican government, and Mexico had had little except a succession of dictators and inconsequential leaders. Benito Juárez showed the most promise, but the French invasion had disrupted his reforms. Even after the Europeans had been expelled, the hopes of the austere Juárez died with him when he suffered a massive heart attack in 1872. The president of the supreme court, Sebastián Lerdo de Tejada followed Juárez to the presidency, and another round of revolutions began. Lerdo had one of the ablest, most intellectual minds in the nation, and was a man with few equals as an orator. But he lacked the ruthless, power-grasping skills needed to govern Mexico.

Lerdo's phobias regarding Americans blinded his political judgment. A more astute man might have foreseen Mexican railroad tracks to the border as an asset. They would have established communications, opened trade, helped unify the country and made it easier to suppress rebellions. Instead, the president considered railroads a steel invitation for Americans to invade.

Revolts against Lerdo broke out. Porfirio Díaz, who evicted the French from Puebla, raised a small force of one hundred ruffians in the United States and captured Matamoros by crossing the border from Brownsville. After enlisting federal soldiers, he attacked Monterrey in April 1876. The attempt failed. Díaz could not recruit sufficient manpower from isolated ranches and tiny villages, so he took ship to the more populous south, organized another army and within a year after the Monterrey fiasco, was president of Mexico.

Díaz possessed the cunning, pragmatic mind a president needed. He understood power, politics and Mexicans. By the middle of his second term, he also understood Americans, and he had a singular ability for exploiting their political weaknesses.

Díaz sought American recognition, and Rutherford B. Hayes could have granted it. But Hayes had just won a questionable presidential victory, and he needed issues to divert the country's attention, to prove his timbre by making things tough for somebody. Hayes needed Texas support, and to obtain it he threatened Mexico. Washington told its minister to Mexico, John W. Foster, that a condition for recognition was "the preservation of peace and order and the protection of life and property" on the border. Texans resented any sanctuary for marauders in Mexico, and they prevailed upon the administration to threaten Díaz with the possibilities of border invasions by American troops.

Secretary of War George W. McCrary sent the following message to General Sherman in 1877. It contained instructions for General E. O. C. Ord, and it has become known as the "Order of June 1."

The President desires that the utmost vigilance on the part of the military forces in Texas be exercised for the suppression of these [Mexican] raids. It is very desirable that efforts . . . be made with the co-operation of the Mexican authorities; and you will instruct General Ord . . . to invite such co-operation on the part of the local Mexican authorities, and to inform them that while the President is anxious to avoid giving offense to Mexico, he is nevertheless convinced that the invasion of our territory by armed and organized bodies of thieves and robbers . . . should no longer be endured.

General Ord will at once notify the Mexican authorities along the Texas border, . . . that if the Government of Mexico shall continue to neglect the duty of suppressing these outrages, that duty shall devolve upon this Government, and will be performed, even it its performance should render necessary the occasional crossing of the border by our troops.

You will, therefore, direct General Ord that . . . he will be at liberty, in the use of his discretion, when in pursuit of a band of marauders, and when his troops are either in sight of them or upon a fresh trail, to follow them across the Rio Grande, and to overtake and punish them, as well as retake stolen property. . . .[2]

The Order of June 1 applied only to Texas. Since the border regions of New Mexico, Arizona and California were underpopulated, raids there did not constitute a serious menace.

Americans believed they were doing Mexico's job in crossing the border to suppress lawlessness, and Mexico should pay the expenses. However, Mexico criticized the Order and refused to accept any financial responsibility, so General Sherman recommended that the United States occupy Veracruz and deduct military expenses by confiscating customs duties. General Ord suggested seizing a mile-wide strip of Mexico along the border, and using it as a buffer against raiders.

Reactions in Mexican newspapers to the Order of June 1 varied from fury to threats. *La Época* denounced the Order as having "neither reason nor right." *Federalista* stormed that such an Order "authorizes the armed invasion of a foreign territory and is equivalent to a declaration of war." *Pájaro Verde* called for "a defense of the flag, the integrity of the country." Mexicans believed the Order was a ruse to annex "the northern Mexican states, and possibly establish a protectorate over the entire country."

A storm of Mexican protests reached Washington, and Ord sensed a weakening of the administration's mind. "If you yield to the demands of these [Mexican] people, they will attribute it to fear, and not to reason or justice," he warned Congress.

Pedro Ogazón, the Mexican Minister of War, ordered General Gerónimo Treviño to the border, directing that under no circumstances should Mexican soldiers cross into the United States, nor should American forces be allowed into Mexico. Furthermore, Treviño would make it unnecessary for American soldiers to consider moving south since he would seal the border against Mexican outlaws and Indian raiders.[3]

Treviño and Ord met at Piedras Negras in late June, and each recognized the other's limitations and pressures. Treviño in particular did not have sufficient manpower and weapons to close the border, and he believed that American crossings, if discretely accomplished, should be quietly permitted, or at least ignored. Ord and Treviño worked out a private understanding whereby American cavalry could penetrate in hot pursuit for 150 miles south of the international line. Ord promised never to cross if Mexican dragoons were in the vicinity, or until he had notified Treviño.[4]

Back in the heartland of the United States, the Order aroused intense controversy. The public perceived it as a stronger power bullying a weaker one. Businessmen and developers wondered how they could invest in Mexican mines and ranches when the Order of June 1 had antagonized the population against Americans.

A year later on April 9, 1878, President Hayes granted recognition to Díaz. He ordered Foster to seek "permanent measures for the preservation of peace and the punishment of outlawry upon the frontier, the better protection of American citizens and their interests in Mexico, and the settlement of complaints made by the Government of the United States."

The discussions went nowhere. Díaz refused to negotiate while the Order of June 1 remained in force. Meanwhile, financial agents argued to Congress and American investors that Mexico anxiously awaited their capital and enterprise. They called for a relaxation of tension, and urged Hayes to be more flexible. The President yielded, taking some comfort that violent conditions along the border had subsided somewhat during the last three years. In February 1880, he rescinded the Order of June 1.[5]

As confrontations slackened along the Rio Grande, Indian threats arose along the land boundary to the west. Few places in North America offered a more suitable region for guerrilla warfare than the United States-Mexican border between El Paso and the Pacific. For a hundred years this area had been a battleground: the Apaches versus Spain, the Apaches versus Mexico, the Apaches versus the United States, the Apaches versus both Mexico and the United States. The boundary gave the Apaches a final opportunity to survive. However, the desert and mountain wilderness would be a refuge only so long as it took the United States and Mexico to agree on a border crossing policy.

Victorio, a Mimbres Apache, had led his people off the San Carlos Reservation in southeastern Arizona. The wily leader slipped back and forth across the Mexican border, chased one week by Mexican forces and the next by American units. Philip H. Morgan, the American Minister to Mexico, told Díaz that American soldiers needed Mexican authority to freely cross the border while in pursuit of Victorio.

Morgan assured the president that "Mexico need apprehend no unpleasant complications from the temporary presence of United States troops on her soil." Díaz agreed, or at least said he did, and permitted a three-month trial from August 30 to November 30, 1880. The agreement authorized American troops to cross the border during close pursuit of Indians six miles or more from the nearest town. They should return home upon losing the trail, or when relieved by Mexican soldiers. Damages had to be paid if any occurred.[6]

Slowly the armies of Mexico and the United States squeezed Victorio into an ever tightening circle. The climactic battle came at Tres Castillos, Chihuahua, ninety miles south of El Paso. Colonel Joaquín Terrazas, the lean, chain-smoking Mexican political leader, ordered home the American cavalry units as well as the Texas Rangers, then defeated and killed Victorio.[7]

The Mexican border quieted for two years until Apache captains Nachez, Cato, Juh and Gerónimo jumped the San Carlos fences and vanished into the Sierra Madre Mountains of Sonora from where they sank the international boundary in a welter of fire and blood. Mexico blamed the United States for her agony, claiming the Americans had not adequately guarded the border. Washington asked for another arrangement to cross the boundary and punish the hostiles.

On July 29, 1882, Mexico signed a "Protocol of An Agreement Concerning Pursuit of Indians Across the Border," originally offering it for two years, then substituting twelve months. The alliance stipulated only the land boundary, and retained the same clauses as the three-month accord of 1880.[8]

American responsibility for implementing the protocols fell on George Crook, the sloppily dressed, mule-riding general who was both the Army's most brilliant and its most inept Indian fighting officer. During the Big Horn and Yellowstone Expeditions of 1876, he planned so poorly for provisions that his soldiers ate their horses to survive.

Crook had uneasy feelings about the "right of close pursuit" understanding, and he telegraphed the adjutant general that "a literal construction of the [protocol] terms . . . will bring about failure in the settlement of pending Indian hostilities." Crook requested permission "to vary the stipulations to the extent required by the best interests of the two governments. . . ." Crook believed that if he waited until he was in close pursuit of the Indians, he would never cross the border. Instead, he proposed an extended search and destroy mission into the

LERDO DE TEJADO
(General Libraries, U.T. Austin)

CAPTAIN EMMET CRAWFORD
(Arizona Historical Society, Tucson)

Sierra Madre country of Sonora. The general had no desire to unnecessarily risk his soldiers, nor kill all the Apaches. His strategy was to apply gradual pressure, flush the Indians from every canyon and ridge, and force their return to the San Carlos Reservation in southeastern Arizona.[9]

Crook did not need unlimited troopers, but requested a contingent of Apache scouts drawn from the reservation, people who were friends and relatives of the renegades. These scouts would track the hostiles down, deprive them of rest and, if necessary, fight them. Therefore, fifty soldiers and nearly two hundred scouts crossed the Arizona-Sonora border in May 1883, plunged into the Sierra Madre fastness, fought a couple of skirmishes and induced the Indians to surrender. A shaky peace lasted until May 1885 when Gerónimo and 150 men, women and children bolted the reservation again and vanished into the remote, boulder-strewn canyons and steep trails of the Sierra Madre. This time Crook sent Captain Emmet Crawford in after him, Crawford being a lieutenant during the Battle of Slim Buttes in the Big Horn and Yellowstone Expedition. Crawford and the 2nd battalion of Indian

scouts made contact with Gerónimo in January 1886, and were awaiting word of possible negotiations when a large force of Mexican irregulars ambushed the American column. Crawford sensed a mistake, but
as he jumped atop a boulder, waved his arms, shouted and pointed to
his beard and military uniform, a bullet struck him in the head, killing
him instantly. An international incident arose.[10]

On April 1, Díaz defined Crawford's death as a regrettable accident.
He defended his soldiers, claiming they had mistaken the scouts for
hostile Indians. Díaz argued that the reciprocal agreement did not apply to Indian scouts retained by the Amerian Army, and he accused
the scouts as being more akin to raiders than military figures. C.
Leivas, Prefect of the District of Moctezuma, Sonora, testified that the
scouts committed murders, that they burned fences, shot cattle and
trampled sugar cane fields. Leivas described the scouts as members of
Gerónimo's band who were only pretending to be associated with the
Army.[11]

The affair ended with Washington accepting Mexico's apology. The
United States wrote off Crawford's death as one of those tragic and in-
explicable incidents. In the meantime, the government replaced Crook
with the testy and pompous Brigadier General Nelson A. Miles, who
lacked the genius of Crook, but not the innovation. He and Washington
believed the border important enough to establish the most elaborate
communications system in the frontier history of the United States Army. The military used a telephone for the first time, the seven-mile wire
hooking Fort Huachuca to the New Mexico and Arizona rail terminal.
With a heliograph operating from several mountain tops, Miles linked
a remote territory two hundred miles wide by three hundred miles
long. While the "talking mirrors" caused no Indians to surrender, and
led to only one skirmish, it at least informed Miles of where the
Apaches were not, and that was an important accomplishment.[12]

Otherwise, Miles applied the same pressure as Crook, although he
retained fewer Indian scouts. Miles forced the surrender of several
women and chidren, and removed them to the reservation, letting
Gerónimo know he would have to give up if he expected to see them
again. He, his family and the families of his followers would be
transferred to the far reaches of the continent. The old warrior knew
now that he had lost, irrevocably lost. He could wander in the wilderness forever, risking death daily, or he could be with his family at a
place where he could cause no more disruptions. Gerónimo surrendered

at Skeleton Canyon, thirty miles east of Douglas, Arizona, within a mile of the border. With the exception of a half-dozen or so braves who remained in the Sierra Madres and became the "Lost Tribe," Gerónimo and his people returned only briefly to San Carlos.

So the Apache wars ended not with a shout or a shot, but with a groan and a rumble as the Army loaded Gerónimo and his followers on to a Southern Pacific train and shipped them east into Florida exile. To its shame, the government included the loyal Indian scouts also.[13]

Neither nation had further need for reciprocal border crossing agreements, and the one covering Gerónimo lapsed on November 1, 1886. Others were not requested until 1890 when both countries hunted the elusive Apache Kid, an outlaw never officially captured or killed. That agreement stayed effective until 1896 when the last border crossing accommodation quietly faded away.

BOOK
FOUR

REVOLUTION
ON THE BORDER

From the beginning it was evident that
the heaviest fighting would be along the
northern tier of border states, and that
the state of Chihuahua would become the
storm center of the revolution.

Ira J. Bush, Gringo Doctor, *162-163*

15

The Struggle Begins

By the end of the 1880s, the Mexican boundary with the United States had become a laboratory for a great economic and cultural experiment. What happened during these years would lead to a blood bath without precedent along the international line, for with some exceptions, the climactic battles of the Mexican Revolution would be fought along the American border.

Mexico had manpower and raw materials but it lacked the financial strength and vocational skills to tap its mines, fields and forests. It failed to exploit its frontiers, particularly in the north. The region was remote, under populated, poorly governed, infested with outlaws. Rich in rangeland and minerals, impoverished in capital but close to the United States, the area attracted American and foreign capitalists with their money and expertise. The revolution therefore had its roots in the Díaz welcome to foreign investors, an invitation to build, develop and get rich. Mexico was supposed to get jobs and self respect, and it did get the former but somehow never obtained the latter.

The American Civil War helped fuse the revolution. The United States sprinted out of the Rebellion on a railroad building spree. By the early 1880s, the Southern Pacific had spun tracks from California to El Paso. Ambitious spur lines snaked into Arizona border towns of

Nogales, Yuma, Naco and Douglas.[1] Magnates wanted tracks in Mexico, so to oblige them, Díaz expropriated the *terrenos baldíos* in Sonora, property farmed for centuries by the Yaqui Indians but classified for this transaction as "national wastelands." When the brutality of taking possession ended, the Yaquis were either dead, in flight, or sold into plantation slavery in the hemp fields of Yucatan.[2] Their land went on the auction block for ten cents an acre as a subsidy to the Sonora Railroad.[3] The plan called for a route from Guaymas to the Arizona border and then east to El Paso. However, as the route was a duplication of the Southern Pacific's efforts, the tracks halted in Nogales.[4]

The *Ferrocarril Kansas City, Mexico & Oriente* ("Northwestern Railroad" in the United States) began as the dream of Albert Kinsey Owen, an American socialist, who wanted rail connections to his utopian "City of Peace" at Topolobampo, Sinaloa. His vision called for a road from Kansas City to cross the border at Presidio, Texas and proceed southwest through Chihuahua to Miñaca, then swing across the Sierra Madre to the Gulf of Lower California. Unfortunately, construction lagged due to insufficient financing.[5]

The Mexican Central was the most important line in Mexico because it extended south from Juarez to Mexico City, tying the United States firmly to the Mexican capital. This 1,200 mile economic artery linked the Mexican interior to the American borderlands. Across these rails pumped the labor of Mexico, grinding north to the absorbing areas of the United States-Mexico border.[6]

An estimated forty American mining corporations were doing business by 1885 near the international boundary in Sonora, Chihuahua and Coahuila. San Dimas, Guarisamey, Sierra Mojada, Santa Eulalia, Batopilas, El Oro, El Boleo, Santa Barbara and San Francisco del Oro were but a few firms familiar to border Americans.[7] However, most smelters were north of the border, and railroads linked them and the mines together.[8]

On average a Mexican miner received one-and-one-half pesos for a ten-hour shift, whereas a hacienda worker earned one peso or less a week. After being issued candles, hammer, scraper and drill, miners removed their clothing and entered the shafts wearing only a breechcloth, leather sandals and (usually) a sombrero. Why the sombrero in a dank, dark pit where neither sunlight nor rain penetrated is a mystery, but Mexicans had fond attachments for headpieces. These men would be assigned specific lengths to be drilled, and they were allowed as much or as little time as needed. Those who finished quickly could idle the remainder of the shift; but those who did not finish were docked wages. While it might seem that shift bosses would assign more work than could reasonably be done in ten hours, their knowledge of worker psychology taught them that being able to finish early usually proved an incentive. After the shift, the boss paid each man with *boletas* (tickets), handing out checks or tokens made of celluloid or brass in denominations of twenty-five centavos, fifty centavos, and one peso. After the boletas were turned in at the mine office, their value was punched on a card divided into squares corresponding to the days of the month. If an employee wished, he could make a purchase at the company store merely by presenting the ticket. At the end of the month, any credits remaining were paid in cash. However, since peons lived so close to their earning level, most workers generally owed the store.[9]

Although miners working for Americans were overpaid by Mexican standards, their living conditions could not have been more miserable and hopeless. Few had even a rudimentary education. They existed in filthy, overcrowded huts without water, heat or sewage, subsisting on corn tortillas and beans. In fairness, they had lived this way throughout their lives, and if mine owners made little effort to improve conditions, they also rarely made them worse. Malaria, typhus, pellagra, hookworm, tuberculosis, and a myriad of ailments sapped strength and mental powers. Two nutritious meals a day at company expense might have done wonders to eliminate absenteeism and upgrade production.

One root of subsequent labor unrest was the paternalistic attitude taken by Americans toward Mexicans. Americans accepted folklorian stereotypes regarding the Mexican culture, a stereotype fed not only by Anglo myths but by a Spanish and Mexican heritage of upper-class superiority. George Griggs mentioned it in his *Mines of Chihuahua:* "They [the Americans] seldom understand the relation which superiors are, by ancient Mexican custom, expected to maintain toward their inferiors, a spirit of affectionate and interested paternalism"[10]

Mexican peasants had always been treated as children by government and religious authorities. The Spaniard and Mexican did it as a means of control. The Americans thought it a natural part of the peon's humanity, but regardless of reasons or intentions, it naturally followed that children could not perform complex tasks or be given too much responsibility. Mexican miners were considered poor mechanics, unsophisticates who could not properly handle a machine drill without breaking it. Mexicans could not timber a mine, for while the shoring might hold, its flimsiness made Americans nervous. Americans admired the Mexicans for being fearless, but believed their gameness also made them careless. No American would work near a Mexican who set powder charges, an act akin to putting loaded weapons in the hands of infants.[11]

This paternalistic thinking would come home to roost at Cananea.

Men had mined the Cananea borderlands in northern Sonora for centuries, extracting the raw surface copper but rarely challenging the veins underground. When the flamboyant Colonel William C. Greene came along, the Spanish and Mexicans had all but given up the process as unprofitable. Greene loved to gamble and drink, and after several years of failing to get rich with cattle near Tombstone, Arizona, he happened upon the Cananea. Greene knew immediately that those thousands of red and brown stained acres had fortunes in copper hidden beneath their rusty surfaces. With a West Virginia corporation handling the financing, Greene took over the *Cobre Grande* (Big Copper) mine in 1898 and organized the Cananea Consolidated Copper Company. The story of this acquisition, and Greene's management and fall from power is an epic adventure as familiar along the border as it was in the steam-heated executive suites along Wall Street.[12]

A narrow-gage railroad zigzagged twelve miles up the Cananea canyons, a track so elaborate in its engineering that admirers dubbed it "the scenic line of the Southwest." By 1906 the company's main transportation tunnel reached six thousand feet, hooking up with thirty-five miles of underground workings. A system of feeder belts, blast furnaces, crushing and sampling mills and concentrators kept the shafts humming.[13]

In some respects, it seems strange that labor unrest would begin at Cananea, for its time the most enlightened mine operation in Mexico. Greene paid his workers three-and-one-half pesos a day, a sum described by the prestigious *Engineering and Mining Journal* as "having been raised to a ridiculous rate."[14]

In years to come, mining barons referred to the Cananea era as the golden age. President Porfirio Díaz welcomed the foreigners, enforced law and order, collected "reasonable" taxes and did not impose what he considered unnecessary restrictions. However, Díaz had remained in office so long that he had lost touch with economic realities. He forced a wage cut of one peso a day, a sum leaving Cananea workers still the most highly paid in the country, but nevertheless bringing them closer to the norm with other Mexican mining companies. For instance, San Francisco del Oro, a gold and silver mine near Parral, had costs of about $11,000 per month, of which only about $1,600 was paid in wages to several hundred employees, including management. Extracting ore ran to about $4,000, freight charges cost nearly $4,000, and the remaining costs went for stables, house rent, interest, assay costs and general expenses. Included in "general expenses" was a fixed government tax of eighty-five cents per kilo of silver, and three-and-one-half cents per gram of gold.[15]

Back at Cananea Copper, its very size and success made it vulnerable. Instead of Greene being identified as progressive, he was vilified as oppressive. The *Partido Liberal Mexicano* (Mexican Liberal Party, or PLM), headed by the intellectual Ricardo Flores Magón, published *Regeneración*, an inflammatory underground newspaper. It indicted Greene as an evil example of American capitalistic exploitation, and used Cananea as a political club to bludgeon Díaz for selling Mexico to the foreigners. In cooperation with the Western Federation of Miners, whose successes in the United States set an example for the PLM, Flores Magón organized fifteen Cananea miners and office workers into a society called *Unión Liberal Humanidad* (Unions for Humanity). From a gradually expanding position of strength, labor unions incited the workers to seek redress for real and imagined grievances.[16]

Labor delegates complained that one-fourth of the work force was American, and Anglos held virtually all the high paying positions: machinists, mechanics, foremen. Americans earned an average of five dollars per shift, compared to three pesos for the Mexican.

The miners struck on June 1, 1906, demanding an increase of two pesos a day, an eight hour shift, an abolition of the company store, and pay parity with the Americans. That afternoon a crowd of workers dressed in their best clothes converged on the lumberyard where proprietors George and William Metcalf met them with rifles and water hoses. Mexican tempers needed cooling off but not wetting down. A brawl ended with several miners killed, the Metcalfs slain, and their lumberyard burned.[17]

William Cornell Greene with daughter Eve. Greene was a swashbuckling, economic freebooter. Without his presence, Cananea would never have been a focal point for Mexican fury. (Arizona Historical Society, Tucson)

Captain Thomas J. Rynning was a Rough Rider, trail herder, champion sprinter, and army scout before joining the Arizona Rangers. (Arizona Historical Society, Tucson)

American employees dressed in their best suits guard the company store in Cananea. (Arizona Historical Society, Tucson)

Telegraph wires flashed the news north amid concerns for American safety. Fort Huachuca in Arizona sent four columns of cavalry to the border town of Naco, and threatened to cross the international line. Meanwhile, President Díaz assured Washington that his *rurales* would shortly bring the riot under control.[18]

Rumor had it that the miners possessed dynamite and firearms, and although this proved false, the managers could hardly be blamed for their fears. Greene wired Governor Rafael Izábal in Hermosillo for assistance, and demanded that General Luís E. Torres send troops from Magdalena. At best, military help was two days away,' so Greene also appealed to Bisbee, Arizona for assistance. Captain Tom Rynning of the Arizona Rangers equipped two hundred civilians and sent them to Naco. While they milled about, anxious to do something, Governor Izábal arrived from Nogales. He gave a brief talk to Rynning's army, explained how he appreciated their assistance, but said he had no authority to lead them across the border.

Rynning, a former Rough Rider, solved the dilemma by disbanding the group on the American side of the border and reforming them on the Mexican side. Izábal swore them in as temporary Mexican Army recruits. Two hours later these "soldiers" were on a train steaming south to Cananea.

All appeared calm when the governor and his unlikely army arrived. Greene and American employees met Izábal with three rousing cheers at the railroad station, and the two men drove among the sullen strikers to reason with them. The Bisbee volunteers stood by with rifles at the ready, perhaps nervously wondering if they had done the sensible thing in coming. The Americans "behaved with complete discretion and followed orders to the letter."[19]

Late that afternoon, Colonel Emilio Kosterlitzky, "the mailed fist of Porfirio Díaz," and his no-nonsense *rurales* rode into Cananea. They relieved the Americans (who went home), declared martial law, allegedly shot several striking ringleaders, and brought calm to the region. Everybody returned to work.[20]

The Cananea strike had been crushed, although how brutally depends upon the sources consulted. In itself the struggle did not reverse government policy or give the aging dictator reason to lie uneasy in his bed. As his arteries continued to harden, Díaz went blithely on as president for another four years. Nothing had been settled, but lessons should have been learned along the border in terms of the forthcoming conflict.

16

The First Battle of Juarez

NEITHER THE BORDER nor the Mexican can be understood unless one takes into account the Revolution. The insurgency will be remembered and revered when floods, outlaw and Indian raids, and controversies about the exact boundary have faded. Along the border, the fires of revolutionary thought nurtured the homeless, the landless, the dispossessed, the hopeless, the unemployed and the exiled.

Ricardo Flores Magón matured in the picturesque country of Oaxaca in southern Mexico, and as a law student embraced the concept of political agitation. His brother Jesús launched *Regeneración* in 1900, a radical newspaper expressing the political views of Ricardo. After spending 1903 in Mexico City's Belen Prison, Ricardo Flores Magón fled to the United States where the weekly circulation of *Regeneración*, by some estimates, rose to three thousand copies by 1906.[1] Here obviously was not a simple man with an uncomplicated philosophy. Harassment and threats failed to quench his revolutionary ardor, as he moved from that of a classic liberal to an outright anarchist, one not satisfied with political reform but demanding nothing short of governmental destruction. Americans gave him an opportunity to rethink his ideologies from the federal prison at Yuma in 1910,[2] but upon release he triumphantly wrote:

Here we are as always in our places of combat. Martyrdom has made us stronger and more resolute: we are ready for greater sacrifices. We say to the Mexican people that the day of liberation is near.[3]

Here we are with the torch of revolution in one hand and the program of the Liberal Party in the other, announcing war. We are not whining messengers of peace: we are revolutionaries. The bullets which we fire from our guns will be our electoral ballots.[4]

Fortunately for Mexico, and perhaps for the United States, the rattled prose of Flores Magón confused more than it clarified. *Regeneración* fell short of uniting the squabbling Mexican factions and their myriad of leaders who could not even agree on revolutionary slogans, let alone dogma. At one time or another they quibbled over "Land and Liberty," "Mexico for the Mexicans," "one-term presidential office," "a guaranteed minimum wage," "abolition of child labor," and a halt to the Church's stranglehold on schooling. Forcing Díaz from his thirty-year presidency was the only practical objective agreed upon by everybody.

The harangues of Flores Magón excited the masses, but his mania for finding enemies behind every establishment bush led him into making poor choices for associates. His relationship with bomb throwers made it easy to track his whereabouts and it gave the authorities a multitude of excuses for arresting him. Ricardo spent as much time in American jails as on American sidewalks.

Francisco Madero represented the moderate precursors, a man more interested in change than ruin. He thought along the lines of graduated pressure, of applying leverage toward specific ends. Madero came from a large and wealthy Coahuila family, professed admiration for the American political system and believed Mexico could be governed by democratic means. He tolerated the Flores Magón brothers, identified with their alienation, but could not accept their theories. Madero wanted Díaz either to resign or quit at the end of his current term. He wanted the country back on the constitutional track, and hoped it could be done peacefully. That dream seemed a possibility in 1908 when American journalist James Creelman, war correspondent and one of the most famous newspapermen of his time, published an interview with Díaz. It quoted the old dictator as planning to retire when his present commitment ended. Díaz said he welcomed political debate, a freedom noted by several aspiring presidential candidates. However, when Díaz changed his mind and started campaigning again, Madero published *La Sucesión Presidencial en 1910*, a tract arguing against an eighth term. Madero himself announced as a candidate of the Anti-reelectionist Party, and he toured Mexico speaking to tumultuous crowds. This radiant do-gooder filled with honesty and charity, a tiny man with a bird-like voice, somehow began uniting the brawling factions, particularly in the northern states with their disgruntled, pistol-toting voters.

But a president seeking an additional term does not want a popular candidate around as a reminder of slipping prestige. So the police arrested Madero in San Luis Potosi, holding him in prison until Díaz had counted the votes. Then, with the mellowing president assured of another victory, he allowed Madero more freedom. Madero used it to dash across the international line at Laredo, Texas, on October 7, 1910.

In San Antonio, Madero formulated his "Plan of San Luis Potosi," an outline for armed rebellion. Yet he had no more military talents than Flores Magón. He plotted an uprising in Pueblo which turned sour. The ringleaders were killed or dispersed. A similar adventure in Ciudad Porfirio Diaz (Piedras Negras) failed. After waiting across the Rio Grande in Texas for shots, and never hearing any, Madero called off an uprising that had never started.[5]

The rebellion might have sputtered and died completely had a call to arms not echoed across the desolate northwestern deserts. Chihuahua had no shortage of field commanders, such as Pascual Orozco, moody and unprincipled, and the cattle thief and murderer, Doroteo Arango, who would become famous as Pancho Villa. Both men had a talent for winning, an ability to make correct decisions from the saddle. Their horsemen could ride great distances and shoot up isolated communities, ranches and mining camps. But though fierce fighters, they would never be anything but brigands until they rallied around a national leader. They were insurgents seeking respectability, and the respectable Madero was seeking an effective army. Together they changed the history of Mexico, and began it along the international boundary.

Madero needed the Mexico-United States border for its sanctuary and crucial railroad linkups. Juarez and El Paso were major ports of entry into and out of their respective countries. Juarez had a direct rail link with Mexico City; El Paso had five rail hookups. Whoever controlled the twin city complex, dominated northern Mexico. As the fourth largest city in Chihuahua, Juarez had over eight thousand people. *Calle del Comercio* (now Sixteenth of September Street), blossomed with elaborate mansions, a post office, an army garrison, the

Pancho Villa rides again. This scene (right) was likely staged for the camera, the event taking place in Juarez or Torreon. (U.T. El Paso Library Archives). Pancho Villa swims again. Villa, (below) in black suit, was visiting in Texas somewhere in the Lower Rio Grande Valley. Other participants are unidentified. (Author's collection)

Aduana Fronteriza (border customs house), and expensive business houses. Ciudad Juarez was an unfailing supply inlet.

However, in many respects it was El Paso and not Juarez that formed the intellectual storm center of the forthcoming Mexican Revolution. It beckoned to the inflamed in spirit. Those unable to find political freedom in Mexico considered El Paso a border mecca for the dissemination of propaganda. *Revista Illustrada, Diario de El Paso, El Clarín del Norte, El Echo del Comercio*, were just a few revolutionary tracts published by articulate Mexican exiles. *La Reforma Social*, for instance, an eight-by-eleven inch sheet printed on one side, posted on its masthead, "We fight for the dignity of high and pure principles, never for races, towns or personalities. We seek the rational truth, the moral law, and finally, progress and goodness."[6] Occasionally, like most of its competitors, *La Reforma Social* anticipated events. On December 26, 1910, its headline screamed, "after hard fighting, the revolutionaries had taken Chihuahua." Not satisfied with this piece of overstatement, the newspaper said, "300 hombres, perfectamente armados y montados" (300 armed men, well armed and mounted) were inside Ciudad Juarez and ready to strike.

As early as 1906, Ricardo Flores Magón and his *Partido Liberal Mexicano* planned to subdue Juarez from El Paso. Flores Magón organized and supported the *Club Liberal* in El Paso, an intellectual organization agitating for social and political reform. The leaders contrived to send two hundred men across the border to dynamite the army garrison, the police station and city hall. If Juarez could be captured, a contingent of revolutionaries would immediately embark by train to Chihuahua City and seize it too.

With so many participants involved, the scheme had no more chance of being secret than it had of being successful. Chihuahua Governor Enrique Creel, through spies infiltrating the rebels, rounded up the Juarez suspects. American authorities did likewise in El Paso, conducting house-to-house searches in *Chihuahuita*. Flores Magón barely escaped by train to California.[7]

Efforts failed to overthrow the Juarez government because of outstanding police work, and because the revolutionary strategy had been poorly developed, funded and directed. Flores Magón could rail against his country's establishment, and he could find maniacal bomb throwers, but he lacked the priceless qualities of Francisco Madero, the ability to raise an army, an ability to appeal to all factions, and an ability to govern. As an anarchist dedicated to the destruction of government, Flores Magón could not impressively offer his credentials to lead one. Madero could. He was a candidate others could support.

As border intrigue continued, questions arose about the strength of the revolutionary movement. How much was power and how much was media build-up? Both Díaz and President William Howard Taft desperately believed it the latter, the old dictator because he wanted to survive and Taft because he wished to continue his "Dollar Diplomacy," a derisive term for government protection of American financial interests in Mexico. A border meeting could demonstrate hemispheric solidarity even though such a conference held risks of presidential assassination.

The border meeting got underway in El Paso on October 16, 1909, the most "eventful Diplomatic Event in the History of the Two Nations," the *El Paso Herald* claimed. That of course was newspaper hype as the conference had no apparent agenda beyond showing the flags. Taft had written Díaz that he planned to be in the Southwest during the fall and hoped to meet the President of Mexico in El Paso or at some convenient place along the boundary.[8] However, he wrote his wife on October 17, saying "I am not quite sure at whose insistence this meeting was held, but I do know that I received a communication, perhaps directly from the old man, of an informal character, saying how glad he would be to have such a meeting brought about. He thinks, and I believe rightly, that the knowledge throughout his country of the friendship of the United States for him and his government will strengthen him with his own people, and tend to discourage revolutionary efforts to establish a different government."[9]

On this basis the two presidents visited the border, although both did little except shuffle back and forth across the international line. One touch of humor occurred at the El Paso Chamber of Commerce when Taft plopped his ponderous bulk into a chair and cracked its leg.[10]

In his only speech, Taft referred to stepping upon foreign soil and enjoying the hospitality of its government. "The prosperity of the United States is largely dependent upon the prosperity of Mexico, and Mexico's prosperity depends upon ours," he said.[11]

Although the meeting created little news worthy of entry into the history books, it was a triumph for Díaz. An hour-and-a-half parade through El Paso brought thunderous applause. "Viva Díaz!" screamed the well-wishers. Even the thousands of American soldiers, police officers, Texas Rangers and Secret Service men joined the enthusiasm. The solemn Díaz, in the full dress of a division general, and with a multiplicity of chest medals glistening in the sun, bowed to the left and right. He had now acquired the American exposure he sought. For his remaining time left as head of state, this would be his finest hour.

But appearances are often deceptive along the border. Truth is a relative measurement. The affection Díaz received was sincere, but the opposition, kept leashed or jailed during the visit, resurfaced after the heads of state had departed.

In Chihuahua the twenty-eight-year-old Pascual Orozco, Jr., demanded revolution in fact as well as in theory. A tough six-footer who looked as American as Mexican, the moody Orozco captured the district capital of Guerrero in November 1910, and shot up a relief column.[12] He won victories with what Mexican historian Calzadíaz Barrera called "an army of rags, without money, without any notions of military discipline . . . some carried axes instead of rifles, others, far from inspiring fear, inspired pity."[13]

Following these successes, Orozco created a loose confederacy of revolutionary powers, tacitly accepting recognition from Pancho Villa and others as the revolutionary commander in the northern district. Certainly he warranted this respect, showing flashes of brilliant strategy by capturing a train on the Kansas City, Mexico and Orient line and then spreading a rumor that he planned to enter Chihuahua City. As Federal soldiers clustered around the capital, Orozco steamed north to the Rio Grande, camped across the river from El Paso and its ASARCO Smelter, and vowed to attack Juarez if Madero would take command. On February 14, Madero crossed the border from El Paso and assumed leadership.

The timetable went awry when Federals reinforced the Juarez military garrison. Madero's confidence sagged, and he thrust a Rebel force south toward Casas Grandes, only to prove that while he might be a rising politician, he was an inept general. He himself led the attack, and suffered a severe defeat as well as superficial wounds. Federals decimated his army, captured sixteen wagons filled with supplies, three hundred horses and numerous prisoners, including Colonel Eduardo Hay of Madero's personal staff. (In spite of seven wounds, Hay escaped from the Chihuahua hospital and rejoined Madero.)

The setback caused Madero not only to regroup but to rethink. Because he had nowhere else to go, he marched north again for an assault upon Juarez. As both sides braced for the expected fighting, Juarez males feared impressment into whichever army they happened to be nearest, so they took their families and fled to El Paso. Business houses closed, a few reopening north of the Rio Grande. The *Banco Minero* and a branch of the *Banco Nacional* transferred their assets to El Paso banks. The post office moved across the border.

Juarez took on the appearance of a ghost town: dark, silent, fearful. The inflexible General Juan Navarro cursed the cold and wondered how long his ragged, poorly armed men could hold out. Even reinforcements were a mixed blessing, as when two hundred additional soldiers broke through the siege and arrived practically without ammunition, half their wives and camp followers barefoot and frostbitten, many in advanced stages of pregnancy.[14]

Meanwhile, on the west bank of the Rio Grande where New Mexico, Texas and old Mexico clasped together at International Boundary Marker No. 1, Francisco Madero established his headquarters in a windowless one-room adobe hut with a dirt floor. Insurgents joined him from remote deserts and mountains. Some were teenage boys with big grins, the butts of their Mauser rifles occasionally dragging the ground. Some were old men with yellow teeth and white, flowing beards. Sixty others were lithe Yaqui warriors with long, stringy, raven hair. Most revolutionaries were in their twenties, ragged, wearing sandals or barefoot, carrying spears, machetes, and firearms of multi-caliber. This odd assortment of humanity shared one common identity, a steadfast belief that at this particular point in time and place they were the best damn fighters in the world.[15]

The bored and restless revolutionaries found themselves reinforced by equally bored and restless soldiers-of-fortune. The tall, austere General Benjamin Johannes Viljoen of Boer War fame strapped on his field glasses and sold his services to Madero. He ranched near La Mesa, New Mexico, and had become a United States citizen in 1910. Yet, he could not resist one last call to battle. Nor could Giuseppe Garibaldi, the canny grandson of "Red Shirt" Garibaldi, the military hero who united Italy. Altogether, between thirty and fifty Americans signed on, individuals not anxious to reveal their identities. Newspapers published names like "Death Valley Scotty," and "Desert Sam." These recruits formed squads called "foreign legions" by the *El Paso Morning Times* and the *El Paso Herald*. Garibaldi called them "groups," whereas Viljoen used "commandos," a Boer term. The Mexican *insurrectos* considered every-

Monument No. 1 at El Paso in May 1911. People in the foreground appear to be American visitors. The man and woman on the right are standing in the United States. The man on the left is either exactly on the international line, or a foot or so inside Mexico. Background individuals are Mexican revolutionaries. (IBWC)

Madero's headquarters at International Boundary Marker No. 1. Adobe building with activity surrounding is headquarters. The Rio Grande is on the right, along with Smeltertown, an appendage of El Paso. Southern Pacific bridges and the El Paso Franklin Mountains are in background. (IBWC)

body including themselves to be *gente*, meaning people or folk. They were the *gente de Orozco*, or the *gente de Villa*.

Starting on April 22, two Federal envoys appeared each day for three weeks of talks in Peace Grove, a clump of trees between the boundary marker and Juarez, almost precisely where the early Spaniards crossed the Rio Grande into the United States. In the end, the talks collapsed, since the surrender of Juarez or the resignation of Díaz were the only negotiable issues.

During the interim, Abraham González, an eventual Chihuahua governor, whose abilities in recruiting, communications and civil government made him one of Madero's most talented and trusted associates, approached the El Paso physician Ira Jefferson Bush. González retained Bush as chief surgeon in Madero's army. The stocky Bush looked like an Indian, and wore a Red Cross band on his left arm. He eagerly accepted, building his first hospital at Samalayuca, thirty miles south of Juarez. However, when the battle started, he moved his *insurrecto* hospital to 410 S. Campbell in El Paso, a mere stagger from the border.[16]

Newspapermen sensed sensational stories, and journalists flocked to the border. On the spot coverage flashed all over the country. John Kenneth Turner, author of *Barbarous Mexico,* put in an appearance. So did Gutiérrez de Lara, a Mexican socialist who practiced "seditious speeches" in El Paso but was so dedicated to pacifism that he allegedly wept during the Madero assault on Casas Grandes.

Other journalists marched to different motivations, the best example being Felix A. Sommerfeld, the barrel-chested, enigmatic German. Although ostensibly a reporter for United Press, he became a mystery figure of the northern revolution, a complex business and intelligence agent for El Paso firms, for Madero and later for Villa.

War correspondents clustered in the Hotel Orndorff (now the Cortez Building) and the Hotel Sheldon bar in El Paso. A favorite after hours saloon was a cellar known as "Bill Reid's Place" under the City National Bank. On any given night (or afternoon or morning), one might encounter L. N. Spears of the *New York Times* (later replaced by Stephen Bonsal). Earl Harding of the *New York World* worried about premature baldness, so he shaved his head and hoped the hair would grow back fuller. Otheman Stevens of the *Los Angeles Examiner* splashed only a drop or two of liquor in his highballs, and thus brought shame on the journalistic tradition of hard drinking. Rodney Gilbert, a Philadelphia newspaperman delighted in wearing the peons'

KKK parade through El Paso. The parade took place around 1920, and the caravan is passing through Pioneer Plaza, the heart of downtown El Paso. (Author's Collection).

straw hats, but gave them up when he acquired lice. Alfred Henry Lewis, a magazine and book writer, rarely sat anywhere if he did not have a stool, and war photographer James Hare tried repeatedly and unsuccessfully to photograph the stiff and formal General Navarro. From south of the border came Gerald Brandon and Leopoldo Zea of *El Diario* in Mexico City, Luís Malvais of *El Pais*, and Ramírez de Aguilar of *Imparciál*. At the slightest encouragement the latter made speeches without much point, but all sounding dramatic. Brandon translated during the bull sessions, shifting back and forth from one language to the other, never missing the proper oratorical touches.

Both the *El Paso Morning Times* and the *El Paso Herald* kept correspondents in the field. While the *Times* is generally credited with the best coverage, it was a slender dandy named Timothy G. Turner of the *Herald* who penned *Bullets, Bottles and Gardenias*, the most significant and memorable eye-witness account of the revolution. "I maintain that never was there such a colorful, romantic, noble and foolish period as the first revolution in northern Mexico," he wrote.[17]

Back in Washington, President Taft and Secretary of State Philander C. Knox vacillated between strict and lax neutrality, a policy unintentionally favoring the revolutionists since only direct intervention would have saved Juarez. Taft sent an additional twenty thousand troops to the border, and a tenuous situation existed. Those soldiers relieved the Texas Rangers and were strung out to intercept guerrillas (and sometimes Federals) trying to slip into Texas. The presence of this army influenced Madero's strategy. With Juarez and El Paso separated by only a narrow Rio Grande, American casualties from stray bullets would be unavoidable as a result of any fighting across the river. At best there would be dead Americans, and at worst the American Army might intervene. Madero weighed the risks, decided they were too great and, never being noted for his decisiveness, ordered a withdrawal south.[18]

However, he reckoned without the influence of Orozco and Villa who would have no part in avoiding a fight. Madero had hardly left the encampment when he heard shooting and was forced to return and act as if he was in command of an assault he had no part in starting. The foreign legionaires stormed Juarez on May 8, 1911. Additional squads of fifteen to twenty Rebels trotted through the dry *acequia madre* (main irrigation ditch) into the heart of town, dynamiting a house holding forty Federals and shooting the survivors as they fled. One by one they captured the Mexican Central Railroad Bridge, the Northwestern Railroad Bridge, and the Stanton Street Bridge. Although several El Pasoans died due to stray bullets, the United States Army remained north of the border.[19]

El Pasoans clustered along the Rio Grande and on buildings and railroad cars as the American army tried to force them back. From atop the El Paso Laundry Building, Judge Joseph Sweeney described the fighting. "It was a beautiful sight to see the shrapnel bursting up in the air and scattering its death-dealing missiles on the hills and valleys surrounding," he said.[20]

As Sweeney wrote, Rebel forces controlled the western, southern and northern portions of Juarez. Desultory firing continued throughout the night. Dynamite bombs and artillery rounds jarred both sides of the boundary.

Villistas entered the city alongside the railroad tracks, and captured the Ketelsen & Degetau warehouse (an armory) near the depot. Other insurgents overran the bull ring, *Nuestra Señora de Guadalupe* (Our Lady of Guadalupe Cathedral), and the post office. Fires burned out of control.

After nearly three days of fighting, Rebels cleared the central plaza and captured the Federal barracks. It was all over. Tired, thirsty and demoralized, Navarro and his men hung out the white flag at one o'clock in the afternoon. Garibaldi accepted the surrender.[21]

A savage scene of suffering greeted El Pasoans as they swarmed across the border. Firing squads enacted their deadly business. This was the hour of brave men, and the camera never focused on a single act of cowardice. The doomed stood stoically, ignoring the bodies of previously executed comrades, and calmly awaited the awful rifles.

Doctors cut and sawed at the city hospital in Juarez. During slack periods they deloused the typhus cases. Dr. John W. Cathcart, a crippled physician, operated a portable X-ray and determined who would undergo the amputation knife. During the early stages of fighting, Cathcart treated wounded in the smelter (ASARCO) hospital. When the shooting stopped, he took his daughter Florence across the border so that she might see first hand the horrors of war. The memory of starving, thirsty *insurrectos* and soldiers, maimed by dynamite bombs and artillery rounds, their arms and legs scattered in the streets, would remain forever vividly etched in her mind.[22]

Orozco and Villa wanted General Navarro added to the corpses. Madero refused to permit his execution. To assure Navarro's safety, Madero arranged to have him smuggled across the border and into the Popular Dry Goods Store where he hid for three days in the chinaware department before quietly registering in Hotel Dieu Hospital.

Ciudad Juarez became the Rebel capital of Mexico, its capture giving enormous prestige to the Madero movement. Back in Washington, President Taft took a philosophical view. He had supported Díaz on principle, but recognized that Mexico had never met its human needs. The president wanted the United States to alleviate the suffering as much as possible, and he ignored requests for closing the El Paso customs ports. Madero's victory "does not change our duty or the right of persons . . . to carry on legitimate business," he said. Supplies of corn, rice, beans and flour started flowing into Juarez from the American people.[23]

With the battle over, Mexico City opened negotiations with Madero. On the night of May 21, 1911, representatives signed the "Treaty of Ciudad Juarez" in the glare of automobile headlights outside the *aduana* (customs house). President Díaz sailed into exile. Madero was elected president, but never lived to bring peace. Mexico's agony had barely begun.

The Border in Flames

WHILE MADERO'S PARTISANS were engaging the Federal troops of President Porfirio Díaz across the Rio Grande from El Paso, the rest of the border was nearly as turbulent. The availability of an easily penetrated international boundary influenced revolutionary activity in the northern Mexican states of Coahuila, Chihuahua and Sonora. Behind this screen, plotters could plot and propagandists could disseminate manifestoes calling for armed rebellion. It provided staging areas for revolutionary leaders to prepare new coups or recover from previous ones. Federal troops crossed the border to outflank the opposition. Merchants sent supplies, volunteers and arms across it. And the boundary was often an international stage from which American audiences watched battles in progress.

A portion of the arms business involved El Paso's McGinty cannon — the old Blue Whistler, sometimes called "Little Tom" — a bronze, twelve-pounder left behind after the Civil War and adopted for ceremonial purposes by a strange and wonderful organization called the McGinty Club. This many-faceted body consisted of musical groups and marching bands. The McGintys fired the cannon during sham battles, its thunder shaking the border. With the demise of the club in 1902, the cannon rested in a triangular park at city hall until the fortunes of war whisked it across the border on April 17, 1911.[1]

Pioneer doctor Ira Bush and his distinguished Chihuahua friend, Abraham González, examined it and concluded it had a couple of good bangs left. They smuggled it out of retirement. Mechanics refurbished the bronze and overhauled the carriage. A local foundry furnished shot. The Shelton Payne Arms Company contributed a barrel of black powder since the gun needed four pounds just for priming. When all was ready, a squad of men loaded the dismantled weapon into hay carts and smuggled it into Mexico.[2]

What happened next is an unsung saga of human endurance. Flores Magón broke with General Antonio I. Villarreal and denounced him as an assassin and homosexual. However, Villarreal still had friends like Abraham González, and González encouraged him to take the McGinty cannon and one hundred men, including thirty-five Americans, to Ojinaga, a downstream border town. Repeatedly the eight-hundred-pound cannon with its fifty-three inch tube crashed into arroyos, slipped from makeshift bridges and toppled into rivulets as exhausted men pushed and pulled it across one scarred ridge after another. Finally, it stood poised two hundred miles southeast of El Paso, pointing its menacing muzzle at the mud walls of Ojinaga.

Ojinaga was little more than a remote border crossroad upstream from the Big Bend. Presidio, Texas, hovered directly across the Rio Grande.

As early as November 1910, the revolutionists had warned the Ojinaga mayor that they intended to behead him. The mayor responded by purchasing the firearms stock of Presidio merchant Ignatz Kleinman. The revolutionaries threatened Kleinman too. The merchant demanded protection but the sheriff had no deputies to spare. Kleinman armed his clerks and used them as bodyguards.

Insurgent activities drew the comments of W. T. Millington, an International Boundary (Water) Commission employee at Presidio, who checked Rio Grande levels and observed boundary shifts. In reports to W. W. Follett, who supervised the commission during the frequent absences of Anson Mills, Millington said he warned Ojinaga of an impending December attack. Since soldiers from Chihuahua City were twenty-four hours away, frightened civilians fled to Presidio, which had no facilities for refugees. After an uncomfortable night on the ground, the refugees returned to Ojinaga when two hundred Federal Mexican soldiers arrived. The military swiftly created a defense perimeter around Ojinaga, and then moved out after the Rebels. Shortly after dark they approached an adobe ruins where obvious cooking fires burned. The confident cavalry lined up and charged, only to encounter rifle fire spurting from the hillsides. In the melee, the soldiers stumbled into barbed wire, and although they lost only one man, most of their horses were later destroyed because of lacerated legs.[3]

Revolutionaries now shifted to El Mulato, thirty miles southeast of Ojinaga and five miles south of the Rio Grande. Again they ambushed the army. Two hundred soldiers and twenty-five *rurales* shot their way out of a box canyon as insurgents fired from boulders and outcroppings. The military lost six conscripts and one officer.[4]

As the conflict stalemated at Ojinaga, President Taft mobilized twenty thousand national guardsmen, promising to support an increasingly beleaguered Díaz by forming a "solid military wall" along the border. The presence "of our forces in the neighborhood [of the border] will have a restraining influence . . . on the fighting in Mexico," Taft said.[5]

The description of a "solid military wall" created an impression among American civilians that United States troops stood shoulder to shoulder on the international line. However, barely 3,500 of the 10,000 troops in Texas ever patrolled the border at any one time.

By law the Army enforced the neutrality laws, and cracked down on smuggling, especially the illegal conveyance of munitions back and forth across the border. However, once Ojinaga fell to the insurgents, munitions were bought and sold freely and legally from American sources.[6]

One hundred troopers of the United States 3rd Cavalry rode into Presidio on February 13, 1911. Until then, Millington, the boundary commission employee, claimed, "it was normal for the rebels to use the road [on the Texas side] . . . as a highway in moving up and down the river and crossing the Rio Grande when they pleased. The Rebels usually traveled on horseback in squads of two or three with their blankets tied back of their saddles and scabbard in place. Never once were the Rebels or their guns seized for a breach of the neutrality laws. They had their way until the American soldiers came. Now we never see a Rebel unless he is in Kleinman's store. Everything is tranquil. Not even a man is now seen distributing an insurrection paper. Had the U.S. soldiers been here some six or eight weeks ago, there would never have been any battles."[7]

But while American soldiers brought peace to the Texas side, by mid March one thousand poorly armed revolutionaries surrounded Ojinaga and its garrison of five hundred Federals and *rurales*. Former

Chihuahua rancher, General José la Cruz Sánchez hammered the Federals until three-fourths of Ojinaga, including the custom port of entry, was in Rebel hands. Meanwhile, an order of Federal food arrived in Presidio. Ordinarily these supplies would now have gone to the insurgents, as they controlled customs. However, American custom officers closed the port of entry and opened a new one at the water's edge. Alfalfa, beans, rice and five hundred sacks of corn were unloaded on the south bank. During the transfer, Sánchez attacked and momentarily seized the ford before Mexican soldiers unlimbered two machine guns. The battle seesawed, with the Federals gradually regaining control of Ojinaga, holding the town even when General Antonio Villarreal and the McGinty cannon reinforced the insurgents.

During the last of April, Colonel José Isabel Robles left Chihuahua City to break the siege of Ojinaga, his six hundred regulars advancing toward Falomir, eighty miles from the border. When Robles was twenty-seven miles short of his goal, Sánchez ambushed and pinned him down in the Peguis Mountains. As the rancher general and his seven hundred men attempted to outflank Robles, Sánchez was himself outflanked by two hundred Indians fighting for the Federals. A disorderly retreat started when a bullet hit Sánchez in the thigh, and he left to get medical attention from the United States Army. The near leaderless revolutionaries abandoned seven wagons of provisions, one wagon of ammunition and two hundred horses.

Federals in town and federals on the road now threatened Villarreal, so he planned to bombard Ojinaga with the Blue Whistler. However, the second round jammed in the tube, and while the explosion did not split the metal, it demolished the carriage when the gun lurched skyward and crashed. Retreating insurgents dragged the smoking, shattered hulk back to Juarez and returned it to El Paso residents who donated it to a scrap metal drive during World War II

Meanwhile, Villarreal's American contingent deserted, explaining to Millington that they "did not come to fight battles in the hills — but to take Ojinaga" and share in the capture of its wealth.[8]

A thousand miles west along the border, events in Sonora and Baja California were as bizarre as they were tragic. Flores Magón, the clarion of anarchism and revolution, wanted to guide without leading, to act without following through, to point the way without specifically defining directions.

Main street of Tijuana, Mexico in 1914. The wooden, false-fronted buildings show a decided American influence. (Imperial Valley Water Irrigation District)

Northwest Mexico had approximately 400,000 potential recruits for Flores Magón. But where were they? Where were the ragged revolutionary armies which by weight of numbers could have easily destroyed the Federals and made it unnecessary for crusaders such as Flores Magón to spend years in American exile? The answer is that the majority of peasants were indifferent; that the bottom line of why Díaz lost and the Insurgents won is that most citizens did not care. Each major battle or shifting of political events saw hundreds of Mexicans not joining the winning side, but fleeing across the border. These refugees would completely redefine the international boundary, not in lines but in cultural, economic and social relationships. They were vanguards of the multitudes to come later.

First came the Flores Magóns with their fiery eyes and burning passions, men whose hand-cranked presses churned out vitriolic, anti-Díaz propaganda. These bitter exiles recruited revolutionaries throughout the Arizona mining camps of Clifton, Morenci and Metcalf. Mexican laborers on the Southern Pacific were encouraged to join. Firebrands such as Francisco Álvarez Tostado traveled the length of the border, haranguing strollers in American and Mexican public plazas on the merits of the struggle.

By spring of 1911, middle and upper-class Sonorans who could not support Díaz and had nothing in common with the Insurgents, swarmed into Arizona. Ures Mayor Francisco Ochoa, Arizpe prefect Ignacio Pesqueira, and the Caborca municipal president Francisco Morineau, all moved into Tucson's Santa Rita Hotel, enjoying its electric elevators and steam heat.[9]

Arizona banks handled flourishing accounts in gold, pesos and bonds. Mexicans stored their private papers, jewels and other valuables in safety deposit boxes.

Lower classes fled the Federals *and* the Insurgents, as each conscripted peons into the army. These destitute people, wailing and terrified, brought their burros, birdcages and religious objects into the United States. Many arrivals needed medical attention. An epidemic of smallpox broke out in Douglas.[10]

During 1910 and 1911, by some estimates 50 percent of the revolutionary forces along the border with New Mexico, Arizona and California were foreign born: Americans (including a large number of blacks), Boers, Germans, French, Russians, English and Australians. Of the remaining 50 percent, many were Mexican by birth, but possessed United States citizenship.[11]

The International Workers of the World (IWW, or Wobblies) recruited foreigners[12] such as Stanley Williams whose razzle-dazzle style of warfare got him killed at Mexicali, and Simon Berthold who was born in Sonora of German parents, but spent most of his life in Los Angeles before becoming an organizer for the IWW. During a skirmish in March 1911, a Federal shot Berthold in the leg. As he lay dying of gangrene in El Alamo, he phoned Governor Celso Vega in Ensenada and demanded the city's surrender. Berthold had no reliable army to attack, and Vega had no suitable forces to defend, so the two officials blustered on the line, the "telephone war" ending in a stalemate. Berthold's replacement was John R. Mosby, reportedly a nephew of the Confederate guerrilla commander, a kindly man but an inept leader.

Caryl Ap Pryce, a welshman, was substantially the only non-Wobbly in a position of authority. This laconic adventurer with a chest of battle ribbons, wore brogan shoes and had a rumpled appearance. A tactician he wasn't, but he could rally fighters to his leadership.[13]

An American sentry (left) stands guard on the American side of the international line across from Tijuana, Mexico. While this individual is obviously a soldier, his dress resembles that of a soldier of fortune. (Imperial Valley Water Irrigation District). (Below) John R. Mosby and adjutant, Bert Laflin, at Tijuana. Insurrectos were doing well when this photo was taken. (Imperial Valley Water Irrigation District)

To keep his forces active, Pryce took two hundred men, only 10 percent being Mexicans, toward Tijuana in early April 1911. On the 18th he attacked and routed the Federals, killing thirty. The survivors fled to California.

However, when Pryce could not pay his men, they looted Tijuana and started charging visitors twenty-five cents each to enter the town. When the casinos reopened, Pryce received 25 percent of the proceeds.

When this failed to provide sufficient funds, a discouraged Pryce conferred with Flores Magón in Los Angeles about disbanding the Wobbly army at Tijuana. Evidently they reached no consensus, as Pryce never returned to Mexico. For a while he worked as a movie extra, later distinguished himself with the Canadian Army in European trench warfare, and then dropped from sight.

When Pryce entered self-exile, his foreign legion chose Jack Mosby as leader. While Mosby remained loyal to the Wobblies and to Flores Magón, he lacked a social consciousness. American newspapers referred to Mosby's men as cutthroats. Mosby possessed barely more military talent than Flores Magón, and in June 1911 his time of testing arrived. Vega left Ensenada with 550 men. Mosby headed south to challenge him with eighty foreign legionnaires and seventy-five Mexicans and Indians. The infantry piled on a train and boisterously waved rifles while the cavalry drunkenly rode alongside. When the forces met in a three-hour battle, Vega won. He scattered the revolutionaries, sending a weeping Mosby and his followers stumbling across the American border as refugees. The American Army arrested several and charged them with desertion.

With the advent of Francisco Madero to the presidency, and the exile of Porfirio Díaz, the insurrection should have been over. Instead, it had barely begun. As Mexico's best hope for peace, Madero vacillated, failing to be either a dictator or a strong democratic leader. In the end, the revolution outran him.

Serious insubordinations flared along the international line, particularly at Ciudad Juarez. Federal troops obeyed Francisco Madero and his revolutionary government. However, disillusioned soldiers in Juarez, receiving neither pay nor assurances of better treatment, declared themselves *Zapatistas* (followers of Emiliano Zapata, a Rebel chieftain in the south of Mexico). Refugees again flocked into El Paso as Federal soldiers looted Juarez. Units from Fort Bliss took up positions along the border.

Taft gave Madero permission to shuttle Mexican troops across the Texas line from other points along the border, to enter Juarez from El Paso and crush the fresh rebellion. However, Texas Governor Oscar Colquitt indignantly countermanded the authority, and Washington backed down.

With the situation tense, Madero sent General Pascual Orozco north to quash the rebellion. Orozco did so with ease, but he too had become disenchanted with the Madero administration, saying it had moved reluctantly on social and land distribution reform. He talked rebellious troopers into swearing allegiance to General José Inéz Salazar, a supporter of General Emilio Vasquez Gómez for president. Gómez was a former member of the Madero cabinet.

Since some Juarez soldiers remained loyal to Madero, Salazar did not have complete control. But he had sufficient men to threaten a Juarez takeover, prompting Max Webber, the German vice-consul, to report that "Most *Juarenses* have gone to El Paso, leaving the houses . . . empty."[14] Violence seemed imminent, and Taft warned Madero against hostilities extending into the United States. Madero had sufficient worries without a confrontation with the Americans, so he ordered the Juarez garrison to surrender. The revolutionaries completely occupied Juarez on February 27 with barely a shot fired. On March 2, a manifesto signed in the Montecarlo Hotel declared Gómez the provisional president. However, Gómez lacked national advocates, so nothing happened. He was president on only an ignored piece of paper signed at a remote point on an isolated border. Salazar's leadership also faded, so Orozco assumed power in Juarez. *Orozquistas* next occupied Chihuahua City, and Madero needed to get them out.[15]

American soldiers of fortune again reacted along the border. Tracy Richardson and his machine gun had fought in Nicaragua, Venezuela and Honduras. Beside him stood his friend, the paunchy "Fighting Jew," Sam Dreben. Dreben had proven his mercenary talents in the Philippines, in China during the Boxer Rebellion and in Honduras. Orozco offered them $500 monthly in gold to fight against Madero, and they accepted.[16]

As Mexico braced itself, President Taft ordered Americans out of northern Mexico, the summons applying to businessmen, ranchers, miners and Mormons. The resultant Mormon exodus was unique in border history. A people in flight throughout most of their turbulent history were now making one more run.

Mormons had fled from New York to Ohio to Illinois to Missouri and to Utah, the promised land. At Salt Lake City, the Mormons established a flourishing religious empire at odds with the 1862 congressional statute forbidding polygamy. United States marshals started rigid enforcement in 1882, and the Mormon church outlawed the practice in 1890. If a Mormon desired plural wives, he would have to leave, and Mexico with its strong Catholic traditions opened its doors to these religious refugees. Wagon trains stretched south from Utah to Deming and Columbus, New Mexico. Emigrants crossed the border at Las Palomas, Chihuahua, and traveled sixty miles to the custom station at La Ascension, north of Casas Grandes. They purchased fifty thousand acres along the Piedras Verdes (Green Rocks) River, and two tracts about the same size a little further north. Mormons named their settlements for Mexican heroes and political figures: Colonia Diaz, Colonia Dublan, Colonia Juarez, Colonia Pacheco, Colonia Garcia and Chuichupa. Where there had formerly been rocks and sand, soon there were vegetable gardens, fruit trees, irrigation ditches, plumbing, rope swings, electric lights, schools and quiet, provincial villages. The colonias looked like rural America.[17]

President Díaz had welcomed the Mormons, and they prospered. Now they existed in the vortex of the Madero movement. The insurgents needed food, money, horses and weapons, and they confiscated freely from the Latter-Day Saints. The Mormons could either fight or leave, so in July 1912, Stake President Junius Romney gave orders to abandon the land. Women and children left first. Within a week the men rode out. The Mormons crossed the border into a land considered foreign by the children. This proud and prosperous people had to accept charity in El Paso, as Congress appropriated $20,000 for their welfare. Fort Bliss furnished army tents. Over five hundred Mormons lived in a lumber shed on Magoffin Avenue. In August another group exited Mexico under a white flag, crossed the border near Hachita, New Mexico, and rode the Southern Pacific to El Paso for a tearful reunion with relatives and friends.[18]

Back in Juarez, hard times had befallen Orozco. *Federales* commanded by the hard-drinking, flint-eyed General Victoriano Huerta entered Juarez and sent the Rebels fleeing. Huerta's stature soared in Mexico City, so upon returning to the capital, he arranged to have Madero murdered, and himself appointed president.

In Coahuila the fussy and pompous Venustiano Carranza hesitated to challenge Huerta until he could organize opposition forces. The insurgent Chihuahua Governor Abraham González withheld recognition, but was not agile enough to avoid execution by Huerta's henchmen.[19] Over in Sonora, Governor José María Maytorena wavered, then took sick leave and slipped across the border into the United States. Ignacio Pesqueira, acting governor, appointed the military genius Alvaro Obregón as commander in chief of the army.[20] And in El Paso, Pancho Villa had recently escaped the execution rifles of Huerta and fled into Texas. For two months he granted interviews, explaining how Huerta had sentenced him to be shot for horse stealing, and how Madero had pardoned him. Now he was eating ice cream in the Elite Confectionary and puttering around town on a motorcycle. With the assassinations of Madero and González, Pancho Villa allied himself with Carranza and Obregón.[21] Together they formed the Constitutionalists, a political war party demanding the country's return to constitutional government.

Carranza appointed himself leader, and named Obregón and Villa his chief officers. Over in Sonora, Obregón chased Emilio Kosterlitzky to Nogales where the old *rurale* put his back to the border. After a twelve hour battle, 285 *rurales* and regulars straggled across the boundary and placed themselves under the protection of Captain Cornelius C. Smith of the United States Army.[22]

Both Federals and Insurgents retained adventurous Americans to bomb and harass each other's positions. The Douglas Flying Club owned a home-made, horse-drawn glider, one the organization outfitted with a motor and dubbed the "Douglas Bomber." A local hardware company furnished five pound bombs, lard pails stuffed with dynamite, scrap metal and chunks of concrete. Understandably, the bombs tumbled when dropped, an awkwardness corrected with four fins soldered on by a tinsmith. The pilots trained by pinning old bedsheets to the ground with rocks to represent railroads. Local hero Charles Ford flew twenty-five miles into Mexico on May 8, 1913, and reportedly blew up a strip of track. The results were not important. The significance lies in the bombing run being the first hostile flight ever to originate from United States soil. In late 1914, two Americans engaged in a dogfight over Naco, Arizona. Dean Ivan Lamb, flying for the Constitutionalists, and Phil Radar, working for Huerta, blazed away with six shooters at 12 o'clock high for twenty minutes with no damage done.[23]

Back in El Paso, several *vaqueros* rode south with Villa in April 1913, but with every stride the chieftain gained reinforcements until several thousand accompanied him. With shouts of *venganza* (vengeance) and *muerte* (death), Villa created the famed *Dorados* (golden ones), a mounted force of three hundred ferocious insurgents whose wild, slashing charges spread terror across the borderlands. By October, Villa's Division of the North, by some accounts ten thousand men, had battered Torreon into a smoldering hulk.

In spite of his potential power, however, Villa was but a loose cannon rolling around in a northern desert still largely controlled by Federal forces. From Torreon he swung north and attacked Chihuahua City, only to be severely mauled by government troops. From this low point, with two thousand men he slithered around the capital, captured a train, loaded his men and steamed north for 240 miles into the heart of a sleeping Ciudad Juarez. When the citizens awoke on November 15, 1913, they were in Rebel hands. As in Torreon, Villa's forces rounded up army officers and Federal supporters, marching them to the cemetery for execution.

Federals counterattacked ten days later and were decisively beaten a few miles outside of town. Villa occupied Chihuahua City on December 8, as government officers fled to Ojinaga. In early January 1914, Villa blitzed the garrison at Ojinaga too, and on the 10th, all resistance ceased.

The Presidio-Ojinaga gateway had now become the exit for fleeing Chihuahua since the railroad between the capital and El Paso had become too dangerous for travel. In December 1911, the richest refugee of all, Don Luís Terrazas, brought out his family, his peons, his friends and whoever wanted to go. Twenty wagons of wealth and personal belongings passed through Ojinaga. In El Paso he rented an entire floor of the Paso del Norte Hotel before moving into Senator A. B. Fall's mansion on Arizona Street.[24]

Meanwhile, thousands of panicked refugees and Federal soldiers crossed the Rio Grande and requested the protection and assistance of Major M. M. McNamee at Presidio. McNamee did not have sufficient quarters for his charges so he marched them in long caravans to the rail station at Marathon, Texas, and shipped them to El Paso. Fort Bliss officials could not allow them to run loose, so General Hugh L. Scott, commander of the Southern Military District, incarcerated them. For four months the army imprisoned between four and five thousand

Refugees streaming across Rio Grande from Ojinaja into Presidio, June 1917. (Harry Ransom Humanities Research Center, U.T. Austin)

Francisco Madero and friends at Madero headquarters, International Boundary Marker No. 1 at El Paso, April 1911. (Standing from left to right) Pancho Villa, Gustavo Madero (brother to Francisco), Francisco Madero, Sr., Giuseppe Garibaldi (Italian soldier of fortune), Federico Garza, Luis Blanco, Juan Sánchez Azcona, Alphonso Madero (brother of Francisco) (others unidentified). (Sitting) Venustiano Carranza (governor of Coahuila), Francisco Vásquez Gómez, Francisco I. Madero, Abraham González (governor of Chihuahua), José María Maytorena (governor of Sonora), Alberto Fuentes (governor of Aguascalientes), and Pascual Orozco. (Harry Ransom Humanities Research Center, U.T. Austin)

Mexicans — men, women and children, civilians and military. Barbed wire surrounded the compounds, armed guards patrolled the perimeters. In May 1914, Scott relocated most to Fort Wingate, New Mexico, and from there gradually repatriated them to Mexico.[25]

Carranza, Obregón and Villa advanced on the capital. By April, Villa had recaptured Torreon, and in late June subdued Zacatecas. President Victoriano Huerta fled into Spanish exile on July 15, 1914.

Carranza and Obregón occupied Mexico City in August, with Villa and Zapata noticeably absent from the celebration. Carranza and Villa had fallen out due to a power struggle, although Obregón, while siding with Carranza, tried to act as peace-maker. In disgust, Villa returned to Juarez, where in August 1914, General John J. Pershing greeted him on the El Paso-Juarez international bridge and provided a personally conducted tour of Fort Bliss. A reception followed in Quarters No. 1, today's Pershing House.

By now Governor José Maytorena had returned to Sonora from the United States, and found his state run by the austere and puritanical schoolteacher, General Elías Calles, who had the support of Carranza and Obregón. Since Maytorena had an ally in Villa, the governor raised a predominately Yaqui fighting force and shoved Calles back against the American boundary. By August of 1914, Maytorena had taken Nogales, Sonora and had trapped Calles in the Mexican border town of Naco.[26]

To halt the fighting, Obregón offered to restrain Calles if Villa would call off Maytorena. However, since Villa's man was winning, and Villa had more to lose by a peaceful solution, Obregón upped the ante by agreeing to a convention of Mexican delegates in Aguascalientes. That conference would determine the next Mexican president. The two leaders agreed and took a train out of El Paso for Naco, Arizona, where they jointly conferred with Maytorena and Calles. When the negotiations ended, the mercurial Maytorena retreated to the Sonoran interior and sulked, while Calles was briefly replaced by the forty-year-old General Benjamin Hill, who would eventually become a Mexican secretary of war before dying of cancer.[27]

Villa, Obregón and Carranza next turned to the peace convention in Aguascalientes, and it failed. The convention ordered Carranza to withdraw as president, and when he refused, the delegates authorized Villa to remove him. Villa and Zapata entered Mexico City in early December, and found Carranza and Obregón gone.

Villa installed the weak Eulalio Gutiérrez as president, but kept real authority for himself. Even so, while the wily Villa understood cow camp politics, he never grasped economics and the myriad necessities essential for complex government. Furthermore, he lost bloody battles to Obregón at Puebla, Leon, Aguascalientes and Zacatecas. Obregón decimated the proud Division of the North. Villa could not even capture Matamoros. Slowly he retreated north into Chihuahua, a stronghold where Obregón could contain but could not defeat him.

Over in Spain, Victoriano Huerta had grown restless in exile. He and his old enemy Pascual Orozco plotted a counter-revolutionary movement. Orozco had been staging raids against the federal government that were more annoying than threatening. With Huerta as titular head of his struggle for country-wide supremacy, however, a national coalition could be organized. Huerta liked the reasoning, so he visited the United States for a "sight seeing trip," and met Orozco in Newman, Texas, barely twenty miles north of El Paso. As the two prepared to depart on horseback for the border, American agents arrested them for violating the neutrality laws. Within hours, Orozco escaped from house confinement in El Paso. Huerta was subsequently moved to Fort Bliss where he drank heavily. His health deteriorated, and the Army released him to doctors in El Paso. Huerta died of cirrhosis on January 13, 1916.[28]

Orozco had an even shorter period of life. Rangers, ranchers and cavalry shot him to death near Sierra Blanca, Texas, eighty miles east of El Paso and twenty miles north of the Rio Grande. The bodies of Orozco and Huerta were placed in a vault in El Paso's Concordia Cemetery. Orozco was later declared a hero of the revolution, and his body returned to Mexican soil. Mexico considered Huerta a traitor to the revolution, and his remains were ignored. During the 1950s, his body was moved to El Paso's Evergreen Cemetery.[29]

Sonora became a pivotal state due to its relationship with the American border and its location as the western neighbor of Chihuahua. While Carranza, Villa and Obregón were distracted with fighting in the south, General Hill tried expanding his perimeters and was challenged by Maytorena. The governor shoved Hill back into Naco, and with the two opposing armies calling themselves *Villistas* and *Carranzistas*, they fought for control of the village. Meanwhile, thirty miles to the east and opposite the border town of Douglas, Arizona, Calles had fortified Agua Prieta.[30]

Americans shored up their side of the line with the black 9th and 10th Cavalry, better known as the Buffalo Soldiers, plus infantry and artillery. Railroad cars acted as a border buffer, and the steel sides deflected a few stray bullets. Nevertheless, two troopers and three civilians fell from indiscriminate Mexican shooting. Yet, the American army never moved even when a 250 bed Red Cross hospital, placed on Arizona soil primarily for the benefit of the *Carranzistas*, was repeatedly shelled by Maytorena loyalists.[31]

Washington sent General Hugh L. Scott, the chubby chief of staff, to the border and Scott offered a five-part armistice calling for a Carranza port of entry at Agua Prieta, and a Maytorena port of entry at Nogales. Naco would be neutral. Both sides would remain in position, and not shell any American communities across the line.[32] The terms appealed to Hill and Calles, primarily because they were losing. Maytorena refused to sign because he had the military advantage.

Since Scott had orders not to cross the border, the general found it vexing to negotiate through intermediaries. Even after enticing Maytorena to Osborne, Arizona, the session ended with Scott unable to get any commitments. Therefore the general turned to Villa as the only third party capable of influencing Maytorena.

Six months later, on January 7, 1915, Villa met with Scott on the international bridge at El Paso, and they moved off to argue for two hours inside a nearby hall. Villa asked why Scott would settle for such a shaky peace along the Arizona border, when Pancho could quickly stabilize the boundary with a hurricane raid on Agua Prieta. Scott replied that he wanted less, not more, fighting, and so Villa reluctantly asked Maytorena to sign.[33]

A jubilant Scott returned to Naco, and an aide hand-carried Villa's order to the governor. Although it reduced Maytorena to tears, he signed. The peace lasted nearly six months until Maytorena sent customs collectors to Naco. A Calles unit invaded Naco in retaliation, killed several Maytorena civil servants and drove the rest into the United States. Calles attacked Nogales, only to be beaten back to Naco and then to Agua Prieta. Pancho Villa telegraphed Scott, complaining that *Carranzistas* had increased the Agua Prieta garrison from eight hundred to almost three thousand. Obviously the armistice was falling apart, and over in Chihuahua, Villa evaluated his options.[34]

18

The Punitive Expedition

WITHIN ONE YEAR Villa had moved from being an acknowledged spokesman for Mexico to being a rebel confined in Chihuahua. His army was in tatters, beaten and disillusioned, rife with desertions. Nevertheless, his immediate problem was not the forces of Carranza and Obregón, but American public opinion. The United States had not yet recognized the government of Mexico, and Villa wanted consideration. However, Villa recognized that the Americans would never pay homage to a bandit chieftain controlling but a small portion of the country. If Villa did not soon re-establish himself as a contender for Mexican national leadership, President Woodrow Wilson might opt for Carranza. To expand his political horizons therefore, Villa needed to govern more than just Chihuahua. So he decided to attack Sonora.[1]

An invasion should have minimal risks. Sonoran Governor José María Maytorena was sympathetic to Villa, as were insurgents who comprised most of Maytorena's army, Indians who occupied the state capital of Hermosillo, plus the seaport of Guaymas. General Plutarco Elías Calles and his three thousand men at Agua Prieta were the only real opposition.

Villa rebuilt his army to twelve thousand men (by some accounts a little less than ten thousand, but still adequate), and by mid-October 1915, he was ready. First he removed all *soldaderas* (wives and camp followers), as their presence would deplete the meager supplies of food and water. In small contingents the army filtered out of the Casas Grandes staging area and crossed Pulpit Pass, forty miles south of the New Mexico line. The weather was brisk but comfortable, and although a cannon or two plunged into *arroyos*, the trek through the high Sierra Madres involved trudging up a steep incline rather than scaling rugged mountain cliffs. However, due to a drought, Villa's cattle herds were butchered before necessary because they consumed too much water. The troops entered Sonora dehydrated and weak.

Villa's primary objective was Agua Prieta, the only significant Federal stronghold in Sonora. However, two events derailed the Villa dream of national glory. He had barely crossed Pulpit Pass when Woodrow Wilson recognized Carranza on October 19 as president of Mexico. Those in violent opposition to Carranza would therefore be considered outlaws by Washington, and this included Pancho Villa.

The second event happened at Agua Prieta. President Wilson authorized its reinforcement by Mexican troops shipped by rail from Eagle Pass, Texas to Douglas, Arizona. Calles now had six thousand soldiers, munitions for a modern war, and supplies still arriving.[2]

Villa engaged Agua Prieta on November 1 and, after a day of sparring, ordered a night assault. Waves of insurgents swarmed across open ground after midnight, and were caught in searchlights, trapped in minefields and slaughtered. After two days, Villa broke off and occupied the undefended Naco where he reacted with bitterness toward Americans. Doctors Rembert H. Thigpen and Charles H. Miller, company surgeons of the American-owned Cananea Consolidated Copper Company, left Bisbee, Arizona to treat the Mexican wounded, and were captured by Villa. The general called them spies, and for the next three mornings awoke them at sunrise with firing squads, the executions always being countermanded as the rifles were cocking. The mining company took the hint, recognizing Villa's subtle way of requesting ransom. Twenty-five thousand dollars in gold changed saddle bags. The copper firm also furnished several tons of food, 1,500 steers and 175 horses.[3]

In the meantime, another army threatened Villa's flank. General Manuel M. Diéguez, a former hard-rock miner, led a Federal force up the coast from Sinaloa, captured Guaymas and Hermosillo, and sent

the Yaquis fleeing. Since Villa could not dislodge Calles from Agua
Prieta, he moved south to engage Diéguez. The main clash came at
Hermosillo, and again Villa sent his men into a slaughterhouse.[4]

By the end of November, a battered Villa aimlessly wandered central Sonora, his ragged, demoralized army reduced by desertion, starvation and death. American agents in Mexico predicted he would surrender Chihuahua to Obregón, and accept Secretary of State William
Jennings Bryan's offer of refuge north of the international border.[5]

But entering the United States as an exile did not interest Villa who
was now a marauder frantically twisting and turning, seeking to escape
back to Chihuahua. His meandering, erratic route led him through the
tiny mining village of La Colorado where he murdered sixteen Chinese
and looted the town. Next, he headed east toward the Rio Moctezuma
and its confluence with the Rio Yaqui. The cannons detoured around
the Agua Verde Mountains by way of San Pedro de la Cueva, approximately two hundred miles south of the American border and an insignificant village even by Sonora standards. Here Villa ordered one of
the cruelest massacres of the revolution.[6]

When the villagers saw horsemen approaching on December 1,
1915, they assumed bandits and ambushed the insurgents. After the
skirmish ended, the residents apologized, saying they mistook Villa's
men for local raiders. Chihuahua officers understood and advised their
commander against reprisals. Villa was not forgiving.

The general ordered every resident executed, then changed the command to include just the men. Firing squads began their awful work at
sunrise, December 2. Two hours later, seventy-seven male residents
lay in stacks. The dead included a priest whom Villa personally shot.[7]

Insurgents then looted and burned the village, abandoned their cannon and crossed the Sierra Madre into Chihuahua. Behind them in
Sonora they left thousands of their own dead, and hundreds of wailing
civilians.

Villa entered Chihuahua nursing revenge, humiliation, hatred and
despair, reacting like a manic-depressive. He raged, sulked, threatened
and wept, blaming the Americans as much as Carranza for his misfortunes. He wired Emiliano Zapata and suggested a joint attack on the
United States.[8]

North of the border, public opinion denounced Villa not so much
for the massacre of San Pedro de la Cueva, the news of which was

slow in leaking out, but for other brutal crimes. In January 1916, *Villistas* summarily shot sixteen American mining engineers at Santa Ysabel, Chihuahua, and El Pasoans reacted with fury. They stormed from the saloons, beating everybody of Mexican extraction on the streets. Civilian and Fort Bliss police worked hours to restore order.

Villa may or may not have been at Santa Ysabel, and may or may not have ordered the executions, but his people were there. His subordinates fired the shots.

Perhaps the same was also true at Columbus, New Mexico. Three or four hundred of his riders milled at Casas Grandes, their numbers perhaps indicative of Villa's slipping prestige even in Chihuahua. During former campaigns he commanded thousands, but all he could gather now was a ragtag assortment of undisciplined rabble. Pancho Villa was a bandit again.

With rumors rife that he planned to seek political refuge in the United States, and other stories indicating that he intended to strike somewhere along the border, Pancho Villa moved north. For several days he hovered near Las Palomas, alongside New Mexico. On the night of March 9, 1916, his raiders spurred into the sleeping village of Columbus, killing innocent civilians and burning much of the town. The reasons why are still not clear. Some say a Columbus merchant had cheated him, but in his long and colorful career, Villa must have been cheated by numerous people. Such betrayals went with the territory.

A fanciful story accused the American government of paying Villa to attack, as the Yankees needed an excuse to train and toughen up their troops by invading Mexico. The truth is likely simple and dull. Villa wasn't thinking well, the American government had abandoned him, the press had turned on him, and he probably never expected any uproar from an attack on an insignificant village. Border raids had always been a fact of life along the international line. Governments filed a few perfunctory complaints, and turned to important matters.[9]

Villa's luck did not change during the attack. It was still bad. Caught by surprise, the American military recovered quickly. Sixty to seventy-five *Villistas* who rode into town did not ride out. Furthermore, in a little known event, eleven of the riders were captured, and six publicly hanged in Deming three months later.[10]

Major Frank Tompkins and thirty-two cavalrymen pursued the raiders into Mexico. They fought a brief battle two hundred yards south of the line, kept up the pursuit for miles and killed nearly a hundred *Villistas*. By some estimates, the strike on Columbus had cost Villa between one-quarter and one-half of his entire force.

On the following day, as Carranza futilely ordered his northern armies to intercept Villa, Washington decided to intervene. It ordered General Frederick Funston, famous for capturing guerrillas in the Philippines, and now commander of the Southern Department, to dispatch troops across the international boundary. General John J. Pershing, commander at Fort Bliss, would lead the charge.[11]

By the 14th, Pershing had organized his Punitive Expedition, and during the early morning hours of the 15th, two regiments of cavalry and a battery of artillery crossed the boundary from Culberson's Ranch near the southwestern corner of New Mexico. The remaining soldiers entered Mexico at Columbus. They found Las Palomas practically empty.

Nearly eleven thousand troops invaded Mexico. Only a hundred thousand comprised the entire United States Army, and most were already distributed along the two thousand mile border.

The Mexico of 1916 was politically bankrupt, presided over by the pompous and opportunistic President Venustiano Carranza who had neither full military nor political control of his country. Pancho Villa had tweaked the nose of Uncle Sam, and overnight changed from a common bandit into a national hero. Carranza could do nothing more imaginative than play the same game. No one could be more anti-American than he. As the defender of Mexican sovereignty, Carranza made it impossible for Americans to use trains or enter large towns. Repeatedly he stridently warned Pershing to go home. When a small column of the 13th Cavalry shot its way out of the Parral outskirts, killing several civilians, Mexican demands accelerated for a United States withdrawal.[12]

Somehow Wilson never quite understood the Mexican temperament. Washington considered the issues logical. The Americans were risking lives and resources to chase down a bandit, to do a job Mexico could not do for itself. Washington did not expect repayment for expenses, but it did expect a sense of gratitude. With the American army charging around in Chihuahua, Secretary of State Robert Lansing suggested a Mexican conference to discuss mutual misunderstandings and he asked generals Scott and Funston to meet with Obregón. The discussions took place mostly in Juarez, but while they were pleasant and spirited, they were also unproductive. The Americans explained their rationales and purposes, and then shifted to railroad problems and a lack of coordination between American and Mexican military units. Obregón refused to discuss anything other than a foreign withdrawal, although he showed flexibility on May 2 by requesting a secret meeting with Scott in the Paso del Norte Hotel in El Paso. It required twelve hours to get an agreement. The Americans would gradually withdraw, and Mexico would intensify its efforts to capture Villa. However, Carranza refused to ratify the document unless Washington set a specific date for removing troops. This Wilson refused to do, and so the conference ended. As Funston and Scott said later, "We evidently came to discuss one question, Obregón another."[13]

For the next two months the Punitive Expedition harried Villa across Chihuahua while sullen Mexican Federals observed American movements. The tense situation worsened with a telegram from General Jacinto B. Treviño warning Pershing that the Yankees could not move in any direction except north. "I communicate this to you," the message read, because you "will be attacked by the Mexican forces if these instructions are not heeded."

Pershing acknowledged the threat, but said Washington had placed no restrictions upon him. "I shall therefore use my own judgment as to when and in what direction I shall move," he replied, and if you assault "any of my columns the responsibility for the consequences will lie with the Mexican government."[14]

Within hours of this exchange, the Battle of Carrizal took place. Nearly a hundred Mexican and United States soldiers lost their lives, as did each commanding officer. Captured Americans were imprisoned in Chihuahua City and released in El Paso a few days later.

On June 18, President Wilson ordered the entire National Guard into active duty on the Mexican border. By July's end, over 100,000 men had detrained at the four border districts: Brownsville, San Antonio, El Paso, Texas and Douglas, Arizona. Those in Douglas battled dust storms, and in San Antonio and Brownsville, they waded through quagmires caused by a hurricane. Nearly forty thousand guardsmen entered El Paso, and their experiences were typical. Twenty-five thousand marched during a massive Flag Day parade. Squads patrolled the Rio Grande for fifty miles from the smelter to Fort Hancock. El Paso's Camp Cotton arose from a sand-flat two miles east of downtown, becoming a sprawling Georgia tent area where a Michigan band played

"Marching Through Georgia." Outraged Southern boys boiled from their tents, and bloody noses, bashed heads and broken knuckles kept the doctors busy for hours. From that time on, bands never played tunes calculated to offend regional sensibilities.

The Americans anticipated an expedition into Mexico as early as April 1914 when a grim Black Jack Pershing took command at Fort Bliss and turned it from an infantry station into the nation's largest cavalry post. Pershing placed his medical corps at the disposal of Mayor Tom Lea, and with the blessings of the city Board of Health, soldiers swept through the narrow streets of *Chihuahuita*, "Little Chihuahua," an area in south El Paso where Mexican immigrants from Chihuahua first settled upon arriving in El Paso. The Army demolished at least 150 adobe shacks, hosed out the trash, removed dead animals and burned the refuse. Such high-handed actions were not considered social and cultural sins in those days.

Guardsmen could have reinforced Pershing, but to their chagrin and disappointment, none of the National Guard entered Mexico. These part-time soldiers never participated in military engagements. Harry Lindauer of Company G in the Wisconsin Guard spoke of their hopes:

> If you want to be a soldier, just come along with me;
> We're going down to Mexico to join the jubilee.
> We'll wipe them off the Border, sweep them off the sea;
> If you want to be a soldier, just come along with me.[15]

Even when fighting occurred near the boundary, the regular army took charge as it did at Glenn Spring, Texas, a tiny community presently within the Big Bend National Park area, and twenty miles north of the Rio Grande. Approximately fifty Mexican-Americans worked in a crude wax factory, and these formed the nucleus of a small settlement. A general store served everyone's needs.

Ten troopers of the 14th Cavalry guarded the village and patrolled the river. At about eleven P.M. on May 4, as two soldiers relaxed in a tent, and seven others slept in an adobe shack, Mexican raiders rode through. A fusillade pinned down the troopers as a fire started on the thatched roof, and three soldiers were shot as they dashed out. One had his clothes afire when he cleared the door. The other four sprinted into the night nursing wounds and blisters. None of the attackers were slain or captured. The Mexican-American community was unharmed.

Between seventy-five and two hundred raiders looted the village store before pausing at Boquillas, where a small group kidnapped five American civilians, forced them into a truck, and crossed the border. As Americans were the only ones who could drive, the Anglos faked a mechanical breakdown and convinced the outlaws to go for water. When the main body left, the captives overpowered three guards and drove back to Texas with the prisoners. According to one account, the captured bandits received life sentences at Huntsville.[16]

Colonel Frederick William Sibley galloped out of Fort Clark with two troops of cavalry and one machine gun platoon. After crossing the international border, he furiously pursued the bandits for forty to sixty miles through the Sierra del Carmen Mountains west of the Coahuila-Chihuahua border. However, General Funston orderd the unit home on May 26, so Sibley terminated his invasion.[17]

The Punitive Expedition had meanwhile boxed itself into a military dilemma. Washington had been patient for years as Mexican brigands and armies accidentally and intentionally killed American citizens and destroyed American property along the border. The United States had exercised self restraint while waiting for Mexico to resolve its internal troubles and restore stability. When Funston and Scott said the Americans wanted to discuss one question at the Juarez meeting, and the Mexicans another, the two generals were referring to withdrawal vs. border security. Mexico wanted the Americans out before other issues were discussed. The Americans said they would like to withdraw, but they wanted assurances of no more Columbus raids. They wanted a relatively tranquil border.

To reach a consensus, Wilson and Carranza appointed a Joint Commission to meet at the Biltmore Hotel in New York City on September 4, 1916. By now the German Kaiser had become far more important than Pancho Villa.

Pershing's force had gone into quarters at Colonia Dublan, north of Casas Grandes, eighty miles south of the border, and did little more than sit on their hands. It had given up even the pretense of chasing Villa, and was pulling guard duty for the Mormon colonies. Boxing dispelled the boredom, as did "The Blue Goose,"[18] an official brothel operating inside the military compound. Otherwise, the troopers cursed the sand and monotony. A printable version of "Tipperary" expressed feelings around the Dublan campfires.

We started to the border and we charged to Parral,
We were after Pancho Villa and Lopez his old pal;
Our horses were starved and dying;
We lived on parched corn.
Oh, it's damn hard living in Chihuahua,
Where Villa was born.[19]

Although the Biltmore talks continued until early January 1917, and broke off without much accomplished, the Americans were preparing to leave. After burning everything including the Blue Goose, the troopers abandoned the charred ruins and marched north on January 29, 1917. With them straggled three refugee groups: Mormons, Mexicans and Chinese. The Mormons had furnished guide service, helped search for Villa, and sold supplies to the army. Great numbers of Mexicans had also collaborated by building roads, providing information, hauling equipment and staffing the Blue Goose. As for the Chinese, Villa in particular had slaughtered them wherever found, and since they had cooked and washed for the Americans, and sought Pershing's military protection, they no longer had a future south of the border.

The withdrawal column extended five dusty miles and included 10,690 soldiers, 2,030 Mexicans, 197 Mormons, 533 Chinese, thousands of animals, and over 300 wagons, trucks, private cars. The weary trek required five days to reach Columbus where Red Cross facilities were waiting. Most of the Mormons left quickly, having relatives to care for them. The Mexicans stayed only a week or so. As for the Chinese, by law they could not even enter the country, and yet there they were, throwing themselves on the mercy of what they hoped would be a benevolent government. It took years for their formal admittance into the United States, and in the meantime Funston and Pershing found jobs for them with the Army.[20]

19

Politics and Peace

MOST AMERICANS assume Pershing's Punitive Expedition ended the border disturbances, but the border remained in constant turmoil, especially at Juarez. Other Mexican border towns sometimes were assaulted, but they were generally so poor, so remote, and so small that their possession was as much a liability as a victory.

Occupying and governing Juarez gave bandits a certain legitimacy, and tended to elevate their status to revolutionaries. In June 1919, Villa had that intention once again in mind. For the last few months he had shot up the interior of Chihuahua, overrunning villages and mining properties while drawing ever closer to Juarez.

The lackadaisical fighter, General Francisco González, defended Juarez from the seclusion of Fort Hidalgo, a half-mile southwest of town. A short distance away, Villa and his brilliant artillery tactician, Felipe Angeles, camped with four thousand men while a nephew of Angeles smuggled ammunition from the *Stand Bueno Bueno* (the Very Good Taxi Stand) in El Paso.[1]

Anticipating the battle might extend across the border, Brigadier General James B. Erwin, commander of the El Paso Military District, reinforced five miles of the river between Ysleta and El Paso with troops. Colonel Selah R. H. "Tommy" Tompkins, the hard-drinking, pink-whiskered, legendary cussing veteran of the 7th Cavalry assumed responsibility for the 2nd Cavalry Brigade. Artillery and black infantrymen took up station near the international bridges.

Villa attacked Juarez on June 14, and within hours controlled the race track and much of the downtown. On the following night, a fusillade struck a command post near the center of El Paso. One private fell dead, another wounded. A furious General Erwin ordered cannon near the intersection of El Paso and 2nd (Paisano) streets to fire, and sixty-four rounds blew holes in the bull ring and race track. The barrage also covered the 24th Infantry, by now double-timing across the Santa Fe Street Bridge. America's black soldiers drove Villa from downtown Juarez, as well as the race track. Some infantry moved south along the river road to intercept fleeing Rebels.

A few miles east of El Paso, Colonel Tommy Tompkins led units of the 7th, 5th and 2nd Cavalry across the Rio Grande. Moving upstream by night, they were mistakenly attacked by the 24th Infantry, although neither side suffered casualties. By now the cavalry had been on alert for two sleepless nights. Although three days' rations had been prepared, the quartermaster had forgotten to include water. The troopers were weary, dirty, suffering from thirst, sleeping in the saddle and unable to identify an enemy. Tompkins ordered a return to the Texas side. However, on the way home, a Mexican informer pinpointed Pancho Villa's location in Zaragoza, ten miles east of Juarez. Tompkins drove them hard, and by 9 A.M. the next morning, June 15, with a relentless sun beating down, the army spotted the Rebels a mile or so distant across an open field. With artillery providing cover, Tompkins aligned his units. The bugles sounded, the horses lunged forward at a canter, changed to a gallop, and the last great cavalry charge in American history was a reality with "Pink Whiskers" Tompkins leading the way.

The charge was momentous in its sweep, beautiful in its perfection, historical in its final grandeur. Then the line collided with an irrigation ditch, and the horses and leading troopers disappeared, sprawling headlong into the water and muck. The remaining cavalry reined up, dismounted and opened fire, sending Villistas scattering. Some units found a bridge, crossed it and pursued the Rebels for fifteen miles. They caught nobody but exhausted so many horses that forty had to be shot on the following day.

The final battle was over. Americans crossed back into El Paso on an engineer-built pontoon bridge after recovering a caisson. They lost one man, and an unspecified number of horses.[2]

Pancho Villa retired to a ranch near Parral shortly after this episode, and was assassinated in 1923. Tommy Tompkins, still as profane as ever, wrote poetry and retired in 1927 after over forty years in the Army. He died of stomach cancer at Fort Sam Houston in 1939, and is buried in San Antonio.[3]

Along the rest of the two thousand mile border with Mexico, sky patrols went into effect. Such a strategy appealed to Brigadier General William "Billy" Mitchell, assistant chief of the air service and director of Military Aeronautics. He reassigned the 12th, 96th and 104th Aero Squadrons to Fort Bliss, and designated them the 1st Bombardment Group. However, since no bombs were carried, he changed the name to the 1st Surveillance Group, or in more popular parlance, the "Border Air Patrol." Twelve DH4 bombers comprised the fleet.[4]

Stacy C. Hinkle described his exciting adventures as a pilot in two engaging monographs, *Wings and Saddles* and *Wings Over the Border*. He told of outlaw sightings, of unpredictable weather, of fiery crashes, of misdirections and unbelievable courage. Hinkle called the DH4 a "Flaming Coffin," and said the oil had a tendency to burn out and freeze the Liberty engine. The wireless reached twenty-five miles, but seldom operated. And while messages could be dropped to troops, the soldiers could not reply except with tediously prepared signals, few of which the pilot had time to read.

A twin-engine blimp comprised the "Lighter than Air Company." However, the hangar entrance should have faced the prevailing westerly winds. Instead, it pointed north. Gusts knocked the gas bag sideways when it entered or left. As a result, the blimp flew only a few "gee whiz" flights over El Paso, and never went on patrol.

With the Fort Bliss Flying Field as headquarters, westbound reconnaissance flights turned around at Douglas, Arizona. To the east, pilots followed the Rio Grande to Presidio, then headed north and spent the night at Marfa. On the following day, the craft retraced its route, or flew to Sanderson and then returned to Bliss by following the Rio Grande home from the Big Bend country. During one of these trips, Lieutenant Harold G. Peterson, the pilot, and Paul H. Davis, the observer gunner, left Marfa for Fort Bliss on August 10, 1919, flying south into Mexico from Presidio after mistaking the Rio Conchos for the Rio Grande. (The Conchos usually had more water in it, and although a tributary to the Rio Grande, it was actually the dominant stream in this area.) Along the way, all four connecting-rod bearings burned out. Both occupants survived the crash, and thinking they were in Texas, sought help. Their rescuers were Mexican bandits, and the leader, Jesús Rentería, demanded $15,000 ransom.

While Washington dallied, Big Bend ranchers raised the money and gave it to Captain Leonard F. Matlack, commander of Troop K, 8th Cavalry at Candelaria, Texas. Matlack went alone into Mexico, and escaped with the prisoners and half the cash. As the three splashed north across the Rio Grande, the 5th and 8th Cavalry slashed south on a punitive expedition. In the confusion, they captured the wrong bandits, and an international furor arose when civilian scouts executed the prisoners. The Army court-martialed Major James P. Yancey, the commanding officer.[5]

As cavalry patrols thrashed through the Mexican brush, the Border Air Patrol circled over Mexico, and Lieutenant Frank S. Estill buzzed three horsemen who fired at him. Estill shot back with two synchronized Marlin machine guns, but missed the targets. The rear gunner, Lieutenant Russell H. Cooper, fired a burst and killed the bandit chieftain, Jesús Rentería.[6]

Mexico protested in 1919 that border aircraft flew unauthorized missions over Chihuahua City, a remarkable feat considering that the capital was two hundred miles south of the border. Mexico also complained of American pilots violating air space over Nogales, Sonora, and firing machine gun bursts. No one was injured.[7]

In mid 1921, several pilots joined Billy Mitchell in demonstrating the impact of air power on German battleships. The Patrol went out of business, and the Fort Bliss Air Terminal became Biggs Field — a refueling stop for cross-country flights.

By the late 1920s, however, United States airplanes returned to the Mexican border in a dramatic response to outbursts of revolution, plus renewed Mexican outlaw forays across the Rio Grande. Since the Army needed an airfield in the Big Bend (Fort Bliss was too distant), civilians scraped out pasture runways on the Johnson Ranch. Once again Uncle Sam swept the border, seeking marauders and refugees, even searching for German spies during World War II.

Meanwhile, Mexican Federals and Insurgents hired American flying mercenaries, although the Insurgents had a tougher time of it due to an American embargo on modern Corsairs. Weapons could be smuggled into Mexico from the United States, but they could not be legally sold. Nevertheless, several American soldiers of fortune sold their talents to the Rebel cause, climbed into the cockpits of whatever would fly, and called themselves the "Yankee Doodle Escadrille." Some of them earned $1,250 a week, plus $600 per mission. While Federal pilots flew modern planes, Americans flying for the Rebel cause had to settle for home-made, back-yard stuff, or what they could steal. While the Federals fired synchronized bullets through the propeller, the insurgents carried rifles and six-shooters. The Federals dropped up-to-date bombs; the Insurgents cradled pipe explosives between their knees, lit the fuse with a cigar and prayed the device did not detonate prematurely.[8]

The roots of Mexico's last (serious) revolt are intertwined with the fall of the Carranza regime in 1920 and the ascension of Alvaro Obregón as president. Obregón was a product of the American borderlands, a *caudillo* (military president or chieftain) known for his diplomatic and military prowess. If he did not take his country to soaring heights, he at least gave it a relatively sound administration. In line with con-stitutional mandates, Obregón stepped aside in 1924 and supported his fellow Sonoran, Plutarco Elías Calles, as president. In spite of good-will professions, neither man liked the other, and Obregón expected Calles to stumble politically due to clashes with the Catholic hierarchy. But Calles survived, became a fine administrator, resumed payments on the foreign debt, started numerous irrigation projects and founded the Bank of Mexico.[9]

However, one term followed by political oblivion never suited the outsized egos of either man. Obregón wanted national prominence again; Calles sought to name his personal successor, a system still used by Mexico. Obregón's friends tinkered with the constitution's fragile wording until it permitted his re-election after an intervening term. This put Calles at a disadvantage, as his hand-picked replacement would have no chance against the popular revolutionary hero, Obregón. Calles therefore did not protest when two army generals, Arnulfo R. Gómez and Francisco R. Serrano, campaigned as Calles successors. When neither showed any grass roots ability, they plotted a revolt as poorly planned as their political crusade. Both men were shot. Gómez was executed by a rising young general, and prominent ladies' man, José Gonzalo Escobar.[10]

Obregón won the election only to be assassinated two weeks later. Calles brilliantly kept the government functioning during the interlude, and although suspicion existed of his complicity in the murder, no evidence surfaced. Meanwhile, he mollified the *Obregonistas*, united the country and opposed the steady procession of generals to the presidency. Carefully he divided and conquered, calling for peace and economic prosperity, and imploring the military to be patient. The generals fumed, but permitted Calles to name Emilio Portes Gil as interim president. The new chief executive was a borderlands attorney and former governor of Tamaulipas.

Calles asked Washington to refrain from selling munitions to Insurgents, and at the same time ordered nine Corsairs equipped with machine guns and bombs. He improved the military system, rewarding generals considered loyal, increasing the pay and allotments of private soldiers. Calles recognized two preeminent sources of political strength: the presidency and the military. For the second highest office in the land, he picked General Joaquin Amaro as secretary of war. However, Amaro stepped aside due to an eye injury, and Calles assumed the position. His cold but steady hand guided the country's military destiny during the next few months.

When José Gonzalo Escobar was bypassed for secretary of war, he assumed supreme command of a consortium of dissatisfied generals on March 3, 1929. The revolution engulfed Chihuahua and Governor Marcelo Caraveo rallied the Insurgents. Only the Juarez garrison commander, General Manuel Limón, remained loyal to the government, but even he wavered until Calles sent General Matías Ramos to steady the Limón nerve.[11]

Caraveo assigned General Miguel Valle to capture Juarez, and as the two armies faced off, General George Van Horn Moseley at Fort Bliss asked Washington for permission to deploy "troops into Mexican territory if necessary." Heavy field artillery and armored cars already nuzzled the international bridges. In response, the War Department assigned Major General William Lassiter to evaluate the situation, and he advised restraint, cautioning Moseley that it "may be possible by artillery fire to drive back the [Rebels] . . . and thus avoid crossing the border." Lassiter otherwise gave Moseley authority to "accomplish the mission . . . regardless of the boundary line."[12]

Moseley alerted Caraveo and Valle that Fort Bliss would take "necessary action for the protection" of El Paso. The governor responded that as Federal troops were incapable of defending the city, pretensions in that regard would "make them exclusively responsible for difficulties with the United States."[13]

Valle prepared to attack, and the sixth battle for Juarez since 1911 commenced on a Friday morning, March 8, 1929. Thousands of Americans clustered on buildings, river levees and railroad cars to watch. The *Literary Digest* called El Paso "the only section of the United States trained to appreciate warfare as a neighborhood spectacle."[14]

General Ramos did not defend Juarez from the southern edge, but from the center of town where he challenged the Rebels to come and get him. The Insurgents promptly drove him to the Rio Grande opposite El Paso. Shots rained into Texas, wounding Luís Chavez, age six, and killing Lydia Rodarte, age two. Fifteen floors of the First National Bank Building drew fire, and employees evacuated to the basement. With southwesterners calling for protection, General Lassiter conferred in Juarez with Ramos and Valle, finally walking both leaders to the Mexican side of the Santa Fe Street Bridge where Ramos accepted refuge in the United States after telephoning Mexico City from El Paso and clearing the arrangement with Calles. The call was made, and shortly after noon, Limón and Ramos, their staff, over three hundred troops (180 regulars, 123 civilian and civil service employees), families, baggage, horses and some motorcars, crossed the international bridge, checked with immigration and customs, surrendered their weapons and transferred by truck to Fort Bliss.[15]

Juarez was the only significant success of the Escobar Revolt. The armies of Calles swept north within a month to overrun Durango, Torreon and Jimenez. Since the United States embargo deprived Escobar of substantial military supplies, the press claimed his disgruntled generals succumbed to the "$50,000 cannon ball," a bribe whereby the Mexican government purchased a rebel commander for $50,000 and amnesty.[16]

Escobar and Caraveo abandoned Juarez and fled to Sonora, only to be outflanked by Ramos soldiers shipped out of Fort Bliss by the Southern Pacific and sent to Arizona. Meanwhile, the Calles forces surged into Sonora, making extensive use of air raids. Federal bombs fell on rebel trains and disrupted troop concentrations along the border. The government accidently dropped a bomb through the roof of the American vice-consul in Ciudad Obregon, but it failed to explode and no one was injured.[17]

The Rebels purchased airplanes when possible but captured them when the opportunity presented itself. In Juarez, they snatched two Federal Stinson Detroiter models, along with the pilots. After repainting the planes, the insurgents apparently believed they had talked the pilots into changing sides. Lieutenants Antonio Cardenas and Arturo Jiménez took off to bomb their own base, but deftly flew the craft across the border and landed at Fort Bliss. The American government released the pilots and turned the airplanes over to the Federal commander at Juarez.[18]

The revolutionaries had no trained pilots, anyway, so they hired American mercenaries. The Federals once lost an airplane, the evidence being unclear if it was shot down in a dogfight, hit by ground fire, or simply ran out of gas. The American pilots also mis-identified the international border, and twice bombed Naco, Arizona, when they were supposed to be striking Naco, Sonora. The bombs were contact-fused artillery shells fitted with tail fins, and were supposed to be hitting the railroad yard in Sonora. The explosives damaged business houses and slightly injured Harry Baker from Alliance, Ohio. Revolutionaries apologized to Washington, arranged Baker's hospitalization and paid him an undisclosed sum.[19]

The border communities of Nogales and Agua Prieta, Sonora were the last revolutionary strongholds when the $50,000 cannon ball hit Nogales Rebel generals Francisco R. Manzo and Benito Bernal. They issued a manifesto claiming to have "been misled by a group of ambitious military leaders and perverse politicians." The Mexican consul in Arizona arranged the surrender of 650 Nogales defenders. The Rebels received two months pay and reinstatement in the Federal army.[20]

Agua Prieta surrendered the next day. Although Federal troops had not yet arrived, William I. Jackson, the American consul in Agua Prieta, said General Victoriano Barcenas deserted to the United States on April 30. Two hours later his next in command, General Jacinto B. Treviño, also fled to Arizona. That left only General Antonio Medina, and he sent an emissary to find the Federals and obtain surrender terms. At two o'clock in the morning of May 1, representatives met in the United States Immigration office at Douglas, Arizona. At 6:30 A.M. the Escobar Revolt ended. Escobar fled to Canada.[21]

The brief revolution cost Mexico two thousand casualties and millions of pesos. Some historians dubbed it the "Railroad and Banking Rebellion," because so many banks were sacked and so much trackage destroyed. But at least the conflict ended, and except for roving bandits, Mexico would know relative peace. After twenty years of near constant warfare, the armies had laid aside their weapons.[22]

Since those days, nothing has so profoundly affected the Mexican psyche as the revolution. It dislocated millions, it crippled the railroads, the mines, the fledgling industries, even the plantations and haciendas. Capital stampeded from the country. English, German and American influences either disappeared or took a low profile. A shaky economic system became even more uncertain. National and local leadership was generally military and warlord, more concerned with self preservation and corruption than education and rebuilding. Land reform inched forward, but what was land without water, without money to purchase seed crop, without finances to employ workers, without a return on investment because few people had enough money to buy produce. In a nation without hope, the farmers abandoned the countryside and sought nonexistent work in the cities.

While their American counterparts had also suffered tens of thousands of casualties on the battlefield during the War Between the States, the Americans came out of the war, at least in the North, with most of their industry intact. Not so in the South. Its factories were destroyed; its plantation system a shambles; its jobs gone. But the Americans were blessed with creative leadership, a system of individual initiative, and a fairly fast resurgence of economic and political power. For those unreconstructed Southerners, there was the West, an opportunity to build, to start over, to recoup. The Mexicans had none of that, none of those advantages, opportunities, possibilities, dreams. The Mexicans had only burdens. So they buried their dead, and for the first time in history, began to look north, north across the American border, north to greater economic security.

For those Mexicans remaining behind, or those who had not yet made up their minds to immigrate, they set about hoping for the best. As the world looks towards a new century the Mexican Revolution is still a searing incident in their mind, as vivid today as it was eighty years ago. There is no such thing as a major speech or address in Mexico which does not make reference to the Mexican Revolution. Yet, to a Mexican politician, the revolution was merely a necessary first phase. The revolution continues for social, cultural, political and economic reform and advancement.

Out of the 1911 chaos emerged the tragic months of Madero, a good-hearted but weak leader who could not even control his own cabinet. He was replaced by the drunken, brutal Huerta, who in turn fell primarily before the wild and elemental Villa, a warrior psychologically unfit for government. The flamboyant, vulgar, rape-oriented, yet pathetically sentimental Villa, was a product of the borderlands, the best-known figure associated with the revolution, a man whose violence still shapes American perceptions of the struggle. Villa became a hero to Mexicans not because they approved of him, but because he dared challenge the Americans. Although Villa shared for a short time the border dynasty with Carranza, Obregón and Calles, his was a primitive, emotional magnetism different from the pragmatic policies of the others.

Next came another borderlander, the vain and self-important Carranza whose victory represented a triumph of the moderates. For a brief period he held together a nation shackled by ruin and desolation, that alone being a tribute to his perseverance. His was not a reign which inspires future generations to erect statues, but Carranza is worth remembering because he sought an efficient, stable government — he established a constitution. While the document was hardly a democratic statement, it was a Mexican Magna Charta representing many divergent leadership views, a beginning.

The outwardly modest and affable Obregón, a borderlander with the most talents for governing, essentially opened his presidential campaign with a trip to the United States. Crossing the border at Nogales, Arizona, he accepted a military parade and then an escort to the railroad station where he traveled to the West Coast, St. Louis, Chicago, New York and then Washington. President Woodrow Wilson received him cordially. While many Americans questioned Obregón's labor support, suspecting Bolshevism, he was a leftist only in comparison to the almost feudal right. During his administration, the firing squads worked overtime as he created a rule of firmness. Ruthlessly, he brought Mexico its first real order since the Díaz regime.[23]

The harsh years of Obregón were tempered by his outward impressions of reasonableness. The scowling and venal Calles who replaced him had no such pleasant mannerisms. He invoked a conflict with the

Church, was gross in his personal habits and merciless in his dealings. Although he appointed his successor, Portes Gil, and remained the dominant power for the next six years, to his credit he never challenged the constitution by resuming the presidency. His greatest accomplishment was a universal political party uniting and encompassing the diverse and rival elements of the nation, a party divorcing itself from strong personalities as its reason for existing. His efforts created the *Partido Nacional Revolucionario* (PNR). While it was never democratic in the American sense of the word, it effectively stabilized and liberalized politics, permitting an orderly transition of government every six years. In 1945, it broadened again, becoming today's *Partido Revolucionario Institucional*, the PRI.

The legacy of the Sonoran dynasty was its relative order and its political institutions, as the borderland chieftains slowly guided the nation to normalcy. In the process, however, they cemented age old corruption practices into an institution gnawing at the nation like a cancer. Payoffs from the highest officials to the lowliest government employee were an unwritten reward of government and municipal service, a curse still locking Mexico into those Third World countries unwilling to admit that corruption is not a negotiable commodity. Alan Riding in *Distant Neighbors*, defined Mexican public life as "the abuse of power to achieve wealth, and the abuse of wealth to achieve power." To know this is to know Mexico.

Just as the American Civil War had created a rootless generation seeking to find itself in a new West, to a large extent, the Mexican Revolution made Mexico a land of wayfarers. It uprooted peasants from the haciendas and plantations. It destroyed mines and industry, and drove out foreign capital. From potentially one of the wealthiest lands on earth, the people migrated to earn a living. The Mexican Revolution started thousands of Mexican laborers on the harsh and hazardous economic road to the United States.

BOOK FIVE

THE COLORADO: A TROUBLED RIVER

We set out to tame the rivers and ended up killing them. We set out to make the future of the American West secure; and what we really did was make ourselves rich and our descendants insecure.

Marc Reisner,
Cadillac Desert

To Chain A River

POETS HAVE WRITTEN colorful prose about the Mississippi, the Ohio, the Shenandoah, the Wabash, and even the Rio Grande. But they shrink from the Colorado because except for riding its rapids and shooting its canyons, there is little romance or poetry locked in its muddy, sluggish waters. It is a bitter river, bitter in taste, bitter in contention. It drains the largest, most arid sector of the North American continent, a quarter-million square mile watershed, and like its eastern neighbor the Rio Grande, it rises high in the Rocky Mountains, then drops two and one-half miles in elevation during its 1,450 mile trip to the Gulf of California, or the Sea of Cortez as it is known in Mexico, irrigating and furnishing utility water for the American Southwest plus portions of northwest Mexico. The Colorado marks the Arizona-Nevada border for 150 miles, and then establishes the Arizona-California line. It twists and turns for another 23.72 miles as the international boundary between Arizona and Mexico before extending eighty tortuous miles through Mexico to its odious demise as smelly brine in the Gulf of California.

Anywhere else in the world, the Colorado might be an inconsequential river. It has negligible traffic. It is alternately torpid and feisty, a river of sediment coming honestly by its name, "Red" in Spanish. The

Colorado is the crucial factor along the United States-Mexico border where an erratic rainfall averages less than three inches a year. Millions of people depend upon its regularity, for if or when the Colorado ceases to flow, Los Angeles may become a ghost town. Lights will go out in much of the West. A fertile Mexican border will revert to desert, and the nation's grocery bill may undergo a startling rise.[1]

No other stream has carved such a remarkable number of deep tren- ches, for where lateral rivers have merged with the Colorado, they have slashed a traverse system of narrow, winding canyons. For eons the Colorado has restlessly sculptured the Grand Canyon, a gorge one mile deep and two hundred miles long. As the scavenging river cuts and dissolves, it supports one of the heaviest silt loads on earth: five times that of the Rio Grande, ten times that of the Nile, and seventeen times that of the Mississippi. Those solids have been dumped on thin crust where heavy pressures have created the San Andreas Fault, and the fault in turn has formed the Gulf of California.[2]

Ages ago the Gulf extended one hundred miles farther north into California, and as the Colorado unloaded its silt, the dirt created a vast natural dam shaped like a saucer lid, which separated the waters on the north (the Salton Sea) from the gulf on the south. For centuries the river emptied into the upper lake by way of what is now the New River and the Alamo River, channels which the Colorado created as it vomited clay and silt to a depth of two miles before abandoning the channels and again seeking the Gulf. Gradually much of the lake evaporated, leaving behind the Salton Sink, more commonly known as the Colorado Desert. Today this area is California's Imperial and Coachella valleys, the fertile soil owing its heritage to the crumbling bulk of the Rockies and the erosion of the Grand Canyon. The Mex- icali Valley is a south-of-the-border extension of the Imperial Valley, a rarely acknowledged portion of the Colorado Desert, a part of the Salton Sink.

Dr. Oliver M. Wozencraft, an Ohio physician traveling to the Sierra gold fields during the 1850s, saw agricultural possibilities in the Col- orado Desert. He wanted Congress to provide irrigation money, and give him the land to develop. But the project folded when the Civil War intervened. Maturation of the region awaited Charles Robinson Rockwood, a burly, imaginative engineer and developer on his way west from Michigan to restore his failing eyesight. He and C. N. Perry, former construction engineer for the Southern Pacific, teamed up with

The Plank Road is leaving Yuma and the Colorado, heading west toward the sand dunes of California. (Spencer Library, Imperial Valley College)

Southern Pacific and hotel overlooking the Colorado River, about 1905. Offering free board for every day the sun did not shine was a safe bet in Yuma. (IBWC)

Anthony H. Heber and Sam Fergusson, promotionalists familiar with luring settlers into land scheme involvements. Dr. W. T. Heffernan, a Fort Yuma physician, joined the group as secretary, and together they formed the California Development Company.[3]

Since the Colorado dumped so much silt that it actually elevated its own channel above the surrounding desert (the alluvial farming areas lay 270 feet below sea level, nearly as deep as Death Valley), a simple canal would direct water downhill from the Colorado to the crops. However, a string of California dunes, generally known as the Yuma Sand Hills, marched parallel to the river, between it and the valley, and threatened to frustrate the vision. A canal on American property would have to go over, under or through the sand hills, and as that was infeasible from an engineering, as well as a financial point of view, the only alternative was the phantom Alamo channel, the ancient river bed which rode the high ground separating the Gulf from the Sink. Millions of years ago, when it carried the Colorado's water, the Alamo looped into the Salton Sink. The channel could be cleared and made to do that again, this time for regulated amounts of water. Unfortunately, in avoiding the sand hills, the canal, or old river bed, extended into Mexico throughout most of its journey.[4]

The firm retained the famous Australian irrigation engineer George Chaffey to work out design problems, and Chaffey quickly realized that he had joined a company vast in dreams but half-vast in integrity. As the organizaton floundered in a financial morass, Chaffey assumed control, demoted or dismissed some of the partners and made himself president. He (or Rockwood) renamed the Salton Sink the more swinging Imperial Valley, and organized a subsidiary known as the Imperial Land Company to divide the valley into parcels and arrange sales. Since the canal had to pass through Mexican territory, the California group created the *Sociedad de Terrenos y Irrigación de la Baja California* (The Lower California Land and Irrigation Company). Guillermo Andrade, a Mexican citizen, became president on paper. On Thanksgiving Day, 1900, construction started on the Imperial Canal, as the irrigation ditch was referred to. It left Hanlon's Crossing on the Colorado River, went south one hundred yards to the border, and plunged six miles deep into Mexico. There it meandered forty-five miles west by way of the normally dry Alamo River channel. The unlined, wavering ditch re-entered the United States at the Imperial Valley in June 1901. Water trickled through miles of distributing canals. At this international crossroads, the desert furnace where the Colorado's irrigation water recrossed the border, two ramshackle border towns arose, each adapting Californian and Mexican names. Calexico formed on the north, and Mexicali on the south.[5] Each had an average annual rainfall of less than three inches.

The California Development Company confined itself primarily to the sale of water, for land had no value without water. The Company sold first rights to its Mexican subsidiary, and Andrade resold it for fifty cents a share to the Imperial Land Company. Whether the farmer had 160 acres under the Homestead Law, or 320 acres under the Desert Land Act, he received no water from the Imperial Land Company without purchasing water shares for $25 each. A share entitled a farmer to one annual foot of water on one acre of ground, and a resident had to purchase a share for every acre, or receive no water at all. The shares made each farmer essentially a partner in the irrigation enterprise. But after buying shares, everybody paid modest prices for all water used.[6]

Farmers and speculators flocked to the region, the Southern Pacific making transportation convenient through the Sink during the early 1880s. By 1904, the Imperial Valley had seven thousand residents. While Calexico remained the prominent village, other tent and board communities evolved into El Centro, Imperial, Holtville and Brawley. Yuma and its five thousand residents anchored the eastern edge of this new American empire.

From south of the border, Mexico nervously observed this irrigation of American farms, and it queried the American Department of Justice in 1902 about possible treaty violations. By international agreement, the Colorado was a navigable river, and would these water diversions not eventually destroy that navigability?[7]

Attorney General P. C. Knox asked Anson Mills, Director of the American section of the International Boundary (Water) Commission, to investigate. Mills in turn dispatched his reliable assistant, the consulting engineer W. W. Follett, down the Colorado in a rowboat. Follett and Zayas, the assistant engineer for the Mexican section, left Yuma on July 4 in the company of Charles Rockwood. They examined the California Company's irrigation project, took numerous measurements and evaluations of the Colorado and the Imperial Canal, traced the river's downstream path, and even interviewed at length two former river boat pilots, Captains Isaac Polhamus, age seventy-four, and J. A.

Mellon, age sixty. Both had been on the river for thirty years, and "were inclined to attach considerable importance to its navigation."[8]

Follett mentioned four active steamers: the *Cochan*, the *Mohave*, the *St. Villier* and the *Retta*. The Southern Pacific owned the first two, and they hauled freight for $75 a ton, or fifty cents a ton-mile. However, Follett did not place much significance in the meager river traffic, and described irrigation as of greater economic value. Anyway, irrigation and steamer traffic could easily coexist.

Follett believed only one inch of water left the river during irrigation season, and the loss did not materially affect navigability. However, Washington sent Follett back for additional evaluations a year later in March. This time the engineer said the irrigation company skimmed off two inches during the peak growing season, and stated there was practically "no navigation on this portion of the river." He recommended that irrigation not be denied, so the The Department of State declared the river navigable as well as acceptable for irrigation.[9]

By now, the Interior Department had created the Reclamation Service (Bureau of Reclamation) in 1902. Reclamation started the Yuma Irrigation Project in 1904, and the Bureau's Yuma Projects Office was the river custodian during the Colorado's last 275 miles in the United States. Out of that came the Northerly International Boundary, where the river met the border between California and Mexico; and the Southerly International Boundary, where the river crossed into Mexico at San Luis, Arizona and San Luis, Sonora. Between the Northerly and Southerly boundaries is the Limitrophe Division (meaning situated on the border). Mexico owns the west side of the river and the United States the east.[10]

In such a dry country, whoever controlled the water controlled the power and status. Those who doled out water could punish as well as reward. They were the technocrats who did not own water, but manipulated it because of an ability to provide water where it was needed, or wanted. In the West, water, unlike land, could not be fenced, and the conflict over water and land created what Donald Worster in his *Rivers of Empire* described as the western predicament: "a struggle between two forms of wealth, symbolized by the land as accumulated capital and the water as accumulated expertise."[11]

Additional Company flare-ups forced out George Chaffey, assigning control again to the heavy-jowled Rockwood and the slick and dapper Heber. Heber appeared in Washington on February 8, 1904, and asked the Congressional Committee on Arid Lands for private enterprise rights to the waters of the Colorado.[12] When the Committee rebuffed him, Heber turned to Mexican President Porfirio Díaz, and obtained an agreement on May 4. Secretary of State Manuel Gonzáles Cosio signed for Mexico and, as the arrangement had to be with a Mexican firm, William T. Heffernan inked as Secretary for the *Sociedad de Terrenos y Irrigación de la Baja California.* Thirty-two wordy and complex articles left no question of Mexican jurisdiction over the Imperial Canal, since it flowed mostly in Mexican territory. Mexico could have fifty percent of the water in payment so that the Mexicali side of the border might blossom. No one suspected the eventual consequences of this agreement.[13]

No sooner had Heffernan signed the contract than the Imperial Canal plugged with silt. Since Article 4 of the agreement allowed an intake on the Colorado River south of the American border, workers made a new and provisory cut from the Colorado into the Imperial Canal, and hoped that the current's strength would flush out the silt. In a time of poor planning, inadequate financing, slipshod construction and terrible luck, the most savage flood in recorded history smashed flimsy river headgates that were never meant to be anything more than temporary.

A rampaging Colorado reinforced by Gila floods swept through the cut in early 1905, this time cleaning out the Imperial Canal's silt as well as destroying the pilings and concrete reinforcements. Farmers awaiting water watched horrified as it arrived all at once. Fields and homes disappeared. Overnight the Salton Sink became the Salton Sea as eighty percent of the Colorado abandoned its channel to the Gulf, took over the Imperial Canal as its new channel, and emptied into the valley.

With an angry river destroying half of Mexicali, threatening Calexico and swirling through El Centro and Imperial, valley farmers hustled by sun and lantern to strip the cantaloupe vines. When the fruit was loaded, the last trains cautiously chugged across swaying trestles jostled by hungry waters.

Rockwood had already sold most of the California Development Company to the Southern Pacific for $200,000. When the floods hit, and Rockwood's repeated efforts failed to stem the break, railroad President Edward H. Harriman took the company into receivership, relieving Rockwood and Heber of any further duties. Harriman placed his shrewd lieutenant, Epes Randolph, in charge of the California firm.

Salton Sea. A Southern Pacific passenger train weaves its way across rising waters of the Salton Sea in 1906. (IBWC)

Colorado River Break. The Southern Pacific Railroad tediously repairs a broken dike in the Colorado River, thus sealing off the Salton Sea from additional flood water. (IBWC)

By now, the "temporary" cut from the river to the Imperial Canal had expanded to a near half-mile in width, and although work crews repeatedly sealed the break, additional massive floods smashed through. Randolph therefore sent for Harry T. Cory, the Southern Pacific's most knowledgeable construction engineer, and it was ultimately Cory who saved the Imperial Valley from becoming part of the Salton Sea. Cory moved the Southern Pacific tracks at least five times to avoid incoming flood waters, and laid several spurs across the border into Mexico. Chinese laborers were rushed in. Cory hired hundreds of Indians for twenty cents an hour: Pimas, Papagos, Maricopas and Yumas from Arizona reservations, and Cocopahs and Dieguenos from Mexico. Even the San Francisco earthquake of April 1906, which placed enormous strain on the Southern Pacific's capacity for relief work, did not deter the Harriman-Randolph-Cory steadfastness to defeat the river.

By December 1906, railroad workers had finally forced the river back into its old channel. But as everyone paused in thanksgiving, the floods came again and the Colorado returned to the Imperial Canal, resuming its odyssey to the Salton Sea. Harrison appealed to Theodore Roosevelt for assistance, but the president could do nothing pending a treaty with Mexico allowing the United States to cross the border. Roosevelt verbally promised to reimburse the railroad if it would close the break. Cory therefore stripped rail traffic off the lines for hundreds of miles to make way for the rock cars, resembling caterpillars inching up a slope, and in a dramatic lunge of February 1907, six work trains hauling nearly five thousand carloads of rock, clay and gravel blocked the river's breakthrough with nearly twenty miles of levee. The Colorado resumed flowing into the Gulf of California, and one of the world's greatest geological disasters, which would never have happened but for the tampering of man, had been thwarted largely by the construction genius of Harry T. Cory and the gritty determination of E. H. Harriman.[14]

As for Mexico, a country ordinarily sensitive about territorial intrusions, it seemed surprisingly unruffled about Southern Pacific activities along its Colorado River border. Of course, that might have been because Guillermo Andrade owned most of the Mexicali Valley, an area twenty miles deep alongside the river, extending fifty miles west along the land border, and largely undeveloped. Andrade had raised cattle since the 1880s, and although the Imperial Canal crossed his property lengthwise, his land remained unproductive because he never utilized the irrigation.

When Edward H. Harriman took control of the California Development Company and its subsidiary, the *Sociedad de Terrenos y Irrigación de la Baja California*, Andrade's valley entered a new era. Harriman acted as go-between for Andrade and Los Angeles investors headed by Harrison Gray Otis, arch conservative and wealthy publisher of the *Los Angeles Times*, and his son-in-law, Harry Chandler. They purchased 832,000 acres of the Mexicali Valley, property extending from the Gulf of California to the "Inter-California Railway," an auxiliary of the Southern Pacific built by Epes Randolph in 1909. The railroad extended southwest from Yuma into Mexico, bisected the Mexicali Valley, and reentered California at Calexico. Randolph purchased sixty to seventy thousand acres of land between the tracks and the United States border, paying twenty-five cents an acre. Such American ownership of Mexican land technically violated Mexican law, but the Otis-Chandler capitalists circumvented the legalities by registering as the Colorado River Land Company in conjunction with a Mexican chartered California-Mexico Land and Cattle Company. Andrade directed the latter corporation.[15]

Randolph leased the land in lots of fifty to one thousand acres at one dollar an acre for undeveloped property and ten dollars for more suitable ground. Although Mexicans took advantage of the opportunity, most of the sales went to Japanese or Chinese nationals, the company preferring Chinese because they formed cooperatives and developed huge expanses of land at their own expense. Then, when the crops were ready, they paid railroads to haul the vegetables to market. In this way the railroad made profits, and it dispensed with the surplus oriental workers from the Southern Pacific. A few Chinese also moved northwest from Cananea.

In early 1910, the river again burst its banks and flooded much of the Mexicali Valley before reaching the Salton Sea. Harriman had since died, and the Southern Pacific refused to intervene. Since the Mexican government had no funds for diverting the Colorado back to its normal channel, President William Howard Taft, prodded by Chandler and Imperial Valley farmers, prevailed upon Congress to appropriate $1 million for flood control in Mexico. All Washington needed now was permission to cross the border and help seal the break.[16]

The Department of Interior dispatched its crack engineer, J. A. Ockerson to the river, and he sent back such promising reports of how easily the break might be contained that Washington suppressed the

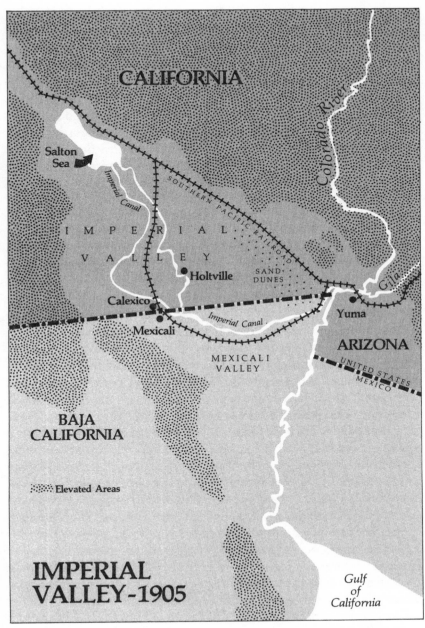

**IMPERIAL
VALLEY-1905**

The most savage Colorado River flood in recorded history smashed into the Imperial Canal. Fields and homes disappeared. Overnight the Salton Sink became the Salton Sea as eighty percent of the Colorado abandoned its channel and emptied into the Imperial Valley.

account, knowing that Mexico, if it had time, would insist upon a treaty guaranteeing it half of the river. Instead, Washington prodded Mexico in November 1910 to make a quick and favorable decision. Work should begin no later than January to intercept the spring floods. Secretary Knox suggested "notes of understanding" so that construction might be expedited.[17]

Mexico approved the suggestion, stipulating that it would not be responsible for construction failures. It insisted that local property rights be respected, that Mexican inspectors endorse construction plans, that the United States government relinquish any sovereignty or jurisdictional claims, and that the work be contracted through a Mexican firm, specifically the Colorado River Land Company — whose chief stockholder was Harry Chandler, owner of the *Los Angeles Times*.

Out in Los Angeles, Ricardo Flores Magón, Mexico's brilliant, ruthless, embittered revolutionist bomb thrower of the intellectual class, shouted his battle cry, "Land and Liberty." He had adopted common cause with the Industrial Workers of the World, the IWW, whose union members, known as "Wobblies," wanted to overthrow the wage system and replace the state with a nationwide industrial syndicate. Their main success lay in organizing migratory labor in lumbering, mining and agriculture, and by 1910 they had a small headquarters in Holtville. Mexican supporters of Flores Magón congregated there, and with moral, financial and physical assistance from the IWW, a small force of revolutionaries attacked Mexicali, a city with barely a thousand residents. It fell on January 29, 1911, to eighteen *insurgentes*.[18]

Within a week, 150 additional Rebels arrived, a tempestuous, rowdy, undisciplined assortment of Mexican exiles, American soldiers of fortune and IWW members. Ockerson accused Insurgent leaders of intending "to raid the grading camps and entice Mexican workmen to join them." According to his statements, the Colorado River suffered "from the depredations of insurrectos who in irregular bands appropriated animals, commandeered supplies, and entered workmen's quarters." American employees are menaced "by threats and a display of firearms. A large percentage have abandoned their work," Ockerson wrote. Washington growled that the United States would use "its military forces for the common good" if Mexico would but consent.[19]

Mexico thanked the Americans for their "benevolent disposition," but chided them for not arresting the Insurgents while they were arming and forming in California. If that had happened, Mexicali would not be in revolutionary hands. Even so, Mexico dispatched the dangerously incompetent Colonel Celso Vega, governor of Baja California, with two hundred men to chastise the insurgents. Vega recruited civilians so poorly armed that the United States offered to equip them from its Yuma arsenal.

Vega never made it to Yuma. The rain poured, the soldiers deserted. The colonel fell ill and had to be borne on a litter. After slogging across a swampy desert, he reached Mexicali on February 15. There the Rebels routed his army, wounded Vega in the neck, and forced him and his litter back to Ensenada.[20]

Ambassador Henry Lane Wilson suggested to Mexico that the United States Department of Interior hire armed American civilians to protect workers along the Mexican portion of the Colorado River. President Díaz approved, provided the guards were carried nominally as employees of the Colorado River Land Corporation. He insisted upon no written notes, and only a verbal agreement.[21]

However, these guards could not be quickly and easily raised, especially in secret, and Secretary Knox hesitated to use American troops posing as civilians. Since Mexico would not dispatch an "overwhelming force" to pacify the region, Knox offered United States soldiers, in uniform. He wanted Díaz to avoid "any absurd distortion of the actual facts." Díaz should officially request American military protection "on the grounds that the levee was being built in a desolate and remote territory [where there existed] no general reason for maintaining [an armed Mexican] force."[22]

Díaz replied that "such a suggestion would not be well received in Mexico." With no other options available, Díaz dispatched the ships *El Democrata* and *General Guerrero* north with five hundred men equipped with four rapid-firing guns.

To save time and expense, after all this was a favor to the Americans and not to himself, Díaz wanted his troops to disembark at San Diego and ride the Southern Pacific to Yuma. From there it would be a short march south to the Mexican trouble spots. However, Washington called the proposal a violation of American neutrality, and forced Colonel Miguel Mayol to land the "Fighting 8th" at Ensenada, Sonora. From there, Mayol stumbled east, having trouble figuring out whether he was supposed to attack the rebels, or just show the flag and hope they surrendered.

Stanley Williams, a Wobbley who preferred to be called General Stanley, foolishly led eighty-five Insurgents, mostly American soldiers of fortune, into battle with Mayol's forces. Mayol's machine guns chopped up the Rebels and killed General Stanley. Colonel Mayol now considered Mexicali safe, but by failing to occupy it, he allowed the village to remain in Insurgent hands. Since he did not know what else to do, he mounted machine guns near the Colorado River, and with no Insurgents within miles, he protected the American construction project.[23]

By now, Ockerson had built twenty-five miles of levee with sand piled upon sand. There were insufficient funds for rock and concrete. The levee showed little promise of restraining a determined flood, and indeed within months it had been breached by surging Colorado waters. But since the $1 million had been spent by May 1911, the Department of Interior withdrew from the Colorado River project and reassigned Ockerson.

The Homestead Act and its variations, the Timber Culture Act and the Desert Land Act, had been designed by eastern politicians who believed it frequently rained everywhere in the world, including the American Southwest. They failed to understand that the land they gave away so charitably was worthless without dependable water, and the question of providing water had, until recently, been the responsibility of individual farmers or private enterprise. However, an ingenius government scientist, John Wesley Powell, was now making his water studies known across the nation. The short, one-armed Powell made up in energy what he lacked in physical appearance. During the 1870s he had twice floated down the Colorado, and out of those incredible explorations and studies came his perceptive, if unimplemented, *Report on the Lands of the Arid Region of the United States.* His 1877 study proposed a plan of irrigation startling in its simplicity: a farmer's right to water should be inherent in his right to land. He should be a land-and-water owner, as well as consumer. Powell urged that arid regions be "organized into natural hydrographic districts," and in 1902 Congress passed the Newlands Reclamation Act, named after its author and principal sponsor, Congressman (later Senator) Francis G. Newlands. It authorized federal reclamation throughout eleven states and territories comprising the West, and was to be financed through the sale of public lands. The Act provided for the creation of

River Boat. The "Searchlight" heads up the Colorado River to reach the construction site of Laguna Dam. (Imperial Valley Water Irrigation District)

John Wesley Powell and an Indian companion and guide. Powell lost his lower right arm during the Civil War. (Imperial Valley Water Irrigation District)

the Bureau of Reclamation. Although the Bureau did not accept all of Powell's proposals, it did adopt the framework and integrity of his essential convictions. Its purposes were basic: Locate and survey all irrigable areas, and construct resources for the storage, diversion and development of water. The government would own and operate the facilities, but they would belong to the people and be responsible to the users.[24]

The Bureau started preliminary surveys of the Yuma area in 1902, and in 1904 Congress authorized irrigation for the Yuma tribe in Arizona. Between 1905 and 1909, the Laguna Diversion Dam went on stream ten miles north of Yuma, the first dam constructed by Reclamation on the Colorado. A complicated siphon system moved water from the California side of the river into Arizona, across the seventeen-mile Yuma Reservation to the Mexican border. At a cost of $9 million, the Yuma Project supplied water for 130,000 acres of alluvial soil.[25]

Meanwhile, California farmers in the Imperial Valley organized into the Imperial Irrigation District on July 14, 1911. However, the District lacked clout because it had to purchase irrigation from the Southern Pacific, which owned the Colorado headgates and canal facilities. The railroad demanded $6 million for its stock. Since the district could not raise sufficient money to purchase the irrigation stock, the valley's tough and resourceful leadership sued in court, and broke the railroad's monopoly. A judge favored the homesteaders, ruling they had no legal obligation to purchase irrigation water from the Southern Pacific, that they could seek other suppliers or construct separate facilities. The best interests of the Southern Pacific now called for a compromise, and it reduced its stock price to $3 million. Then it financed the paper.[26]

Overnight the Imperial Irrigation District became an economic and political entity with only one threat to its power: Mexico. The Imperial Valley irrigation canal, recently purchased from the Southern Pacific, extended south of the border throughout most of its length. Americans spent $500,000 a year on that portion, supporting an expensive standing army of alert crews and fast work trains, material and men to constantly observe and repair the dikes, levees, canals and headgates. Mexico spent nothing, but had physical possession of the facilities, as well as options for fifty percent of the water. Californians feared any foreign hands on the water valve, and their anxieties were not relieved knowing that Mexico City was only half aware of events on its remote northern frontier. Mexico could close that valve for many reasons:

The Colorado River where it empties into the Gulf of Lower California. (IBWC)

All American Canal as it cuts through sand dunes west of Yuma, 1986.
(Author's Collection)

money, reserving additional water for itself, political or economic demands, ignorance, blackmail, capriciousness, or revolutionary activity. Insurgents could seal the ditch, or dynamite levees and channels, sending the Colorado flushing back into the Salton Sea.

The solution was an American Canal on California soil, one which Mexico could neither touch, control nor threaten. However, such a mammoth project required enormous financial capabilities. The District did not have that kind of money. Fortunately, Washington did.

By now a subtle but clearly recognizable shift was transforming the West. It had been a conservative land, a land of individuals living an American dream. It had been an empire welcoming and testing men, and it had no place for whiners unprepared to fend for themselves. This was the Marlboro Man image that twentieth century Americans imagine the West to have been. Reality was different. By 1902, the noble individual who made things happen was vanishing from everywhere except in literature, replaced by politicians, businessmen and civic clubs, people who still touted their celebrated sense of independence, but began to accept — and even demand — federal assistance.

The irrigation district insisted upon government aid for an All-American Canal, and Phil Swing, the articulate chief council, went to Washington in 1919, where the heavy-shouldered dirt farmer, Mark Rose, joined him. Swing and Rose convinced the "Committee on Irrigation of Arid Lands" to support the project.

Arthur Powell Davis, director of the Bureau of Reclamation and nephew of John Wesley Powell, opposed what became the William Kettner bill. Kettner did not include a storage dam in his legislation, since the expense might have caused Congress to reject the package. Davis, who argued for reclamation of the entire river, insisted that the Imperial Valley was "inseparably linked with the problem of water storage in the Colorado Basin as a whole." When the Kettner bill failed in committee, the Fall-Davis Report, *Problems of the Imperial Valley and Vicinity*, emerged as the "Bible of the Colorado River." Named for Albert Bacon Fall, Secretary of Interior, and Davis of the Reclamation Service, it recommended the All-American Canal, a storage reservoir at Boulder Canyon, and hydroelectric power to pay dam expenses.[27]

Although the Imperial Irrigation District had shown strength in Washington, a Los Angeles demand for electric power (utility water would come later), also pushed the project along. None of the other states bordering on the Colorado had thus far, because of small populations and different economic priorities, shown much interest in river reclamation. Suddenly they realized that according to "arid states" doctrine, a priority of river rights went to the first user. After the first right had been established, future water projects of other states took secondary status, and California, which contributed no run-off to the Colorado, was not only out in front with demands, but was positioning itself to legally snatch the whole stream.

Several congressmen whose states contributed water to the Colorado had powerful committee positions, and that meant trouble for California if it refused to compromise. Colorado furnished a whopping 62 percent of all the water in the Colorado River. Utah followed with 13, Arizona with 12, Wyoming with 11, New Mexico and Nevada each with one percent.[28]

The best interests of everyone called for cooperation, so the seven Colorado River Basin states, including California, petitioned Congress in 1921 for permission to enter into a compact. Because the Colorado was an international stream, and Mexico had special rights not yet defined, Secretary of Commerce Herbert Hoover chaired the conference. While Hoover occasionally drew slashing criticism for his views, most representatives considered him fair and moderate. His keen judgment prevailed over the acrimonious proceedings, and when the convoluted entanglements could not be resolved regarding water quotas for each state, Hoover advocated dividing the river into Upper and Lower basins. Lee's Ferry, in northern Arizona, was a natural division point. Colorado, Utah, Wyoming and New Mexico formed the Upper Basin; California, Nevada and Arizona the Lower.[29]

The Upper Basin briskly ratified the 1922 compact, as did Nevada of the Lower Basin. However, as the compact did little except divide water into upper and lower sections, California insisted that a Boulder Canyon Dam and an All-American Canal be approved by Congress before California ratified. Those projects gave California a leg-up when it came to dividing the lower river water, or solving the remaining issues. The demand infuriated Arizona, and it also refused to ratify, claiming it had practically no protection against the voracious water appetite of California. A hustling California, with its immediate power and irrigation requirements, could quickly consume most rights to the Lower Basin, and Arizona rights and needs would disappear entirely into the West Coast's insatiable maw.

Construction of the All American Canal was, for the time and place, one of America's great engineering feats. In both of these photographs, the canal work is slowly proceeding through the Yuma sand hills east of Calexico. 1938. (Imperial Valley Water Irrigation District)

Arizona fears were not unfounded. Ten years earlier the Los Angeles Water and Power District had built the gargantuan two hundred and fifty mile aqueduct north from Los Angeles to the Owens Valley, in the high sierras of California. But even that failed to supply future water requirements, and the burgeoning metropolis by 1923 was thinking of a 240 mile aqueduct from the Colorado River to southern California. While Arizona fumed, California requested an annual 1,000,000 acre-feet allotment from the Lower Basin. Out of this petition grew the Metropolitan Water District, and the passage of a $220 million bond issue, an awesome figure for its time. California voters approved it in 1931.[30]

In the meantime, six long years had passed as the compact states quarreled, and Congress dallied. Finally, on December 21, 1928, President Calvin Coolidge signed the Boulder Canyon Act. It promised Boulder Dam in the canyon, the Imperial Dam near Yuma to store and desilt water for the Imperial Valley, and the All-American Canal. Parker Dam would retain water for southern California and the Colorado River Aqueduct.

Boulder Dam was not completed until 1936, but was christened in 1931 as Hoover Dam in honor of President Herbert Hoover. When the Franklin D. Roosevelt administration assumed office in 1933, the Department of Interior referred to the project as the Boulder Dam, or Boulder Canyon Dam, although it was actually constructed in Black Canyon, twenty miles downstream from Boulder. After the Roosevelt era had ended, however, Congress permanently named the project "Hoover Dam" in 1947. It stored and regulated water for all reclamation projects in the Lower Colorado Basin. Hoover Dam provided the first reliable protection against downstream floods. It produced power to lift water 1,600 feet and pump it across mountains and deserts for 240 miles to California.[31]

Congress approved the Colorado Compact, and Arizona rejoined the organization in February 1944. However, Arizona continued filing legal suits, and losing them all, until it won one in March 1964. At that point, the court divided the 7,500,000 acre-feet of lower river mainstream water. Approximately 4,400,000 acre-feet went to California, and 2,800,000 to Arizona. Nevada received 300,000 acre-feet. The Secretary of Interior would divide future surpluses and shortages. Mexico, which not only bordered on the river, but owned the final portion, had no guarantees at all.[32]

21

A Call for Partnership

MEXICO HAD LONG IGNORED the Mexicali Valley and Baja California, and the Americans not only lived in it (nearly to the total exclusion of Mexicans), but had quasi-control. In particular, the California-Mexico Land and Cattle Company, totally American dominated, employed five thousand Chinese before 1917 to harvest virtually the only crop, cotton.

Major Estéban Cantú, military and civil governor of the northern district of Baja California, cooperated with the Americans and kept his region financially solvent by encouraging gambling and prostitution, then heavily taxing it. He also coaxed over twenty thousand Mexican citizens into the district, but the population dilution was only partly successful because many Mexicans crossed into the Imperial Valley where employment conditions and pay furnished more incentive. Nevertheless, when the federal government forced Cantú from office in 1920, he had increased the Mexicali population to twenty-four thousand people, a ten year climb of 240 percent. The numbers included four hundred Japanese, three thousand Chinese and 1,400 Americans, most of the latter making their living from vice or land ownership.[1]

Mexicali had become so Americanized as to be the equivalent of United States-South. Stories circulated that Harry Chandler plotted to overthrow the peninsula, and name his new state "Otis" in honor of his father-in-law. The American government filed charges against him and six others in 1915 for violations of the neutrality laws. Even though all were acquitted, that did not diminish speculation of a United States annexation.[2]

Senator Henry F. Ashurst of Arizona five times introduced resolutions in Congress for the acquisition of ten thousand square miles of Mexico. What he and other Arizonans wanted was a salt-water seaport. The Mexican border went west from Arizona's southeast corner along the 31° 20′ parallel of latitude for approximately 125 miles until about ten miles west of Nogales where the line abutted the 111th meridian. From there the border arced slightly northwest until intersecting the Colorado River south of the Gila confluence. Arizona wanted this changed, specifically requesting a new boundary continuing west from Nogales along the 31° 20′ line through Sonora to the Gulf of Lower California at the Bahía de Adair (Bay of Adair). The Arizona border would then follow the gulf shore north for one hundred miles until reaching the mouth of the Colorado. At that junction, the river would become the international boundary between Arizona and Baja California. This proposal meant adding a northwest Sonoran triangle onto Arizona that was 240 miles long and fifty miles wide at the greatest width. In addition to a sea outlet, Arizona would also acquire a desolate region of sand hills and extinct volcanos known as "Papagueria," a land inhabited by wandering tribes of Papago Indians.[3]

Although the State Department and Congress ignored Arizona's pleas, the possibility of Mexico losing its northwest provinces caused mass colonization. The Mexican Secretary of Communications, Juan Andreu Almazan, called for an immediate halt to American land purchases, and for the acquisition of foreign-owned properties. Orientals were not welcome. The peso would become the official unit of exchange instead of the dollar. Signs had to be in Spanish. Parks and plazas would have Mexican names. In his patriotic zeal, President Lázaro Cárdenas prohibited gambling in 1935, figuring this would drive out the Americans. However, far more Mexicans than Americans joined the unemployed. Peasants migrated to the United States, and Mexico's colonization efforts suffered a temporary setback.[4]

Mexicali Port of Entry during the 1930s. Mexicali was probably the most
Americanized of all Mexican towns. (Spencer Library, Imperial Valley College)

Cárdenas took the ultimate step of Mexicanization on April 14, 1936
by expropriating, with a generous settlement, the California-Mexico
Land and Cattle Company. The property was distributed among colonists, most of whom received between 50 and 150 hectares (124 to 371
acres), and by 1940, nearly 80,000 Mexicans occupied the northern territory. While United States cultural and economic influences remained
and made Mexicali one of the most Americanized of Mexican towns,
the days of American land monopolies were over.[5]

In terms of irrigation, Mexico had sufficient land in the Mexicali
Valley for the country to insist upon its share of the Colorado River
water. Washington initially stonewalled the request, saying there was
insufficient water even to irrigate American properties. Furthermore,
the government said Mexico's portion of the river contributed only
minutely to the stream. The tributaries, the snow packs and rainfall
were hundreds of miles upstream from the border. Still, the state department grudgingly recognized Mexico's entitlement, even though early
negotiations for a treaty faltered because of the Mexican Revolution
and because Mexico had embraced near anarchy with the assassination

of Carranza and the emergence of Alvaro Obregón as president. Washington withheld recognition until 1923.

To get things moving again, and to keep everybody's rights and needs in perspective, Mexico appointed a "Mexican Water Commission" in May 1927. Since the United States was the source of the Colorado River, and Mexico was the source of the Rio Conchos, which kept the Rio Grande flowing to the sea, Mexico believed it could get better terms on the Colorado by considering the two rivers as a package when negotiating a treaty.

When discussions commenced in August 1929, Fortunato Dozal, Chairman of the Mexican delegation, appealed for 4,500,000 acre-feet of Colorado water, six times more than the Mexicali Valley had ever consumed in one year. Elwood Mead, chief of the American team and director of the Reclamation Bureau, countered with an offer of 750,000 acre-feet, the largest annual amount ever used by the Mexicali Valley, and argued that Mexico could not demand more water than it could presently consume. Mead planned to increase the offer to 1,000,000 acre-feet as a negotiating gesture, anyway. In the meantime he extolled the free benefits Mexico would receive from flood and silt control at Hoover Dam.[6]

Dozal reminded Mead of the Imperial Canal agreement of 1904. Approximately 7,200,000 acre-feet had crossed Mexican territory each year. Since Mexico was entitled to half (3,600,000) during those hungry years, it should be allowed no less now. Mexico then complained about the 60,000 acre-feet settlement from New Mexico's Elephant Butte Dam on the Rio Grande, and how it had denied the Juarez valley any potential for future growth.[7]

The United States countered with its doctrine of prior use. Americans had used the Colorado first, and since most of the river was already apportioned by the compact states, Mexico was entitled only to surplus, and there wasn't much.

The negotiations broke off as a determined Mexico began strengthening its bargaining position. Gradually it invested the region with concentrations of industrious Mexican farmers. Since Mead placed great value in the concept of present use, when negotiations resumed, the United States would find Mexico had vastly increased its irrigable acreage. Furthermore, Mexico's President Lázaro Cárdenas, a politically brilliant personality, moved Mexico determinedly toward the twentieth century. He furnished credit to farmers and began a sincere effort at land distribution. Dams spouted on the Salado, Conchos and San Juan Rivers, tributaries of the Rio Grande. Mexican engineers considered cutting into the Rio Grande upstream from the Lower Rio Grande Valley, and draining the river onto Mexican farms through a ditch called the Retamal Canal.[8]

The diversion threatened Texas farmers in much the same manner that Boulder Dam and the All-American Canal imperiled Baja California. Only a treaty could protect both countries from each other, but Mexico continued to insist upon a treaty for both rivers. The Colorado Compact frustrated Washington by refusing compromises and balking at anything other than Mead's previous 750,000 acre-feet offer. Occasionally its leaders trotted out Arizona's Senator Henry Ashurst who snorted, "Mexico has no right to any waters in the Colorado River, by treaty or otherwise."[9]

Arizona sent Hugo Farmer, an investigator, to examine the Mexican delta in 1938, while American Boundary Commissioner Lawson dispatched Joseph Friedkin from El Paso to the Imperial Valley. Friedkin, a brilliant engineer and hydrographer who would eventually become boundary commissioner, was to determine the amount of Mexican acreage currently under irrigation. Since aerial surveys did not exist, he measured what he could get access to on the ground. He also utilized the records of American finance companies backing the Mexican farmers. Friedkin's figures were remarkably accurate and used as a basis for the forthcoming water treaty even though Friedkin entered the Army during World War II and never testified before Congress.

Farmer reported an astonishing number of roads and ditches under construction. Large numbers of settlers filled the towns and farms. Irrigable acres expanded everywhere. Actually, Farmer probably evaluated the situation too positively, for much of what he saw by other accounts reflected confusion rather than progress. But there was sufficient activity to worry Arizona, and its Compact neighbors too. They met in Phoenix in June 1938, passed resolutions against providing Colorado River water to Mexico, and formed a Committee of Fourteen, two members from each of the seven basin states, to look after the Compact's interests.[10]

Events and time supported the Committee of Fourteen. Mexico had expropriated the American-owned oil properties, and intense American anger made it unlikely that any treaty opposed by the Committee could pass Congress. The basin states had the legislative clout to block most Mexican settlements, including one plan by the Interior Department guaranteeing Mexico 1,200,000 annual acre-feet of "return flow" (drainage from farms that had already used the water, usually in the reclamation projects), plus an additional 385,000 acre-feet of water released from the dam.[11]

During a negotiating lull, Secretary Cordell Hull ordered a study of possible counter measures to the Retamal Canal, the plan by Mexico whereby water would be removed from the Rio Grande channel and used in the Mexican interior. He learned that a "Valley Gravity Canal and Storage Project" in Texas was feasible, that a concrete ditch placed upstream from the proposed Mexican Canal could route water 169 miles across Texas parallel to the Rio Grande. It could drain off the river before Mexico's Retamal facilities ever got wet.

Texas obviously had the power to strangle Mexican agricultural interests in portions of the Rio Grande Valley, and Mexico was in danger of being locked out of both the Rio Grande *and* the Colorado. Furthermore, Mexico's threat to dam the Conchos seemed a little hollow as the dam would be in the worst possible place for Mexico's own people. While the dam would practically shut down the Texas bank of the Lower Rio Grande, it would do likewise to intensive farming on the Mexican side of the river.

But Mexico had things going for it that even its own leaders had not considered. President Franklin Roosevelt needed a hemispheric partnership to thwart Germany and Japan. Mexico was a defensive cornerstone of that marriage, and the president aggressively sought its cooperation. As for the Compact, its cohesion was slipping. California had taken the toughest stand against Mexico, and for a while the other states, including Arizona, had stoutly supported it. The result was an overconfident, even cocky, California which took its partners so much for granted that it made plain its plan to consume the Colorado's surplus, the size of that surplus being dependent upon Mexico's agreed-upon share. The other states angrily now saw the common enemy not only as Mexico, but California. In reaching for security, California was threatening to turn the Colorado into its private preserve. Thereafter, when California sought assistance against Mexico, Arizona in particular felt victimized by its colleague's imperialism, and furnished only token collaboration.[12]

Still, when the Committee of Fourteen met in El Paso during June 1942, it had adequate solidarity to offer Mexico 800,000 acre-feet a year, plus the irrigation seepage back into the river, the return flow. But Secretary Cordell Hull never submitted the proposal, knowing it would be refused.

Instead, Hull sent Laurence Duggan, political adviser for Latin-American affairs, to explain the diplomatic facts of life to the Committee. Duggan said the United States needed to strike "a fair bargain under international law." Acreage increases in Mexico had to be given consideration. Mexico should not become a martyr in South American eyes. Duggan explained how he and Francisco Castillo Nájera, the Mexican ambassador, had recently discussed possible Colorado allotments, and how the ambassador had refused to budge from 2,000,000 acre-feet as his country's bare minimum needs. The Mexicali Valley claimed to have 125,000 acres under cultivation, with that much more available should additional water be found. With adequate water, even the immense salt regions of the valley could be recovered.

Nájera termed unacceptable a tentative state department offer of 1,150,000 acre-feet, and Duggan called it "unthinkable that the United States Senate would approve a treaty providing an allocation anywhere near the Mexican figures." He stressed the merit of a controlled, scheduled water supply from Hoover Dam, but the ambassador scoffed, replying that while controlled water did have greater value than natural flow, it "did not add enough value to make 1,250,000 acre-feet equivalent to Mexico's just share of the water supply." Nájera warned that his country planned to take the issue to binding arbitration if a settlement did not come soon.[13]

With Mexican negotiations on hold, the State Department called another meeting of the Committee of Fourteen for April 1943 at Santa Fe, New Mexico. This time the exasperated government said it was offering Mexico a minimum of 1,500,000 acre-feet with a possibility of increases to 2,000,000 acre-feet. California furiously denounced the proposal as a "first mortgage" on the river, which it was, because a Mexican water treaty would override any interstate agreements. While Mexico's water portion might be small as compared to the Compact states, the treaty would give it "first call" on the available supply. Half of that 1,500,000 would be "return flow" previously used by Arizona and California. California remained adamantly opposed, but when the votes were counted, the West Coast state stood alone.[14]

Arizona then asked the Compact for exclusive rights to the Gila River. That request collided with California's interests in the Gila as a Lower Basin tributary of the Colorado. But the other states approved, and the Gila became part of Arizona's jurisdiction.[15]

What happened next was just as devastating for California. New Mexico urged a resolution, which passed, placing the Pilot Knob and All-American Canal diversions under government control instead of the Imperial Irrigation District. The move effectively denied California any claim to canal "surplus." Arizona was delighted.[16]

Salty River, Thirsty Land

WHEN THE COMMITTEE OF FOURTEEN finally agreed on a fair share of water to offer Mexico, much had already happened along the Rio Colorado. Hoover Dam and its power plant had become a reality (1936), as had Parker Dam (1938), a diversion dam for the Los Angeles aqueduct. Imperial Dam, the southernmost diversion structure on the river for the United States, and twenty miles north of Yuma, was finished in 1938.

Irrigation water diverted down from Parker was diverted again by Imperial into the concrete-lined All-American Canal on the California side, and hence to the Imperial Valley, the Bard Water District, the Quechan Indian Reservation and the Coachella Valley. By way of a siphon under the Colorado River, water flowed to the Gila Gravity Main Canal on the Arizona side. The Main Canal supplied the Yuma Mesa, the North and South Gila valleys, and the Wellton-Mohawk Valley. These ventures, and more to come, marked the Colorado as the most regulated river on earth.

By now Mexico, with nearly equal amounts of chagrin and horror, realized that the Americans were allocating more and more water to themselves. Mexican political realities were self-evident. As time passed, Mexico's chances of striking an equitable deal for a fair share of the river moved inexorably from "not much" toward "none at all." While the United States had made progress in what it could and should offer its neighbor, Mexican stubbornness kept the diplomats talking but not negotiating. Mexico needed an agreement, so in 1943 it suggested to Cordell Hull that negotiations shift to boundary commissioners, as they were familiar with the strengths and limitations of the Colorado.

Mexico had two outstanding water representatives in Boundary Commissioner Rafael Fernández MacGregor and his advisor, Adolfo Orive Alba, executive director of the Mexican Commission on Irrigation. Alba had studied engineering in the United States, and had experience on reclamation projects. For the other side, Lawrence Lawson guided the American contingent as boundary commissioner and was assisted by Laurence Duggan and Charles Timm, specialists for boundary and Latin-American affairs. In 1941, Timm wrote a complex, scholarly book, *The International Boundary Commission, United States and Mexico*. While Timm's tortured academic semantics left readers groping in confusion, few would dispute that he understood the diplomatic and engineering complexities of rivers as boundaries.

Upon completion of the Santa Fe Conference with the Committee of Fourteen, Secretary Hull authorized the boundary commission to seek an equitable alliance with Mexico regarding the Tijuana, Rio Grande and Colorado. Commissioners met in the El Paso-Juarez complex in September 1943 and nimbly reached agreement on the Rio Grande and Tijuana. Lawson proposed 1,250,000 acre-feet for the Colorado, and Fernández MacGregor countered with 1,700,000 acre-feet *to be delivered at the All-American Canal* (emphasis added). The question had now reversed from one of amounts, as both sides were within range of a compromise, to where to make delivery and take possession. A subtle shift had maneuvered the negotiations from *quantity* to *quality* of water.[1]

Ignoring such modern-day factors as "acid rain," moisture falling from the clouds is nearly pure. After it strikes the ground, however, each droplet becomes polluted, and the more that water is used, the more contaminated it becomes. As it flows south from Colorado, it is less pristine, containing considerable silt, but is still "good" water. But salinity is a naturally occurring phenomenon in rivers. Before the beginning of this century, the salinity of the Colorado at its source was about fifty parts per million, and only about four hundred parts per million when it reached Mexico. By the early 1990s, over twenty reservoirs will store approximately 62 million acre-feet of water when full, and these dams have tremendously increased the river's evaporative potential. When water evaporates, its dissolved salts are left behind. As these salts accumulate, the water becomes less fit to drink. Then it is unsuitable for certain kinds of crops. Finally it is so saline that it will kill any growth. If the water is not eventually cleaned (the minerals and salts removed), it is suitable only for dumping, and that too can be a difficult, complex, expensive, smelly problem.

Once the Colorado River leaves Hoover dam, it becomes a working, productive force. Irrigation spreads out onto the Arizona and California farmlands. Water not absorbed by the crops either drains off, evaporates, or percolates down through the soil to the groundwater. Water which evaporates leaves its salt behind, a white sheet draping the ground. Water percolating into the earth accumulates these salts, plus others naturally occurring in the West's mineral-rich soils, with the resultant salinity of the groundwater. If the groundwater is allowed to accumulate and rise toward the surface, it will drown the plants or strangle them with salt. Meanwhile, the fields can also become waterlogged with irrigation. Good irrigation practice, therefore, calls for the excess water to be drained off, and for high levels of groundwater, whether saline or not, to be pumped into the river channel. This surplus is released as "return flow."

As an analogy, using human excretions rather than salt, imagine a neighbor's house at the corner of the block. The good water comes to his residence first, and he flushes his toilet. The water is now on its way to the sewer, but first it stops at the next door neighbor, who in turn flushes it to the third residence, and so on. That is a graphic, and not altogether exaggerated, description of return flow — with one important distinction. A city dweller need not tolerate return flow. A farmer does. After rainfall hits the ground, all flow in one way or another is return flow. The man at the end of the line, such as the farmer in the Mexicali Valley, knows that he will get the return flow, because it has nowhere else to go. Therefore, when return flow is so saline that it kills plants instead of nourishing them, then a farmer justifiably demands that the return flow either be cleaned (desalinated) before it is released to him, or that large amounts of "good" water be provided to dilute the bad.

Mexico now realized that it would never get the amount of water it wanted or needed, because those figures were impossible to fulfill. The attention was therefore placed on quality, because an acre-foot of the good might be worth several acre-feet of the bad.

When Commissioner Lawson offered 1,250,000 acre-feet annually to Mexico, he thought in terms of return flow, for return flow might satisfy a treaty pledge. Should the return flow be insufficient, then "fresh" water would make up the difference. Eventually, of course, a method might be found to scrub salt from the return flow, but the committee assumed that would be Mexico's expense and responsibility. So the Americans side-stepped Mexico's request for delivery at the Imperial Canal, which would dip too much into the relatively fresh water, and offered to supply Mexican allocations at the border, thirty miles south of the canal.

Mexico tried to split the difference, to take *most* of its guarantee at the boundary. But *some* had to be released at the All-American Canal. After considerable haggling, Lawson upped his commitment to 1,500,000 acre-feet "from any and all sources," and 500,000 acre-feet from the All-American Canal until 1980. Thereafter, Mexico would get only 375,000 acre-feet annually through that diversion dam.[2]

The Mexican team accepted the stipulations. Lawson reported to Secretary Hull, and Hull met with the Committee of Fourteen. All except California were relieved that the negotiations were completed, and it complained because Mexico had not compensated the Imperial Irrigation District for the old Alamo Canal facilities. Furthermore, it believed Mexico should have shared costs of the Imperial Dam and All-American Canal conveniences.

On February 14, 1944, the treaty headed for confirmation by the United States Senate, and ran into formidable political opposition, again from California. Governor Earl Warren, State Attorney General Robert Kenny, and Senators Hiram Johnson and Sheridan Downey described the treaty as a "stab in the back," a "disservice to the nation." Brochures displayed threatening south-of-the-border hands reaching out to snatch American farms, homes and businesses.

When hearings commenced in the Senate Office Building on January 22, 1945, discussions lasted a month and filled 1,800 pages of testimony. President Franklin D. Roosevelt claimed "the United States would lose much more than it could reasonably hope to gain by further delays in negotiations." But California denounced the weak treaty language, especially a clause pertaining to "extraordinary drought." What was the difference between an extraordinary drought and one not so extraordinary? Treaty supporters responded that all water allotments, including Mexico's, would be decreased proportionately when a drought threatened.[3]

The sharp-tongued Senator Downey did not believe Mexico would accept the salt-heavy return flow. "Is there any statement in the treaty as to the quality of water that must be delivered by the United States to Mexico?" he asked Colorado's Royce Tipton, a supporter of the treaty.

"We are protected on the quality, sir," Tipton replied.

"You mean . . . we could [satisfy] the terms of our treaty by delivering water that would not be usable?" Downey inquired, rather incredulously.

"Yes sir."

"And you think," said Downey, "that some court in the future would uphold that kind of interpretation, that we could satisfy our obligation to Mexico . . . even though some or all of [the water was] not usable for irrigation purposes?"

"That is my interpretation of the treaty," responded Tipton. He claimed the issue of water quality was intensely discussed during negotiations, and all delegates agreed on the understanding of "from any and all sources." However, Charles Timm admitted that Mexico frequently expressed concern about "the omission of quality," but said "we succeed in evading it."[4]

Commissioner Lawson said everybody understood that at sometime in the future, the return flow would probably need "some dilution with fresher water." Future Boundary Commissioner Joe Friedkin expanded further: "The Mexican negotiators did not insist upon a water quality provision because they thought that the treaty as written would protect their rights. . . ."[5]

Frank Clayton, Counsel for the American section of the International Boundary Commission, elaborated:

The representatives of the United States insisted upon those words in the treaty. They were objected to by Mexico, for the simple and obvious reason that the United States wanted to secure credit for all water of any kind, wherever it might come from, that actually flowed across the boundary line, whether it was drainage water from projects within the United States or whether it was used for sluicing upstream and could not be put to beneficial use below, or floodwaters, or waste waters of whatever kind.[6]

Assistant Secretary of State Dean Acheson called the treaty a "question of maintaining the Good Neighbor Policy and world peace." It is unthinkable, he said, "that we could continue to let this matter go unsettled until . . . it could begin to raise issues of international hostility, and even more unthinkable that we should ever rely on superior strength to prevent a settlement."[7]

Roosevelt's death now gave the passage its final impetus. According to historian Norris Hundley, Jr., whose *Dividing the Waters: A Century of Controversy Between the United States and Mexico*, is a standard on the Colorado and Rio Grande rivers, the acceptance of the treaty now "took on the appearance of a deathbed wish." Harry Truman pushed it through Congress. The Senate approved the "1944 Treaty Relating to the Utilization of Waters of the Colorado and Tijuana Rivers and of the Rio Grande."[8]

The Mexican Senate examined the treaty, and its delegates were just as concerned about language as some of the Americans. Several senators worried about an unusable, highly saline supply of water, and Orive Alba agreed that Mexican water would not likely be as pure as California's. However, since the treaty specified that the water delivered to Mexico would be used for municipal purposes as well as for irrigation, "it is understood that the water must be of good quality." With some uneasiness, the Mexican Senate ratified the document on September 27, 1945.[9]

A little known but highly significant by-product of the 1944 treaty was the restructuring of the International Boundary (Water) Commission, and renaming it the International Boundary and Water Commission. With greatly expanded jurisdiction and authority, it would provide leadership in future border disputes.

One of its initial acts of cooperation involved a Mexican project named the Morelos Diversion Dam, 1.1 mile downstream from the California-Mexico border, the "Northerly International Boundary," on the Colorado River. Mexico named the dam after José María Morelos, a priest and heroic leader in the country's fight for independence. Upon its completion in 1950, the dam routed water into the Alamo Canal (old Imperial Canal). The dam's eastern edge abutted Arizona. To prevent floods from inundating American farmlands, the International Boundary and Water Commission (hereafter IBWC) raised the height of nearby levees. Mexico paid construction and maintenance costs.[10]

This led to the Colorado River Flood Control Project in 1964 when both governments cleared vegetation downstream twenty miles along the "Southerly International Boundary." River levees protected both sides. The effort proved effective in 1980 when rain-induced floods scoured and even improved the channel, but did not breach the banks.[11]

To the east in Arizona, southwesterners since 1880 had farmed the Wellton-Mohawk Valley, a strip extending east from Yuma alongside the Gila River for fifty miles. Groundwater supplemented the oftentimes parched Gila, but by 1940 the valley underground supplies had deteriorated because of heavy salt concentrations caused by circulating the same water too many times.

Had Congress suspected what this region would eventually cost in money and Mexican good will, it might have bought out the farmers and allowed the land to remain a desert. Instead, Washington sanctioned the Wellton-Mohawk Irrigation & Drainage District in 1947. In 1952, the government completed a twenty-one-mile Gila Main Gravity Canal from the Imperial Dam to the Wellton-Mohawk Canal. That put relatively fresh water onto the crops, but new troubles arose when the land waterlogged due to insufficient drainage, the problem being solved by draining the excess irrigation water back into the Colorado.

Mexico's irrigation quandary increased. For years, the average annual salinity level ranged from 700 to 920 parts per million, not much higher than the average for Imperial Dam. Wellton-Mohawk took good water which Mexico might have received, and increased the salinity with return flows, which Mexico definitely received. Nevertheless, the Mexicali Valley struggled along until 1961. By then, a drought and an exceptionally light snow pack, combined with Lake Powell filling behind the recently constructed Glen Canyon Dam, and the result was a shortage of irrigation water. The Wellton-Mohawk drainage, pumped into the Gila, which then flowed into the Colorado and consequently to Mexico, soared to 6,000 salt parts per million. There was little supplemental water for dilution. Overnight the Mexicali Valley resembled a giant green, threadbare carpet. North America's largest cotton producing area stumbled in mid-growth, the plants stunted and withered. A blistering desert sun baked the white salt deposits blanketing the soil.[12]

Admittedly Mexico's irrigation practices had never set standards for excellence. A panel of State Department experts concluded that the Mexicali Valley had spread the water too thin, and made no allowances for drainage. Water evaporated instead of running off, and salt soured the soil. Poor farming methods, combined with outrageous water salinity, sent portions of the Mexicali Valley back to the desert. But Mexico hesitated to find blame with its methods. Instead, it denounced the Wellton-Mohawk drainage, refused to accept additional water supplies, and snapped, "the delivery of water that is harmful for the purposes stated in the Treaty constitutes a violation of the Treaty."[13]

The Americans shrugged, implying that Mexico knew what it was getting, or was liable to get, when it accepted the Treaty of 1944 wordage of water delivery "from any and all sources." Clinton P. Anderson, President Harry S. Truman's Secretary of Agriculture from 1945 to 1948, and Chairman of the Committee on Interior and Insular Affairs during the early 1960s, opposed any concessions to Mexico as his widely-touted liberalism ended at the Mexican border. Since his Committee had legislative oversight of the Interior Department with its Reclamation Bureau and its myriad dams, reservoirs and canals, he had the necessary clout to get attention.

Even more powerful was Arizona's Senator Carl Hayden. As an ex-sheriff of Maricopa County turned congressman, Hayden had entered the House of Representatives in 1912, the same year Arizona became a state. He accepted an immediate seat on the Committee on Irrigation of Arid Lands and Public Lands, Indian Affairs, Mines and Mining, and later as a senator would chair the Senate Rules Committee and then the Senate Appropriations Committee. Gradually he became third in line of succession to the presidency, and one of the most powerful politicians in the country. For a time he blocked the Boulder Canyon Act because he regarded it as too favorable to California, and he repeatedly fought the California water cartel to a standstill. Hayden more than any other person created the Central Arizona Project. John F. Kennedy said of Hayden's fifty-six years in Congress, that "Every federal program which has contributed to the West — irrigation, power and reclamation — bears his mark." Senators Hayden and Anderson regarded Mexico's claims as nonsense, and growled that the United States had no obligations. They suspected the Colorado River runoff had been grossly overestimated in times past, and feared any drainage replacement by mainstream water would cause shortages for Americans. The senators called it ridiculous to subsidize such inferior irrigation practices and insisted that Mexico install an effective drainage system throughout the Mexicali Valley.[14]

These and other political attitudes inflamed Mexican leftists and Communist groups, all of whom recognized a villain when they saw one. They thundered "Yankee Imperialism," threatened violence in Baja California, and marched on the American Embassy. Mexico retained Chapman and Friedman, a Washington, D.C. law firm. The attorneys believed the United States could be held accountable in the World Court for damages, but "urged Mexico to seek a solution through the normal channels of diplomacy and, if that failed, to request arbitration by invoking the Inter-American Arbitration Treaty of 1929."[15]

Chapman and Friedman correctly read the political realities, because moderate American and Mexican politicians foresaw no benefits in arbitration prior to diplomacy. There was no certainty of an ultimate satisfactory judgment for either side, and a court approach would probably delay a negotiated settlement to the disadvantage of everyone involved. However, the Americans had even greater reasons to hesitate. They had already evaluated their courtroom chances, and concluded that public and legal opinion would support Mexico.

According to the 1944 treaty, the responsibility for settling disputes should have fallen upon the IBWC, but the issues were so complex and the possibilities so expensive, that negotiations shifted to the capitals. President John F. Kennedy worried about his Alliance for Progress, so he and Adolfo López Mateos declared a national policy of finding mutually satisfactory solutions.[16]

Secretary of Interior Stewart Udall, conferring almost daily with the Reclamation Bureau and the IBWC, prevailed upon Mexico in 1965 to sign a five-year agreement (actually a moratorium) while Americans installed expensive tile drains at Wellton-Mohawk and drilled wells to reduce the groundwater level. The Reclamation Bureau constructed a twelve-mile bypass canal capable of emptying the drainage either downstream from the Morelos Dam, or upstream where Mexico could mix it with arriving water. Even though Washington spent $11 million on the systems, and salinity levels never again reached the peaks of 1961-62, dropping to an average of 1,240 parts per million by 1971, the controversy would not go away. While Mexico refused the most saline of the Wellton-Mohawk drainage, the United States replaced it only to the extent of furnishing another 40,000 to 50,000 acre-feet of mainstream water. Otherwise, everything Mexico discarded counted against her guarantee of 1,500,000 acre-feet a year.[17]

Obviously the 1944 treaty phrase of "from any and all sources" called for broader interpretation because Mexico was shifting its basic negotiating position. It did not want water only slightly more saline than the Imperial Valley supply, it wanted water just as good.

In 1970, President Luís Echeverría Alvarez took over the government as the "new Echeverría," his image different from that of old when as minister of interior he had crushed the student revolts of 1968. With Mexico teetering on revolution, guerrilla bands robbing banks and bombing cities, Echeverría moved his administration to the left and sought Third World leadership. The salinity issue was a natural. Using "World Court" buzz words to make Americans nervous, he visited Washington in June 1972. Echeverría complained that Wellton-Mohawk drainage did not qualify as Colorado River water under the 1944 treaty, and he touched a tender spot in the American psyche when he asked why the United States would spend billions in Vietnam and practically nothing to help a friendly neighbor. During an emotional speech to Congress, he described damage in the Mexicali Valley as heart-rending. Mexican public opinion "is becoming increasingly impatient about this important matter that has been going on for more than a decade without any satisfactory solution,"[18] he said. The Louisville *Courier-Journal* supported his stand, calling it embarrassing, "that the Mexican president has to ask Congress personally to do something about our poisoning of water that Mexican citizens depend upon for their lives."[19]

Following long discussions with Henry Kissinger, security-affairs adviser, President Richard M. Nixon pledged in a joint communique with Echeverría to:

(a) undertake prompt action to improve the quality of water going to Mexico;

(b) designate a special representative to find a permanent, definitive and just solution;

(c) instruct the special representative to report by the end of the year;

(d) submit this proposal, when approved, to President Echeverría for his consideration and acceptance.[20]

While Echeverría appreciated the Nixon administration efforts to reach an accommodation, the Mexican president nevertheless announced that the Mexicali Valley would bypass all further Wellton-Mohawk drainage until the United States found a solution. Echeverría had raised the salinity issue to such an emotional pitch that only a quick and generous agreement could salvage his prestige as a Third World leader. He also needed a moral victory in the middle of his six-year term so he could hopefully propel the triumph on to a presidency of the United Nations. Nixon then took the near ultimate step of a good neighbor. He ordered 118,000 acre-feet of Wellton-Mohawk drainage discharged into the Gulf each year, and replaced with an equal amount of Colorado water taken from above Imperial Dam as well as from wells on Yuma Mesa. The gesture became a part of Minute 241 of the International Boundary and Water Commission and it meant Mexico was getting water as good as, and perhaps superior to, irrigation supplying the Imperial Valley.

The United States had now placed itself under intense pressure to solve the drainage dilemma because it could not forever afford this generosity. Nixon appointed Yale graduate and former United States Attorney General Herbert Brownell as his special representative, and it was an excellent selection. Brownell possessed a superb legal mind; he had not antagonized the Mexicans, and he did not hold any impassioned views about the Colorado River. He understood the political clout of the Committee of Fourteen, and he could reason with them in diplomatic, as well as blunt, pragmatic language.

Nevertheless, Brownell could not reach a negotiated settlement with the Committee of Fourteen, or any of the basin states. The water from Hoover Dam had been allocated, and if Wellton-Mohawk drainage was flushed into the Gulf, the basin states had no replacement. Brownell could work only on improving the *quality* of water available to Mexico. His final report recommended a desalting plant.[21]

By now, Nixon had become so ensnarled in Watergate that Brownell doubted the president ever read the suggestions. But others did. The Office of Management and Budget inquired why the ordinary taxpayer should pay for such an expensive distillation plant when Arizona and California would benefit as well as Mexico. Philip L. Fradkin quoted Brownell in *A River No More* as replying that "the attitude of the Basin states" explains it all. "This is the critical point," Brownell said, "because without their support one does not have a solution to the problem with Mexico. Their Congressional delegation can hold up appropriations . . . and their public reaction could undermine the credibility of our negotiations."[22]

Henry Kissinger, acting for President Nixon, understood the political realities, and he accepted the Brownell recommendations in May 1973. The final agreement, contained in Minute 242 of the IBWC, stipulated:

- That 1,360,000 acre-feet delivered to Mexico would have an average of no more than 115 (plus or minus 30) parts per million over the average salinity of the Colorado River water at Imperial Dam.
- That a concrete-lined bypass drain at United States expense would carry Wellton-Mohawk saline drainage from the desalting plant to the Santa Clara Slough on the Gulf of California.
- That the United States would support Mexican efforts to obtain financing for the improvement and rehabilitation of the Mexicali Valley.
- That there would be a mutual limitation on ground water pumping within five miles on each side of the border.
- That the United States and Mexico would consult prior to undertaking any new developments. . . .
- That the Department of Interior would begin construction of the world's largest desalting plant just west of Yuma, and that it would be capable of seventy percent water recovery and ninety percent salt recovery.
- That Minute 242 would constitute a permanent and definitive solution to the salinity problem.[23]

Manuel López, Jr., Director of the Reclamation Bureau's Lower Colorado Region, described the 1973 Mexican negotiations as filled with secrecy. The Bureau had sixty days to prepare plans and cost estimates, and thirty days to get them printed. "The difficulty was that we could not tell anybody what we were doing. We hired a consultant, told him we thought we needed a desalting plant, [and] gave him the salinity of the water to be treated," López said. But we "did not tell him where it would be located or any of the other facts."[24] Out of this confusion and haste came the 1974 Colorado River Basin Salinity Control Act, and a proposed desalting plant at Yuma ten times larger than any in the world. It had an initial estimated expenditure of $121,500,000, and an optimistic dream of treating 129 million gallons of drainage a day.

The basic design was faulty, and law suits further delayed construction contracts. The plant was scheduled to be on stream by 1979, but the date came and went with only the fifty-two mile bypass drain complete. This brine ordinarily would have gone to Mexico as part of the treaty commitment, but the United States borrowed mainstream water from the basin states, planning to repay it either through above normal runoffs or through financial assistance such as concrete-lining the Coachella Canal to prevent seepage. Except for some fish and wildlife migration features and the Coachella Canal lining, the project was essentially complete by 1987 at a cost of nearly $48 million.[25]

Back in Washington, the economic enormity of Minute 242 started penetrating. Desalination was an extraordinarily expensive and power-consumptive process, to say nothing of inefficient. The system would cost twice as much as Hoover Dam, the largest structure on the river, and its desalted water would be three times more expensive than mainstream water.

Construction rates jumped to $211 million. Other figures mention $356,400,000, but these estimates represent the desalting plant, plus the bypass drain as well as other Title One features.

Although the plant has been revised downward from 129 million gallons a day to 73 million (with an expansion capacity to 93 million), good economic justification was involved. The water going to Mexico must be between 600-900 parts per million, and that has a 115 plus or minus formula. Therefore, if 73 million gallons are desalted to 285 ppm, and then mixed with the untreated raw drainage water, the overall salinity level will fulfill treaty obligations.

While the desalting plant was originally planned for completion in 1984, due to wet years, the Colorado River and its reservoirs were unusually full. Mexico's commitment was easily met without resorting to desalted water. The facility's completion was scheduled for 1992, with $25 million budgeted annually for operations and maintenance.[26]

Congress appropriated over $10 million to preserve the fish and wildlife, a concession to the environmentalists. Over three thousand acres in Arizona and California were set aside for wildlife and water-fowl feed crops — a replacement for a habitat lost by the narrowing of the Colorado River.[27]

During the 1970s, a few congressmen and several environmentalists flirted with buying out the Wellton-Mohawk district and removing it as farmland, as that would obviate any need for a desalting plant. However, the government already owned eighty-six percent of Yuma County, and Washington would have to displace nearly 10,000 people, plus businesses and schools. The remaining part of the county might not survive the tax loss, so Wellton-Mohawk, as inefficient and expensive and unnecessary as it is, will continue as an irrigation entity.[28]

With the options slim, and with many congressmen expressing guilt about Mexico, desalination proceeded because nobody knew how to stop it and still keep faith with Wellton-Mohawk and Mexico. Representative George Brown of California, perhaps the most vociferous critic of the Yuma plant, estimated eventual construction costs of a half-billion dollars. "How can we get out of this mess?" he cried. "While I'm no expert, the experts I've consulted believe the key is how we develop our arid lands, and how we irrigate our crops."[29]

What Brown had in mind was a long range solution, irrigation and salinity answers tied to scientific research and self-discipline. Eventually, farming would come down to that anyhow, but in the meantime, only a desalting plant, with its expenses and shortcomings, offered any immediate relief from the salinity quagmire. After all, even with desalting facilities, the salinity present will still cost farmers and metropolitan users multi-millions a year.[30]

Eventually, as more and more farms use more and more irrigation, mainstream water will become as sour as Wellton-Mohawk. Mexico, California and Arizona may eventually seek common cause against the United States to solve these embarrassments of their own making. Congressman Brown's plaintive question may yet return to haunt us. "How can we get out of this mess?"

Short of admitting we do not need all of that irrigation, which will happen when the river learns to flow backwards, the solution is more desalting projects. The Yuma Desalting Plant is designed only to treat the Wellton-Mohawk drainage. It will not treat water at the Imperial Dam, nor the return flow from the Imperial Valley, or any of the irrigation districts and upstream users. Therefore, Title 2 of the Salinity Control Act of 1974 calls for projects in the Upper Basin of the Colorado, specifically at Grand Valley, Paradox Valley and Las Vegas Wash.[31]

And the electrical requirements. There is no greater irony in reclamation than Hoover Dam, with its huge potential for power output sitting idle since its giant turbines run only when water is released for downstream irrigation — which mean they almost never operate at full capacity for extended periods. While water is less expensive than electricity, water is at such a premium that it is never released through the Hoover turbines solely for the purpose of generating power. Instead of good clean hydropower keeping our southwestern cities humming, the border prosperous, and the Colorado River empire functioning, it is the pollutive but dependable steam power plants that operates and maintains them.

Moreover, the enormous salinity dilemma pales in comparison with the *real* question of from where the necessary water for a multitude of contractual uses is going to come? Journalist George Sibley defined the Colorado as "about 120 percent committed and 85 percent used."[32] When the compact states made their division in 1921, they assumed an average annual flow of nearly 17 million acre-feet. So giving themselves a little flexibility, they reduced the figure to 15 million and divided it, 7.5 million acre-feet for each of the two divisions. The long-term average total since has been 13.9 million acre-feet. When we extract 1.5 million for Mexico, and another 1.5 million for evaporation, that leaves a yearly deficit of 4-million acre-feet. The river hasn't already been reduced to a gurgle and a belch because the Upper Basin states, especially Colorado, have not yet used their shares.

To prolong the reckoning, the Colorado has been turned into an engineering and scientific miracle, a graded ditch between dams, a 1,400 mile plumbing system. It nourishes the lush grazing meadows of the Rockies, over 1,200,000 acres of agricultural splendor along the borderlands, and the green lawns of Los Angeles and San Diego. Hardly a drop escapes use. The river is so well run that its efficiency is mind-boggling. Millions of acre-feet work to create electricity, prepare foods and flush sewage. Farmers harvest two, and sometimes three crops a year in what has become known as the nation's "winter salad bowl." Crops range from cotton, lettuce, carrots and citrus, to wheat, garlic and sesame seeds. The Colorado River does its job, and a portion is recaught, filtered, desalted, wrung out and recycled. The Colorado is the hardest working river on earth. It may occasionally rage, but it never sleeps.[33]

Since the Colorado is over-subscribed, eventual water shortages are as certain as the forthcoming arguments about who is to blame. The Colorado River Basin Project Act of 1968, which included the Central Arizona Project (CAP), bringing Colorado water into the Phoenix and Tucson basins, where underground water was disappearing, contained an obscure statement that the 1.5-million acre-feet pledge to Mexico was a "national obligation." Those two words could mean that the basin states had no further responsibility, that Washington may have

Hoover Dam and Lake Mead. The Boulder Canyon Project in Arizona and Nevada helps make the Colorado the hardest working river on earth. (Bureau of Reclamation)

to look elsewhere to fulfill its international obligations. Should the water come in from the northwestern states, or Canada or Alaska, the cost would be more palatable to Americans if they were fulfilling Big Neighbor commitments. And when that northern water arrived, there would be sufficient amounts not only for Mexico, but for the Lower Basin to continue its spiraling growth. As usage escalated, so would development and its accompanying demands for additional water.

With the Colorado already over-allocated, Navajos and Mojaves are threatening to notch the apportionments ever narrower. The Navajo Indian Reservation, encompassing 25,000 square miles, most of it in northeast Arizona, is insisting on its Navajo *Winters* rights, which in general terms means that land set aside by the federal government for the benefit of an Indian tribe carries with it an implicit obligation of water, the amount of which is determined by the purpose and size of the reservation. A best guess is that the Navajos will get a minimum of 50,000 acre-feet of irrigation, and a maximum of two million.

The big question is whether the Navajos will be treated as an eighth Compact member. Since Indian promises predate the Compact, by law they could have first rights. Will they share equally with the others, or will their portion be taken from the Arizona allotment? In either event, one historian believes the effect could be a final yank on the Colorado River plug.[34]

Meanwhile, the United States has made utility water available on an emergency basis for Tijuana, Baja California. In cooperation with several southern California water authorities, especially in San Diego and Los Angeles, water can be diverted from Parker Dam and conveyed 322 miles by aqueduct and canal to the city. This has happened at least twice, and although American facilities are available should deficits occur again, Mexico is installing a line across its own territory from the Colorado westward. Today the river terminates not only in the Gulf of Baja California, but at the end of a pipe near Tijuana.[35]

So how does the Colorado fulfill all of its obligations? What happens during the dry years, when the water shortages come? A partial answer is to reduce shares to the states even though farmers would have to restrict acreage and cities would have to consider rationing. There are educational programs alerting farmers and city-dwellers to the benefits of conservation, although only in a few isolated, imaginative and forward-thinking communities are the best in water conservation techniques going into effect. Instead, solutions are sought to make it look as if water is being created rather than used.

There have been experiments at cloud seeding, and cutting forests into quiltlike patterns to increase runoff. Every now and then the idea surfaces to pump water south from the Columbia River, or to tow icebergs south to Los Angeles and San Diego, melting them for drinking water. These possibilities stem from an American belief, in spite of genuflections to private enterprise, that at the last moment the government will save us, that civilization along the border will grow until the water is gone, and then it will expand even more because Washington will "do something."[36]

But barring a breakthrough in purifying sea water, or "teaching" snow and rain to fall in specific, designated places, or in entering a wet cycle for the next few decades, the time of atonement is approaching. Sustained droughts could hasten it, and such calamities as forty-year droughts are not unheard of. Population is another ticking bomb. Sunbelt cities take great pride in their expansion. Chambers of Commerce publicize new people, jobs, businesses, phone connections, houses and industries. Yet, all this cannot be sustained without eventual sacrifice. Americans can live where they wish, and every year tens of thousands more opt to live in the Southwest. The only dispute about a day of reckoning is when.

The first casualty would be irrigation which cannot likely continue with its disproportionate use of water. Farming in the desert is an endangered species, and while there is much we might do to slow its demise, the end seems clearly certain. While southern California and western Arizona produce foods helpful to the feeding of America, many experts believe these areas can be closed with little impact upon diet.

Furthermore, there is a point beyond which growth, and its costs, will become unacceptable. During the last few decades the Lower Basin has furnished municipal water to several hundred thousand people in Los Angeles and San Diego. Los Angeles now has millions. San Diego is booming. Phoenix and Tucson are undergoing phenomenal development. All of these and dozens of other southwestern towns consider the Colorado their primary source of fresh water. They too have pumped ground water like it would last forever, and it will not.

Nor can the burgeoning cities of Mexicali and Tijuana be overlooked. Mexicali's population took a thirty-percent increase between

1970 and 1980, from 400,000 to over 500,000. Tijuana soared almost ninety-percent during the same period, from 340,000 to 640,000. Each will have a million-plus people by the mid 1990s. Although the Mexicali Valley is diversifying its crops from cotton to vegetables, it too is expending water like it is endless. Roughly twelve thousand farmers irrigate plots nearly fifty-acres in size (about half the valley is *ejidos* — federally owned sections), and the farmers share a common belief with Americans that the Colorado will always have sufficient water.[37]

Neither will Mexico's border forever be satisfied with 1.5 million acre-feet of the Colorado, although Mexico will never get more irrigation water than it does now. Irrigation is not the potential problem. Americans are fortunate that Tijuana and Mexicali use such primitive methods for domestic water consumption. Many Mexicans do not have faucets, or toilets that flush. Nor do they have green yards, bath tubs and swimming pools. However, if and when these mushrooming bordertowns catch up in sanitary improvements to where they use even a third as much water per person as an American, then a United States that naively believes it can ignore teeming millions of people short of "good" water is fooling itself.

So in spite of the Colorado Compact, the dams, reservoirs, irrigation and aqueduct systems, in spite of international and regional treaties and agreements, there is not enough future water for everybody's needs unless the region enters an exceptionally wet cycle (such as the late 1980s), or unless dramatic advances are made in desalting procedures — not altogether an impossibility. Until that time, realistic divisions, quotas and expectations for the Colorado River are in order. The great and bitter controversies have not yet even started.

BOOK SIX

THE RIO GRANDE

The river is so big, so diverse,
it overwhelms. How do you really
know the Rio Grande?

Thaddeus Herrick & Carolyn Cole,
El Paso Herald-Post. *August 17, 1987*

Great River,
Great Problems

SPANISH EXPLORERS originally believed the Rio Grande was several different streams. They called it the *Rio Grande* (Great, or Big, River), *Rio de Las Palmas* (River of Palms — as seen from the Gulf), and *Rio Bravo del Norte* (Bold, or Wild, River of the North). In Mexico, it is still the *Rio Bravo*.

The Rio Grande is the second longest river entirely within, or bordering on, the United States, and the fifth longest river in North America. The International Boundary and Water Commission considers its *official* boundary length as 1,254 miles, over half of the border distance between the Gulf of Mexico and the Pacific.[1]

It begins 11,600 feet high on the eastern slopes of the Continental Divide in southwestern Colorado. The Rio Grande slices New Mexico down the middle from north to south, plunging six hundred miles from its source to El Paso, but once past El Paso the river fades rapidly because of irrigation, often threatening to disappear completely if not replenished primarily by Mexico's Rio Conchos, the Rio Grande's major tributary. The Conchos enters at Presidio-Ojinaga. The river now shoots through the canyons of the Big Bend, flowing between three hundred and four hundred miles east from Presidio through hilly country until reaching the Pecos and then the Devils River, each flowing out of Texas. In the vicinity of Rio Grande City, the Rio Salado, Alamo and San Juan, all from Mexico, supplement the Rio Grande. In decades past, before reclamation came to the river, the flow then split into three delta channels, one of them rendezvousing with the Gulf, the other two oozing into lagoons.

During its long journey, the Rio Grande enters several geographical zones. Northern New Mexico is pine and granite, the clear water storming through rocky channels prior to reaching the desert country of Albuquerque. From Albuquerque to a hundred miles past El Paso, the banks are soft and the river has carved a valley of green. Canyons and solid banks identify the river until it exits the Big Bend and even then there are reefs and falls until Del Rio and Eagle Pass. Once the river passes Laredo, the land flattens and can be considered semitropical. The Rio Grande has become sluggish, salty (although never as saline as the Rio Colorado) and meandering. According to Pat Kelley in his *River of Lost Dreams*, there was a time before irrigation, when steamboat navigation almost reached Presidio from the Gulf. Boats with a draft of two-and-a-half feet regularly made it to Laredo (377 miles from the sea), and even beyond, before unloading and turning back.[2]

From social, engineering and geographical points of view, rivers are the worst possible boundaries. They may separate nations and societies, yet people who live on opposite sides of a river usually have more in common than they have with fellow citizens residing farther away. Furthermore, rivers are never *absolutely* permanent. They evaporate, flood, change channels, shrink, expand and even disappear. Rivers are by nature, capricious.

Mountain crests, or lines of longitude and latitude, define boundaries much more effectively. They are more exact and reliable, their form altering almost imperceptibly in human terms of reference. Because of this, Colonel John James Abert, chief of Topographical Engineers during the Emory surveys of the 1850s, described the land border "as permanent and unwavering."

The "other parts of the boundary are already marked by the rivers," Albert wrote. On the other hand, General E. O. C. Ord considered the Rio Grande as more complex than that. He told a congressional committee in 1876 that the river "is not looked upon as the real boundary line . . . as there are bolsas or pockets, . . . which have been cut off from one side or the other, leaving . . . little pieces of Mexico all along our side of the river." Mexico enforces its own laws in these regions, Ord reported, and the population refuses American control. "Raiding parties can rendezvous on [our] side of the river . . . and we cannot disturb them without [entering] Mexican territory."[3]

General William Steele, adjutant general of Texas, confirmed Ord's evaluation, testifying before Congress that "what is in Mexico at one time is in Texas at another. These bits and pieces of transferred Mexican soil make it easy for raiders to congregate and strike."[4]

A portion of disputed territory involved *La Isla de San Elizario* (the Island of San Elizario), usually just referred to as "the island," or sometimes "Pirate Island," twenty miles downstream from El Paso. The island extended nine miles and comprised thirteen thousand acres, two hundred in cultivation, the rest in tangled *bosque* (thickets). Nearly 250 residents, living in thirty-nine huts, existed by farming and/or outlawry. The Rio Grande flowed near the southern edge during the 1850s, which meant the island belonged to the United States. After Emory's boundary surveys, however, the river meandered north. Both countries still considered the border as following the original channel even though that bed was nearly obliterated by underbrush.

Pirate Island became a border flash point in 1892. Texas Ranger Captain Frank Jones, an intrepid officer and widower, married the former Helen Baylor Gillett (ex-wife of former Texas Ranger James Gillett), and left her pregnant on June 30, 1893 when he and five rangers entered the island to arrest Jesús Holguín and his two sons, Severino and Antonio. The old man faced charges of cattle rustling and attempted murder. Antonio was an accused rapist.

As Americans born and raised in San Elizario, the Holguíns lived as "pirates" on the island. They knew the thicket trails, so they easily avoided the rangers, leading them in so many circles that the rangers, plus their guide, became hopelessly lost. As the lawmen gave up the search, and groped toward Ysleta, wandering in the wrong direction, they inadvertently crossed into Mexico. Here they unexpectedly encountered a Holguín who dashed toward the village of Tres Jacales (Three Shacks). Jones vigorously pursued him, but died from chest and thigh wounds received during a brief gunfight. The other rangers were unable to retrieve the body, so they withdrew to Ysleta.

Sheriff F. B. Simmons of El Paso County and Lieutenant Rafael García Martínez, a Juarez political and police figure, recovered the badly decomposed Jones. Although a Mexican posse captured the Holguins as they fled the *bosque*, Mexico refused extradition because the rangers had no legal authority in Tres Jacales.[5]

A furor started regarding national jurisdiction and whether American officers had deliberately violated Mexican sovereignty. That reopened debate on the exact boundary, and politicians offered contradictory opinions. The Treaty of Guadalupe Hidalgo provided no language or guidance regarding the border if the river abandoned one bed and created another. "The boundary line . . . shall be religiously respected by each of the two republics, and no change shall ever be made therein," the document stated. Everyone agreed that the river had shifted since the original surveys. They further agreed that the treaty made no provisions for redefining the boundary after those changes. Treaty diplomats who wrote the document expressed no concern about channel realignments, evidently because nobody in 1848 suspected that within a generation the Rio Grande would contain a dozen or so communities on both banks.

Early boundary commissions held various opinions about what should happen if the river changed course or channels. Andrew B. Gray sent his thoughts to Secretary of Interior Stuart in 1851:

The Rio Grande changes its bed almost annually, in some part or another, and if we do not mark it without some delay, there is imminent danger of the loss of important ground to us. The flourishing city of Brownsville . . . is one instance where . . . in a few years the river may change. And sir, after we have marked the course of the river now, could it then belong to Mexico [at a later date]?[6]

Emory cited the Gila River as the international line prior to the Gadsden Purchase. "The Gila does not always run in the same bed," he wrote, but "whenever it changes, the boundary must change [with it]. The survey of that [Gila] River, therefore, as it fixes nothing — determines nothing."[7] By late 1856, however, Emory had accepted Gray's point of view, writing Secretary of Interior McClelland that "solid losses of land [caused whenever the river makes a major channel adjustment] does not change the [national] jurisdiction."

Attorney General Caleb Cushing modified these views, establishing the official position of the United States when an international river shifts its channel. *Gradual* modifications or adjustments, such as erosion or accretion (increase in land by gradual natural additions) of the river channel would not affect the international line, he wrote in 1856, as the boundary would remain with the river; but any *sudden or violent* shifting (avulsion), would leave the border precisely in the former bed, even though that empty channel might thereafter be dry. Cushing had provided a policy of border adjustment based on whether an international river changed its channel in a rapid or gradual manner. But he did not define speed. How fast was fast, and how slow was slow? How much did accretion have to do with erosion? Cushing's flawed opinion formed the bedrock of American policy even though it signified a shift from the 1848 Treaty of Guadalupe Hidalgo.[8]

By the 1870s the Rio Grande was frequently outside its "legal" channel as determined and mapped during the Emory-Salazar surveys. Mexico called for a boundary convention to re-evaluate the river border. The United States rejected the request because Mexico had not stopped the Lower Rio Grande Valley cattle raids.

Then came the Morteritos Island incident.

Actually, there were two islands, Morteritos and Sabinos, lying end-to-end in the Rio Grande near Roma, Texas and Mier, Tamaulipas. The Emory-Salazar surveys gave Morteritos (the largest) to the United States, and Sabinos to Mexico. Within a few years, however, the two islands joined, then attached themselves to Mexico. The entire strip now became Morteritos, although in local parlance it was Beaver Island. Mexican residents bought out the Americans inhabitants, paid taxes and voted in Mexico, and considered themselves Mexican citizens.

Local tenants could not establish national jurisdiction, however, and the former island, even though it formed a part of Mexico, legally belonged to the United States. On February 27, 1884, United States customs agents, Luciano Munoz and George Lowe crossed the Rio Grande and confiscated twelve oxen, two horses and one mare because the animals had been "smuggled" into the country. Mexican officials angrily refuted the charge and removed twenty-five head of cattle from Morteritos. Americans denounced the "official" rustling by Mexico, and a contingent of United States troops occupied the island. Although Mexico responded with soldiers also, it preferred the diplomatic approach and called for a new convention to settle boundary disputes. Washington refused pending the Beaver Island resolution, so Mexico relinquished its claim in October 1884. One month later the two nations met at the conference table.[9]

The Convention of 1884 applied only to the Rio Grande and Colorado River. It contained six articles. The first reaffirmed the center of the deepest channel as the international line, and stated that gradual erosion would not change it. The second referred to sudden and violent shifts of the bed. When that happened, the border remained in the former channel even if it was "wholly dry or obstructed by deposits." The third forbade artificial channel adjustments with jetties, piers or dredging of waterways to shorten the navigable distances. Number four created the border exactly in the middle of the international bridges. The fifth referred to bends *(bancos)* severed at the neck by violent action of the river, the channel simply straightening itself. Land now on the other side of the river belonged to the country with original jurisdiction. Article six merely called for treaty ratification.[10]

The agreement became the "Morteritos Treaty," although it fell short of untangling the complex web of disagreements regarding the precise international line as it applied to the Rio Grande. The treaty did not, and could not, determine the boundary when controversies arose because the pact ignored the creation of a commission to settle disputes.

Up at El Paso, where river and land boundaries collided, the earth resembled southern California, New Mexico and Arizona more than it did Texas, and in fact its history had developed along the same lines. Land grants in the those days resembled a checkerboard without specific pattern. Generally they were located near mines, springs or grazing areas.

Most California grants supported mission Indians, and since the padres had a remarkable ability to get free labor from their charges, church properties for a while were productive, if not wealthy. After secularization, however, the lands fell into disuse and decay until *dons* (landed aristocracy) generally took control. When California became a state and tried resolving the land grant labyrinth, an investigative commission in San Francisco presumed all claims false until proven legitimate. Of 813 presented, the judges confirmed 521, rejected 273 and discontinued 19. Losers in 132 cases appealed, and 98 won.

A majority of the Arizona grants lay alongside the San Pedro and Santa Cruz rivers, the grants having been acquired between 1820 and 1833.[11] However, Apaches swept the region so clean of inhabitants that many owners either abandoned their property or were buried on it. Conditions did not materially change until the 1870s and 1880s when the United States Army reduced the Apaches to more of a nuisance than a threat. By then, several of the land grant owners hesitated to return, figuring the time and expense to prove a claim would not be worthwhile.

The discouraged owners may have had a point. The history of land grants in Arizona and New Mexico is a case study in chicanery. The strong and politically powerful took advantage of the weak and politically dispossessed. Many grants changed hands from Mexican to American owners within a few decades of the Treaty of Guadalupe Hidalgo, the original owners not being so much intimidated as preferring to sell while the opportunity seemed available and promising. Considering the circumstances, sellers might have made the wise choice. They unloaded property of no great value (then), made at least some profit, and were spared the expense, time and effort of proving a claim. As a result, most court cases were rarely between the original owner and the government, but between an American purchaser and the government.

Documents of doubtful authenticity flooded the territory, one of the best known frauds involving the Peralta Grant of 10,467,456 acres claimed by James Addison Reavis, the self-styled "Baron of Arizona." Railroads paid him huge sums for right-of-way across property the Baron did not own. Ranchers repurchased their own land, and municipalities considered paying him for undisputed community titles. Until he went to prison for six years, the Baron was one of the most imaginative confidence men in southwestern history.[12]

New Mexico and Arizona had fascinating land grant approaches to the court. In Arizona, false claimants tried to swindle the honest government. In New Mexico, the crooked government tried to swindle the honest claimants.

A portion of the grant often went in lieu of legal fees.[13] The power and wealth of Thomas B. Catron, attorney and leader of the Santa Fe Ring, rested on his ability to be paid in territory from claimants he represented. In 1893 he itemized his landed estate:

> 50,000 acres of the Mora Grant
> 80,000 acres of the Beck Grant
> 2/3 of the 78,000 acres of the Espiritu Santo Grant
> 1/2 of the 21,500 acres of the Tocolote Grant
> 7,600 acres of the Juana López Grant
> 24,000 acres of the Piedra Lumber Grant

11,000 acres of the Gabaldon Grant
15,000 acres of the Baca Grant
A portion of the Tierra Amarilla Grant
8,000 acres of patented homesteads.[14]

Historian Howard Lamar explained how these situations could occur: "The tradition of large land-holding *patrones* with almost the power of life and death over a village continued to exist. What made New Mexico unique was that in such a subsistence frontier its only medium of currency was land, and that was in the hands of a few people. Finally, the tradition of a passive, relatively illiterate electorate willing to sell its vote, obey the local *patron,* or simply to cooperate, made it easy to get away with extraordinary abuses and with an unusual concentration of power."[15]

Issues of who owned what caused settlers to hesitate about filing for, or purchasing land for fear the property might be taken from them when the grants were adjudicated. Scandals escalated so outrageously that President Grover Cleveland appointed Edmund G. Ross and Surveyor General George W. Julian to clean up the New Mexico infractions.

After separate investigations, Julian said 90 percent of all claims were fraudulent and recommended that the secretary of interior have final approval. Ross advocated a court of private land grant claims.

Congress created it on March 3, 1891, its chief justice and associate justices approved by the President and Congress. Although a claimant had to prove his case, rather than have the government disprove it, the procedures were fair. American justice and legalisms did not count before the bench. The question was whether or not a claimant had a right to a specific grant under Spanish or Mexican law.[16]

The court remained active until 1904. While it never completely resolved the land grant questions, it did calm, if not settle, most controversies. In New Mexico, it passed judgment on 231 claims and confirmed eighty. In Arizona, it handled seventeen and approved eight. Obviously the judges took a skeptical view of most land grant claimants, but considering the fraud so prevalent in both territories, it had an obligation to be critical of every statement and document. The court system was as fair and impartial as reasonable people might expect. To its credit, the Court of Private Land Grant Claims moved the Territories of Arizona and New Mexico off dead center and permitted normal development to restart.

To its discredit, the decisions smacked of haste and a certain inconsistency. Nobody could foresee the radical "liberators" of the 1960s with their demands that former land grants (over half of New Mexico) be returned to them. Their rallying cries reflected a keen perception of media grandstanding coupled with a valid sense of discrimination and outrage. Nevertheless, they either did not know, or did not want to admit that they knew, how the grant and court system operated. The nation should have been spared the embarrassment of army tanks and helicopters chasing a ragged band of Reies López Tijerina revolutionaries through the high mountain country of New Mexico.

Grants also influenced the El Paso del Norte (Juarez) region, the town dating its existence from 1659. In 1827 Juan María Ponce de León, a wealthy Chihuahua trader with interests in several Spanish grants, purchased two *caballerías* (211 acres) of mud flats for eighty pesos on the opposite side of the Rio Grande, in what is now south El Paso. It included "all land that could be cultivated," and the river elbow formed the southern and western boundaries.[17]

Ponce planted vineyards and orchards, plus extensive fields of corn and wheat. All went well until the spring floods of 1830. The river shifted south into Mexico and Ponce requested and obtained the section between his former grant and the new bed (today's downtown), roughly doubling his holdings.

When the 1848 Treaty of Guadalupe Hidalgo relinquished the northeastern bank of the Rio Grande to the United States, Ponce leased his grant for $18,000 to Benjamin Franklin Coons, merchant, trader and (some say) confidence man. Coons rented the Ponce buildings to the United States Army for the "Post Opposite El Paso" (the first Fort Bliss), but could not avoid ensuing financial reverses. Ponce repossessed everything. When he died in July 1852, his heirs sold the grant to William T. "Uncle Billy" Smith, a freighter, for $10,000. Smith hired W. L. Diffenderfer, district surveyor for El Paso, to determine the exact metes and bounds. Diffenderfer discovered a 150 yard difference between the El Paso portions of the José Salazar river boundary of August 1851, and the William Emory survey of February 1852.[18] When Diffenderfer ran the line in March 1853, the grant included an additional sixty-nine feet.[19] This did not necessarily mean any mistakes in measurement. It probably meant that the Rio Grande had gradually eroded south during those years.

Smith sold the grant to five businessmen calling themselves the El Paso Company. They in turn retained Anson Mills to subdivide a town site. Mills surveyed and platted El Paso in February 1859. Since the Rio Grande had shifted even further south by this time, Mills acquired an extra thirty-five acres.[20]

The Civil War and Reconstruction, plus the French invasion of Mexico, delayed any bi-national discussion. In the meantime, Robert Campbell of St. Louis purchased three-fourths of the El Paso Company. When he died, W. H. Hills, his attorney, turned the southeastern section of the old Ponce grant into the Campbell Addition. A courthouse sprouted on Ponce's former wheat fields.

It wasn't until 1867 that Matías Romero, Mexico's minister in Washington, protested a partial loss of the El Paso del Norte community. The land had gone to El Paso, Texas. Mexico wanted recognition of its territorial rights north of the Rio Grande, and requested that Fort Bliss and El Paso authorities acknowledge Mexican sovereignty.

Washington fell back on Cushing's opinion regarding rapid and gradual channel changes — and pointed out that Mexico had accepted Cushing's concept. But how fast was fast, and how slow was slow? Americans called the channel changes imperceptible; Mexico described them as violent and instantaneous.

The two-nation struggle for a mutually acceptable boundary soon had a side issue of water rights. Forty-five residents of San Elizario petitioned El Paso County Commissioners in April 1880 for relief from taxes due to drought. The farmers had no water, so they could not farm; and if they could not farm, they could not pay taxes. County Judge H. C. Cook accused Juarez of utilizing a stick-and-stone dam that unfairly diverted portions of the Rio Grande to Mexican use. Cook asked Governor Oran M. Roberts for assistance, and Roberts implored Washington to censure Mexico. However, Mexico documented the dam's existence of nearly three centuries, and by international agreement, prior use made it legal. El Paso County residents grumbled, but moderate rains and more river water temporarily relieved the issue and the incident passed.

Meanwhile, Mexico claimed six hundred acres of Mexican territory in El Paso, land accumulating during the last forty years. Juarez accused El Paso of taking illegal control of foreign property with nonchalant moves amounting to ownership on a gradual basis. Furthermore, a twelve-inch El Paso municipal pipe emptied raw sewage into the Rio Grande. Matías Romero said the contamination affected "the health of the towns lying opposite, without the consent of the two governments." He further complained that the pipe crossed Mexican property (the Chamizal) to reach the river.

Washington asked Texas Governor Lawrence Sullivan Ross to investigate, and Ross ordered John M. Dean, District Attorney for the 34th Judicial District, to examine the issue. Six weeks later Ross denied the pipeline crossed any Mexican territory because the area did not belong to Mexico. He further denied that the sewage detrimentally affected the health of Juarez because it entered downstream from the drinking water. No inhabitants existed for another twenty miles, and experts testified that the river's current would purify the sewage within two miles.

Mexico lashed back, calling the pollution "criminal and anti-humanitarian," predicting it would "convert the salubrious . . . Rio Grande into death-breeding regions . . . which would decimate the population on the banks of the river, and carry deadly germs to distant locations." The condemnation cited nearby villages affected, including Senecu, Zaragoza and the hacienda of San Agustin.

Although the United States ignored Mexican complaints, El Paso could not ignore Ysleta, Texas, twelve miles downstream. Ysleta took no comfort from allegations of germ-free sewage within two miles. It had clout in Texas affairs, and stopped the disposal with court actions.[21]

As the controversial El Paso open-sewage system entered a temporary lull, the city incorporated the disputed land into its Second Ward. In the meantime, the high Juarez banks were continuously undercut by a strong current. Mexican vice consul in El Paso, Mariano O. Samaniego, said the Rio Grande movements had caused the "flowery and productive part [of Juarez] to disappear, carrying with it the ruin and desolation of a multitude of families." To retard the process, Juarez constructed "wing dams" to deflect water. Juarez laborers fashioned them of willow branches, odds-and-ends of trash, and attached one end to the Mexican bank. The dam floated obliquely downstream to a selected position, and was anchored with heavy rocks. Projected at an angle in the water, it deflected the current. In theory the water ricocheted off the porous wing dams and undermined the opposite (American) bank.

In November 1888, the Mexicans fastened a wing dam onto a dry channel and awaited the spring floods. El Pasoans complained, of course, and both countries dispatched investigators. Each submitted an *impartial* report, one especially difficult for the Mexicans as their chief inspector, *Ingeniero* (Engineer) Ignacio Garfias, had designed and constructed the object causing the fuss.[22]

The American team, headed by Major Oswald H. Ernst of the Engineering Corps, called the dam aggressive in character and a violation of American sovereignty. *Ingeniero* Garfias considered it just the opposite: defensive. Garfias denied it would affect American territory because the river eroded only what was known as the Chamizal portion of the El Paso bank, and the Chamizal belonged to Juarez. If the river could take the Chamizal from Mexico, why could the river not return it?[23]

The stand-off illuminated shortcomings in the Mexican-American relationship. The only authority for settling boundary disputes existed with the diplomatic corps in Washington and Mexico City, and those bureaucracies moved ponderously, with no real concept of events happening on location — and with but limited concern.

On March 1, 1889, Minister Romero and Secretary of State Thomas Bayard signed a convention creating the International (Water) Boundary Commission. Both nations considered the commission temporary, and having no jurisdiction over the land boundary. It would implement the Convention of 1884, evaluate border problems along the river and devise solutions acceptable to both sides.[24]

Washington appointed Major Anson Mills, a brevet lieutenant colonel in the 10th Cavalry. The brilliant but irascible Mills had mapped the town thirty years earlier. In April 1888, he suggested an international dam at the Pass three miles north of El Paso. What happened to that promotion will be explained later.

Like former commissioner John Barlow, Mills had difficulty holding a military and civilian position simultaneously. The War Department arranged his promotion to colonel, and authorized the pay and allowances of an officer on duty along the border. When the border tasks took longer than expected, however, the government upgraded him to brigadier general and retired him to full-time boundary commissioner.

Mills took the oath of office in the Mexican Consulate at El Paso on January 8, 1894. José M. Canalizo did likewise for Mexico, although he died within a few weeks. F. Javier Osorno replaced him.

Besides the Chamizal, the two commissioners had other border responsibilities, especially "La Isla de San Elizario," "the island," or

"Pirate Island" where Captain Frank Jones lost his life. During the four decades since the Emory-Salazar surveys, the river shifted north. Fortunately the original bed, overgrown with brush, could be identified by local farmers. By August 1896, an acceptable international line had been drawn where the river bed "used" to be, and marked with twenty-one monuments. For the first time in history, the Mexican border along the Rio Grande had moved away from the river.[25]

Another boundary issue involved the *Bosque de Cordova* at El Paso, an enclave abutting the Chamizal. The Rio Grande curved like a worn horseshoe, forming the *Bosque de Cordova*, the western edge rubbing against southeast El Paso. During ordinary times, water flowed lazily around the sand-choked bend. When floods hit, however, Cordova retarded the current. On May 8, 1897, high water entered *Chihuahuita* (Little Chihuahua), portions of which comprised the Chamizal. The torrent swept away tracks of the Texas and Pacific, the Galveston and Harrisburg, and the Atchison, Topeka and Santa Fe.

The river receded on the 13th, El Pasoans little realizing that a more severe flood would crest on the 24th and breach the levees. Water lapped over the Santa Fe Bridge, and El Paso police evacuated the jail when floods broke through sandbags. Over 120 homes in *Chihuahuita* dissolved or went downstream, forcing weary refugees into empty Texas and Pacific railroad cars. As an added irony, a nasty dust storm engulfed the town.

Over two thousand residents greeted the 25th without homes, having spent the night with friends or in municipal buildings, soggy tents and boxcars. Nearly 250 jammed abandoned barracks at old Fort Bliss. Congress appropriated $10,000 for flood relief, and Austin sent another $5,000.[26]

When the water finally retreated, refugees moved onto the mesa north of town and established Stormsville (present-day Rim Road), not named for the flood but for the developer, D. Storms. While the residents escaped future devastation by the Rio Grande, their problems on this high, remote plateau stemmed from too little water. At the time of Stormsville's condemnation in 1928, it had a population of four hundred, four toilets and no sewers.

Commissioner Mills criticized Mexico for the El Paso flood damage, referring to "mattresses" torn loose from the Mexican bank and lodged against pilings supporting the streetcar bridges. These mattresses, like the wing dams, contained brush and trash tied together and anchored

W. W. FOLLETT
(Author's Collection)

ANSON MILLS
(U.S. Military Academy Archives)

with rocks or stakes. They were supposed to prevent additional soil from eroding to El Paso and joining the Chamizal.

The Cordova Curve, the "great bend of the river," also contributed to the El Paso flood. When water reached its neck, the surge not only went up and over the embankment, it went up and over El Paso.

Boundary engineers W. W. Follett for the United States and E. Corella for Mexico, called for severing Cordova's horseshoe neck, and diminishing the flood threat to El Paso. A cut would shorten the flow and give the Rio Grande a steeper fall or grade. Mayor Joseph Magoffin offered to meet expenses with El Paso municipal funds if the boundary commissioners could determine who owned Cordova after the surgery. Mills believed all 370 acres should join the United States since the land would be north of the Rio Grande. But Commissioner Javier Osorno insisted on a retention of Mexican sovereignty, and Mills reluctantly conceded.

Later, when Osorno hesitated to authorize the work, an irked Mills referred to him as "inclined to a degree of procrastination extraordinary even for a Mexican." Mills accused the Mexican commissioner of delaying decisions. Even routine correspondence received "in due course" replies. The testy Mills chided Osorno, asking if "in due course" meant a day, a month, or years. He finally concluded that it meant eventually.[27]

In defense of the dapper Osorno, Mills had practically a Washington power of attorney compared to the Mexican's limitations. Osorno shared local authority with Juarez Mayor Valentín Oñate, who owed his position to Chihuahua governor Miguel Ahumada, who in turn bowed to Mexico City. So while Osorno might sanction the Cordova work, digging could not commence without the permission of Oñate, and the two officials rarely spoke. Magoffin tried to expedite matters with an official request. Oñate referred it to the governor. That transaction alone took weeks because, as Oñate explained to Mills, he could get more words in a letter than he could in a telegram. Ahumada hesitated too, and passed the responsibility to Mexico City. It in turn conferred with Osorno, and so it went.

Eventually all parties agreed. Magoffin cajoled $4,500 out of the El Paso City Council and paid all expenses. Juarez furnished the labor. Boundary commissioners marked the former channel around the Cordova oxbow with nineteen monuments and declared it the international line.[28]

Cordova became an island of Mexico inside the United States, an island irritating local and international relations. It blocked El Paso's growth and transportation arteries, and was a foreign protrusion protecting smugglers and illegal aliens, a haven for lawbreakers during prohibition. Mexico retained national jurisdiction as a matter of pride even though it ignored the enclave. Cordova Island's presence caused as many resentments in El Paso as the Chamizal did in Juarez.

The disputed territory headed for adjudication on November 14, 1895 when Pedro I. García filed suit in the Juarez Primary Court of Claims for the return of 7.82 acres of El Paso. He referred to his property as "El Chamizal," which translates, roughly, into "weed patch." The name stuck. A variety of other claimants also entered the controversy, and the amount of contested land soared to 630 acres. However, in February the Mexican tribunal declared it lacked jurisdiction and transferred its transcripts to the International (Water) Boundary Commission. According to rules previously established, boundary commissioners would examine the evidence, listen to testimony, discuss the options and reach a decision acceptable to each of them. Chamizal deliberations started in April 1896.

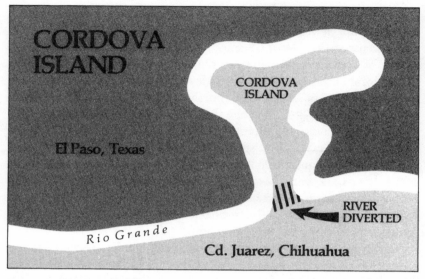

During ordinary times, the Rio Grande flowed lazily around the sand-choked bend of the Cordova Bosque. Because of problems caused by flooding, the horseshoe neck was severed by international agreement and Cordova became an island of Mexico inside the United States.

Seventy-seven-year-old Jesús Serna of Juarez described the floods of 1854, 1864 and 1868. He worked as a Rio Grande ferryman, and watched the torrents destroy "trees, crops and houses."[29]

Ynocente Ochoa, who had provided refuge to Benito Juarez during the French invasion, followed Serna. He recalled the floods of 1858, 1860 and 1864, and described how the water undermined the high Mexican banks. He said the collapsing noise "seemed like the boom of a cannon, and it was frightful."[30]

Landowner Espiridon Provencio assisted families to higher ground. The river resembled a moving thing, he said, and "up to fifty yards would be washed away at certain points."[31]

Mexico rested while the United States called its first witness. José M. Flores, a Juarez businessman who lived in El Paso and crossed the river daily to work, said the Rio Grande's southward shifts were "imperceptible." Merchant and former mayor Solomon Schutz admitted that the Mexican banks had been worn away, but insisted their erosion had been slow and gradual because jetties (mattresses of brush) protected them.[32]

Joseph Magoffin, State National banker and former El Paso mayor, testified last for Mills. He explained how his father James Magoffin had created Magoffinsville, and how Fort Bliss existed there for several years. The Rio Grande ravaged Fort Bliss in 1867, the point being that El Paso and Juarez both lost land on occasions, the losses balancing each other out.[33]

Mexico's final witness was Mariano Samaniego, former Juarez mayor, former Chihuahua governor, landowner, physician and great-grandfather of 1980s El Paso Sheriff Leo Samaniego. He claimed the river had consumed the flowery and productive parts of Juarez. When flood waters got behind or under the mattresses, damage was even more severe. The community once lost 150 acres during a single onslaught.[34]

When the testimony ended, Mills and Osorno reviewed engineering reports and prepared final arguments for each other. Osorno presented his oral and written statements on July 13 and demanded the entire Chamizal. According to his logic, channel changes were due "to the force of the water's current, not to slow and gradual erosion." No one seriously believes "that a river so inconsistent as the Bravo does its work step by step and degree by degree," he said.[35]

Four days later Mills rebutted, believing his logic would prevail and Osorno would concede. All seven witnesses had emphasized how the Rio Grande cut into the Juarez banks, but no one had observed Mexican land actually under water. Instead, while Juarez lost some soil, only in El Paso had floods driven residents to higher ground. For a channel change to be rapid, Mills argued, the river must carve a new bed and leave behind landmarks. No witnesses testified to any. Furthermore, Mills called attention to the Mexican lack of concern for the Chamizal from 1852 until present times, and he reminded Mexico of the 1884 and 1888 international agreements whereby bridges across the Rio Grande were divided in the middle for jurisdictional purposes. By that very act, Mexico had accepted the present Rio Grande as the border, Mills said. It could not now come forward and claim the boundary was not the river, but was an unidentified line running near the heart of downtown El Paso.

As might be expected, neither Mills nor Osorno accepted the other's arguments, and the disagreement remained. Mills notified Secretary of State Richard Olney on August 4, 1895, of failure to reach an understanding, saying he was ashamed of the long and fruitless discussions. He urged the State Department to continue the Chamizal talks and try for a settlement at another diplomatic level.

By now, many El Pasoans assumed a victory for the United States, and squatters settled on Chamizal land claimed by the Southern Pacific between the river and 11th Street. The railroad filed suit to remove them. United States Marshal H. R. Hillerbrand ordered fifty families out in 1907, and ringed the area with barbed wire. "This enclosure is in the hands of the U. S. Marshal and trespassing is forbidden," a sign warned.[36]

Ordinarily news of American law officers evicting squatters might have cheered Mexico, for the fewer families on the land, the easier for the United States to eventually relinquish it. However, evictions raised the spectre of American civil actions causing the Chamizal to be resolved in American courts rather than by the Boundary Commission. Mexico complained, and Washington halted the proceedings and dispossessions.

Three years later presidents William Howard Taft and Porfirio Díaz met in El Paso. Díaz wanted American support for his tottering regime, so he evidently brought pressure on Taft to settle the festering Chamizal issue. A few months later, both governments announced for arbitration. A Canadian jurist would sit with Mills and the new Mexican commissioner, Ingeniero Fernando Beltran y Puga. The two commissioners and M. Eugene Lafleur would act as judges, but as Mills and Beltran were apt to split their vote and cancel each other out, as Mills and Osorno had done, Lafleur as presiding commissioner would cast the deciding nod. For this he had excellent qualifications. He was the author of two studies in international law, a professor of civil and criminal law at McGill University, and a respected member of the Montreal Bar.[37]

The judges would not present testimony, but would listen patiently as others tried the case. The United States chose William Cullen Dennis as its chief attorney, Dennis being the assistant solicitor of the Department of State and American delegate to the Hague. Assistants were Walter B. Grant and Richard Fenner Burges, the latter a distinguished member of the El Paso Bar.[38]

Mexico chose Joaquín D. Casasús, attorney and former Mexican minister to Washington. Assistants were W. J. White of Montreal, Seymour Thurmond and W. J. Warder of El Paso. Also included was historian Alberto María Carreño.

The Chamizal Arbitration Commission commenced its proceedings in the El Paso Federal Courthouse on May 15, 1911. The United States and Mexico dispensed with witnesses, and prepared their cases with oral arguments and the presentation of documents, reports, maps and related records. Thus began a legal struggle not without humor and irony.

Theories and legalisms abounded. Nobody was certain if the differences in the Emory-Salazar surveys were because of surveying errors, or because the river shifted. For that matter, the river had meandered so much during the last fifty years that it could not correctly be defined at any particular time. Furthermore, treaties and agreements were argued not so much for what they said, but for what they did not say, and for what they should have said.

In the meantime, Porfirio Díaz abdicated as president of Mexico, and Francisco Madero assumed the government. He gave the Chamizal no priority whatsoever. No instructions or messages went to Beltran or his council, and neither he nor his associates knew if they had been retained, dismissed, forgotten, or were liable to be shot as enemy agents. In the absence of guidance, the Mexicans nervously continued as before.

In terms of these Mexican participants, Charles Dickens could not have created a more disparate cast of absurd characters. The commission chose W. J. White as its chief counsel, and opened itself up to accusations of unfair influence since White was a close friend of Lafleur's. It picked Seymour Thurmond as assistant council, an attorney so fond of colorful and long-winded platitudes that Mexican lawyers kept him off the stand. (As it turned out, several Americans believed Lafleur felt sorry for him.) Finally, there was the former Mexican minister to Washington, Joaquín Casasús. Although he spoke fluent English, and each side had agreed to conduct arguments in English as a courtesy to Lafleur, Casasús insisted on coequality in Spanish. He gave his best speech in Spanish, the effect being lost when neither Lafleur nor Mills understood it and waited days for a written translation. Then, when two-thirds through the arbitration, Casasús decided he should be in exile with Díaz, and he did what most wealthy exiles were supposed to do. He went to live in New York.

By contrast the American commission presented practically a letter-perfect case. It was sound, logical, thorough, organized and detailed. It did everything except win.

Lafleur divided the Chamizal along the 1864 river bed. The arbitrator ruled that the river's 1864 shift to the south amounted to "rapid erosion." Therefore any changes prior to 1864 were gradual, so the United States retained that part of the disputed district. Mexico won everything

Chamizal Arbitration Commission in El Paso. (Standing left to right) P. D. Cunningham, John A. Happer, Salvador
F. Mallefert (Sec.), Cuellar. (Sitting) Frank B. Dabney, Anson Mills, F. Javier Osorno, Col. E. Corella. (IBWC)

between the 1864 channel and the present (1911) river bed. Of the 630 acres in contention, Mexico received approximately two-thirds.[39]

Beltran expressed disappointment, as he anticipated winning the entire Chamizal. But he accepted the decision.

Anson Mills rejected the arbitrator's finding. He claimed Lafleur had authority to decide who owned the entire Chamizal but he had no authority to divide it. Lafleur injected "rapid erosion" (fast-slow) into the case, the term having no meaning. The 1864 river bed had never been positively identified, and was impossible to precisely outline on the ground. Since its location could not be determined, a splitting of the Chamizal along an undetermined line amounted to such a vague decision that it could not properly be executed.[40]

From a historical point of view, Mills probably did the United States and Mexico a favor. The American government lacked a financial commitment and the sense of social justice necessary to relocate numerous residents. Law suits would have kept both countries in constant litigation. The new boundary would have left the river in place but moved Mexican jurisdiction into the city limits of El Paso. The line would have divided streets and parks, jobs and workers, friends and neighbors, families and relatives. Law enforcement, customs and immigration restrictions would have been impossible. During those troublesome years, with revolutionaries capturing Juarez six times during the next two decades, American public opinion would never have permitted guerrilla forces to shoot their way to within a few blocks of downtown El Paso.

To no one's surprise, the only parts of the continent interested in the 1911 arbitration were El Paso and Ciudad Juarez. Except for isolated Mexican intellectuals who wrote seldom-read articles decrying the loss of national patrimony, most Mexicans were unaware there had even been a controversy. The *New York World* described the Chamizal Arbitration Commission as practicing "an astuteness worthy of the celebrated tariff ruling on frog legs," and said the "differences between tweedledum and tweedledee was never before so accurately defined in diplomacy. A comic-opera librettist never created a more diverting situation," the *World* chuckled.[41]

For the next half-century, the wrangling continued at a more muted beat as Mexico asked Americans to honor the arbitrator's decision. Meanwhile, the Chamizal awaited propitious international conditions that would not arrive until the 1960s.

24

A Banco Here,
A Banco There

CORDOVA ISLAND, La Isla de San Elizario and the Chamizal were but outward indications of something out of adjustment with the river border. Around El Paso, these meanderings affected relatively large numbers of people, but other, remote *bancos*, as intrusions, horseshoe or oxbow curves came to be called, were important and frequently just as complex.

Everyone knew the Rio Grande had shifted in various places during its border trip to the Gulf. Unlike the Colorado, which had few sharp curves, the Rio Grande not only had dozens of bancos but had bancos of different sizes and shapes on top of former bancos. Over a period of decades or centuries, a curve might dry as the river adjusted and changed direction. Later a fresh flood could send the river back into that bend again, but since part of the former channel might have silted, or become overgrown with brush, the river cut a different course, laying a new, different patterned banco on top of an older banco. In places where the river had meandered frequently, former channels were everywhere. Which ones represented the true border? Only the Boundary Commission could decide.

The Lower Rio Grande Valley had the most acute difficulties. East of Rio Grande City the river twisted so relentlessly that it seemed reluctant to reach the Gulf. On the basis of a straight line, the channel averaged a two foot drop per straight mile; but miles of curves often represented a drop of only a few inches.

The Customs Department was frustrated. J. J. Cocke, the inspector at Brownsville, complained that his officers could not observe the river without intruding upon isolated bancos. No one knew which country owned them, and their presence forced agents to withdraw a mile inland and wait for law-breakers to come out. Cocke asked the government to reinstate the river as the boundary, straighten the channel, and eliminate the bancos. Those north of the Rio Grande should go to the United States, those south to Mexico.[1]

Mills and Osorno did not know it yet but they were struggling toward the same realizations. In the fall of 1894, the commissioners reexamined four bancos: Camargo, Vela, Santa Margarita and Granjeno, all in the Lower Rio Grande Valley. These tracts had been troublemakers for a quarter century, longtime caseloads on the commission agenda. National jurisdictions overlapped in some instances, and there had been arrests on Vela by both countries when officials disagreed about the banco's "legal" ownership.

From Laredo east the American commission mapped the four bancos and recorded local testimony regarding the river's fluctuations. Drifting downstream on a rented, two-peso-per-day flatboat, Mills described the villagers as almost exclusively Mexican in speech, mannerisms, culture and general characteristics. They are "densely ignorant," the "poorest and least progressive [people] I have seen except [for] the North American Indian," he wrote. The majority did not know their age, and took little note of time.[2]

The commissioner portrayed the Rio Grande as having three divisions. From El Paso to Presidio the river had cut new channels and formed islands. From Presidio to Rio Grande City, the fall was steep, the channel consistent, and the banks usually solid. However, from Rio Grande City to the Gulf, a distance of 108 miles in a direct line, the river meandered through 241 miles of twisting curves (bancos) to reach the coast. The soil was alluvial, the fall measured in inches. Channels constantly eroded, the river frequently turning back upon itself, creating cut-offs.

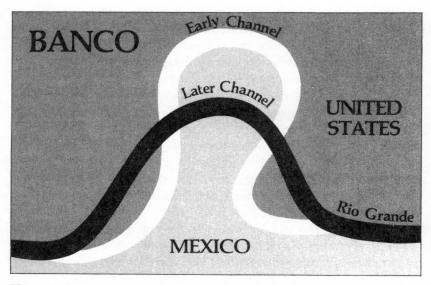

This example shows an overlapping of two bancos on the Rio Grande.
Overlapping bancos sometimes amounted to a dozen or more intermingled beds.

Engineers mapped the four bancos while Mills estimated another forty or fifty in the vicinity. To resurvey these, to identify and mark the Emory-Salazar line would take years. Monuments would cost altogether between one hundred and one hundred fifty thousand dollars. Even when the surveys were complete, bancos on both sides would still create complex legal and cultural problems. Agricultural products could not always be sold to citizens of the country owning the bancos without violating the customs and revenue laws. Without special extradition statutes, law violators could not always be arrested and conveyed to the courts which should have jurisdiction.

Mills and Osorno recommended that Articles I and II of the 1884 treaty be amended. The present river should continue as the boundary, but the bancos (the four already mapped, plus others recently discovered) should be transferred to the nation they protruded into.

Washington found this acceptable, but Mexico City did not. It insisted upon detailed drawings of all bancos, so engineers located and mapped fifty-four additional ones in late 1897 and early 1898. A total of fifty-eight lay between Rio Grande City and the Gulf. Mills and Osorno recommended that a new treaty or convention eliminate them, plus others that might originate or be determined in the future.

Two months later Osorno resigned and the distinguished Jacobo Blanco replaced him. Mills now pushed for a banco treaty covering the entire river border. He further advised Secretary of State Richard Olney to stop dreaming about the "short life of the commission."[3]

Unfortunately, Mexico had sour memories regarding territorial losses to the United States, and it especially recalled the Gadsden Purchase. To prevent further occurrences, the Mexican constitution had been amended. That was prudent, but at a time when the deletion of bancos was in the best interest of Mexico, its constitution blocked progress. Diplomats finally circumvented it by substituting *transfer of jurisdiction* for *transfer of territory*.[4]

The 1905 Convention for the Elimination of Bancos erased the fifty-eight bancos in the lower Rio Grande. Since the treaty applied to the entire river, future bancos would be transferred in the same fashion. Residents kept ownership rights. Citizenship could either be retained or changed. Furthermore, the treaty did not eliminate bancos containing cities or towns, nor did it change jurisdiction for populations in excess of two hundred. In those instances, the abandoned river bed would become the boundary, and the sovereignty would not change.

Officials removed thirty-one additional bancos in the Lower Rio Grande Valley between 1910 and 1912 before the Mexican Revolution sent the boundary commission into near limbo.

In 1922 the colorful George Curry, a former territorial governor of New Mexico, a past Rough Rider and lawman, accepted the position as commissioner. Mexico selected Gustavo P. Serrano. Although Curry considered Serrano a "competent and reasonable man," Secretary of State Charles E. Hughes cautioned Curry to keep "contacts on a strictly unofficial basis," as the United States had not recognized the Mexican government. Within a short time, however, normal diplomatic relations resumed. Curry continued the banco elimination program until 1927 when his long friendship with the former Secretary of Interior A. B. Fall,[5] who was indicted in the Teapot Dome Scandal, cost him his position. Curry resigned and was replaced by the able Lawrence Milton Lawson, who remained until 1954. By 1940 the IBC had eliminated 172 bancos, two in the Colorado River south of Yuma. Twenty bancos were erased in the El Paso-Juarez valley, the last ever found there. During the 1940s, thirteen were deleted in Quitman Canyon, southeast of El Paso, and several also were struck from the Presidio Valley. By 1970, with the Banco treaty phased out, 241 bancos had been eliminated, the land amounting to slightly over 30,000 acres. The United States acquired over sixty percent, getting 18,505 acres while Mexico picked up 11,662.[6]

In the meantime, border emphasis shifted from bancos to water divisions. Such thinking called for dams.

25

Dams for the River

A CONGRESSIONAL COMMITTEE investigating the Salt War in 1878, closed its inquiry with:

> The Salt War is probably ended, but . . . questions . . . of water, as to its diversions and distribution the board regards as serious. The Rio Grande . . . often shifting, always erratic, . . . sometimes dry, affords . . . a scant and variable supply of water to the people of both nationalities, but is utterly insufficient to irrigate this extensive valley where the yearly rainfall measures but a few inches. As time progresses . . . the question must grow in importance and may occasion trouble beyond the reach of diplomacy to settle.[1]

Congress approved the Homestead Act in 1862, and opened the West to 160 acre farms. The mandate's purposes were noble, but the plan's weakness lay in congressional ignorance regarding desert productivity. Unlike the humid East, where crops thrived on rainfall, natural fertility meant nothing in the West without accessibility to streams or underground water. A tract of land had value only in proportion to available irrigation.

John Wesley Powell had directed a federal geological and geographical survey of the Colorado River from 1871 to 1879. That experience propelled him into the fledgling Geological Survey for mapping water resources and assessing the possibilities of storage dams.

Powell foresaw the international complexities of the Rio Grande, and arranged the transfer of Major Anson Mills to Fort Bliss, Texas, and hence to El Paso. Due to drought and a momentous increase in Rio Grande usage by Colorado and northern New Mexico (Mexico accused the two states of stealing water), the border country wanted solutions. Mills rejected complaints of excessive water use in upstream areas, a position he amended when his assistant, W. W. Follett, completed an engineering study. Until then, Mills blamed scant water supplies on the drought, on the natural evolution of wet and dry cycles. The solution was to capture water in years of plenty and store it until years of scarcity.

Mills advocated a sixty-foot-high stone-and-concrete dam at the Pass, a monolith submerging sixty thousand acres (later reduced to twenty-seven thousand acres), and creating a lake fifteen miles long and seven (later four) miles wide. It would store water, release controlled amounts when necessary, stabilize the river and provide electrical power and irrigation free from whims of season and weather. The United States and Mexico would equally divide the water, and Mills anticipated enough to irrigate annually one hundred thousand acres. The major hesitated about sharing construction costs, as Mexico would have an equal right in operations, an option Mills believed should be retained by the United States. A substantial dam would cost about $300,000: $100,000 for construction materials, $100,000 for land, and $100,000 for relocating tracks of the Southern Pacific and Atchison, Topeka, and Santa Fe. By 1896, however, with engineering reports less optimistic and acquisition costs rising, the estimate soared to nearly $2.5 million.[2]

Congress approved the proposal in April 1890, but appropriated no funds. In 1894, Mexican Minister Matías Romero filed a $35 million damage claim against the United States. His suit spoke of evils "suffered by the inhabitants of the Mexican bank" due to water shortages caused by Colorado and New Mexico. Americans had violated the treaty of 1853, Romero claimed, as well as Article VII of the treaty of 1848 which prohibited interfering with navigation. By international law the Rio Grande was navigable, and Romero believed the upper river diversions had decreased the river's flow by sixty percent along the border . . . thus hindering navigation.[3]

United States Attorney General Judson Harmon disputed Mexico's allegations. The United States could not give greater rights to foreigners than to its own citizens, he rebutted in December 1895. If Juarez ran short of water for irrigation, that was regrettable but of no significance. Harmon denied that the Rio Grande's navigability extended from the Gulf to El Paso, but even if that were so, the United States had "absolute [Rio Grande] sovereignty."[4]

Harmon's decision angered El Paso as well as Mexico. If New Mexico and Colorado had unlimited authority to divert Rio Grande water, then El Paso, plus Juarez and miles of the Texas-Mexico border might eventually strangle on their own dust. The Senate committee on "Irrigation and Reclamation of Arid Lands" made an inspection trip to hear border complaints, and it endorsed the international dam suggested by Mills.[5]

On the strength of this testimonial, Mills assigned the old reliable Follett to survey the upper Rio Grande. Follett submitted his report in 1896, his findings and conclusions hampered by a lack of statistics regarding past-flows. Still, Follett explained more about the river than anyone except an engineer would want to know.[6]

Armed with Follett's findings, the joint commission agreed that Mexico "has been wrongfully deprived for many years of . . . a portion of her equitable rights to . . . one-half of the Rio Grande, . . . and it is apparent . . . that the dying fruit trees and the vines, the abandoned fields and dry canals," had been responsible for a population decrease. A proposed treaty drafted by Mills and Osorno called for an equal distribution of Rio Grande waters and the construction of an international dam at El Paso. It called for a New Mexico cession of ninety-eight acres so that Mexico could border on the south end of the dam, making the lake truly international. The United States would absorb all costs.[7]

Article VI of the Joint Commission's proposed treaty was particularly significant. It forbade the construction "of new works or canals on the Rio Bravo del Norte and its tributaries, on that part passing through the territory of the United States of America." This barred Colorado and New Mexico from further diverting or regulating the Rio Grande.

Secretary of State Olney and Mexican Minister Romero tentatively approved the draft even though Olney cited existing "embarrassments."

A private firm had a license to build the Engle Dam, called the "Boyd Dam" by southwesterners. It was scheduled for construction 115 miles north of El Paso, at a location at or near present-day Elephant Butte Dam.

This refueled a classic, long-simmering dispute between government ownership vs. private enterprise. Prevailing philosophies expected such undertakings to be financed privately. However, far-sighted people such as John Wesley Powell insisted that only government had the power and money to build and operate adequate dams. But Powell lost. In the ensuing political struggles, disposing of the West's natural resources shifted to the secretary of interior, and he supported private efforts for irrigational purposes. The Department merely insisted that investors complete their projects within five years.[8]

A battle of ideologies shook El Paso when Mills accused city engineer John L. Campbell of conspiring against the region's best interests with realtor Albert M. Loomis and casket salesman Edward V. Berrien. The three developers brought in the First National Bank and the law firm of Davis, Beall & Kemp. They formed the Rio Grande Dam and Irrigation Company in 1893, retaining the fiery Nathan E. Boyd, President of the Mesilla Valley Irrigation Company of New Mexico. On February 1, 1895, Secretary of the Interior Hoke Smith granted Boyd permission to build a dam at Engle, New Mexico.

Due to a decline of American gold reserves, the Panic of 1893, a drop in stock prices and a repeal of the Sherman Silver Purchase Act, Boyd lacked sufficient financing, so he prevailed upon a British group to purchase the charter. It did so, and reorganized the firm into The Rio Grande Irrigation and Land Company, Limited. Local directors and bankers remained a part of it. Based on experiences in the Nile Valley, the English committed themselves to the largest artificial lake in the world. While they promised electricity to cities, farms and ranches, their primary income would depend upon the management and sale of land, plus water rights. "The company will obtain control of the entire flow of the Rio Grande in southern New Mexico . . . [and] in controlling the water the company will, to a great extent, control the irrigable lands," the prospectus read. Property owners would "convey to the vendor company one-half of their lands in return for water rights to the other half, and . . . pay a water rent of $1.50 per acre per annum for every acre of land irrigated." The firm anticipated an income of $15 million a year.[9]

Mexico would be guaranteed *no* water, although it could purchase water on an availability basis. Furthermore, the Boyd Dam would obviate any need for another dam at the Pass.

A furious Mills and a frustrated Mexico demanded that Washington revoke the British contract.

Secretary of State Olney asked Interior Secretary David Rowland Francis to rescind the agreement. Instead, Francis consulted with his attorneys, who told him "Congress has never granted . . . nor authorized this Department [to grant] . . . a monopoly on the entire flow . . . of the Rio Grande." Practices like that would "reduce to servitude landowners, citizens of New Mexico, Texas and Mexico, living on the river below the reservoir proposed."[10]

The lawyers suggested that the Interior Department cancel the private license for the Engle Dam. Nevertheless, Francis refused to void an act of his predecessor. To do so, he explained, would be improper.

Olney next huddled with Daniel S. Lamont, secretary of war, for a discussion of the Rivers and Harbors Act of September 19, 1890. The Act forbade man-made obstructions on a navigable river, and by terms of the 1848 Treaty, the river was navigable. The secretary of war could block those diversions.

That the Rio Grande was navigable in *law* and by treaty with Mexico, no one disputed. But was it navigable in fact? Determining such evidence fell upon Anson Mills, who cited instances of the river's use for commercial purposes. Flatboats had plied the river north of Juarez before Colorado and New Mexico diverted the water. Logs had floated downstream. In 1882 and 1888, Congress authorized two international bridges at El Paso, and Mills believed that act in itself supported the river's navigability. Under his prodding, army engineer Captain George McDerby and Major A. M. Miller swore that the Rio Grande would float ships near El Paso during specific seasons, and that a dam at Engle would paralyze commercial traffic.[11]

With this evidence, Acting Attorney General Holmes Conrad on May 7, 1897, instructed his Albuquerque office to file an injunction against the British company.

The syndicate failed to immediately realize its peril, believing the dispute was a matter of inadequate communications, a subject for negotiation and compromise. "It must not be supposed that the United States government is antagonistic to the company," one memorandum said. "To the contrary, we have reason to believe the United States government is the reverse of unfriendly." Boyd of course had some rationale for his optimism. He won his case repeatedly in New Mexico's federal courts only to have the decision reversed by the Supreme Court. Yet, he still expected to prevail, having confidence that deep down the Americans would never opt for a dam at the Pass. Costs would be excessive, and valuable farm land submerged. He considered the Pass too wide for an adequate dam, and expressed doubts about the bedrock's stability.[12]

Mexico was the British firm's primary obstacle to a settlement, and Boyd anticipated that Mexican needs and American desires for accommodation would eventually work in the Engle dam's favor. Ultimately, Washington would ask Boyd to supply the Juarez requirements. Mexico would either "have to pay, or the United States would have to subsidize the company . . . $250,000 a year for twenty years."[13]

While the English awaited negotiations that never started, Mills launched a survey to determine navigability between San Marcial, New Mexico (fifty miles north of the proposed Engle site), and Laredo, Texas. Should the river prove to be navigable, then there would be no dams anywhere because the Treaty of Guadalupe Hidalgo, which strictly denied any hindrances to navigation, took precedence over all laws and dam building schemes. Yet, neither New Mexico, Colorado, Texas or the United States and Mexico wanted the river to be found navigable. Everybody had too much at stake in irrigation. Therefore, the survey would be of the Rio Grande as it existed in 1901. Engineers would not factor-in the flow of the river before irrigation started.

Commission engineers floated downstream in two skiffs throughout May, June and July, 1901, taking measurements and photographs. The trip turned into an ordeal. Boat crews battled quicksand, dry channels, floods, mosquitoes and monotony. A rattlesnake bit consulting engineer P. D. Cunningham on the toe as he slept near Langtry, Texas, and he spent a week waiting for the swelling and pain to subside. As it was, Cunningham's time had come. When twenty-five miles from Eagle Pass on July 13, his skiff struck a submerged boulder. Cunningham drowned.[14]

The navigability report, in a classic case of figures proving whatever one wants them to prove, buttressed the government case, indicating to Mills' satisfaction, at least, that the Rio Grande was navigable north and south of El Paso. The engineers found that only sixteen percent of the water leaving San Marcial, New Mexico ever reached Roma, Texas

Santa Helena Canyon in the Big Bend of the Rio Grande in 1901.
P. D. Cunningham drowned near here. (IBWC)

(in 1901). If irrigation figures had been included, or factored-in, then fifty-five percent of the water would have made it. This meant that without irrigation, the upper river could have contributed to the lower river's navigability. But the report didn't say that because nobody asked for it. Based on convoluted reasoning, Mills contended that a dam at Engle would destroy El Paso's river traffic, although left discreetly unsaid was why a dam at the Pass would not do the same.

The quixotic Dr. Boyd finally recognized that the full weight of the government was slowly marshalling against him. Bitterly he attacked Mexico, Mills and the secretary of state. Calling it treasonous to even consider free water for Mexico, he asked why Mexicans shouldn't pay a fair price just like Americans?

Boyd leveled twelve charges at Mills, the severe ones including perjury, treason, fraud and conspiracy. Boyd's greatest wrath, however, fell upon Secretary John Hay whom Boyd accused of having a "long and full knowledge of the facts of the case . . . and [he] has deliberately condoned General Mills' crime. If I cannot bring this official crime to the President's notice in any other manner, I shall . . . horsewhip

Secretary Hay in some public place and thereby secure my own arrest and the necessary publicity." Boyd swore that if Mills were cross-examined, "it would not be necessary for me to sacrifice myself further by publicly pulling John Hay's nose or caning him, or putting a bullet through him, in order to arouse sufficient public interest in my charges to ensure their proper investigation."[15]

But then suddenly on May 23, 1903, the case dramatically closed. A federal court in New Mexico cancelled the Engle contract because the company had failed to build a dam within five years as required by law. Of course, the United States had kept the syndicate in litigation during that time.[16]

The firm went bankrupt and then lost its breach of contract suit against the United States. Colonel W. J. Engledue, designer for the British Imperial Irrigation Company in India and a consultant for the Engle Dam, committed suicide. Boyd blamed Mills for Engledue's death, and J. P. Cunningham's as well.[17]

It would seem that a victorious United States and an exultant Anson Mills would commence an international dam at El Paso. But Washington stalled, primarily because reclamation thinking was revolutionizing water control. Congressman John H. Stephens of Texas introduced a bill calling for the equitable distribution of the Rio Grande, placing responsibility for the cost on the United States. New Mexico and the Rio Grande Dam and Irrigation Company denounced the measure as a ruse to build a dam at the Pass and prevent construction of one farther north.

Ira G. Clark, whose *Water in New Mexico* is a final word on the subject, said the committee believed "a dam at El Paso would discipline a river whose erratic behavior was a constant source of trouble, [and that a dam would] preserve and restore the navigability of the Rio Grande, assure to the El Paso-Juarez area its just share of water, and release the United States from Mexican claims." A congressional committee concluded that reclamation involving more than one state or territory, and having international complications, should become a commitment of the federal government. This led to the National Reclamation Act of 1902, a responsibility of the Interior Department, which created the Bureau of Reclamation to administer it.[18]

Theodore Roosevelt urged its passage, and the Act swept Congress, promising harbor improvements in the East and South, as well as dams and canals for the far West and Southwest. A much needed common

Elephant Butte Dam, New Mexico, in 1966. On the Rio Grande, 150 miles south of Albuquerque, it is named for the land mass in upper center, which was said to resemble a reclining elephant. (Bureau of Reclamation)

sense approach came to Western development. Under the Act's auspices, farmers paid for water rights in return for federal construction. The fund would replenish itself, and after expenses were met, local water users associations would assume control. The government retained title only to the dam and auxiliaries.

The Bureau of Reclamation investigated possible Rio Grande reservoir sites, and reached two conclusions. The El Paso bedrock had potentially serious weaknesses, and a dam at the Pass would flood approximately eighty-eight thousand acres of the Mesilla Valley in New Mexico. Furthermore, since no federal public lands existed in Texas, a dam at El Paso would not qualify for reclamation funds. Engineers approved the Engle, New Mexico region, where the British firm had washed out, calling for a dam at Elephant Butte. The Bureau asked for public support as the 13th Annual Convention of the National Irrigation Congress met in El Paso during November 1904. A committee endorsed Elephant Butte Dam, and the entire membership roared its approval.[19]

The convention took no action regarding Mexican demands for a portion of the Rio Grande, and New Mexico fretted that it might yet win the dam and lose the water. Governor Miguel Otero testified in Congress that "the people within this Territory are greatly discouraged . . . [because] no definite assurance has been given them that they will not be robbed of their surplus waters through the claims of a foreign government."[20]

Mexico vigorously complained about conspiracies depriving it of just water rights, and Secretary of State Elihu Root reacted with "principles of the highest equity and comity." He offered a treaty providing Rio Grande water as far east as Fort Quitman, Texas (about ninety miles), the eastern end of the El Paso-Juarez valley. Americans would build and finance a dam at Elephant Butte and provide Mexico with sixty thousand acre-feet per year at the *Acequia Madre* (the principal irrigation ditch) in Juarez. During periods of drought and a low reservoir, Mexico's share would be reduced on a percentage basis just like the Americans.

Mexico rebutted with a demand for seventy-five thousand acre-feet annually, and delivery at the diversion canals. The Mexican minister also requested one-half of storm and drainage waters.[21]

The United States rejected each request, and Mexico, anxious for an agreement on paper, accepted the American offer. An "Equitable Distribution of the Waters of the Rio Grande" was signed in Washington on May 21, 1906.[22]

The Upper River
Becomes a Ditch

THE RECLAMATION ACT OF 1902 lacked jurisdiction in Texas because the federal government owned no public lands there. Three years later, however, Congress included the El Paso Valley as a part of the Rio Grande Project for reclamation purposes. In 1906 the Act embraced the entire state.

Elephant Butte Dam ended all speculation about navigation on the river, as the Rio Grande Project, which included the dam and reclamation area, extended from 175 miles north of El Paso to one hundred miles southeast of El Paso along the international line. By the late 1980s, the cumulative annual crop value for the Project exceeded $2 billion, with cotton the largest contributor. Five diversion dams deflected the water into the fields. Canal systems unfurled for six hundred miles, and were enlarged by an additional five hundred miles of drainage ditches. The Elephant Butte reservoir, with its capacity of 2,195,000 acre-feet, became the largest and best known lake in New Mexico, eventually attracting more than a million tourists and sportsmen annually.[1]

While Elephant Butte brought agricultural prosperity to El Paso, carelessness of the city council prevented El Paso from sharing extensively in the Rio Grande for utility water. Project Director Lawrence

M. Lawson advised the city in 1917 that water rights on eight thousand acres of undeveloped lands could be claimed by assuming a share of the Project construction costs. The city council called it too expensive, meaning it was easier and cheaper to remove vast amounts of good quality underground water from the nearby Hueco Bolson. In 1928, the city reconsidered, but the Project Limits Board ruled that the Elephant Butte storage capacity was already appropriated. It wasn't until 1941 that El Paso worked out leases with the Bureau of Reclamation for water rights to two thousand acres of land, and more was added in the mid 1960s. The city may eventually acquire rights to four thousand acres.

As the turn of the century approached, the city has authority to remove river water equaling about thirteen percent of its needs, or roughly twenty thousand acre-feet annually. Unfortunately, its two water treatment plants cannot handle that much, another is under consideration near the Riverside Diversion Dam. While it also has a "wild water" (generally conceded as rain water) agreement with the Bureau, giving the community title to whatever water enters the Rio Grande south of Elephant Butte Dam and upstream from El Paso, it has never constructed a reservoir for storage, nor has it made much effort to process and utilize the water because of the low treatment plant capacity. It is still cheaper to pump dwindling supplies from the ground.[2]

A few miles north of El Paso, Mesilla Valley farmers organized the Elephant Butte Irrigation District of New Mexico. West Texas farmers created the El Paso County Water Users Association. They figured formulas for sharing construction, operations and maintenance costs, which totaled out to nearly $28,800,000. Heavier expenses fell on farmers with the most irrigable land. The Reclamation Act limited participants to 160 acres, and the farmers estimated that $40 per irrigated acre would be a fair reimbursement to the government since the Bureau also would collect income from electrical power.

Friendly suits against water users determined property ownership. Reclamation engineers resurveyed the old Spanish land grants, and in some instances found tenants who did not know their landlord's name. Several families squatted without titles, and had to be removed.[3]

Water from Elephant Butte reservoir irrigated the Mesilla Valley, and then swept downstream for El Paso and Mexican distribution at the *Acequia Madre Dam*, now frequently called the "International

Dam," a dirt and stone structure two miles northwest of downtown Juarez. Mexico diverted its sixty thousand annual acre-feet when needed, whereas *all* of the remaining water was allocated to El Paso valley farmers. The Bureau of Reclamation purchased the ancient but dilapidated Franklin Canal, whose channel extended from the International Dam to the El Paso Lower Valley, although the canal banks were frequently just barely traceable ridges. The canal's right-of-way saved the government time plus expensive condemnation procedures.

A delicate link in the irrigation chain was the El Paso Water Users' Association, although it lacked authority to tax and legally obligate its members. It reorganized into the El Paso County Water Improvement District No. 1 with the power to raise money.[4]

In the meantime, President Theodore Roosevelt had lost confidence in Mills, and the commissioner came under slashing attack by Colorado Senator Charles Spalding Thomas who claimed Mills paid his assistants too much salary. Thomas also accused Mills of averaging but two trips a year to the border. Mills knew what the politicians wanted, so he resigned on July 1, 1914. Even that did not prevent a 1915 congressional drubbing.[5]

The construction of Elephant Butte Dam ended in 1916. The ultimate development, as it now exists, was not finished until 1925. Three intermediate New Mexico diversion dams were either in place or in the process of construction when controlled amounts of water left Elephant Butte. The first was Leasburg, finished in 1908-09. The Mesilla Dam near Las Cruces (1916-1917) was second, and Percha last. Leasburg and Mesilla dams served the Mesilla Valley, while Percha irrigated the Rincon Valley, thirty miles south of Elephant Butte.[6]

Nevertheless, the Rio Grande Project was merely a step in the right direction and not the entire journey. Tension arose between Texas, New Mexico and Colorado over an equitable disposition of the upper Rio Grande.

New Mexico in particular had been suspicious of Texas water acquisitions ever since the Boyd Dam fiasco, and a dispute opened regarding each state's share of the remaining water. Colorado and New Mexico were not inclined to restrict their own development to assist Texas, and Texas feared her northern neighbors might leave little more than a sandy ditch. Agreements and understandings were necessary, and Secretary of Commerce Herbert Hoover chaired an organizational meeting in Colorado Springs. These deliberations produced a temporary Rio Grande Compact (popularly called the Santa Fe Agreement) of 1929, and a permanent one in 1939.[7]

The Compact assured each state a share in the Rio Grande, and made allowances for a system of debits and credits to balance out the lean vs. the abundant years. Colorado and New Mexico went almost immediately into debit status, using more than they were entitled to, and a deficit of Compact deliveries to Elephant Butte amounted to three years of stream flow by 1965. With reserves less than anticipated, the United States decreased Mexico's annual allotment proportionately.[8]

Meanwhile, Elephant Butte Dam brought complexities as well as blessings to the border. The Rio Grande carried a heavy load of sediment, and even though it accumulated slower than projected, over periods of time it often forced the river to seek lower beds.

While the current acted as its own scouring agent, especially in times of high and fast water, Elephant Butte reduced the floods which meant the channel tended to fill with blow sand. The Rio Grande meandered even more intensely, and such serpentine wanderings wasted water, destroyed crops, increased scrub vegetation and shifted the boundary. A rain-swollen river swamped south El Paso in 1925, in the process inundating Washington Park and the Island of San Elizario.

An analysis called for straightening the Rio Grande from El Paso ninety miles downstream to the Quitman Mountains, installing several international bridges and dividing land (bancos) sliced from the river curves. The International Boundary Commission described these bancos as "parcels."

On February 1, 1933, both countries approved the Rio Grande Rectification treaty, and Lawrence M. Lawson, a scholarly fifty-three-year-old Washington, D.C. engineer, directed the program. Lawson had been Rio Grande Project manager in 1917, guiding the operations of Elephant Butte and seeing that the irrigators in New Mexico, Texas and Mexico received their allotments of water. He became commissioner of the American section of the International Boundary and Water Commission in 1927, and he and Mexican Commissioner Gustavo P. Serrano conceived, planned and directed the rectification of the Rio Grande throughout the El Paso-Juarez Valley.[9]

Prior to now, the boundary commissions had expended their energies in solving disputes. Now they were involved in building a $6 million channel, the construction of which started in 1934 and ended in 1941. The United States paid eighty-eight percent of the cost. Seven

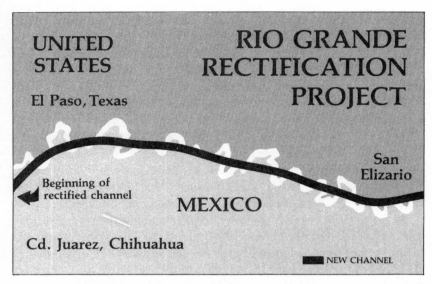

UNITED
STATES

El Paso, Texas

RIO GRANDE
RECTIFICATION
PROJECT

Beginning of
rectified channel

MEXICO

San
Elizario

Cd. Juarez, Chihuahua

NEW CHANNEL

The rectified line became the new U.S.-Mexico boundary. Land (bancos) cut south
of the new riverbed went to Mexico. Land lying north of the line was assigned to
the United States (Texas). (Arnulfo Oliveira Memorial Library, Brownsville)

foot parallel levees doubled as maintenance roadways as well as barriers against future floods.

The center of the artificial channel, now a relatively straight ditch,
became the international boundary. In straightening the border,
engineers shortened the river in the El Paso Lower Valley from 155.2
miles to 85.6 miles, and divided over ten thousand acres of parcels
equally in accordance with the 1905 Banco Treaty. Sixty-nine went to
the United States, and eighty-five to Mexico. The remaining twenty-
four parcels stayed in the floodway channel. Those assumed by the
United States were given either to municipalities or sold. Ascarate Park
in El Paso is a former parcel.[10]

Toll-free international bridges were erected between Ysleta and
Zaragoza, Fabens and Guadalupe, and Fort Hancock and El Porvenir.

The Rectification Treaty provided for the construction of Caballo
Dam, with a capacity of 344,000 acre-feet, an earthfill structure ninety-
six feet high and twenty-two miles south of Elephant Butte. Studies in-
dicated that fifty percent of the drainage entering the river between
Elephant Butte and El Paso did so within thirty miles downstream of

the reservoir. The secondary storage facility would reduce potential downstream floods, and hoard additional water for border irrigation. With Caballo as a catch basin for drainage as well as water released for winter power generators at Elephant Butte, a considerable amount of water could be preserved that might otherwise be lost.[11]

And of course if water could be saved by straightening the Rio Grande throughout the El Paso valley, the same might happen by aligning the 108 miles of river between Caballo Dam and El Paso. In this instance, banco distributions were of no consequence because both sides of the river belonged to New Mexico. A straightening of the channel would reduce New Mexico floods. Water releases for the Mexican border would be more controllable and regulated.

By an act of Congress in June 1936, the Canalization Project went into effect. Washington removed a 108 mile strip from private ownership, the reasoning being that since the commission was charged with allocating an annual sixty thousand acre-feet of water from Elephant Butte to Mexico, the transfer could not judiciously be done without also controlling flows into the southern New Mexico diversion dams. Boundary commission employees gouged out a straight channel, raised levees, planted two thousand trees and installed ten bridges, plus miscellaneous structures.[12]

When irrigation water reached the border and the International Dam, Mexico measured its sixty thousand acre-feet and dumped the remainder back into the river channel or into the Franklin Canal for use by farmers in the El Paso valley. However, according to Bureau of Reclamation estimates, Mexico frequently diverted more than its allotment.[13] To compensate, Elephant Butte released excessive amounts to make up the difference. That depleted the reserves and denied Texas its "proper share of the Rio Grande."[14]

Primitive Mexican facilities contributed to the problem. The diversion dam was porous and insubstantial, two feet short of a height needed to properly reroute water. Instead of adequately raising the height, the Mexicans piled stones and brush on top. Their makeshift construction permitted them to divert their own water while wasting the rest.[15]

By treaty terms, Mexico had no legal right to any Rio Grande water in this upper portion of the river except the sixty thousand acre-feet commitment. All other water in the channel was United States property. But when El Pasoans erected diversion dams for better access,

Lawrence Lawson (left) former American boundary commissioner. (IBWC). (Below) the Rio Grande pauses at the American Dam near El Paso. Mexico is at the upper right (New Mexico enclosed by lower right road), and Texas on the left. The dam measures and releases Mexico's water into the river channel. The American Canal is left of the dam, and most of the water is dispatched through it and earmarked for Texas farmers in the El Paso Lower Valley. (IBWC)

furious Mexican farmers threatened dam destructions, even though no attempts took place. Mexican authorities took more water out of the Acequia Madre headgates than authorized, and Mexican farmers installed illegal diversion pumps in the river channel. The Mexican boundary commissioner could do nothing because the allocation had become a political issue. The unauthorized thefts equaled at least "three times the amount [of water] allocated."[16]

Americans had only themselves to blame because while the United States had assumed responsibilities for water delivery to the International Dam at the Acequia Madre, Washington waited thirty years to appoint an administering agency. In 1935 Congress authorized the American Dam, 3.5 miles northwest of downtown El Paso, 140 feet north of the international boundary, and two miles north of the International Dam. The American section of the Boundary Commission installed sensitive measuring equipment, and from 1936 forward, Mexico no longer estimated its own allotment of water. The American Dam did that for them, metering and releasing water into the river channel. The American Dam diverted the remaining flow into the American Canal, a two-mile-long feeder for the Franklin Canal, which carried water for irrigation to the El Paso side of the valley.[17]

The Franklin Canal was narrow and shallow, its maintenance and cleaning barely adequate. While the American Canal had a flow capacity of 1,200 cubic feet per second, the Franklin Canal had seven hundred and in places barely four hundred. The Franklin lacked a capacity to carry the American Canal's full volume, so the American Canal dumped portions of its load back into the river channel downstream from Mexico's *Acequia Madre* at the old International Dam. Water emptied back into the river provided Mexican farmers with opportunities for illegal pumping. These activities have been ignored by the American Section of the boundary commission because to raise the issue would likely mean reopening the 1906 treaty. To reopen the treaty would mean a Mexican insistence on more water.[18]

Mexico has always felt cheated anyway, believing it deserved more than sixty thousand acre-feet annually, the estimated maximum annual use prior to the 1906 treaty. While Mexico averaged 42,737 acre-feet of water annually during the thirty-three years between 1951 and 1983, El Paso farmers averaged 250,000 acre-feet.

During this period, the Rio Grande watershed languished through a severe drought, with Mexico in 1964 receiving only 6,614 acre-feet.

However, it received a full allotment for fifteen of those thirty-three years, including every year since 1979. During the mid and late 1980s (as in the early 1940s, especially 1942), so much water ran over the dams and through the spillways, most of it due to heavy snowfall in Colorado, that Mexico not only received its full share, but a lot more. The channels ran loaded, and in places between El Paso and Del Rio, minor flooding happened.

Still, full reservoirs are forty year phenomenons, on average. Even during less than peak years, however, there may be more water in the reservoirs than needed by the United States. That extra water is not given to Mexico because 1), Mexico is not entitled to it by treaty, and 2) to provide additional water on occasion would encourage Mexico to enlarge its acreage, and to expect, and even demand, extra water each year. Therefore, Mexican illegal diversions leave the United States with two options, besides disregarding it. The American Boundary Commission could charge the unauthorized thefts against Mexico's guarantee, which would be tantamount to reopening the 1906 treaty, or the Americans could expand and enlarge the Franklin Canal, and divert all of the water away from the river channel. Neither option seems likely in the near future.[19]

The Lower
Rio Grande Valley

FOR A TIME, at least, the needs of the upper Rio Grande had been met, and attention turned to the Lower Valley of Texas and its massive potential for cotton, vegetables and citrus. The lower Rio Grande extended from Roma, Texas to the Gulf, a distance of 250 miles, roughly twice the length of a direct line.

Seventy percent of all tributary water reaching Texas came from Mexican streams, the principal ones being the Rio Conchos near Presidio, Texas, the Rio Salado between Laredo and Roma, and the Rio San Juan, downstream from Roma. The Devils and Pecos rivers in Texas furnished a majority of the remaining thirty percent, and they entered the Rio Grande a short distance upstream from Del Rio.

The people could be just as intemperate as the rivers, and José de Escandón, a forty-seven-year-old Spaniard, conquistador and governor of Nuevo Santander soon found that out. He went by the title of Conde de la Sierra Gorda (Count of Fat Mountain), and he was a tough, intelligent administrator and organizer. As a royal agent for Mexico, Don José de Escandón brought hundreds of *criollo-mestizo* families out of the Queretaro region and in early 1747 converged on the Lower Rio Grande Valley. Two years later he established Camargo. With great pomp he awarded one hundred pesos to each of forty families. Next he built Nuestra Señora de Guadalupe de Reynosa, forty-one miles downstream from Camargo. In neither Camargo nor Reynosa did he provide for individual grants. Instead, he set aside a large "common" for community agriculture and grazing.[1]

In August 1751, José Vásquez Borrego, a Coahuila rancher, opened a ranch headquarters north of the Rio Grande, and at the western terminal of what would come to be called the Nueces Strip. He named the headquarters Nuestra Señora de los Delores, and staffed it with thirteen families.

Borrego talked Coahuila neighbor Tomás Sánchez into building a nearby ranch, and Escandón assisted with a grant of fifteen leagues. Sánchez was supposed to start a town and a mission, but did neither. His grant remained a ranch headquarters, but from it a town eventually arose which became Laredo, the only village on the north bank of the Rio Grande.[2]

In 1757 Spain conducted a census. Reynosa had 279 persons of European ancestry, and nearly three hundred Indians. Camargo counted 637 Mexicans and 245 Indians representing five different tribes. Meanwhile, two more Rio Grande communities started. Mier had thirty-five families of Spanish descent, and 250 Indians. Revilla (later Guerrero) had 150 people, residents described as Spanish, *mestizo* (half Spanish and half Indian), and mulatto (Spanish and black, or Indian and black).

The government assigned a six-square-league jurisdiction to these towns, with authority similar to counties in the United States. Surveyors measured town plats with a fifty *vara* leather cord (162½ feet) stretched one hundred times from the central plaza. Streets were a standard ten varas in width. Residents who preferred living outside the community were given a specific lot, plus an obligation of improvements within two years.

Inhabitants fell into three categories: original settlers with over six years along the river; settlers with between two and six; and those with less than two years. The government gave original owners, including heirs, two leagues (8,856 acres) of grazing land or twelve *caballerías* (1,500 acres) of agricultural soil. Six caballerías for farming went to the middle classifications. Newcomers received two leagues of pasture. Of course, none of these units had value without water, so surveyors laid out grants end-to-end along the Rio Grande. (In Revilla, allotments fronted on the Rio Salado.) At the time of possession, the grantee symbolically pulled a few weeds, tossed a handful of dirt into the air, and gave thanks to God and majesty. He then signed or marked the necessary documents and dispatched them to Mexico City.[3]

By modern standards none of these properties had precisely defined boundaries. The fifty vara cord stretched or shrank depending upon wet or dry grass. Allowances had to be made for arroyos, hills, trees, boulders and other obstacles. There were odd-shaped wedges, and portions often overlapped as the surveyors avoided geological or natural intrusions. Later as sections were sold, abandoned, broken up or given to heirs, as settlers moved in and out, as scenery or the river bed changed, the complications regarding who owned what turned into a legal quagmire.

By 1810 few people of humble origin still owned a grant. Most had sold out, or left. Portions were divided, subdivided, multiplied, expanded, rented, abandoned, forgotten and repossessed. In Reynosa, practicaly all grants ended up in the possession of six families. Hardly a section belonged to an original owner by 1800, and absentee landlords ruled. Captain Juan José Hinojosa, chief justice of Reynosa, had land eleven and one-half leagues wide and fifteen leagues long. It all fronted on the Rio Grande. His son-in-law José María de Ballí owned La Feria grant on twelve and one-half leagues to the east. Their heirs increased those holdings to nearly the entire Lower Rio Grande Valley.[4]

After the Mexican War and after the land grants north of the Rio Grande had passed to the United States, grant recipients were oftentimes aliens on their own soil. They had title problems, political problems, tax problems, language problems, cultural, social and customs problems. Texas created Nueces County out of the Strip, then in 1848 broke it into Webb (with Laredo as the county seat), Starr (with its seat in Rio Grande City), and Cameron (first Santa Rita, then Brownsville becoming the county seat). Zapata and Hidalgo counties were created later. The legislature appointed a commission on February 8, 1850, to investigate Mexican grants, a move Governor Peter Hansborough Bell said was "to quiet and not to disturb or invalidate the land titles."

By 1848 treaty terms the United States had agreed to recognize legitimate land grants. But first the courts had to determine which land grants were legitimate, for until legitimatized, the grants could not legally be sold, rented or taxed. Proper ownership remained in doubt. Just as any American was not entitled to land just because he lived there, so former Mexican citizens were not entitled to property simply because they laid claim to a Spanish or Mexican land grant. In short, while the United States agreed to recognize these grants, that recognition depended upon the evidence produced. Documents were the most desirable and positive proof, but oral testimony from claimants, family and witnesses was duly evaluated.

Land commissioners W. H. Bourland and James R. Miller inspected Webb, Starr and Cameron counties, heard twenty applicants from the valley around Laredo and 115 from Rio Grande City. Cameron had only a couple of cases although both involved huge amounts of property. On occasion the commissioners arbitrated boundaries between rival grants, as in the claim of Francisco Guerra of Hidalgo County who sued for eight-and-one-half leagues from the jurisdicton of Reynosa. After examining the evidence, they ignored both claimants and reverted the land back to the Hinojosa heirs.[5]

Numerous Lower Rio Grande Valley land grant cases have since come and gone. In some instances legal considerations have given way to practical necessities, as in the lower valley where every community on the American bank of the Rio Grande lies on a former grant, or portion thereof. The United States recognized, as had Mexico, that grants sometimes had to be revised for the common good. The Espíritu Santo Grant, which dated back to 1781 when José Salvador de la Garza took possession, was expropriated in 1826 by Tamaulipas so that the village of Matamoros might be created. The Matamoros common lands extended across the river and became the foundation of Brownsville in 1850.

Strangely, while only one family originally owned all this, its partial loss became an emotional factor in the Cortina War. Juan Cortina, attracted to his cause illiterate peasants whose ancestors had for the most part never been property owners in Spanish Texas, but who now fervently believed the region had been stolen from them by the Americans.

As for American farmers, they started arriving in Brownsville with the Missouri-Pacific in 1904. Potential buyers paid $49.50 round trip from Chicago. A typical acre sold for $325 during the 1920s, and farms averaged between fifteen and twenty acres. Add $50 per acre for clearing, plowing and ditching, another $110 for citrus trees, plus the cost of buildings and equipment, and one could understand why developers working out of Chicago disregarded people with less than $5,000. The average purchaser had a net worth of $50,000.[6]

Within a couple of decades, Texas had one hundred thousand acres in crops alongside the lower Rio Grande and was dependent upon river irrigation. While the Rio Grande valley had an average yearly rainfall of twenty-four inches, it fell at the wrong time for thee growing season.

So farmers called for Washington to negotiate a treaty recognizing Rio Grande water amounts already in use for Texas, and permitting expansions.[7]

The State Department created an international commission separate from the boundary commission in 1908 to evaluate the lower Rio Grande, as well as the Colorado. Mexican representative, Fernando Beltrán y Puga of Mexico, stymied all agreement efforts on the lower Rio Grande, however, insisting that "Mexico should have all the water she needs before the United States gets one drop." Beltrán must have enjoyed saying that since it echoed and mocked American opinions regarding the Colorado. To drive home its point, Mexico put its own tributaries to more accelerated use, spending millions for a dam on the Rio Salado and canals on the Conchos.[8]

Congress requested a treaty again in 1924, asking Mexico to negotiate an equitable division of water in the lower Rio Grande. But Mexico refused to participate without the Rio Colorado's inclusion. Mexico considered itself a giver regarding the Rio Grande, but a taker regarding the Colorado, and it did not wish to give without first seeing what it would receive.

But the discussions failed. Compact states could not harmonize on sharing the Colorado, and until that happened, Mexico received little satisfaction. This left nothing to debate except the Rio Grande and the Tijuana, the latter not arousing much interest and the former having no chance for settlement before the Colorado. The commission busied itself with discussions of flood control and engineering evaluations. The American Section of the commission published its findings, two-thirds of which described the Colorado.[9]

While everybody argued, an estimated four million acre-feet of water annually flowed down the lower Rio Grande and wasted itself in the Gulf. The United States proposed a series of dams on the river, but could not implement the plan because Mexico owned the south bank. Meanwhile, a gravity canal, called the Retamal, threatened to tap the lower Rio Grande and divert the entire river onto Mexican crop lands. Subtract that water from the United States, seal off some of the Mexican tributaries (as Mexico was threatening to do by building El Azucar Dam on the San Juan River), and South Texas might become a desert, which was what the ancient Spanish considered it anyway.

In 1930, the Texas Valley Gravity Canal and Storage Project essentially destroyed the Retamal Canal concept because it could intersect

F. Beltran y Puga, (left)
Mexican boundary
commissioner. (IBWC).
Early day Fort Brown
(below) at Brownsville,
Texas, looking across the
Rio Grande toward
Matamoros.

the river farther west than the Retamal, and divert much of the Rio Grande through a 169 mile-long concrete ditch. Over four hundred thousand acre-feet might be captured annually. Even if Mexico fully utilized her tributaries, the proposed Texas action could deprive nearly one million acres of fertile Mexican farmland from the Rio Grande. Each country now threatened the other's productivity, so both nations finally recognized the advantages of a negotiated settlement.[10]

Lawrence Lawson, American Boundary Commissioner, and Rafael Fernández MacGregor, Mexico's counterpart, drafted the Treaty of February 3, 1944, for "Utilization of Waters of the Colorado and Tijuana Rivers and of the Rio Grande." It allocated to Mexico: (1) all of the waters reaching the main channel of the Rio Grande from the San Juan and Alamo rivers, including return flows; as well as (2) two-thirds of the flow in the main channel of the Rio Grande from the Conchos, San Diego, San Rodrigo, Encondido and Salado rivers, plus that of the Las Vacas Arroyo, and (3) one-half of all other flows downstream on the Rio Grande from Fort Quitman.[11]

Commissioner Lawson explained to an incredulous Senate Committee on Foreign Relations, that the United States would get fifty percent of the flow even though it provided only thirty percent of the water. The two governments would jointly construct, operate and maintain dams on the lower Rio Grande. These would conserve, store and regulate the annual flow.[12]

In the meantime, a power struggle arose between Secretary of State Cordell Hull and Secretary of the Interior Harold L. Ickes. Ickes believed the river work should be handled by his Bureau of Reclamation. By implication he called American Boundary Commissioner Lawson an "empire builder," and said that unless stopped, Lawson would "continue and expand his engineering and construction organization." Ickes snapped that the Department of State, of which the International Boundary and Water Commission was a branch, should "have no desire to build up an engineering organization."

The issue was resolved on July 3, 1944, when President Franklin D. Roosevelt sent Ickes the second of two bristling letters, bluntly explaining his support of the secretary of state. With this issue resolved, the IBWC moved into a position of political, diplomatic and engineering strength along the border.[13]

Out of the 1944 treaty came a commitment to construct dams on the lower Rio Grande, giant storage containers designed to anchor a treaty stipulation known as the Lower Rio Grande Flood Control Project. This part of the border extended 180 river miles between Penitas, Texas and the Gulf, a delta given immense fertility by river sediment laid down in ages past.

Because the shallow, twisting channel had only a slight drop or fall, a normal rainfall often sent the Rio Grande surging over its banks. Several natural overflow channels, or arroyos, caught the floods and directed them toward the Gulf. Nevertheless, floods still devastated Tamaulipas, and the extreme eastern Texas counties of Cameron, Hidalgo and Willacy. Although delta counties invested over $5 million in Rio Grande levees, it was insufficient. Their efforts frequently caused worse flooding in Mexico.

In response to this economic gutting, Mexico and the United States cooperated on the multi-purpose Anzalduas (diversion) Dam in Hidalgo County, eleven river miles upstream from the border cities of Hidalgo, Texas and Reynosa, Tamaulipas. Work commenced in early 1956, and by 1960, the structure rerouted high water into the interior Texas floodways, and away from American farms. However, even Anzalduas could not altogether staunch the floods of 1958, and Hurricane Beulah in 1967. The powerful storms dropped colossal amounts of moisture on the delta, and torrents washed away crops and villages in northeastern Mexico, as well as Harlingen and McAllen, Texas. When the destruction subsided, each state restored its levees, and in 1976 adopted further safeguards by building the Retamal Dam, thirty-eight miles downstream from Anzalduas. It restricted the Rio Grande at Brownsville and Matamoros to safe channel capacities by diverting the excess water into Mexican floodways.[14]

Even those improvements failed to save man from himself. Roads and bridges encroached on the Rio Grande flood plain. The boundary and water commissions could not get federal ownership of floodways, and local courts determined design specifications for buildings on those plains. Each government spent billions to restrict flooding, yet vast property values were endangered as housing and businesses built in exposed areas.[15]

Another aspect of the Lower Rio Grande Flood Control Project commenced seventy-five miles downstream from Laredo where presidents Dwight D. Eisenhower and Aldolfo Ruíz Cortines dedicated Falcon Dam in October 1953. The structure cost $46 million, the United States picking up 58.6 percent by claiming a greater share of the stored water.

To build Falcon Dam, Washington relocated the town of Zapata, Texas, the county seat of Zapata County, with its two thousand people, along with the villages of Falcon and Lopeno (plus twenty-four cemeteries), to higher ground. Workmen built a new Zapata, including a modern courthouse on an 846 acre site. Mexico uprooted Guerrero and established Nueva Ciudad Guerrero.[16]

During its first five years of existence, the reservoir met all water deliveries. However, an estimated 16.6 percent shortage occurred during the second five years, 1958 and 1963, the figures being guesses as the IBWC did not install scientific measuring devices for twenty years. Engineers could not accurately determine how much stream flow belonged to Texas and how much to Mexico. Both nations often pumped water belonging to the other. Even hydroelectric income fell eight percent below anticipated revenue for twelve years.[17]

Mexico put seventy-five percent more land into irrigation before the dam was completed, and Texas increased its acreage by fifteen percent. Today, a delta water shortage is anticipated forty-six percent of the time.

In spite of shortcomings, the dam paid for itself during its first year, 1954, when Falcon restrained and stored the largest flood on record. Thundering waters rumbled out of the Devils and Pecos rivers, swamping Del Rio, Laredo and numerous other Texas and Mexican towns. American Boundary Commissioner Joseph Friedkin described the devastation as sickening, but was impressed and gratified when, from the air, he watched dark and muddy waters rolling to a standstill at Falcon Dam. And beyond the dam, the scene was tranquil.[18]

Amistad was the last dam of consequence, and was downstream from the Devils and Pecos rivers, and upstream twelve miles from Del Rio, Texas. The United States controls 56.2 percent of the dam and its water. The Friendship Dam attracted the interest of more presidents than any other border project. Eisenhower and Adolfo López Mateos agreed to its erection when they conferred in Ciudad Acuna during 1960. Six years later, presidents Lyndon B. Johnson and Gustavo Díaz Ordaz met during construction to pledge additional friendship. Presidents Richard M. Nixon and Ordaz dedicated the structure in 1969.[19]

Falcon and Amistad are probably the best border investments ever made. By taming the floods, they stabilized the lower Rio Grande Valley, allowing a firm agricultural economy to develop. Prior to the dams, Texas had about 300,000 acres in cultivation. Now the figure exceeds 700,000.[20]

The Kennedy Give-Away
and Other Border Oddities

SECRETARY OF STATE Philander Knox in 1913 tried to trade strips of border territory for the Chamizal, but Mexico refused. Nineteen years later, Washington offered to return the Pious Fund, if Mexico would relinquish all claims to the Chamizal. The Pious Fund originated in 1697 when Spain and church officials collected money for Jesuit missions in California. The United States annexed California, as well as the Fund in 1848, when the figure was in excess of a million dollars. Mexico refused to swap the Pius Fund for the Chamizal, believing it already owned both. Anyway, the Chamizal controversy had become a moral issue, and Mexico even rebuffed the free benefits of Rio Grande rectification, plus offers of other land, in exchange for the Chamizal.[1]

The issue clamored for what historian Gladys Gregory called "a decision cutting through the accumulation of historical, legal and technical flotsam. . . ." It needed statesmanship.[2]

President John Fitzgerald Kennedy sought a more productive relationship with Mexico in June 1962 when he and President López Mateos met in Mexico City. The Americans recognized that if they wanted better relations with their neighbors, the Chamizal would have to be resolved on Mexican terms. Out of their deliberations came resolutions for a "complete solution" to the Chamizal. Two weeks later Ambassador Thomas C. Mann advised El Paso authorities of the discussions.

While Lafleur's 1911 decision gave Mexico everything south of the 1864 river channel, that bed had never been surveyed and its location could only be surmised. Engineering estimates of the Chamizal's size amounted to 437 acres, about two-thirds of a square mile. The property contained 5,600 residents and hundreds of businesses, homes, apartments and tenements. Within that narrow framework, determined Washington diplomats worked the best deal possible.

American Ambassador Thomas C. Mann conceived the basic settlement and moved it efficiently through multilayers of government. Along the way, Chamizal acquired the support of Texas senators John Tower and Ralph Yarborough. When El Paso Congressman Ed Foreman had trouble making up his mind, Richard White replaced him and gave Chamizal his commitment.

American Boundary Commissioner Joseph F. Friedkin coordinated communications between Washington and Mexico City, between El Paso and Juarez, and between El Paso, Austin and Washington. He coalesced diplomatic compromise and engineering practicalities. The tireless and fair Friedkin defended the Chamizal to Congress, and explained exactly how the transaction would be implemented. He argued for appropriations, explaining why Congress needed to purchase 770 acres. A separate deal had to be worked out between Washington and El Paso, a deal involving more land than just the Chamizal compromise. The 770 acres included not only Chamizal properties, but right-of-way for a new channel for the Rio Grande through downtown El Paso, transferring nine miles of railroad track, building a border highway and relocating federal facilities. Friedkin also pacified the nerves of three hundred thousand apprehensive El Paso residents who had serious reservations about the "Kennedy give-away."

The *El Paso Times* and the *El Paso Herald-Post* soothed the unease with vigorous editorials of support. The Chamber of Commerce passed resounding resolutions, and local governments pledged assistance.

Mayor Judson F. Williams, a statesman modest in height but tall in ideas and integrity, deftly guided the Chamizal locally through the shoals of misunderstanding and hostility. The articulate, persuasive Williams rallied community leaders and persuaded them to speak with one voice.

Local Chamizal adversaries were consistently outflanked and reduced to venting their frustration through letters to the editor. Only Shirley Abbott and Feliciano Hinojosa emerged as spokesmen for the opposition, and even they seemed reluctant. The conservative Abbott insisted to a Senate Foreign Relations Committee that the Chamizal had no legality. Hinojosa, President of the Chamizal Civic Association, wanted specific assurances that displaced Americans would receive a just and adequate settlement.[3]

Generally, in depressed areas, such as south El Paso where the Chamizal was located, property was worth less. In a normal situation, the property would have brought what a willing seller would have received from a willing buyer. But Chamizal residents were not willing sellers. Few wished to move, since it meant selling low and purchasing high when they entered a better class neighborhood. Therefore, the government paid the owners not the value of their home, but the replacement value in areas where residents planned to relocate.

Federal District Judge R. E. Thomason stated repeatedly that residents would get an honest price for their Chamizal land. Thomason had been a former El Paso mayor as well as congressman, and from his bench he asserted that "Uncle Sam doesn't mistreat his citizens. If any of them doesn't obtain a fair value for their property," he thundered, "then come to my court and I'll see they get it."[4]

Judson Williams, in cooperation with Mann and Friedkin, made the fears of Hinojosa and others his own. They obtained a four-point program for El Paso.

1. Adequate compensation for displaced property owners.
2. A six-lane border highway.
3. A national monument park and cultural center.
4. Relocation of the Franklin Canal, preferably underground.[5]

The Franklin Canal started near the present-day Hacienda Cafe (old Hart's Mill) and meandered through the city to El Paso's lower valley. This irrigation ditch had long been a dangerous eyesore, a filthy stream where young children swam, waded and often drowned.

A Chamizal cultural center would add class and beauty to the region. A six-lane border highway would ease El Paso's transportation impediment, and open arteries along the congested southeastern edge of the city and the international boundary.

Williams, Mann and Friedkin obtained these concessions primarily by demonstrating what the Chamizal settlement would cost El Paso in lost revenue. The assessed value of El Paso's taxable Chamizal amounted to $9,211,000 in 1960 dollars. Annual revenue losses to the county, state, hospital and school districts ran to $202,000. City and county public investment equaled $10 million. Five hundred and ninety-six residential homes, eighty commercial and industrial structures, and several miles of railroad would be lost. Navarro Elementary School went to Mexico, as did a city dump and Border Patrol administration and detention facilities. Bridges would need replacement.[6]

The Chamizal had benefits too. It amounted to a vast slum clearance, the destruction of nineteen tenements so foul that even New Yorkers would blanch. While some businesses such as the Mine and Smelter Supply were lost forever, most companies, as well as 5,600 Chamizal residents, purchased offices or homes in other parts of the city.

The best deal meant including Cordova Island in negotiations, and Washington believed if the United States was generous regarding Chamizal, Mexico would be equally flexible regarding Cordova. Mexico had never developed this 287 acre protrusion into El Paso, and had little emotional baggage attached. Since the Rio Grande would need relocating as the international border, to force the river around Cordova Island would require sharp turns. Why not sever Cordova on an east-west line, the United States taking the top half (193 acres). This meant the Americans owed Mexico 437 acres for Chamizal, plus 193 acres for Cordova. However, to straighten the Rio Grande even more, the United States gave Mexico 264 acres east of Cordova. By subtracting the 193 acres from the 264 acres, it left an imbalance of 71 acres in favor of Mexico. In order to bring the swap back to an even 437 acres, 71 acres were removed from the Chamizal, making it amount to 366 acres.[7]

The United States cited a flurry of numbers, all meaning the same, but used for different purposes with different audiences. Just keep in mind that Mexico received *exactly* 437.18 acres in the final settlement, nothing more and nothing less. Nevertheless, the most popular quote in El Paso was 630 acres. By subtracting the 193 acres of Cordova Island, the sum is back to 437 again. When officials testified before Congress, they generally cited the 437 acres. However, the Chamizal

Convention, signed in Mexico on August 29, 1963, and proclaimed in the United States on January 16, 1964, refers to 823 acres. It included 366 acres of Chamizal, the 264 acres east of Cordova which helped straighten the river channel, and the 193 acres of southern Cordova which had always belonged to Mexico anyhow and had never been in dispute.

The six point agreement came down to this:

1. The center of the Rio Grande would become the international boundary [after the channel was relocated].
2. Neither country would pay the other for land transferred. However, the National Bank of Mexico would purchase structures left standing on the Chamizal portion passing to Mexico.
3. The United States would acquire [purchase] the Chamizal land [from American citizens] and order the evacuation of occupants.
4. The cost of a river channel lined with concrete [to keep the channel from ever changing again between Juarez and El Paso] would be borne equally by both governments.
5. The existing international bridges would be replaced, and the cost shared.
6. Boundary changes would have no effect on the legal, criminal, or citizenship status of anyone living in, or doing business with, any portion of the exchanged territories.[8]

Mexico did not allocate the Chamizal to squatters, as Americans and Mexicans had predicted. Instead it cleared the property, planted more than 750,000 shrubs and trees, built a plant nursery, a botanical garden, an innovative archaeological museum and created a range of sports facilities from tennis courts, baseball stadiums, soccer fields and handball courts to a major stadium and a public fairgrounds. Mexico used the Chamizal settlement lands as a continuation of the National Border Program (PRONAF) and extended developments into an upgrading of several miles of the border through the Chamizal area.

The initial commemorative structure and a large amount of landscaping was in place at the time of the Johnson-Díaz Ordaz meeting in October 1967. Today, the largest park in Juarez, a city with over a million people, is its Chamizal. Thousands of picnickers daily utilize the shade, the green, soft meadows and the cultural complexes.[9]

In contrast, development on the American portion of the Chamizal was limited at first to the facilities for the new port of entry at Cordova

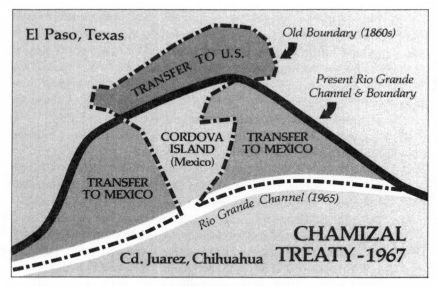

The Chamizal Treaty between the U.S. and Mexico called for (among other things) the relocation of the Rio Grande at El Paso. This map shows subsequent transfer of disputed territory.

Bridge, renamed Bridge of the Americas. Development and manage-ment of the park facilities were assigned to the National Park Service of the Department of the Interior, a Bureau that restricted in-advance-planning prior to gaining title to the land in October 1967. In October of 1973, ten years after the original agreement was presented to the Senate for ratification, the Chamizal National Memorial opened to the public.[10]

Along the way, there were matters of jurisdiction to be settled. Since the Cordova Island tract had never been a part of the United States or Texas, legal responsibility rested solely with the federal government. Texas did not contest jurisdiction, although the state legislature finally requested that the tract be included inside Texas boundaries. The United States ceded jurisdiction.[11]

Even when the initial development of the Memorial was completed, it represented less than half of what had been promised to, and an-ticipated by, the public. A cultural center with limited facilities opened to commemorate the Chamizal settlement. Chris Fox, State National banker and "Mr. El Paso," angrily called attention to Mexico's cultural center, and said El Paso's memorial was "for the birds and a constant source of embarrassment." Civic leaders tended to agree with Fox. Today's memorial is still small, but due to the impressive leadership of National Park Service Superintendent Franklin Smith, the Chamizal National Memorial has become a class achievement.[12]

The border highway was four-lane, not six. However, a new Bowie High School arose on Mexico's former Cordova Island. It is a monument to education.

The alien detention facilities never returned. A holding camp near Chamizal for undocumented Mexicans seemed inconsistent with the spirit of neighborly relations, so the City of El Paso released twenty acres several miles from the border, donating it to the Immigration and Naturalization Service.[13]

Only the ultimate swap remained, and the trauma of John F. Kennedy's assassination did not stop presidents Lyndon Baines Johnson and López Mateos from gathering in El Paso at Bowie High School on September 25, 1964. Their ceremony commemorated the reconciliation. On October 28, 1967, Johnson and President Díaz Ordaz greeted each other at the Chamizal Memorial in Juarez and signed the final Minute of the agreement, formally transferring lands. The Rio Grande was locked inside 4.3 miles of concrete bed, and on December 13, 1968, Johnson and Díaz Ordaz diverted the river into its present channel. That completed a settlement costing the United States in excess of $43 million.[14]

But Chamizal did more than redress a jurisdictional cancer. It added incentives for mending the remaining boundary grievances. Disputes involving the exact international line would no longer throttle amicable relations, for on November 20, 1970, negotiators signed the "Treaty With Mexico Resolving Boundary Differences."[15] It embraced three major issues.

First, it ratified a maritime boundary. An exact line extended seaward from the Atlantic and Pacific shores for twelve nautical miles.

Second, the governments agreed to restore and maintain the Rio Grande and Colorado rivers as natural boundaries. When the channel shifted and transferred no more than 617.76 acres and one hundred inhabitants, the country suffering the loss could restore the river to its original bed within three years. Otherwise, sovereignty passed to the nation having possession, and the river remained the border. The losing country had a "credit" when the stream displaced land to the other

side. When the affected area exceeded 617.76 acres or one hundred inhabitants, the river would be *jointly* reinstated to its prior channel and
continued as the boundary.

Third, the governments agreed to resolve all remaining questions
pertaining to the international line. Over three hundred islands dotted
the Rio Grande channel, with a single exception all of them tiny and of
little consequence. The exception was Beaver (Morteritos) Island which
belonged to the United States.[16]

A similar but different situation existed at the Horcón Tract, Horcón
meaning a forked pole which supports the branches of fruit trees.
Horcón's 419 acres were thirty miles west of Brownsville in the Rio
Grande valley, a steamy, brushy, meandering strip of river making a
lazy U-turn to the right and paralleling itself for a short distance before
circling to the left and returning to near the original starting point. The
two thousand-foot-wide neck might have eventually severed itself naturally, but the parallel channels, five hundred feet apart, could have
linked even sooner.

The Rio Grande Land and Irrigation Company preferred to manage
events rather than wait for nature. The firm operated pumps on the
western side of the neck, but if the parallel beds should merge, the
channel leading to the neck would go dry, and the pumps would have
no water. By straightening the river's flow with a trench across the
neck, the company assured itself of a continuous feed to the pumps.
The ditch shortened the channel, created a steeper grade and strengthened the current.[17]

The former banco now lay south of the international line. As for
Mexico's Horcón Ranch, a fruit farm for whom the tract was named, it
had fronted on the Rio Grande. When the irrigation company severed
the banco, the ranch had no water because the river thereafter flowed
five hundred feet north.

The Texas company had violated the Treaty of 1884 by unauthorized tinkering with the border. The American Boundary Commission
filed charges and the United States District Court for the Southern
District of Texas ordered the Rio Grande Land and Irrigation Company to pay damages of $5,000 to the Horcón Ranch for loss of water.
The firm also paid $10,000 for violating the treaty, and another $2,000
to survey and mark the Horcón banco as United States territory.[18]

For the next half-century, a solitary monument identified "Horcón
Cutoff Banco No. 93," the only evidence of American jurisdiction. The

fines paid for several markers to fully outline the strip quietly disappeared into the United States treasury.

Meanwhile, the Rio Grande meandered north, further landlocking the Horcón Tract inside Mexico but keeping it indisputably American. The United States never relinquished title, but it never enforced its authority or jurisdiction either. For its part, Mexico acknowledged American ownership while gradually assuming de facto control.

During the 1930s, Brownsville and McAllen residents crossed the Rio Grande from Weslaco, Texas to Rio Rico (Rich River), Tamaulipas, a modest Mexican bordertown created to avoid American prohibition laws. Restaurants, souvenir shops, bars, liquor stores, a dog track, and seamy vice contributed to the pleasures. In 1941, two floods washed away the bridge and portions of Rio Rico. The community retreated a brief distance, intruding unknowingly on the Horcón Tract. The American government ignored the silent invasion, perhaps not realizing it had happened, or perhaps not caring that American property existed south of the border. A new Progreso International Bridge spanned the river between Rio Rico and Texas.[19]

When the United States and Mexico implemented the 1970 treaty, Mexico traded 481.68 acres near Hidalgo-Reynosa for 481.68 acres comprising the Horcón Tract and Beaver Island. The swap permitted a straightening of the border with a 1.6 mile (3 kilometer) channel, which also provided flood control. This strip of river contained one of the largest segments of subtropical forest remaining in south Texas, and the Interior Department incorporated the brush-covered countryside into its Division of Sport Fisheries and Wildlife. Aside from aesthetic values, the region protected twenty-four species of birds peripheral to the "Rare and Endangered" list. Included were green jays, kiskadee flycatchers, tropical kingbirds and red-billed pigeons.[20]

Mexico assumed jurisdiction of Horcón and Beaver Island in 1977, the United States granting "absolute ownership, free from any private titles or encumbrances. . . ." While Article I of the treaty promised an "orderly evacuation of the occupants," neither government paid attention. No one lived on Beaver Island and the United States and Mexico had always considered the hundred or so residents of Horcón to be Mexicans. The "evacuation . . . of the Horcón Tract would cause unnecessary hardship," Mexico claimed, and both boundary commissions concluded that the people "should remain undisturbed."[21]

Another rationale may have involved legal processes already at work in determining the citizenship of 130 residents of Horcón, people whom Edinburg, Texas attorney Laurier B. McDonald called "the lost Americans."

McDonald had been a marine and an FBI agent, a lawyer possessing experience with immigration matters as far away as China. He accepted the case of Homero Cantu-Treviño, a forty-year-old man born in Rio Rico on August 25, 1935. The diminutive, graying Cantu-Treviño entered the United States with a three-day visitor's pass in 1972 and stayed four years. When the immigration service caught him, he claimed American citizenship. The case went to trial in Harlingen, Texas on May 11, 1976, and Cantu-Treviño's claim dissolved before immigration Judge Carl Craig's stern but reasoned opinion. Craig insisted that since the disruption of the river channel in 1906, "no country, state or United States official exercised authority within the Horcón Cutoff. No American state, federal or local taxes were collected, nor were any of those laws enforced. Citizens of Mexico passed freely, without documents, from the Horcón Strip into other parts of Mexico. Residents and persons born there were not subject to military service or civil and criminal laws in the United States. Nor was there any United States protection, the final essential."[22]

Judge Craig ordered Cantu-Treviño deported, and the case seemed a natural for the United States Supreme Court. However, Craig's decision went first to the Immigration Board for approval (which it received), and then to the Attorney General for review. On December 18, 1978, Griffin B. Bell overruled the Board and the judge, saying the Immigration and Naturalization Service had failed to prove Cantu-Treviño an alien. His American citizenship was "restored." All other Rio Rico residents born in the Horcón Strip before 1977 were Americans. "Homero Cantu-Treviño is the first person in American history to be born on United States soil though the place he was born was generally accepted as being part of another country," McDonald said.[23]

While the Cantu-Treviño case traveled through the courts, not far away the International Boundary and Water Commission faced its most compelling impasse since Chamizal. It involved the border controversy at Presidio, Texas and Ojinaga, Chihuahua.

In 1913, journalist John Reed called Presidio "a straggling and indescribably desolate village."[24] Sixty years later, Congressman Richard

C. White referred to the one thousand residents of Presidio as living in a depressed area but not knowing they were depressed.[25]

Presidio residents paid no city taxes, had no city officials, and no municipal property. The Lion's Club owned the water system. The only paved street was Highway 67. Scorching summer temperatures, often the highest in the nation, provided the few newsworthy announcements. Presidio was seventy miles west of Big Bend National Park, and not much farther from the county seat at Marfa. The entire county had less than 5,000 people, the meager economic base being the cattle herds near Marfa and 5,400 acres comprising the agricultural strip along the Rio Grande border at Presidio.[26]

Across the river, Ojinaga had thirteen thousand residents. It had rail connections with the Sonora coast and an unpaved highway to Chihuahua City. Author Tom Miller described Ojinaga as having "the rhythm of a *pueblito* in Mexico's interior rather than a town facing its northern neighbor." He called Ojinaga the "Mexican West," a village with "more cowboy hats than sombreros, more flour tortillas than corn."[27] Its valley had five thousand acres under cultivation by 1970. The long, hot growing season produced bumper crops of cotton, grain, cantaloupes and onions.

Actually, there were two valleys here at the border, the 18.6 mile strip of the Rio Grande, and the 3.7 mile lowland of the Rio Conchos, which intersected the Rio Grande and provided most of the water. When the Conchos flooded, it not only swamped its own 2.5 mile-wide-valley, but the two-mile-wide border as well. The Conchos in flood nudged the Rio Grande north, and into erratic patterns. The Rio Grande in flood, did equally capricious things to the Conchos. From the air, bancos carved twisted, overlapping patterns in the soft, fertile soil.

Emory and Salizar established the 1850s border near the Presidio sand hills, which meant Mexico owned most of the irrigable land. However, when floods battered the boundary and eroded the Rio Grande south into Mexico, the Mexicans could do nothing because the two countries did not have diplomatic relations. When talks resumed, the American boundary commission negotiated only the question of bancos, and removed twenty-six.[28]

The Chamizal settlement led to the 1970 treaty authorizing a land swap re-establishing the Rio Grande as the international line. Engineers dug two channels called the Ojinaga Cut (or Tract), totaling 8.3 miles.

In the process, the United States relinquished 1,606.9 acres, which amounted to thirty-one pieces of land owned by twenty-three people. For its part, Mexico gave up 252 acres.

To further stabilize the border, a flood control project invigorated the Presidio-Ojinaga valley. An international floodway extended fifteen miles.[29]

By now, no serious jurisdictional problems remained anywhere along the border. The burning issues had shifted to people and of their right to cross the border unimpeded and unmolested.

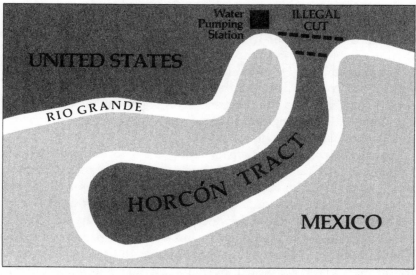

This is the only time in history when a piece of United States territory literally disappeared from the records.

BOOK SEVEN

THE TIRED AND THE POOR

By 1910 Mexican Americans as a group seemed fated to remain foreigners in a land that had been native to their ancestors.

David J. Weber (editor),
Foreigners In Their Native Land

I Lift My Lamp

In 1986 PRESIDENT RONALD REAGAN signed the Immigration Control and Reform Act, a basic provision granting amnesty to an anticipated four million illegal immigrants, most of them Mexicans who could prove United States residence prior to January 1, 1982. It also promised fines and jail terms to Americans henceforth guilty of knowingly employing undocumented aliens. The Act provided the most sweeping immigration reform ever enacted in the United States, a long-debated law which came to grips with the widely-held suspicion that the United States had lost control of its Mexican border.[1]

Still, in spite of reforms, and after a century of controversy, the immigration issue badly needs perspective. Amidst the thunder from left and right, the call for totally open borders versus the call for totally closed borders, lost among the rhetoric are historical signposts pointing out how we got to where we are today. Contrary to what some journalists, politicians and even borderlanders suspect, immigration issues are not just a twentieth century phenomenon.

The right to migrate anywhere on earth is the most ancient of all freedoms, and the human species has dominated the planet because of an ability to roam, to explore oceans, mountains and plains. That restlessness has led man across boundaries imagined, implied and established. Immigration settled the valleys of the Nile, the Indus and Yellow rivers.

It brought early man to the Mediterranean, to Europe and the wind-swept steppes of Russia. If one ignores a few Norsemen and Egyptians who might have arrived in North and South America as prehistoric travelers, Asiatics migrated across the Bering Strait between fifteen and thirty thousand years ago, eventually reaching Tierra del Fuego, the southern tip of South America. They approached not in one mighty surge, but across thousands of years, and were eventually called "Indians" because of a Columbus error in geography. Each arrival, Indian *and* European, was an invader to the continent; each came as an immigrant, without papers.[2]

While the Indians never recognized the concept of private property, they staked out tribal territories that shifted, expanded, shrank or disappeared. Indian prehistory is a bloody story of boundaries overrun by other Indians, and tribes either driven out, absorbed or vanishing. Only the white man's borders effectively yoked the Indian's freedom to wander, and it was the white man's fences, the reservation boundaries, that finally brought the Indian to heel.

To the south, as the Aztec had violated the boundaries of his neighbors, so the Spanish overran the fabled Aztec empire. Incas, Mayas, Chichimecs, Yaquis, Pueblos, and lesser tribes fell before the Spanish sword. Yet, the Spanish bid for near continental conquest stalled on the bloody rim of Apacheria and Comancheria. Apaches and Comanches made a mockery of the Spanish borderlands with deep, slashing raids into the interior.

On the East Coast of North America, the British pushed the French beyond the Alleghenies and out of Canada. The Americans retired the English, then prevailed upon the Spanish to relinquish the Floridas. The Spanish complied because they had already essentially relinquished jurisdiction of their borders, and had the unhappy choice of either selling or facing extinction through absorption by American colonization.

Daniel Boone led pioneers west beyond the Alleghenies to the Mississippi. Settlers poured through the Cumberland Gap, sailed down the Ohio and crossed territory disputed and divided by Indian, French and British boundaries. Practically every ridge and river represented a border to someone, but in less than a generation, Americans took control.

In 1803 the United States purchased the Louisiana Territory. Had the French waited another two decades, the Americans would likely have controlled that huge expanse anyway, all by right of occupation. So much for legitimate borders.

The Louisiana Purchase put the United States on the northern rim of Spanish Texas, a near vacuum. The Red, Arkansas and Sabine rivers formed the boundaries. Spain feared the French might occupy Texas, so through empresarios (private land agents), with Stephen F. Austin the best-known and most successful, the Spanish invited in the Americans. These Yankees would hopefully accomplish what Spain, and then Mexico, could not. They would secure the border not only against the French, English and Comanches, but against the United States as well.

Thousands of American colonists became responsible Mexican citizens. Unfortunately, the Mexicans had no contingency plan for an onslaught of "illegal" aliens, Americans who had not been invited to Texas, but had migrated anyway. Austin called them "leather-stockings," a sneering reference to hunters, trappers, wanderers and ne'er-do-wells. It is an obscure irony of history that the first major groups of modern undocumented immigrants into Texas were not Mexicans but Americans. Mexico, emerging from a ruinous war for independence with Spain, had few soldiers to guard its border with the United States. Since American colonists resented the intrusions, they occasionally helped Mexico expel them. However, as a misguided Mexican government cracked down on legal and illegal alike, the Anglos had little choice except cooperation with each other. The 1836 War for Texas Independence made the Red, Arkansas and Sabine rivers the international line between the United States and the Republic of Texas.

For the next ten years, neither Texas nor Mexico respected the other's boundaries. Texans in particular unleashed filibusters, and these marauding buccaneers of the desert carved momentary empires at the expense of legitimate Mexican borders. Following the Mexican War, filibusters violated American neutrality, and the forays gradually ceased only as United States military power made itself felt.

After surveyors marked the Gadsden Purchase lands in 1856, a two thousand mile international line stretched from the Gulf Coast to south of San Diego, a boundary rarely guarded except against Indian predators. For nearly three-quarters of a century, citizens of both countries crossed each other's border with few delays. The United States fashioned its immigration rules only to check the Europeans because 98 percent of immigrants coming to the United States originated from across the Atlantic.

Chinese visitors were another matter. The Chinese were economic precursors to the Mexicans. The Chinese immigrated to the United States primarily from Kwangtung Province around Canton where they had a centuries-old heritage of seamanship, trade and exploration. They fought the Mongols and the Manchus, and paid a bloody price for brief periods of independence. When the English launched their Opium Wars by invading Kwangtung, the resistance was fierce but futile. Not long afterwards, in the midst of their despair and defeat, the Cantonese started migrating to America, disembarking at San Francisco. By 1870, an estimated thirty-five thousand lived in California.[3]

Chinese labor constructed part of every railroad in the West. Coolies generally remained three to ten years in the United States, saved their seventy-five cents to a dollar-a-day wages, rarely attempted to become citizens, and usually returned to China. Although the Chinese were a West Coast oddity seldom encountered by easterners, the peril of a "yellow scourge" frightened the nation.[4] Trade unions insisted that Americans would labor "in the kitchens or restaurants and hotels if the Chinamen were not working for less wages. . . ."[5]

On March 2, 1875, the United States Supreme Court placed immigration under the jurisdiction of the federal government, and Congress quickly passed a law barring Chinese prostitutes and contract labor. The Chinese Exclusion Act of 1882 (which established the principle of denial by race) suspended the orientals for ten years. A similar prohibition followed a decade later. In 1902 the ban became permanent, not to be rescinded until the Immigration and Nationality Act of 1952.

A 1907 "Gentlemen's Agreement" with Japan was in some respects even more bizarre. It was an illegal understanding between Japan, which wished to avoid the humiliation of having its nationals restricted from the United States, and the executive branch of the United States government.[6] Congress objected to this abridgement of its treaty authority, and passed the "National Origins Act" of 1924, which barred the Japanese altogether. The National Origins Act further contributed to American hysteria of "Asiatic hordes" at a time when American and European gunboats were patrolling the Yangtze River to enforce the white man's authority.

Chinese circumvented the exclusion laws by disembarking at British Columbia and crossing the border into Washington. When Canada banned the practice, ships paused a few miles off California and placed their Chinese cargo on Mexican boats, which usually unloaded at Ensenada, Mazatlan or Guaymas. For five dollars a head, guides took them to the American border where Americans or Mexicans charged the coolies between twenty and forty dollars each to be smuggled into San Diego's Chinatown. Only three inspectors of Chinese patrolled the California border with Mexico. Even so, the inspectors had a fair success rate because of Mexican informants ranging from consular officers to politicians and *vaqueros.*[7]

As it grew more difficult to enter the United States through California, the Chinese trekked into the Mexican interior and infiltrated El Paso, Texas, by way of Chihuahua. Tales still circulate of a smugglers tunnel under the Rio Grande, linking Juarez with the Sunset Heights district of El Paso. Such an awesome engineering achievement never happened, of course, because the Chinese easily slipped across the unguarded border. Once inside El Paso, they worked as cooks and waiters, servants and laundrymen, and were nearly impossible to detect. In their own quarters they frequently moved from one residence or place of business to another through a system of mole-like intercity tunnels. Some authorities believed such passageways reflected the furtive nature of the Chinese, but a more likely analysis is that a Chinaman not on the street was unlikely to be questioned by authorities, and perhaps deported.[8]

During the early 1900s, southwestern newspapers rarely mentioned Mexican aliens. Instead, the articles reported "Chinese wetbacks" attempting to slip across the desert to California. While the smuggling of Chinese was held in low repute even by hog rustlers, the practice may have led to the most sensational murders along the border. Emmanuel "Mannie" Clements, Jr., a brother-in-law of the notorious Jim Miller, was shot dead in an El Paso saloon in 1908. The killing was connected to Chinese smuggling, as well as the recent murder of two American agents investigating the racket. Meanwhile, Miller was in Mexico supposedly purchasing cattle to graze on a remote New Mexico ranch owned by former sheriff, Pat Garrett, famous as the taciturn slayer of outlaw Billy the Kid. Garrett was murdered in 1908 while in the company of a Miller relative by marriage, Carl Adamson. A few months later, Adamson was caught smuggling a wagonload of Chinese into the United States from Mexico, and was sentenced to eighteen months. Someday, perhaps, the threads of these murders will be followed to some startling conclusions involving the smuggling of Chinese.

Back east, the United States perceived itself at the turn of the century as awash in European migrants, and in danger of losing its national identity. Just how many foreigners could the nation absorb? From the 1890s through the early 1900s, concern mounted against European Jews, Slavs, Russians, English, Germans, Italians and Irish, their countries being charged, with some credibility, of dumping convicts, lunatics and paupers on American shores. On the West Coast, the Italians were more universally despised than the Chinese because the Italians took the better paying labor and mechanic jobs.

Legrand Atwood, superintendent of the St. Louis Insane Asylum as well as a specialist in "brain troubles," testified in May 1890 before a congressional committee investigating immigration practices. Atwood treated four thousand patients during a quarter-century, and nearly two-thirds were foreign born. He believed insanity often stemmed from immigrants who "did not find things as pleasant here as they anticipated. . . ." Atwood and the Association of Superintendents recommended "action to prevent the influx of insane foreigners, [because they were] becoming an alarming factor in the insanity of this country." Cities such as Chicago, St. Louis, New York and Cincinnati had predominant foreign populations who allegedly contributed to an erosion of the country's values.

Between 1820 and 1950, the United States admitted six million immigrants from Germany, nearly five million from Italy, four and one-half million from Ireland, and nearly four million from Great Britain. Poles, Hungarians, Czechs, Croats, Slovenes, Serbs and Slovaks accounted for four million. Russia sent four million of its Jews, Ukrainians and Lithuanians. Two million homeless came from the Scandinavian countries, half a million from Greece, and a quarter-million from the Netherlands. Asia sent four hundred thousand Chinese and two hundred and eighty thousand Japanese. There were three million Canadians and a half-million West Indians. Only one million arrived from Mexico, a suspiciously low figure since it was easier to count arrivals at Ellis Island and San Francisco than to keep track of wanderers across a lightly observed southern border. Nevertheless, therein lies our story.

Miners from Zacatecas, Sonora and Lower California crossed the border after the Mexican War and headed for the gold fields of California, or the mines at Bisbee, Clifton, Morenci, Tombstone and Silver

City in Arizona and New Mexico. Others made it to the mining camps of Colorado and Nevada. They were not illegal aliens but citizens of North America living and working where they pleased. Immigration restrictions did not exist. Unions were the major impediments to Mexican workers. With some exceptions, unions kept the Mexicans confined to pick-and-shovel work. Except as strike breakers, Mexicans rarely figured prominently in labor difficulties so prevalent in the mines.

On March 3, 1891, Congress provided for a superintendent of immigration reporting to the secretary of the treasury. He counted foreign noses until 1903 when the Bureau of Immigration was formed and placed in the Department of Labor and Commerce. In 1906, it became the Bureau of Immigration and Naturalization, and in 1933 the Immigration and Naturalization Service. Americans today call it the INS, whereas most Mexicans use *La Migra*.

Mexicans did not feel the bite of *La Migra* until after the railroads had turned Mexico into a third-world country, an appendage of its American neighbor. Rails locked the American Southwest into an intricate eastern industrial system. Mexican bordertowns, lacking a commercial and industrial base, and effectively isolated from their own country's center of population, stagnated.

American railroads created additional American settlements. They made transportation convenient and cheap, they imported products from all over the world, and they produced a market for southwestern crops, cattle, citrus, mining and smelting. When the railroads needed workers, Mexico came into its own. It had a surplus of hungry, willing-to-work people.

In the meantime, William Williams, commissioner of immigration, warned a congressional committee that "thousands of foreigners [Europeans] keep pouring into our cities, declining to go where they might be needed because they are neither physically nor mentally fitted to go to these underdeveloped parts of our country." He accused Europe of having "millions of undesirable people,' and said 'agencies are constantly at work to send part of them here [to the United States]."⁹

In 1911, a Senate Committee published the classic Dillingham Report, a massive investigation of "Immigrants in Industries," with the emphasis on Europeans. The report identified Americans and Irish as the best workers (the Italians and Greeks were the worst — the Italians because of feuds and fighting, and the Greeks because they would bribe their bosses to keep from working), but they had priced themselves out of the market and were replaced by the Chinese. However, by 1900 the exclusion laws made the Chinese all but a memory. And while there were not many Japanese in the country, they became prized railroad workers. Only the Mexicans, when they started arriving in sufficient numbers to make an impact, offered serious competition to the Japanese. "They [the Mexicans] are stronger and superior in every way except in progressiveness and sobriety," the congressional report stated. The Japanese were sober, tractable and industrious. On the downside, they were regarded as "crafty," and when one was dismissed, the entire Japanese labor force usually walked off the job. The Mexicans were "passive and easily satisfied." However, "due to a lack of ambition" they seldom became foremen, according to reports, rarely rising beyond trackwalkers who earned $1.25 daily. Drunkenness and absenteeism were the Mexican's worst traits, and when he collected his pay at month's end, he usually "layed off" or "quit work" until his money was spent.[10]

The Mexican Central Railroad built south from Juarez to Mexico City, its purpose to open Mexico's interior to Mexican, American and European development. Because it touched mines, towns, haciendas and businesses, the railroad brought job opportunities and markets. Nevertheless, it achieved fame for reasons few anticipated. The Mexican Central sought to stimulate Mexico, but as a practical matter those Mexicans hauled north to work in the borderlands of their own country were delivered close enough to the boundary to respond to the call of opportunity. One representative said he brought eight thousand men from Zacatecas to the mines of Chihuahua, and within a year eighty percent had quit and left for New Mexico or Arizona.[11] The Mexican Central became a conduit for dispensing labor north to the United States.[12]

Because Juarez was the largest town on the south side of the border, and the only bordertown with direct rail connections to the Mexican capital, and because El Paso was the largest bordertown on the American side, and for a while the only bordertown with any railroads at all (it soon had five), the thrust of Mexican labor into and out of Mexico focused at this international complex. Railroad offices flourished near the international bridges, although the lines also retained independent firms such as "The Holmes Supply Company" or "Manning and Company." Their "rustlers" (agents) prowled the streets and cantinas, hustling labor for the railroads. From July 1908 to February

1909, five agencies processed 16,471 workers, while the Department of Immigration recorded only 12,292 as crossing the border. The Mexican Central delivered them; the Southern Pacific and others carried them away. Ugly boxcar villages became "Mexican Town," "Sonora Town" or "Chihuahua Town." Many obscure railroad communities throughout the American Southwest still have high percentages of Hispanic populations, descendants of the original workers.[13]

Although Brownsville and Laredo were active labor centers too, most Mexicans made initial contact with employment agencies at El Paso. From El Paso the workers fanned out to San Antonio, a major distribution point. Kansas City, Missouri was another center, as was Los Angeles. Tucson, Trinidad and Denver handled large numbers.[14]

The supply of willing, hard-working, passive Mexican labor was seemingly inexhaustible, and if a Mexican could cross the bridge, he could work for the railroads. At times the need for Mexican labor soared to such desperate straits that the Santa Fe Street Bridge resembled a madhouse with agents wrestling with whatever Mexicans they could reach. Eleven "rustlers" were arrested for disturbing the peace in September 1907, the newspapers snickering that one "tried to pull his laborers one way and another another. One had a laborer by the coat, another by his sleeve, and another by his hair, each shouting in loud tones the advantages of his particular agency. In a compact mass the group swayed back and forth, completely blocking the sidewalk on South El Paso Street as well as attracting quite a crowd."[15]

Most Mexicans were destitute, so the agencies kept them fed, off the streets and living in warehouses until the railroads hauled them to distant work areas. Even then, the Mexican was not free of the agencies, for the railroads provided only a salary. Agencies sold supplies and food. The cost of beans cooked with a little meat amounted to $8 a month for the average single Mexican. Personal items were supplied at agency rates ten to fifteen percent higher than retail in Los Angeles. The railroads docked agency deductions from the worker pay, a sum (including a fifty cent "hospital fee") amounting to roughly one-third of the average $26 a month salary. (Workers put in a ten hour day, six day week.)[16]

The Mexicans preferred seasonal work. The Valley of Mexico and the central plateau (called "Peon country" by the agencies), especially the areas of Jalisco (which furnished the preferred laborers), Michoacan, Guanajuato, Aguascalientes and Zacatecas, had a crop-growing

Mexican and Chinese workers camped along the west side of the main irrigation canal in the Imperial Valley. Their only pause was at high noon for lunch. 1913. (Imperial Valley Water Irrigation District)

Agricultural workers bed down for the night outside Imperial Valley fields. (Spencer Library, Imperial Valley College)

heritage. The peasants worked from January until May, then went home to plant crops. During the growing period they returned to the United States, but left again during August and September to harvest the Mexican fields. Fiestas consumed the holiday season through December, which meant labor was scarce during that period in the United States.[17]

The crisscrossing of labor walking back and forth across the bridges helped explain lax American immigration procedures at the Mexican border. Since few Mexican immigrants were anything other than temporary working visitors, it hardly made sense to constantly monitor their comings and goings.

By returning the worker to El Paso, the railroad dispensed with part-time employees who might get disgruntled if abandoned north of the border. The United States was pleased because it had few out-of-work paupers burdening its private, and meager, welfare systems. Yet, while a seasonal employee might be delighted to be shipped home, other foot-loose men waited at the border. During slow railroad periods, job seekers aimlessly wandered the Juarez streets. When thousands jammed the Mexican side of the bridges, American officials closed the border to prevent an influx of paupers. Juarez mayors sought local jobs, and the Mexican federal government sometimes offered work on Chihuahua railroads for a peso-and-one-half a day. Most laborers spurned the offer, preferring to await better times in the United States.[18]

The era of open public lands ended in the 1890s, and historian Frederick Jackson Turner signed its death certificate with "The Significance of the Frontier in American History." For decades the United States had vast expanses of farmland, too much to be plowed by the native-born alone. In spite of resentment against the Irish for Catholicism and depressing of wages, and against the Germans and Scandinavians because they did not speak English, and against southern Europeans because of feuds and immorality, the nation opened its doors and sought to fulfill its mystical "manifest destiny," to stock the farmland from sea to shining sea. When the frontier symbolically closed, and the age of industrialization commenced, European immigrants started thinking less about working in the fields and more about careers with the Ford Motor Company. That left the Mexican almost alone in competing for field jobs.

The Newlands Reclamation Act of 1902 inspired the construction of irrigation projects. Former desert lands produced cantaloupes, cotton, lettuce, cabbages. Sophisticated canning and food preservation techniques, combined with the development of the refrigerated railroad car, suddenly freed formerly worthless acres for production. Developers got rich, homesteaders made a living, and Mexican workers had jobs. Not only did Mexicans pick the crops, they cleared the mesquite and thorny undergrowth. The $12 million Elephant Butte Dam in New Mexico released thousands of acres for development near El Paso, and practically all of the labor was Mexican. Irrigation doubled and tripled the amount of California land in cultivation, especially in the Imperial Valley. California petitioned Congress for a relaxation of the Chinese Exclusion laws, and when that failed, the state turned to Mexicans. By 1927 immigrants from Jalisco and the populous central plateau of Mexico caught the railroad linking Guadalajara with Nogales, Arizona. That solved any lingering labor shortages troubling California and Arizona.[19]

During the growing season in Texas, hundreds crossed the Rio Grande on the National Railroad at Laredo and earned a few weekly dollars as stoop labor in the emerging vegetable and citrus industry. They also worked as vaqueros, sheepherders and domestics. Migrant labor colonies lined the Rio Grande from El Paso to Brownsville, the farm workers earning $2 daily in Texas compared to $.50 in Mexico. They crossed the Red River and picked cotton in Oklahoma, and drifted southeast to Louisiana and worked in the sugar cane fields. A cotton picker might get fifty cents per hundred pounds, with two or three hundred pounds being a good day's work. When a whole family collaborated, children included, a family might earn five dollars in a single day.

The cost of living for Mexicans was about the same in both countries. Peons wore clothes bought in Mexico, and lived in housing generally supplied by the employer or built from the earth. They consumed a traditional diet of corn, meat and beans, the cheaper, plentiful foods.[20]

An irony is that the United States had immigration laws standard for the country, but the only rigid enforcement was on the east and west coasts. Contract labor in particular aroused Washington, and Congress investigated its origins in Europe, and blocked it when possible at the eastern ports of entry. Yet, it flourished blatantly at the Mexican border because no outcry existed for its suppression. Everybody, including the Mexicans, accepted it, wanted it, considered it a normal way of

Chile pickers in the Mesilla Valley of New Mexico. *(El Paso Herald-Post)*

doing business, and made money off it. In eastern America, contract labor from Europe cost American jobs, and the unions stoutly opposed it; in the Southwest, contract work took jobs nobody wanted, and except for in the mines, unions hardly existed.

While the push of Mexican poverty and the pull of American jobs frequently worked to the economic benefit of the border, violent factors often changed the ratios. The Mexican Revolution of 1910-1920 rocketed that unhappy nation to the brink of anarchy. Streams of Mexican political exiles arrived in the Southwest during the early 1900s, most of them headquartering in El Paso, San Antonio or Los Angeles. Anarchists pleaded political persecution in their home country, gained grudged admittance to the United States and thereafter severely strained the patience of benefactors with their maniacal bomb throwing and ungrateful statements. With the surrender of Juarez to revolutionary forces in 1911, and the fall of the federal government, the Díaz politicians took their turn in exile. Add to this the pitiful civilian refuse, plus revolutionaries driven out by marauding Federals, and Federals sent packing by vengeful Insurgents.

Yet, at the same time, there were serious factors discouraging immigration. A rumor swept the Southwest that Mexican immigrants would be conscripted to help America fight in Europe. Overnight hundreds returned to Mexico. Meanwhile, cholera and typhus struck portions of Juarez, and Mexicans crossing the border into the United States were forced to bathe in a mixture of vinegar and gasoline to kill germs and lice. The fumigation did not stop immigration; it just made it more humiliating.[21]

European immigrants paid a head tax of $4 each in 1907, but the regulation was never enforced at the Mexican border. However, an $8 head tax and a literacy test in 1917 did apply at the border as well as Ellis Island. (The literacy test required reading a paragraph from the Bible in an immigrant's own language.) The 1917 law wasn't written as a punitive measure against Mexico, although it was obviously meant to reduce and stabilize the number of border crossings. Authorities hoped the law would upgrade immigration procedures.

These new regulations momentarily stalled the worst classes of Europeans, but they inadvertently slowed *legal* crossings by Mexicans except for the wealthy. Mexico had no educated middle class. Between the very rich and the very poor, a vacuum existed, and the well-meaning 1917 restrictions denied entrance to the intelligent, hardworking, honest but poor and illiterate individuals that Americans needed most. Over ninety percent of the Mexican population fit into a poverty category where $8 purchased a month's supply of groceries. So the Mexican immigrant, who seldom regarded himself as an immigrant in the same sense that Europeans did (the European was immediately at home; the Mexican was a visitor commuting to a job), had a choice. He could pay $8 to cross the bridge and work, or he could pay two cents and walk over as a visitor. The decision was easy. He paid the two cents and went to work anyway. That he was an illegal alien probably never occurred to him, as he was simply defeating an oppressive and silly system. Besides, who would deport or punish him?

An amendment to the 1917 law required American border officials to take individual immigrant pictures and keep records. Laborers received identification cards. However, as the law made legal immigration increasingly expensive and difficult, American employers seldom had enough help. Mine owners, businessmen, military contractors, the Arizona Cotton Pickers Association, the Colorado Beet Growers, the

Texas cotton farmers, all demanded more Mexican participants. Food administrator Herbert Hoover asked the secretary of labor to waive all restrictions against the Mexican, including having his picture taken since "the Mexican has a primitive suspicion of the camera."[22] Congress did not enact all of Hoover's recommendations, especially the removal of pictures, but laborers were allowed to remain for the duration of the First World War.

In January 1920, Claude B. Hudspeth of Texas introduced a joint resolution in Congress calling for an end to the literacy test, the $8 head tax, and suspension of the contract labor laws, as applied to Mexicans. Hudspeth and other witnesses assured congressmen that nobody wanted the Mexicans forever. W. W. Knox, representing the Arizona Cotton Growers Association, admitted it would be a mistake for Mexicans to become American citizens, for when a white man "marries with a Mexican it is an absolute tragedy." Hudspeth called the Mexicans "an inferior race," stating "If I believed that by bringing these people in you were going to permanently increase the Mexican population down there [in Texas], I would say to keep them out." Ninety percent of everything they do is peon labor, he commented, and it "is a class of labor that knows nothing about the value of money other than to get enough to live on." Twenty thousand laborers, including women and children, "will stay here four or five months, save perhaps $150, and go back to Mexico, spend the money, and then return to the United States for four or five more months."[23]

One year later, an economic decline struck the United States. Southwestern farmers were going bankrupt, and out of work Mexicans were stranded in remote hamlets without food or means of returning to Mexico. Arizona appealed to the federal government to deport the Mexicans, but Washington refused, saying it was the grower responsibility to send them home.[24]

The economic downturn of 1921 and 1922 revealed homeless, starving Mexicans all over the United States, people frequently terrorized by night-riders vowing to drive them from the country. The federal government provided neither protection nor aid. Yet, when the economy resurged in 1923, it was as if neither nation had learned from the traumatic experience. A thousand Mexicans daily entered Juarez with intentions of migrating to the United States. Fleets of trucks left El Paso hauling workers to Texas, New Mexico, Arizona and California. Petitions flooded Congress for a relaxation of controls, and a congressional study returned the first sensible response to the chaos. The report called for "an amply financed and staffed federal agency to coordinate the distribution of unskilled labor. A proper distribution of Mexican workers rather than unrestricted immigration . . . was the only solution."

But the government wasn't ready for common sense, and the confusion stumbled on. By now, the Midwest wanted Mexican labor, and offered higher wages. Mexicans spread more intensely around the country. Texas reacted by fining labor agents $1,000 for recruiting people to work outside the state.[25]

Congress passed the Quota Acts of 1921 and 1924, the former being an emergency measure temporarily imposing a three percent limitation on European immigration, a figure charged against each country according to nationality in the 1910 United States census. European immigration plummeted by 500,000 the first year. In 1924, the government set a quota of two percent on unskilled workers from southern Europe, specifically Italy, Poland, Greece and Romania. This figure was based on the census of 1890. America had now slammed the door on European immigration, the United States believing, in the words of President Calvin Coolidge, that the nation was limited in its capacity to absorb immigrants.[26]

The 1921 and 1924 laws did not apply to Mexico or other hemispheric nations for several reasons: part of them generosity and good will toward a southern neighbor and part of them a matter of economic self-interest. Mexicans needed work; the United States needed workers. Since most Mexicans had no interest in remaining forever in the United States, they were not perceived as a flood tide threatening American civilization, as the Europeans were. However, the Americans needed to control the southern border in a more orderly fashion. To this end, a Mexican seeking work had to pay $10 for a visa from an American consul, in addition to the pre-existing $8 head tax. However, what the American saw as reasonable, the Mexican saw as intolerable. The era of the illegal immigrant again took a dramatic upswing, and some estimates say as many as 100,000 illegals crossed the Mexican border each year during the 1920s.[27]

Congress anticipated some of this, and it appropriated $1 million in 1924 to create a Border Patrol for the Mexican and Canadian boundaries. The Patrol's mission called for the prevention of illegal European and Chinese immigration along the Mexican border. Initially the Patrol ignored illegal Mexicans and enforced customs and prohibition violations.[28]

Customs officers Wood and Ash ride the Rio Grande border in 1938 in search of smugglers. Both were former Rough Riders. Ash later became a police officer in El Paso. (Author's Collection)

This group of Yaqui Indians lured a troop of Mexican cavalry into a Sonoran canyon and killed them. They then crossed the border into the United States and surrendered to immigration officials. (Harry Ransom Humanities Research Center, U.T. Austin)

As the lawmen turned to illegal Mexicans, and made modest deportations, alarmed growers in the Imperial Valley complained bitterly to the Labor Department, which sent I. F. Wixon, an Immigration Bureau supervisor, to investigate. Wixon suggested a "gentleman's agreement." Instead of deporting the aliens, as the law stipulated, he gave the workers identification cards. That protected them from deportation. Next, the workers paid the $10 visa fee, plus the $8 head tax. However, since few laborers had $18, the money was deducted in $3 weekly installments. Finally, the workers were escorted to the nearest border station and 6,500 were legalized.[29]

The well-intentioned but ill-considered plan drew dour criticism from Congress and labor leaders who argued that the Wixon deal encouraged illegal immigration. Furthermore, the compromise could be terminated at any time by the Labor Department. It made no allowances for incomplete payment of fees. Nobody accounted for the funds. It ignored the law.

Suddenly the Mexican worker had come to the attention of the entire United States and while the Labor Department squirmed, the American Federation of Labor (AFL) called Mexicans "a menace to American workers." But the criticism merely made the union seem even-handed, when in reality the Mexican workers had not threatened union strongholds in the east, and were not substantially perceived as a union threat anywhere in the country. Union leaders worried primarily about industrial workers, and while unions insisted upon a two-year suspension of immigration from anywhere in the world — they actually meant Europe. So while Congress tightened European immigration, it made no changes regarding the Mexican border.[30]

Thus the Mexican labor problem lurched in contradictory fashion from one crisis to another, the shock coming in 1929 when the Great Depression forced an agonizing reappraisal of the worker dilemma.

The Deportations

By THE LATE 1920s, chaotic Mexican emigration figures provided little insight into population shifts along the international line. A lack of instructions, a lack of political concern, a lack of facilities and a lack of trained manpower, all on the part of American immigration officials, made a correct count and assessment of those crossing the border from Mexico as impossible as it was meaningless. Those who crossed without permits rarely considered themselves as violating the law. They were avoiding red tape and unjust, discriminatory costs. To the Mexican, it was not disobeying the law but utilizing survival techniques. Furthermore, few Mexican laborers had any concept of what these rules and regulations were all about, and as they did not understand the rules, and the reasons for them, they were only a step away from disregarding them. Furthermore, legals recrossed into Mexico without checking in with American border agencies, or they checked in at different ports than they had checked out of, and then they would cross again, perhaps several times, legally and/or illegally. All this legal-illegal business was considered nonsense anyway, a method of expunging money. If a Mexican had a job, he was legal.

Mexican workers crossing into the United States for the first time were generally uneducated, unsophisticated, impoverished, scared, docile, untrained and homesick. Offers of $1.25 a day from border labor agents seemed as fortunes, and part of the worker's learning process began with the discovery that he rarely got that much money, and all too soon it vanished . . . and the work ended. Such experiences evolved the Mexican into a seasoned and cynical worker realizing quickly that American employers rarely had his best interests uppermost in mind. The Mexican laborer often went home a different person than the one who entered with hat-in-hand a year earlier.

Even the stereotype of the Mexican worker always returning home was not true, and perhaps never had been. While picking cotton, he heard strange and wonderful stories of higher wages in the beet fields of Michigan and Colorado. Those dazzling sums earned in the Detroit automotive plants intrigued him, as did money possibilities in the clothing mills of Chicago and St. Louis. By the end of his first few years in the cotton fields, the laborer knew enough about the United States to risk traveling to regions remote from the border. Since he could not return home easily, he brought his family. His children saw less and less of Mexico, and thought of it as a foreign country. Pockets of Mexican culture evolved in the United States. Flourishing Mexican colonies surfaced in Los Angeles, Denver, Chicago, St. Louis, Dallas, Atlanta, New Orleans, Philadelphia, New York and Boston. A few Mexicans found steady, full-time jobs in business and industry.[1]

Because of poor pay and atrocious working conditions, farms from Texas to California gradually became little more than way stations for Mexican laborers migrating to something better. Border areas usually attracted the initial illegal immigrants, and since field hands had to be replenished each year, border regions suffered chronic labor shortages. Farms alongside the border could not agriculturally exist without labor from Mexico. Southwestern legislators understood this, and kept their positions by advocating open Mexican immigration.

Not all citizens around the United States considered unrestricted immigration to be in the nation's best interests, however, and they needed constant reminders that cheap lettuce was the direct result of those Mexicans. Some described the immigration as an invasion similar to the "yellow peril." Since a precedent existed for restricting the Chinese and severely curtailing Europeans, and the country had survived in spite of doomsayers, concerned citizens demanded a tightening of immigration along the border. Congress compromised. It did not establish quotas but did stiffen entry requirements. Most Mexicans had large families, and were poor and illiterate, so a 1924 head tax of $8, a visa fee of $10, a literacy test and a physical briefly slowed the exodus from below the border. It amounted to closing a door without actually slamming it. Add to that a fledgling Border Patrol, and the boundaries seemed secure. But the Mexicans rose to the challenge. In 1924 there were 87,000 legal immigrants. In 1925 it dropped to 25,000 but had stormed back to 66,000 in 1927, and illegal immigration was out of control.[2]

Congressman John C. Box of Texas, who considered Mexico a Bolshevist society, chaired the House Immigration Committee and opposed an unregulated influx of Mexicans. Those who testified at his hearings represented farmers, stock growers, chambers of commerce and agricultural associations along the Mexican border. To a man, they demanded open immigration. A frustrated Box responded with what he perceived as the real issues. In Los Angeles where 7 percent of the population was Hispanic, 27.44 percent of the relief cases were Mexican. At Pasadena, with a 2.8 percent Mexican population, 6 percent of the welfare cases involved them. In Long Beach with 1 percent, Mexican welfare absorbed 21 percent of the cases. In Orange County, with a 10 percent Hispanic population, county aid for them amounted to 50 percent of the budget.[3]

Knowing and fearing the strength of Box on the committee, most speakers philosophically adopted a sympathetic and understanding attitude toward him, wishing they could think of another way to get the farm work done without using Mexicans. They profoundly agreed with immigration laws barring the miserable Europeans and the immoral Chinese. They described the Mexican worker as nearly as bad, someone the country had to be careful about. "We . . . are not anxious to build the Civilization of California . . . upon a Mexican foundation. We take him because there is nothing else available," said S. Parker Frisselle, chairman of the Agricultural Committee of the Fresno County, California, Chamber of Commerce. As the testimony turned derogatory, filled with how any farmer would rather have a "white" worker than a Mexican, but none would work for the wages, an exasperated Judge Box suggested that southwestern businessmen needed a road filled with ever-moving Mexicans. The employers could pick one out, work him for a while, and when finished, toss him back into the line. "What you really want," Box angrily told J. T. Whitehead, representing federal reclamation projects, "are a class of people who have not the ability to rise, who have no initiative, who are children, who do not want to own land, and who can be directed by men in the upper stratum of society." Whitehead replied, "I believe that is right."[4]

To make matters more complex, neither legal nor illegal Mexicans were melting into the immigration pot. Their faulty English, low social status, plus an inadequate grasp of customs and judicial systems, made American citizenship a hindrance rather than an advantage. To be a citizen meant taxation, draft registration, jury service, schooling; it meant the authorities knew who you were and where you were; it meant that you were no longer anonymous. To become an American carried with it responsibilities and accountabilities that few Mexicans wanted or understood. Authorities meant trouble, and so the Mexican preferred the periphery of the American system, rather than its core.

This reluctance to assimilate, plus the inane prejudice of the American, plus the approaching world-wide Great Depression, brought grief to the Mexican laborer. The Irish, the Italians, the Greeks, the Germans, the French, the Chinese, they had all taken their discriminatory turns as responsible for the demise of American jobs. Now the Mexican's time had arrived, and in a way it started with *The Saturday Evening Post* of February 28, 1928. "It is a strange and unusual state of affairs," the author wrote, "to find the United States . . . in a position to be economically annihilated by another nation. In the years since European immigration was cut from a rushing, overwhelming torrent, to an orderly river by the application of the quota law — the immigration of Mexican Indians, and Mexican mestizos or halfbreeds — has risen from year to year, creeping up on a new mark one year, receding the next, then rising higher and higher, and spreading further and further, north and east and west."

If the *Post* had waited another three months, it might have reinforced its arguments by pointing to the May 1928 strike of twenty thousand Hispanic workers in the Imperial Valley cantaloupe fields. Although the rumblings lasted but a week before growers and lawmen broke the strike and had everybody working again, an irony was that most of the pickers, if not United States citizens, were year-around illegal Mexican residents of Imperial County. They wanted more money, a more equal share of the American dream.[5]

Meanwhile, congressmen failed to get a Mexican quota out of Committee. Box repeatedly watched his bills die. Senate attempts fared no better. Yet, legal immigration from Mexico dropped an incredible 94 percent by 1930 when consular officials reduced the number of visas on the grounds of illiteracy, the possibility of becoming a public charge, and contract labor violations. No one knows how many rejected Mexicans subsequently became illegal aliens, but estimates run into the tens of thousands.[6]

The stock market crashed, and people blamed immigrants for a large share of the unemployment. Business leaders worked in kitchens, and those who formerly worked in the kitchens sought jobs in the fields. Farmers, mine owners and railroad magnates dismissed their Mexican help and hired Americans, who now accepted the menial jobs. The Mexican had no place to go, except home, back to Mexico.[7]

Repatriations began, voluntary and otherwise. For the first time in its history, the United States lost more population than it took in. Mexico invited back its people, creating work projects in Coahuila, Aguascalientes, Durango, Hidalgo, Chihuahua and Sonora. Private and government lands were redistributed. When Mexico expropriated the American-owned oil fields in 1938, President Lázaro Cárdenas established agrarian colonies for Mexicans formerly living in Texas, California and southwestern states. Colonies in Chihuahua and Lower California doled out twenty-five acres to each returning farmer, and a loan from Mexico's Agricultural Bank permitted farmers to buy seed, tools and supplies until their first cotton crop matured.[8]

Back in the United States, relief agencies changed the population patterns of America. Since people had to prove a legal residence to obtain aid, millions of poor blacks and whites retreated to their southern homes. Mexicans and other foreigners had the same options, an irony being that even though they might have lived in a specific area for years, their very reluctance to accept citizenship cost them their relief checks.

Between November 1929 and December 1930, over 200,000 Mexican laborers left the United States and re-entered Mexico, most of them voluntarily. In 1931, welfare agencies frequently provided transportation, often including box lunches and even cash inducements. Nearly 150,000 Mexicans crossed the border going south that year, the heaviest traffic of the decade.[9]

In Washington, President Herbert Hoover appointed William N. Doak as Secretary of Labor, and Doak promised to deport a hundred thousand illegal aliens, thus providing opportunities for Americans. However, only 7,116 Mexicans were expelled, the government relying on voluntary departures from those "who could walk home." During the first month of his campaign, Doak deported over a thousand illegal aliens from New York alone, announcing in the process that he was not "directing any campaign against Communists or any other special class," a reference to the Red Scare of 1920 when so many Communists were rounded up and deported. Nevertheless, Doak's methods seemed so extreme that the National Commission on Law Observance and Enforcement, commonly known as the Wickersham Commission, denounced the Labor Department tactics.[10]

Although most deportees were Europeans, the Report noted that no law existed, except against the Chinese, which required anyone, legal or illegal, to produce a certificate of birth or naturalization on demand. It accused the Labor Department of acting as investigator, prosecutor and judge, of arresting suspects first and having warrants telegraphed from Washington, of allowing no appeals, and of deporting people who had a right to remain in the country.[11]

However, by 1933 the great thrust of repatriations had passed. Although 500,000 Mexicans (some of them Americans by birth) returned to Mexico during the decade, the figure needs to be kept in perspective since it represented but a fraction of the total Mexicans in the United States. Gradually the nation turned to other subjects: the plight of the Okies, the looming war in Europe, Franklin D. Roosevelt and the promise of economic recovery. However, before America would again open wide its doors to Mexican immigrants, there would be substantial changes in admittance procedures.

31

The Braceros

1940 FOUND THE UNITED STATES untangling from the Great Depression, with agriculture becoming agribusiness as the family farm struggled to stay solvent. It was the era of the "labor pool," a floating supply of Mexicans, poor whites, blacks and Japanese. Workers drew the "prevailing wage rates," which meant they could not bargain for pay, and farmers need not worry that competitors would lure away their best hands with offers of more money.

World War II changed that. The Japanese went into detention camps, and the poor whites, blacks and resident (and some non-resident) Mexicans went into the army. Southwest agribusinesses suddenly had few people to harvest crops. Mexican labor could still be imported, of course, but the time had passed for lackadaisical processing. Imported Mexicans would have to be regulated and accounted for, not only to protect the border and give the United States better control, but to weed out undesirables as well as potential Fifth Columnists.

Other important factors had a place too. Whereas better paying jobs had always siphoned off a tiny percentage of Mexican labor, industry and big eastern businesses had rarely sought the peons. However, with war shortages the Mexican immigrant represented an acceptable labor source, one temptingly lured from farms by the siren of more money.

Yet, while the government was sympathetic to defense industries and business manpower shortages, Washington denied any relief through Mexican labor. If the Mexican was to be brought into the United States, his importation and return would have to be assured and regulated and supervised by the government. Such tasks would be easier if Mexicans were employed near the border and assigned jobs where they could be easily counted and observed. Agriculture, and to a certain extent railroads, fitted this category. Furthermore, since labor pools no longer existed, and government as well as farmers wanted to keep crop prices low, the worker would be paid a prevailing, non-negotiable wage.

Mexico had ambivalent feelings about the "official" employment of its citizens in the United States. It had always criticized the "wetback" system (although Mexico curiously took little action to prevent wetbacks from crossing the border), and urged Washington to make it illegal for American employers to hire them. As for furnishing a legal labor supply, the program was an admission of the PRI's failure on economic policies. Yet, the nation needed dollars to balance its population pressures, and to create new jobs. So reluctantly the Mexican government negotiated, insisting that Mexican workers deserved certain guarantees: fair treatment, housing, medical facilities, food, transportation, freedom from exploitation and discrimination. The ensuing agreement was the Mexican Farm Labor Supply Program, the "Bracero Program." ("Bracero" comes from the Spanish word *brazo*, which means arm. A bracero was a hired arm, or hand.)[1]

Dealing on such a massive scale with people, especially foreigners, however, took Mexican employment out of the free enterprise market place system, of one individual dealing with another, and made the concept a hot topic for negotiation between governments. The United States and Mexico believed a solution had been found with adequate controls. The United States had facilities for organization, for the recruitment and transportation of large numbers of employees. Mexico insisted upon a written contract between the worker and his employer, round trip transportation guaranteed, freedom to purchase merchandise at a place of the worker's choice, wages at the prevailing rate, and deduction of 10 percent of the salary to be held in savings and paid on termination of employment.

Mexico realized it could not end worker exploitation, but it could set limits on it. Both sides agreed that Mexicans would not replace American workers or, by their presence, lower wage rates. The arrangements would be temporary. Mexicans would work only in agriculture (and railroads until 1946, the duration of World War II); and they would be returned across the border immediately at the end of the contract. Either party could abolish the agreement upon ninety days notice. Negotiations were completed in the summer of 1942.[2]

The Bracero Program extended through two periods, from August 1942 until December 1947, and from February 1948 until December 1964. During the first period, the number of imported workers did not exceed 250,000; the seventeen year second period, however, brought nearly 5 million Mexican nationals into the United States on a temporary basis.

The United States and its growers accepted the terms, the growers reluctantly because of their expenses and the issue of worker rights. The Farm Security Administration initially administered the program, and the bracero agreement functioned according to its idealistic design. However, in 1943, the War Food Administration (a grower-dominated agency) took charge, and bracero guarantees suffered from a lack of enforcement. Nowhere was this more apparent than in Texas, notorious for its discrimination. Mexico was reluctant to accept Texas participation anyway, and Texas ignored the program, refusing to hire workers by contract, preferring an "open border" policy allowing the Mexican to freely cross, a practice repudiated by the United States-Mexico agreement. In such a situation, Washington had an obligation to support and defend the understandings just inked with Mexico, but on May 11, 1943, the Immigration Department, fully realizing Mexican fears, broke the agreement and issued one-year work permits to Mexican nationals willing to illegally ford the river into Texas. Over official Mexican protests, two thousand of its own citizens quickly crossed the Rio Grande and took advantage of the work opportunity.

In June 1943, Ezequiel Padilla, Secretary of Foreign Affairs for Mexico, angrily and "officially" denied braceros to Texas. He cited an excessive number of discrimination complaints.

Texas responded with a growing concern about its world-wide racial reputation. In May 1944, Austin legislators passed the "Caucasian Race Resolution," promising equal rights for all caucasians in public places. But most braceros refused to enter the state, and Texas recruited Mexican-Americans, school children, college students and even prisoners of war to tend its crops.[3]

Governor Coke Stevenson created the "Good Neighbor Commission," a state agency battling the evils of discrimination. However,

Governor Beauford H. Jester, who succeeded Stevenson, turned it into a ceremonial circus content with espousing good will. The commission rarely had Hispanics on its board. During the 1980s, Governor William Clements created "The Border Commission," whereby governors of all states bordering the Rio Grande met and discussed common issues. Today, almost any Texas border city large enough for a chamber of commerce is actively trying to improve relations with its Mexican neighbors.

Mexico took Texas off the black list in 1947, with the exception of selected counties. By 1948, with an improved Mexico-United States bracero agreement, cotton harvesting time arrived in Texas and, as customary, the Department of Labor accepted Texas figures of $2.50 per hundred pounds of cotton picked, as the prevailing wage. An indignant Mexico demanded $3 before releasing its braceros, a demand startling to the United States as well as Texas, because it broke the bracero agreement. Prevailing wages were established by the American government, and were not subject to negotiation or adjustment by Mexico. Prevailing wages were the pay that Americans might draw had there been any available for work. Prevailing wages were non-negotiable guarantees provided to the braceros.

However, Mexico knew what everybody else knew, that prevailing wages were not set by the government but by the growers. Furthermore, prevailing wages were considerably below what an American might earn while doing the same labor.

Planters deliberately established pay scales unattractive to domestic workers, and when none showed up, Washington declared a labor shortage and opened the region for braceros. American officials tolerated this fraud because it kept the growers happy, and housewives pleased at the grocery stores. An indignant Mexico refused to go along with the sham, and tried to raise the prevailing wage which, in spite of moral issues involved, still violated the agreement. But although legally wrong, Mexico had influence because it could close the border, and threatened to do so. Texas responded by encouraging peon labor to enter illegally, and over six thousand Mexican workers stormed across the Rio Grande at El Paso between October 13-16, 1948. The United States Border Patrol formally received the laborers, herded them into temporary enclosures and paroled them to farmers whose trucks hauled them away. Mexican nationals so glutted the market that wages fell to $1.50 per hundred pounds. Mexico of course complained, threatening to terminate the bracero agreement, and the United States admitted that American encouragement of recent crossings had violated the pact, and apologized. The program continued.[4]

The Bracero Program, designed to fill American warpower needs and to eliminate the entry of illegal entrants, met the first goal but failed miserably on the second. Instead of retarding the flow of illegals, the agreement stimulated it. Part of the problem involved Mexico's choice of bracero recruiting centers. Since Americans paid transportation costs, the United States wanted locations on the border. Mexico preferred the interior, correctly perceiving that centers on the border would overwhelm available agencies and community relief services.

The National Stadium in Mexico City recruited first, and over fifty thousand transients and laborers applied. With additional unemployed arriving daily, Mexico shifted the responsibility to several cities, specifically Hermosillo, Chihuahua and Monterey. Even so, the red tape, corruption (bribery), and delays proved disheartening. Many applicants ignored the stations, flooded the border anyway, taking illegal jobs in the United States.[5]

Although the United States paid bracero expenses averaging $450 a person, the growers had expenses too, a $25 bond and housing for each bracero. These private costs, plus government demands for acceptable bracero treatment, made illegal workers more of a bargain. Illegals were easily accessible, particularly along the border, and their presence and availability were reflected in Border Patrol arrest numbers. For the years between 1940 and 1943, the arrests averaged 7,000 a year. In 1944, they exceeded 29,000, in 1946 they reached 100,000 and in 1947 200,000. By 1950, the number was over 500,000.

During these years, not more than two hundred Border Patrolmen guarded the international line at any one time. Illegal entry was not a crime (punishable by prison), nor was the employment of illegals a criminal offense. The number of "wetbacks" (especially in Texas which in a technical sense had the *only* wetbacks because Mexican nationals had to ford the Rio Grande to qualify), took a soaring upturn in 1947 and 1949-50. The Border Patrol now had two aggravations: one of embarrassment because so many peons had slipped through the patrol screen, and one of facing grower wrath for deporting their help. All of this could of course be solved by making the illegals legal.

In informal agreements with Mexico, wetbacks were "dried out." The United States reduced its call for braceros, and "legalized" the illegal

Border Patrolmen relieve Mexican smugglers of pistol and contraband near the Rio Grande in 1926. (Harry Ransom Humanities Research Center, U.T. Austin)

Pete Crawford, Texas state game warden and later Texas Ranger (on ground), shakes hands with Mexican customs officer, Chief Hernandez. The scene took place along Rio Grande south of Alpine, Texas. (Harry Ransom Humanities Research Center, U.T. Austin)

aliens already working. Over a hundred thousand undocumented Mexicans became legitimate braceros practically overnight.[6]

Instead of easing the illegal numbers in the United States, however, the drying out process aggravated it. Legal Mexicans realized the practice of hiring illegals had its rewards after all. Wetback arrivals continued to increase.

During negotiations to renew the bracero agreements, Mexico insisted on more precise wage determinations. To break the deadlock, and to get the laborers started, Americans opened the border at Calexico, San Ysidro and San Diego on January 18, 1954. Crowds of Mexican workers, all illegals, roughtly 3,500 men, stormed across the border, assisted by willing hands of the Border Patrol. For ten days the laborers were processed and declared braceros. At that time the American labor shortage was declared over, and the border closed. Anyone else caught slipping over was illegal, and deported.[7]

But men out of work and desperate to enter the United States were like a faucet which, once opened, could not easily be shut off. Thousands of illegals had been encouraged to cross the border and accept legal work; thousands had been processed and "dried out," but thousands were waiting along the international line, and thousands more from the interior hearing the news, and especially the rumors, of unlimited jobs in the United States, were on their way. They would not be denied by a line which few men watched. Nor would they be deterred by the term "illegal" or "wetback," which, judging by recent United States's actions, had meanings that changed on a day-by-day basis.

As for unilateral recruiting, even though illegal by United States law, it had been successful. It had worked. With the precedent set, Congress amended Public Law 78, giving authorities a heavy-handed permission to ignore Mexico and recruit at the border anytime an agreement regarding braceros could not be negotiated on American terms.[8]

The amendment further brought about "Operation Wetback," the mass deportation of Mexican illegals. By assuring farmers that regardless of future disagreements between Mexico and the United States, with unilateral recruiting at the border, there would never be a shortage of braceros, Washington got the grower's reluctant acceptance that the immigration laws would have to be enforced. The day of the illegal Mexican worker was thought to be ending.

In 1952, an exasperated United States senator was quoted as saying, "We shall be using more than a million dollars in the next two and one-half months to get Mexican laborers into our country legally, and at the same time the Department of Immigration is asking for $4 million for the next two and one-half months to keep illegal aliens out." The senator had identified one of the curious contradictions of American immigration policy, a contradiction Attorney General Herbert Brownell wanted to eliminate with military support. His undermanned Border Patrol could not guard the entire international line, but if the Army would seal the boundary along the 250 mile California-Arizona border with Mexico, the patrolmen could stifle illegal crossings from western New Mexico to the southeastern tip of Texas. With undocumented workers no longer getting in, a campaign would open to expel those already here.

Although the Army snubbed his request, an undismayed Brownell toured the border and determined that deportations could be accomplished if the Border Patrol had the right leadership. To this end he appointed recently retired Lieutenant General Joseph Swing as commissioner of immigration. While Swing had the little-deserved reputation as a "Mexican hater," he brought a strong sense of organization to the patrol. He restructured and streamlined its administrative staff, instituted mobile task forces and made plans for an airlift, buslift, trainlift and boatlift. The concept called for transporting illegals deep into Mexico, the hope being that they would not turn north again.

To the din of intense publicity, "Operation Wetback" started in June 1954. Roadblocks went up all over California and Arizona, New Mexico and Texas. Patrolmen swept the farms and ranches, the sweatshops, bars, clothing and construction industries. Thousands of illegal Mexicans crossed the border and went south of their own accord. In 1954 alone, over a million (which includes a lot of official guesswork) Mexican deportations took place. In 1955 the figure fell to a quarter-million, and would not reach that number again for nearly fifteen years. In spite of the financial costs, in spite of repatriation memories, in spite of resistance from southeast Texas farmers, Operation Wetback had several accomplishments. It demonstrated that for a price, the borders could be controlled, if not tightly contained. It also demonstrated that the operation had been a stopgap measure with a brief, ambiguous success. It momentarily slowed, but did not halt, the illegal immigration.[9]

Early in 1951, the United States opened negotiations for an extension of the Bracero Program, and with its passage amendments were added in 1952, 1954, 1955, and 1959. Mexico improved its position with regards to worker guarantees, and expressed pleasure with the success of Operation Wetback. It also believed that "the day the United States makes it impossible for employers to hire Wetbacks the problem will be settled."

Both countries strained to find reasons for continuing the bracero agreement. It had started as a World War II need, and everyone assumed the braceros would be phased out when the global struggle ended. Once that terminated, however, the growers argued that returning employees now had a taste for higher wages, so braceros needed to be retained. Then the Korean conflict started, and suddenly agriculture needed bracero labor to feed the country during another patriotic struggle.[10]

The success of the "farm bloc" in keeping the Bracero Program going is the story of marketing more than just cotton and melons. Farm leaders and their organizations were a lot like politicians. They quarreled and clashed even while sharing certain attitudes and drawing upon common sources of power. On an individual or regional basis, they worked out compromises, obtained allies, subordinated internal differences and built coalitions. A small segment of American agriculture kept special ventures like the Bracero Program functioning for over two decades in a manner benefiting primarily itself.

By 1961, however, the Bracero Program was collapsing and becoming an embarrassment to support. While there had been voices of conscience in the past, they stemmed generally from the ranks of social workers and religious leaders. The decade of the 60s, however, was the decade of the television documentary, "Harvest of Shame." The nation witnessed pay and living conditions of the field hands, and the nation was ashamed. Few liked it, and few dared defend it. Because of television, religious, welfare and liberal organizations suddenly had a podium for talking directly to the American people. While their visions of bracero "slavery," "inhumane treatment" and "moral outrages" were just as excessive as the grower versions of "happy, well paid workers," it stirred unease in the American conscience. The era of John F. Kennedy, Martin Luther King and Lyndon Johnson arose, an era of idealism and social justice. The nation wanted to feel good about itself, and it wanted the excesses of bracero labor to cease.

Support for Public Law 78 declined as citizens grew suspicious of "labor shortages" and "prevailing wages." The Bracero Program struggled through the early 1960s, and by late 1964, in spite of pleas from Mexico for its retention, it was all over. California farmers complained, but eventually took steps to recruit and attract domestic help. Mechanization increased, and the legal bracero went back to being an illegal wetback.[11]

A Place To Work

OUT OF THE BRACERO ORDEAL, a historic truth emerged. Whenever legal channels for entry are severed or reduced in the United States, the number of undocumented workers entering the country rises. It was true with the elimination of the Bracero Program, and it was true of the. Immigration and Nationality Act Amendments of 1976, which reduced legal Mexican immigration from 62,000 to 40,000 a year. The Mexican kept coming. In 1964, when the Bracero Program stopped, the government expelled 104,500 illegals, ninety percent of them Mexican. By the end of the decade, the deportations had shot to over 400,000.[1]

And while the Mexicans were stereotyped as lazy, shiftless, passive siesta-seekers, people who patronized *mañana*, those who knew them realized that just the opposite was true. The Mexican was one of the hardest working individuals on earth, and he proved it just to get into the United States. He walked for weary weeks, forded muddy and violent rivers, clung to the tenuous underside of trucks and trains, stuffed himself into the sizzling engine compartment of automobiles, slipped through and over jagged fences, risked being murdered by his own people, flattened by traffic as he darted across the freeway, suffocated in tightly enclosed vans and railroad cars, arrested by the Border Patrol, all so he could earn minimum wages toiling with a short hoe from dawn to dusk. If he wasn't an illegal, he would surely have deserved commendation for bravery, perseverance and endurance. Such are the people whom we expel from our borders.

Pressures built for decades in the United States as reformers sought more rigid immigration controls. From Henry Kissinger's "Tortilla Curtain" (an imposing fence along portions of the border) to the Simpson-Mazzoli bill, various groups have sought workable, humane solutions to the illegal immigration problem. Simpson-Mazzoli repeatedly bogged down on the issue of employer penalties for the hiring of illegal aliens. Businessmen and farmers argued that it made them, in a sense, immigration agents. In an unexpected move, however, Hispanic leaders across the United States bitterly opposed employer sanctions, their rationale being that legal Mexicans, and especially Americans of Mexican descent, would find discrimination in the work place. Why should an employer hire any Hispanic and risk jail and heavy fines if the worker turned out to be an illegal? Safeguards plugged into the law had no effect on adamant Hispanic leaders, but when it finally occurred to legislators that the Mexican-American leadership was out of touch with its followers, that most Hispanic citizens favored employer restrictions because illegals took jobs away from Mexican-Americans, an immigration bill with employer penalties passed.

Meanwhile, how many illegals have slipped through the net and remain? How many have been caught once, twice, five, ten, twenty, one hundred times, and have been deported and return, frequently beating the patrol vehicle back to the highway? Nobody knows, and depending upon who does the estimating, the figure ranges from four to twelve million. The 1987-88 amnesty provided numbers to analyze, and it came up with nearly two million. Some experts believe that three times that many are still out there, insisting that millions of illegal aliens have lived in the United States for years, perhaps decades, and have full time jobs. Many have American-born children, who by law are citizens, even while their parents are not. Most live in near poverty, frequently in low-income housing supported by taxpayers. A few will be on welfare, their offspring in schools and getting their best meal of the day. The adults will learn broken English from their children and from television, and exist in constant fear of deportation.

Occasionally a circumstance will surface which, upon learning of it, Americans don't know whether to be proud, angry, or just frustrated. The *El Paso Times* of May 2, 1987, printed a front page story (including photo) about nineteen-year-old Cesar Salas. Cesar and his parents, plus an older brother and sister, illegally crossed the Rio Grande from Juarez in 1979 and settled in Roswell, New Mexico, 180 miles northeast of El Paso. Within a few years Cesar enrolled at Goddard High School, was named to "Who's Who in American Football," and became a cross-country track star. His accomplishments earned him national recognition as one of the top fifty high school leaders in the country. Young Cesar was invited to the White House, but as an undocumented alien, he lacked a social security number and other papers. However, since he and his parents admitted their illegal status and applied for amnesty, the Immigration and Naturalization Service furnished the family temporary permits of legal residence, which allowed Cesar to visit Washington. Chances are that the Salas family will be approved for amnesty, based on information published in the newspaper, and that they will become good citizens, as some might argue that they already have. Nevertheless, this case brings into poignant focus a portion of the illegal alien dilemma.

But do illegals hold jobs that Americans will not fill? Do they pay more in taxes than they consume in benefits? Are they a burden on the welfare system? Are they apt to commit crimes? Academics have analyzed the issues, and if their reports were water, the Southwest could grow crops on every acre of its deserts. Never have so many studied so much, and come up with so little that had practical benefits.[2]

As for either stopping or throwing back the prohibited alien, the history of these attempts proves only that deportations, in themselves, only momentarily slow the tide. The illegal keeps returning, and he keeps returning because he is the victim, not the problem. He enters the United States because he has no other choice. He will cease crossing the border illegally in record numbers when 1), American employers, because of stiff, enforceable fines and jail sentences, are fearful of hiring him, or 2) the Mexican economic incentives are worth remaining home for.

The first was enacted with the 1987 immigration act. Within weeks the illegal flow started to subside. Ed Miller of the Texas Employment Commission in Austin noting that by late 1987, El Paso employers alone had increased their requests for citizen workers by "some 30-35 percent," the surge being attributed to the new laws. However, the illegal numbers have fluctuated before, so it remains to be seen if this is merely a temporary lull before the onslaught of fresh undocumented floods.

The second possibility suggests a Marshall Plan for Mexico, a virtual impossibility. The European Recovery Program was successful because the defeated countries had no alternatives other than the hard, progressive choices the Plan offered. A Marshall Plan for Mexico would likely vanish into a Black Hole of corruption and political chicanery.

But if a Marshall Plan of old for Mexico is impractical, today's changing economic forces are offering new alternatives. An off-shoot of World War II was the subsequent erosion and decline of American workmanship and pride of mechanical skill. The "bottom line" emerged as a new buzz word, synonymous with profit. American icons were no longer the mechanical geniuses, tinkerers like Henry Ford and Thomas Edison, but the accountants, leaders with no concept of how cars, or cameras, or light bulbs were made, but managers who could omit a part, eliminate an employee, cheapen the material, or avoid new engineering designs, and create an attractively packaged product manufactured with less money. Managerial concerns had less to do with quality or customer satisfaction, and more with how well the company stock was selling.

Prideful maintenance fell by the wayside, service was deemphasized, and replacement of aging equipment deleted from the budget. Manufacturers encouraged customers to buy new cars each year because quality need not be a serious consideration when automobiles were purchased on an annual basis. And the profit stayed high. Public relations campaigns were so successful that manufacturers became their victims as well as their advocates. Big business believed the American buyer would remain devoted. He didn't, and when the Japanese brought a better automobile onto the market, and the gasoline shortages hit, the consumer threatened to turn Detroit into a ghost town.

Industrial America reacted by blaming the unions and, in the case of Ford at least, seeking employee and legislative help for restricting the Japanese, while at the same time escalating its importation of overseas engines and transmissions. As Congress showed a reluctance to pass trade deterrents, the titans of finance sacrificed an American industrial lead in order to generate the same, or more, profit. They abandoned product, factory and employee loyalties. With hardly a whimper and rarely a show of concern, the United States turned its face toward becoming a service-oriented society.[3]

In the beginning, few industries other than the candy and garment (needle trades) gave serious consideration to moving to Mexico. Mexico was "protectionist"-oriented, manufacturing almost nothing for export, and producing some of the world's shoddiest products for internal consumption. The country was perceived as politically dissolute, hostile toward foreign ownership, and to foreign eyes, frequently poised on the brink of revolution. It tolerated and even supported left wing if not outright Communist causes. Finally, Mexico had its unions, and although they usually were puppets of government and business, and only nominal supporters of employees, the leaders felt a periodic itch (and still do) to encourage labor unrest. American manufacturers rarely understood the topsy-turvy world of Mexican politics and business, and felt more secure with the oriental attitude of industriousness and pragmaticism.

Mexico developed a National Border Program (PRONAF) in 1961, and followed it in 1965 with a Border Industrial Program to utilize Mexican labor for the assembly of American products in northern Mexico. Instead of importing the workers, the United States would export the industries. These factories were originally characterized as Twin Plants, because there was a Mexican plant on its side of the border, and an American structure on the other. However, the Mexican plant frequently employed hundreds, whereas the American border facility was usually a warehouse or office with less than a half-dozen employees. In reality, the American border facility, when it existed, was frequently just a shipping port for its Mexican neighbor. The "twins" never actually existed. The border facilities, on both sides of the boundary, were subsidiaries, or support, plants for the manufacturing firms primarily in the United States East and Midwest.

The industry is called "in-bond" or, more generally, *maquiladoras*, or *maquilas*. The word comes from the verb *maquilar*, meaning to collect a toll. *Maquila* is a toll of corn collected by the miller. Foreign assembly plants import raw materials, components or machinery on a duty free basis. The products are assembled in Mexico and then shipped back to the United States, custom's duties being assessed only on the Mexican value added.

The United States and Mexico signed no maquila agreements, as the project was strictly a Mexican enterprise. Mexico and American industries took advantage of laws already in place.

By 1973, maquila plants started moving into the interior of Mexico, although eighty percent have remained along the border. From the onset, the government permitted complete foreign ownership, and today Mexico is the world's major exporter of assembled items to the United States.[4]

Only twelve plants had entered Mexico by the end of 1965, but by 1982 the figure had jumped to 588 plants employing 122,493 people. Automotive and electronic industries did not show much interest in Mexico until the government of President José López Portillo collapsed economically, the peso tumbling from 26 to 115 to the dollar. By 1986 the peso had plunged to over 500 to one, and a year later to over 2,000 to one. Mexico could barely make its national debt payments, and faced bankruptcy. Its trade balances fell, austerity programs started, and capital fled the country. In spite of repeated pay raises, the real value of a worker's salary continued to drop. By 1982, it was even more economically advantageous for labor intensive maquila plants to enter the country.[5]

Prior to 1982, neither the Mexican nor American governments had ever applauded the Border Industrial Program. Mexico treated it as an embarrassment, an admission that it could not provide for its northern border. In the desperation of economic chaos, however, incoming President Miguel de la Madríd made the maquiladoras a cornerstone of his recovery policy. On August 14, Madríd met with President Ronald Reagan, and both pledged support for the border phenomenon. By the late 1980s, Mexico had in excess of a thousand plants employing over 300,000 workers.[6]

The industry had passed beyond its "needle trades" status by the late 1980s, and garments constituted but fifteen percent of the total. The remainder are mostly electronic and automotive, the parent companies having familiar names like General Electric, RCA, Motorola, Ford, Hughes Aircraft. Most electrical harnesses for Chrysler and small GMC cars and trucks are assembled in Mexico, as are some of America's most highly sophisticated defense products.[7]

Nevertheless, the maquiladoras are not without their detractors. Mattel Toys, weary from its struggle with Mexican unions, pulled out of Mexicali and returned to the United States in 1975, leaving behind three thousand embittered workers. During American recessions, as in 1977, other industries closed for lack of work, or moved to Asia or the Caribbean. While a majority of American plant managers are satisfied, that figure could change with future Mexican and United States union pressures.

The maquilas began as "light industry." However, while the program is still dominated by this kind of operation, more and more plants are purchasing state-of-the-art assembly processes. Computers

Workers leaving a Juarez maquila plant for home. Note that most are well dressed and young. Note also a preponderance of women. *(El Paso Herald-Post)*

are finding their niche, and a few plants have installed assembly machines worth millions. Electrical boards are rarely ever assembled by hand. In the process, such upgradings require a higher level of employee skills, a level Mexico is struggling to meet because training facilities, except for on the job, have rarely existed. That is now changing as Monterrey Institute of Technology, one of the better technical schools in the world, is moving branches into cities such as Juarez. A shortage of mid-level management personnel also is critical, although these leaders are also being trained and educated.[8]

For a while, most factories employed only women because, as one manager said, they had a high ratio of immunity to tedium. Suddenly, along a border where the wife seldom was employed except as a maid, women became the wage earners while their husbands cared for the children, or hung out with the boys. Macho Mexican men preferred masculine work such as construction. Sociologists had a new field to study, but it tapered off as employers overcame their initial reluctance regarding males, and males themselves started applying for the jobs.

Today, the factories are about evenly divided between men and women, the ratio being similar to anywhere else in the world, including the United States.[9]

Back in the United States, the flight of American industry aroused envy and anger, with Congress making frequent threats to restrict the maquiladoras through the removal of tax advantages. Unions claimed, with closed eastern and midwestern assembly plants as evidence, that American jobs were lost to Mexico. Union leaders derided the maquilas as "run-away plants" because they ran away from the United States. Maquila supporters responded that corporate headquarters never transferred to Mexico, and assembly products were still manufactured in the United States, as well as returned there for further processing once the assembly was completed. Industrialists cited the savings of labor costs in Mexico, for without those benefits, the corporation could not exist. If the raw material assembly products did not flow to Mexico, they would go overseas. Since it would be economically impractical for American firms to ship manufactured goods across the ocean, the materials needing assembly would be manufactured across the ocean also. So the United States would not only lose the assembly plant, but the manufacturing plant on the East Coast or in the Midwest as well.[10]

The big question about the maquiladoras, of course, is will they last? And for how long? If they pull out, what will happen to the border? Will there be chaos, or will Mexico have put its economic house in order, and be capable of functioning without them? There are no positive answers. A rule of thumb says that when and if Mexican wages becomes competitive with American labor, the maquilas will leave.

However, the maquilas will likely remain in Mexico at least throughout the rest of this century. The border is easier and less expensive to reach from plants or headquarters in the United States; the border causes less American employment disruption than an assembly plant located anywhere else; and in case of rising world tensions, the border area is easier called to account than more remote and distant world locations. The border is accessible to water, transportation and relatively easy communications. An infrastructure is in place. The major factor in any industrial decision to transfer assembly operations to a foreign country is labor costs well below rates in southeast Asia. Mexican maquila wages will probably remain world competitive because Mexican minimum wages are well under one fourth the American wage.

Maquila jobs are readily available. Since a majority of new workers are in their late teens or early twenties, an average of eight percent quit *each month* (a few years ago it was fifteen to twenty percent), leaving whenever the spirit moves them. Employees who terminate can usually work for another maquila, or when they finish traveling or visiting, they can often return to the same plant.[11]

Officially Mexico's unemployment is four percent; unofficially it is closer to thirty, and maquilas can never solve, or even notably reduce, that awesome tragedy. Mexico needs 900,000 new jobs each year just to stay even with its population growth. Yet, the maquilas run newspaper ads almost every day, and the best assembly jobs in Mexico are rarely filled to capacity.

Because of the maquilas, the border in Mexico could be described as an island of prosperity in a Mexican sea of economic misery. While maquila working conditions are the best in Mexico, the pay is abysmally low compared to what a Mexican citizen with a work permit (called a Green Card) might earn in the United States. Green-Card holders generally are employed in agriculture or construction. While a maquila worker might get seventy cents an hour (which includes the benefits), a Green-Carder earns two to five dollars. Add these figures to the wages Mexicans get who cross the border ostensibly for shopping or visiting, and work as maids from $20 to $100 a week, plus the illegals who furtively work in construction, agriculture, cantinas, or as domestic servants, and there are Mexicans earning considerably more money than that paid by the maquilas.

All of this has created an air of unreality because the American side of the Mexican border is in itself a low-wage area. Refineries, construction and clothing plants represent the closest approach to manufacturing. Agriculture is strong, although river farm land is disappearing under concrete housing slabs. There is a vibrant service industry (hamburgers, cleaners, tourism). Employees for the federal, state, county and city government shore up the economy. The military is especially strong in communities like El Paso, and a robust border climate attracts retired people. So in cities where the highest paid people are often federal workers, thousands of Mexicans want in because the living is so good. Such an odd paradox could exist only along the border.

The Art of Pulling Together

THE MOST OBVIOUS SHORTCOMING about the border is that no one is in charge, although along any part of the international line, be it river or sand, every government agency except the Patent Office seems to have jurisdiction. The bridges in particular are an asylum belonging to the inmates. Customs, Immigration, FBI, DEA, Boundary Commission, Public Health, Reclamation Bureau, plus an unbelievable assortment of city, state and county bureaus all exercise a certain fiefdom, some of these agencies having little concept of what it all means, or amounts to. Between these federal and local bureaucracies, they control, in one form or another, half the bridge. Then there are the Mexican operations on the other half.

Although millions of people live on both sides of the border, it is the federal agencies, Mexican and American, especially Immigration and Customs, who establish the ground rules between neighbors. Major decisions are made not in El Paso, San Diego, Laredo, Brownsville, Matamoros, Juarez or Tijuana, but in Washington and Mexico City. The regulations are inviolate, intricate, complex, comprehensive and everywhere.

Comedian Mark Russell once described the American-Mexican boundary as a spot where north meets south, after a two hour wait. When access through both border crossings is swift and easy, as it usually is when entering Mexico, then the two cities function on a more personal level: officials talk, art blossoms. When access through the border crossings continues to be difficult and time consuming, as it usually is when entering the United States, then interpersonal, city-to-city relationships stagnate.

Even without federal interference, neighboring cities seem uncertain and edgy when officially dealing with one another. It is not unusual for elected officers to be unfamiliar with the other's language. Politicians and business leaders tend to approach discussions as if negotiating with an antagonistic foreign potentate, instead of a friend who lives next door.

Even so, local Mexican officials are more politicized than their American counterparts. Mayors and governors are ordinarily hand-picked by the federal government. The cities and states have few funds because the only tax is essentially a federal tax. Local officials and governors line up and pay homage to the PRI for the financing of state and municipal projects.

For these reasons, it is difficult for rival Mexican political parties to gain power, and that explains why elections in Mexico are more free and honest than most Americans suspect. A governor or mayor who belongs to a different political party, such as PAN, rarely gets anything more than superficial support from the federal government. When elections roll around again, it is anticipated by the PRI that the citizens will vote the right way.

On the American side, especially in Texas, there is more talk about English as an official language than about the conservation of water. There is more concern about the loss of maids than the control of boundaries. There is more emotion about poor learners whose grades prevent them from playing high school football than about the quality of education. There is more discussion about "cultural" heritage than about pragmatic economic decisions and opportunities.

While there is debate about political rights, less than a third of the eligible citizens vote. Hispanics lead the nation in the number of school dropouts. Residents insist upon more industry and jobs, yet sizeable segments of the population have no professional training, and often can neither read nor write. El Paso, a city of a half-million, the largest community on the American side of the Mexican border, supports less than a dozen book stores, tiny by national standards. (Juarez, with over a million people, the fourth largest city in Mexico, and the biggest community on either side of the border, has only a handful of bookstores.)

The vast American import along the Mexican border is people, Spanish speaking people, an expensive "poor" population frequently into the second or third generation before English becomes common and employment skills have been upgraded beyond manual labor or domestic service. Yet, there is no serious discussion of the long term effects of this immigration on the borderlands. There is scant dialogue regarding the social, economic, educational and cultural goals that should be overriding the conflicting interests of all parties.

Cities along the border brag about their compatible race relations, and certainly the Hispanic and Anglo populations have learned to "get along," but they have done so at a price of shying away from sensitive subjects. To feel strongly about controversial ethnic matters, and to voice these disquieting concerns, is to risk the label of racist.

Crime has become the leading growth industry along the border. South of San Diego, the borderlands have become a killing ground where illegals prey on one another and the situation isn't much different in El Paso and other cities. While violence has always flourished along the border, there are disturbing connections between the steadily inflating brutality, the increasing flow of aliens, and the deteriorating Mexican economic situation. As long as these basically docile people pass this way, because as illegals they have no other routes to take, thugs from both sides of the boundary will profit from their misery. Because they are breaking the law in order to enter the United States, they rarely complain unless seriously injured or apprehended. They fall between the cracks in the system, because the massive forces that should be protecting them are geared only for their arrest and incarceration.

Eight hundred miles to the east in Juarez, a middle-aged mother kisses her five children good-by and if she has money, and if the water is deep, she pays a "mule" fifty cents to ferry her across the Rio Grande in a rubber boat, or carry her on his shoulders. If she has no money, or the weather is warm, she may strip to panties and brassiere, then wade. (Men will cross naked.) At that point, she either pays a bribe, or provides a "free feel" to Mexican hooligans guarding holes in the fence, or blocking the northern exit of makeshift bridges. Authorities rarely intervene because the thugs fade back and forth across the interna-

The "mules" ferry illegal workers (left) across the Rio Grande into El Paso. The woman will probably work as a maid, the men as laborers in construction. The mules earn twenty-five cents to one dollar a trip. 1988. *(El Paso Herald-Post).* A rubber raft (below) carries illegals across a swollen Rio Grande into El Paso. 1987. *(El Paso Herald-Post)*

tional line. Even if the terrorists (and this is precisely what they are, since bodies floating in irrigation canals can often be traced to their activities) are captured, who will testify against them? Their success and relative immunity prove that even with all these overlapping jurisdictions at the boundary, the exact center of the border remains a no man's land, a mine field for shattered lives.

Upon reaching the northern side, illegals hesitate like tense football players anticipating the whistle. Everybody instinctively knows when the Border Patrolmen are visiting the bathroom. Then these undocumented workers dash for downtown El Paso, a few blocks distant, where comparative security exists as they blend in with resident, bronze-skinned people.

One of the great boundary ironies is that any United States resident can enter any Mexican border town with only the wave of his hand as credentials. And he can remain there essentially as long as he wishes, although he cannot work except in select occupations and industries. If an American desires to visit the interior, the formalities involve presenting a birth certificate or voter's card. There is also a fifteen minute delay: fourteen minutes of standing in line, and one minute for processing.

As for the demise of the illegal invasion, if and when it comes, that will depend upon several factors. The law enacting punishment for employers knowingly hiring illegal aliens has yet to be constitutionally tested. If it stands, *and is enforced*, the swarms of undocumented aliens will cease. The Department of Immigration and Naturalization, specifically the Border Patrol, has identified major violators. The authorities know the predominantly guilty businessmen, bar owners, construction foremen, sweat shop operators, farmers. Those in the past who have regularly flouted the law will likely become the first luckless recipients of the government's clout.

Meanwhile, jealousies over jurisdictions and responsibilities, the mountains of red tape, the difficulties of language and the lack of historical knowledge and cultural sensibilities, have driven wedges between neighboring cities whose single greatest problems are each other. Juarez is a city with no automotive exhaust laws, miles of dirt streets, unregulated cement plants and a million-plus population — many of whom burn discarded oil filters because they give surprisingly good heat transfer, to cook and keep warm. Tijuana and San Diego share the same paradox, as do Laredo and Nuevo Laredo. Since pollutants are not respecters of international boundaries, neighboring border cities gag on each other's filth.

Yet, while part of the Mexican border is arguably the most polluted strip in North America,[1] occasional spasms of inter-city cooperation do occur. The El Paso-Juarez complex has almost no mosquitoes because the El Paso Department of Health sprays both communities. It is a little known, quiet piece of effective diplomacy.

To the west, the New River flows out of Mexicali (Mexico) into Calexico (U.S.) and is one of the world's most virulent streams. It looks like an irrigation ditch, but with dead animals, laundry suds, human feces, slaughterhouse wastes, agricultural fertilizer and barrels of toxic chemicals, it smells like what it actually is: an open, foul, ugly, dangerous sewer. Since 1970, Mexicali has doubled in size to nearly a million people, and cannot handle its own unregulated growth. Experts believe a thorough cleanup of the New River may cost $400 million, money which authorities are not likely to allocate until local residents start dying at a faster rate. Altogether, the New River flows seventy-five miles into the Salton Sea, which may eventually become the "Pollutant Sea." Mexico in particular, and the United States in general, act as if the environment is a renewable resource.[2]

Other environmental disasters in the formative stage are the Colorado, the Salado, the Rio Grande, the Pecos, the Conchos and the Tia Juana. They carry tons of fertilizer solvents, chemical wastes and raw sewage. When President Lyndon Johnson pushed a button routing the Rio Grande through a new (and concrete) channel between El Paso and Juarez, all by virtue of the Chamizal agreement, it should have come as no surprise when the initial weak surge of water swept a dead dog past the dignitaries.

Over in Nogales, Sonora, the land slopes "down" to the north, and the sewage of a mushrooming Mexican Nogales is visited upon its American neighbor, Nogales, Arizona. Back in the early 1950s, the boundary commission built a treatment plant on the American side to take care of both cities. Mexico paid its share. By the 1970s, the plant was inadequate, so the commission constructed a larger one outside of town. Mexico paid a portion. Now, Mexican sewage overloads the plant, and Mexico refuses to cooperate in another treatment facility because of major costs and a lack of concern.

A couple of hundred miles west, a burgeoning Tijuana also has massive waste disposal problems. Yet, Tijuana has an outlet that

Joseph F. Friedkin, (left) former U.S. Commissioner, International Boundary and Water Commission, United States and Mexico. (Below) Secretary of State George P. Shultz presents the Department of State's Distinguished Honor Award to Commissioner Friedkin. With Friedkin is his wife Nellie May.

NARENDRA N. GUNAJI
American Commissioner, International
Boundary and Water Commission, 1989.

CARLOS SANTIBAÑEZ MATA
Mexican Commissioner, International
Boundary and Water Commission, 1989.

Nogales does not: an ocean. The city flushes its raw sewage through a pipe into the Pacific where it is out of sight and out of mind for Tijuana but not for San Diego. Ocean currents carry the sewage northward and deposit it on California beaches.

Are there solutions? Not really. None completely satisfactory, anyway. Anyone who has traveled in Mexico knows that sewage disposal is not a national priority. Mexico City, known for outstanding accomplishments and breathtaking features, does not advertise clean, efficient restrooms. Mexico will not build a first-class treatment center at Nogales, Tijuana or Mexicali because the nation has other priorities, and construction of such a project along the border would be perceived as benefiting Americans.

Other Mexican border towns, like Nuevo Laredo, dump their sewage into the Rio Grande for downstream communities to worry about. Farther up-river, Juarez solves its problems by using the sewage for irrigation. As a fertilizer and dispenser of liquid sludge, it works. As a deodorant, it has certain disadvantages.

All rivers along the border have as their special purpose the watering of land. Yet, the onion fields of Laredo, the citrus and cotton crops in the Lower Rio Grande Valley, and the melons in the Imperial Valley (with substantially the same produce grown by neighbors to the south) may someday bow to a greater need, a human, city need. A decision will have to be made whether water will be available for farmers, or for people. Population pressures are transforming the border. Juarez is the fourth largest city in Mexico, and Mexicali, Tijuana and Matamoros are not far behind. On the American side, San Diego is moving incessantly south;[3] El Paso is (according to the 1980 census) the 23rd biggest city in the United States and one of the fastest growing. The Lower Rio Grande Valley is exploding with growth, and Laredo approaches one hundred thousand residents. Many people desire to live on valley land, to have grass and trees. But as soaring populations force out agriculture, it also deprives people of greenery. The American Southwest and northern Mexico will eventually use their rivers solely for drinking, cooking and washing.

Cities like El Paso and Juarez currently tap the Hueco Bolson, an underground water source going dry. If Juarez residents consumed as much water per capita as El Pasoans do, the bolson would have emptied years ago. That would leave the Rio Grande as a supplier of basic needs. Yet, neither city sees fit to discuss mutual issues involving the finding and sharing (and sharing is what they will eventually have to do) of new water. Both towns showed a blithe unconcern about the abundant water in 1986 and 1987, when the Rio Grande ran full and belched its wasted resources into the Gulf. Enough water possibly rolled between the two cities to have satisfied twin needs for decades.

Elsewhere, thirty-five percent of the heroin and almost twenty percent of the cocaine and thirty percent of the marijuana entering the United States comes across the international line. And the percentages are increasing. Yet, drug officials before Congress testified that "even if they had every piece of equipment that had been requested, it would be impossible for them to intercept more than 10 to 15 percent of the drugs pouring into the United States over the border."[4]

Short of massive budget increases, American federal agencies have done all they can to stifle the traffic. Not only has the effort failed, it has contributed to deteriorating relations along the border. Long lines started forming at the bridges in the 1970s as American immigration and customs authorities suddenly subjected each motor vehicle to intense inspection. Trained dogs sniffed for drugs while urinating on tires. An hour wait in a hot sun was not uncommon for motorists, and as tempers flared and cars overheated, Americans without compelling reasons to cross the border, stopped doing so.

Since then, Congress has questioned why the armed services should not contribute toward tightening the border. The quest has stalled thus far, not for a lack of merit, as additional radar has been offered and accepted, but because the Army was never meant to be a police force. The same suggestion will no doubt surface again, for in terms of drug eradication, there are only three options: increase the Immigration-Customs budget by at least ten fold (and be prepared to do it again if that doesn't work); turn the full resources of the Army loose and close the border; or make drugs legal in the United States.

The Mexicans are never going to seal their side of the border against narcotics, and whoever waits for a significant stiffening of a Mexican drug policy is dreaming. Corruption is an important factor, especially since it has shifted from serious in the 1970s to pervasive and even outrageous in the late 1980s. Of more significance, however, is the fact that Mexico lacks the financial resources to blockade the border. Mexicans see the narcotics dilemma as an American problem, knowing that the United States has the most insatiable market for drugs in history.

Mexican school children (left) pose at the last International Boundary Monument (No. 258) on the Pacific Coast. They are on the United States side of the border, and therefore illegal aliens. 1986. (Author's Collection). The United States-Mexico border (below) ends with a grubby fence protruding into the Pacific. The people in this picture are illegal Mexican workers entering the United States. They waded around the fence. 1986. (Author's Collection)

Americans encourage it, they pay the price and they countenance the blood that's spilled.

In Mexico, a country that cannot feed its people, nor create sufficient jobs, a country whose hospitals frequently cannot find the money for X-ray film, whose children die of dehydration because they cannot get pure drinking water, for it to channel scarce resources into programs perceived as solving an American addiction is political and economic nuttiness. Hysterical sanctions against Mexico for failing to do what Americans refuse to do for themselves, are hardly a solution.

And speaking of money, Mexico has not forgotten, and most Americans are only dimly aware, that Mexico has a very serious capital shortage. During the peso devaluations of the seventies and eighties, billions of dollars fled the country, much of it deposited in border banks. American bankers have far more Mexican money in their vaults than they have on loan to that unhappy country, and it scarcely behooves United States officials to insist that Mexico fulfill its crushing loan payments after the bankers have sucked up gigantic portions of their capital.

Meanwhile, just as the United States showed imagination in its amnesty program of the late 1980s, in order to achieve a larger goal of regaining control of its borders, and Mexico showed imagination in opening its borders to maquilas, the times now cry for additional leadership. Author Carlos Fuentes referred to the border as, "the next frontier of American consciousness." It is the "most difficult frontier of all," he wrote, "because it is the closest and therefore the one most often forgotten, most often ignored, and most feared when it is stirred from its long lethargy."

Still, the border has no priorities in either national capital, or among the cities that so identify and give it character. Furthermore, it has never spoken with one voice. The border is bereft of leadership.

Cathryn Thorup, Director of the United States-Mexico Project of the Overseas Council (ODC) urged the establishment of an "Eminent Persons Group." Although she had in mind using it for all of the United States and Mexico, it should work just as well strictly along the border. The committee would be composed of respected and knowledgeable representatives from the United States and Mexico. With presidents George Bush leading the United States, and Carlos Salinas de Gortari doing likewise for Mexico, perhaps a start will be made for a two country plan of progressive action along the respective borders.[5]

For as bad as some things seem to be, the Mexican-American border is an area rich in history, an area romanticized for centuries. The Rio Grande, polluted and diverted as it is, remains one of the world's fascinating, foremost rivers.

Tall palms still wave over the coastal prairie, the sub-tropical country we call the Lower Rio Grande Valley. In spite of serious problems, it remains a citrus and winter vegetable source for much of the country. In the fall of each year, "snowbirds" arrive by the thousands, they and their motor homes and trailers escaping the snow and ice of mid-America.

Traveling farther west, some of America's most isolated and craggy mountains take shape near the Big Bend. The canyon walls of sheer rock have retained their weird, beautiful scenery.

West Texas, New Mexico, Arizona and southern California may have scanty rainfall, but they have abundant sunshine. On clear days, one can see snow-capped peaks a hundred and fifty miles distant. This magnificent land remains the home of the cowboy and vaquero, the hard-rock miner, the scraggly ghost towns, the two cultures, and the historic, Old West gunfighters — Billy the Kid, John Wesley Hardin, Wyatt Earp — to name a few, who have so immortalized America's frontier past.

In western Arizona and eastern California, one can find desert, mountains and pine forests, all within a short drive of each other. The huge dunes are still used by Hollywood to depict the Sahara. Oasis-like towns still have their date groves. And the one hundred and twenty-five degree summer heat is not for sissies.

Finally, after two thousand miles from the Gulf of Mexico, San Diego is still bathed in the Pacific surf, sunny and mild and booming and fleet headquarters for the United States Navy. Not too cool in winter, nor too hot in summer, a land which many suspect contains America's most ideal climate.

From San Diego to Brownsville, from Tijuana to Matamoros, the beginning and the end, or the ending and the beginning. That's the Mexican-American international line. That's what we call the Border.

ACKNOWLEDGMENTS

Joseph Friedkin, former United States boundary commissioner, gave me an early boundary tour along the Rio Grande and opened the historical possibilities. Present United States Boundary Commissioner Narendra Gunaji has also been very helpful. Former American Boundary Commission Secretary Ray Daguerre, and present secretary, Robert Ybarra, made boundary commission files and photos accessible. They read manuscripts, and were always available for advice and assistance. I'm grateful to Al Giugni, district director, U.S. Immigration and Naturalization Service for several hours of discussion.

Dan Page and Bill Sidell (retired) from the El Paso Bureau of Reclamation were very helpful. So was Peggy Goiner, who initially ran the necessary interference. My thanks to Robert Steele, public affairs officer for the Yuma Bureau of Reclamation, who read the Colorado River portion of the manuscript.

My old friend Dale L. Walker read manuscripts and gave his usual outstanding advice. The same can be said of James M. Day, a longtime associate and confidant. Others who read and commented on manuscripts were Pat Kelley, David Overvold, Robert Ybarra, Ray Daguerre, and my father-in-law, William Schilling. Thanks also to Martha Peterson, a fine writer with a discerning eye for misspellings and typos, who gave of her time to read everything.

Mary Sarber, of the El Paso Public Library, has freely shared her knowledge. The staff in the Southwest Room was particularly helpful.

Robert Seal, U.T. El Paso librarian was helpful, and many of his staff deserve special thanks: Helen Bell (now a librarian in the El Paso public schools), Tom Burdett, Cesar Caballero, Yvonne Greear, Hatsuyo Hawkins, Susan Hicks, Mary Keckley, Dan Miller, S. H. "Bud" Newman, Dolores Sweezey, and Louise Tenner.

My Mexican maquila experts provided hours of evaluation and conversation. Those most active were Don Shuffstall, private Mexican consultant; Sam Drake, executive director of El Paso Industrial Development Corporation; William L. Mitchell, vice president Grupo Bermudez; attorney Carmen Leal; Ellwyn Stoddard, sociology professor, U.T. El Paso.

Outside of the library, others I turned to from U.T. El Paso were: Howard Applegate (especially helpful during the violent border years), Nancy Hamilton, Oscar Martinez, W. H. Timmons, John West, and Sue Wimberly.

Others who contributed mightily were author T. H. Fehrenbach, Peggy Boone, Pat Brink, Richard Estrada, Don Lavash, Taft Lyon, Pat Pierce, Sue Turner, Marta Durón Hernández, Myrna Zanetell. Myrna opened doors in southern California.

My appreciation to Susan Clarke Spater, director of the Pimeria Alta Historical Society in Nogales; to Austin Hoover, director of University Archives at New Mexico State University; to George Gause, Jr., Special Collections librarian at Pan American University; the San Diego Historical Society and its Junípero Serra Museum; the Columbus (NM) Historical Society; the Cochise County Historical and Archaeological Society; the Sul Ross State University and its Big Bend Museum; to Craig McStravick and the Imperial Irrigation District; the Douglas Chamber of Commerce; the Arizona Historical Society and its Museum; the New Mexico State Records Center; the Texas State Archives; the numerous archival collections at U.T. Austin; and to public libraries the length and breadth of the border, beginning with the one in Brownsville.

Finally I want to thank Frank and Judy Mangan, El Paso publishers of Mangan Books, who had confidence in this manuscript, and to express a special word of appreciation to my wife, Cheryl. She was my best proofreader and editor. Cheryl repeatedly rallied my spirits throughout the many trying years that it took to research and write this border history.

In spite of all this assistance, however, the responsibility for errors lies solely with myself.

ABBREVIATIONS FOR NOTES AND BIBLIOGRAPHY

HED — House Executive Document
HR — House Report
SB — Senate Bill
SED — Senate Executive Document
CG — Congressional Globe
FRUS — Foreign Relations of the
    United States
IBC — International Boundary
    Commission
IBWC — International Boundary and
    Water Commission
NA — National Archives
RG — Record Group
PL — Public Law

AH — *Arizona Highways*
AJIL — *American Journal of
    International Law*
AW — *American West*
A&W — *Arizona and the West*
BBL — *Bulletin of the Bureau of
    Labor*
CHSQ — *California Historical
    Society Quarterly*
CO — *Chronicles of Oklahoma*
CQ — *Cochise Quarterly*
EMJ — *Engineering and Mining
    Journal*
FA — *Foreign Affairs*
HAHR — *Hispanic American
    Historical Review*

H — *Harpers*
HM — *Harpers Monthly*
HW — *Harpers Weekly*
IAEA — *Inter-American Economic
    Affairs*
JAH — *Journal of Arizona History*
JEH — *Journal of Economic History*
JSDH — *Journal of San Diego
    History*
JS — *Journal of the Southwest*
MM — *The Mexican American*
MSP — *Mining and Scientific Press*
MVHR — *Mississippi Valley
    Historical Review*
NAR — *North American Review*
NMHR — *New Mexico Historical
    Review*
NRJ — *Natural Resources Journal*
OR — *Orders of the Rebellion*
PHR — *Pacific Historical Review*
SA — *Southwestern Agriculture*
SES — *Southwest Economy &
    Society*
SHQ — *Southwestern Historical
    Quarterly*
TMH — *Texas Military History*
WHQ — *Western Historical
    Quarterly*
WRB — *Water Resources Bulletin*

NOTES

1. To Establish a Border

1. There were many reasons for the collapse of northern Mexico, but David J. Weber suspects that the greatest cause lay in "Mexico's failure to tie her frontier to the rest of the nation through the building of strong institutional, economic, and even social ties." David J. Weber, "From Hell Itself: The Americanization of Mexico's Northern Frontier, 1821-1846," *CQ*, 4.
2. SED 52, "The Treaty Between the United States and Mexico," 1-306.

2. A Commissioner Falls

1. HED 135 (Part 1), *Report on the United States and Mexican Boundary Survey*, by William E. Emory, 1. Hereafter cited as Emory, *Report*.
2. SED 34 (Part 1), "Emory to Sec. of State John M. Clayton," Sept. 15, 1849, 28-29; Ross Calvin (ed.), *Lt. Emory Reports*. Except for the introduction, this book is a copy of SED 7.
3. SED 34, 2-6.
4. Ibid.; Joseph Richard Werne, "Partisan Politics and the Mexican Boundary Survey, 1848-1853," *SHQ*, 329-330.
5. SED 34, "Whipple to Emory," May 17, 1849; to "Maj. Vinton, Quartermaster of the U.S. Army," May 17; "William Nelson, Consul for the U.S. at Panama," May 22; to "Sec. of State John M. Clayton," May 23; to "John Weller," May 14, 2-6.
6. Richard F. Pourade, *The History of San Diego: the Explorers*, 94-95.
7. R. P. Effinger to his mother, Aug. 29, 1849, R. P. Effinger Papers, San Diego Historical Soc. Hereafter cited as *Effinger*.
8. Lewis B. Lesley, "The International Boundary Survey from San Diego to the Gila River, 1849-1850," *CHSQ*, 6; SED 34, 2-6.
9. There is controversy about the spelling of Ylarregui's name. Emory spelled it Larregui. Most Mexican publications spell it Ilarregui. For his memoirs regarding this episode in his career, see José Salazar Ylarregui, *Datos de los Trabajos Astrónomicos y Topográficos Dispuestos en Forma de Diario. Practicadós Durante el Año de 1849 y Principios de 1850 Por la Comision de Límites Mexicana en la Línea Que Divide Esta República de la de Los Estados Unidos . . . .* (Mexico, 1850)
10. Emory to Maj. E. R. S. Canby, July 5, 1849, Emory Papers.

11. *Effinger*, Aug. 11, 1849. Effinger said there were 250 Mexican soldiers.
12. Ibid.
13. *Effinger*, Aug. 29, 1949.
14. Records of Office of the Judge Advocate General (Army), Court Martial of J. McKinstry; J. McKinstry to Emory, Sept. 2, & George F. Evans to Emory, Sept. 2, 1849, Emory Papers.
15. Abert to Emory, July 5, 1849, Emory Papers.
16. SED 34, 29-31; Salazar, *Datos*, 21; Lesley, "The International Boundary Survey," 10.
17. Salazar, *Datos*, 21.
18. Cave J. Couts, *The Journal of Cave Johnson Couts*, 27.
19. Arthur Woodard, *Feud on the Colorado*, 75.
20. Clifford E. Trafzer, *The Yuma Crossing*, 8-11; Jay Wagoner, *Early Arizona*, 304-307; Rosalie Crowe and Sidney B. Brinckerhoff (eds.), *Early Yuma*, 2; Douglas D. Martin, *Yuma Crossing*, 128-136.
21. Salazar, *Datos*, 24-25.
22. SED 34, 3-4.
23. Emory, *Report*, 4. For an outstanding nature study of the U.S.-Mexico borderlands, read, *Mountain Islands and Desert Seas*, by Frederick R. Gehlbach.
24. SED 34, 3-4; and SED 34, "Gray to Weller," Nov. 7, 1849, "Weller to Gray," Nov. 8, 1849, 45-47.
25. *Effinger*, Nov. 3, 1849.
26. SED 34, 9-10.
27. Jesse Benton Frémont MS, 112.
28. John Bigelow, *Memoir of the Life and Public Services of John Charles Frémont*, quoting from Frémont to Jacob R. Snyder, Dec. 11, 1849, 389-396.
29. CG, 31st Cong., 2d Sess., 78-84; Emory, *Report*, 5.
30. Ibid.
31. Ibid.; SED 34, "Clayton to Frémont,"June 20, 1849, "Clayton to Weller," June 20, 1849, "T. Ewing to Weller," Dec. 19, 1849, 9-15.
32. SED 119 (Part 2), 74-76; Werne, "Partisan Politics . . . .," 337-343.
33. Ibid., "Emory to Clayton,"Sept. 15, 1851, 28-29; Draft of "A Communication of the Boundary Commission," undated, Emory Papers.
34. Hardcastle to Emory, July 17, 1851, Emory Papers. This communication conflicts with Emory's *Report*, p. 4, which states that the two surveys met "nearly on the same line."
35. Salazar, *Datos*, 32-38.

3. A Boundary Too Far North

1. Bartlett's physical description in this book differs with most biographies. Some writers seem to have ignored the photographs in favor of the paintings, which are more flattering.
2. Robert V. Hine, *Bartlett's West*, 7
3. SED 60, "Report of the Sec. of Interior Communicating . . . a Copy of the Charges Preferred Against the Present Commissioner Appointed to Run and Mark the Boundary Line Between the United States and Mexico," 52-58.
4. Ibid.; John R. Bartlett, *Personal Narrative of Exploration and Incidents*, 20. Hereafter cited as Bartlett, *Narrative*.
5. SED 119, "Bartlett to Sec. of Interior," Sept. 29, 1850, 377-78.
6. John C. Cremony, *Life Among the Apaches*, 18-19; Bartlett, *Narrative*, 48.
7. SED 119, "Bartlett to Maj. Van Horne," Nov. 7, 1850, 20-21.
8. Benjamin Franklin Coons came to El Paso in 1849 and established the first mercantile business in what is now the downtown area. He had leased the Ponce Rancho, and named the village that grew up around it, "Franklin." In 1859 it became El Paso. See Rex Strickland, *Six Who Came to El Paso*, 7-8.
9. Frederick Augustus Percy was an Englishman born in 1827 who apparently came to El Paso as wagonmaster for Benjamin Franklin Coons. In 1854 he handwrote a thirty page newspaper, *El Sabio Sembrador* (The Wise Sower), and filled its pages with much of what we presently know about El Paso in 1854.
10. SED 119, "Stuart to Bartlett," 94; SED 60, "Bartlett to McClellan," Dec. 16, 1851, 12-13.
11. SED 119, 497.
12. Ibid., 25.
13. SED 60, 2-5, 42-43, 51-52.
14. SED 89, 2.
15. SED 119, 42-48.
16. Ibid., 396-9, 403.
17. Ibid., 396-97; Bartlett, *Narrative*, 156-167 *New Orleans Picayune*, undated, and *Providence Journal*, undated, both in Bartlett's, *Scrapbook: The Mexican Boundary Commission Papers of John Russell Bartlett*, reel 11.
18. The Spanish and Mexicans considered these mountains as part of *Los Organos* (the Organs). After Doniphan's conquest in 1846, many maps carried them as the White Mountains, a likely reference to Customs Collector Frank White. Franklin was probably adopted as the mountain name during the late 1840s or early 1850s. They were named for Benjamin Franklin Coons.
19. Magoffinsville was 115 feet east and 16 feet south of the present-day intersection of Magoffin and Willow streets. The geographic position of the hacienda was very nearly 31 46° 12' latitude and 106 27° 53' longitude. The 1850 boundary commission calibrated it.
20. Ysleta is now a part of El Paso. Socorro and San Elizario will eventually be annexed to El Paso.
21. Dr. Hunter Miller (ed.), *Treaties and Other International Acts of the USA*, Vol. 5; William H. Goetzmann, *Army Exploration in the American West*, 155-156, 173-179.
22. *El Faro*, Chihuahua City newspaper, Nov. 26, 1850. The issue carried a story about the boundary commission, and García Conde's presence in the Chihuahua capital.
23. SED 119, "Bartlett to Stuart," Dec. 18, 1850, 386-390.
24. Ibid., "Whipple to Bartlett," Dec. 12, 1850, 247.
25. Ibid., "Arguments of General Conde," Dec. 20, 1850, 277-278.
26. Ibid., "Bartlett to Whipple," Dec. 30, 1850, 248.
27. Ibid., "Copy of Document Deposited at Initial Point," 233-234; Bartlett, *Narrative*, 2-5, 206.
28. Mario T. García, "Merchants and Dons: San Diego's Attempt at Modernization, 1850-1860," *JSDH*, 52-77; Robert W. Frazer, "Military Posts in San Diego," Ibid., 44-52.
29. Radzyminski was born in Warsaw, Poland in 1805. He served in the Polish Revolutionary Army and was granted asylum in the U.S. when Russia crushed the rebellion. After fighting in the Mexican War, he worked with the Northeast Boundary Commission during the border dispute between Maine and New Brunswick, Canada. As Gray's assistant in the El Paso Southwest, he was the principal surveyor for the boundary commission. When the surveys were completed, he became a first lieutenant in the 2d Cavalry Division at Jefferson Barracks, Missouri. He died in Memphis, Tennessee of tuberculosis on Aug. 18, 1858. Camp Radzyminski in southeastern Oklahoma was named in his honor. See Stanley F. Radzyminski, "Charles F. Radzyminski: Patriot, Exile, Pioneer," *CO*, 354-384.
30. SED 119, "Gray to Bartlett," July 25, 1851, 279-284.
31. Ibid., "Bartlett to Stuart," Aug. 8, 1851, 145-150.
32. Bartlett, *Narrative*, 348.
33. SED 119, "Graham to Bartlett," July 10, 13, 1851, 195-196.
34. Ibid., "Conde to Bartlett," July 7, 1851,

142-143, "Bartlett to Conde," July 11, 1851, 143-144.

35. Ibid., "Graham to Bartlett," Aug. 7, 1851, 208-210.

36. *Correspondence Book of Lt. Col. J. D. Graham, USBC, 1850-1852*, "Graham to Bartlett," Aug. 13, 1851, no pagination.

37. SED 119, "Stuart to Gray," Oct. 8, 1851, 92-93, "Gray to Bartlett," Aug. 9, 1851, 213-214.

38. *Correspondence Book of Graham*, Aug. 16, 1851.

39. SED 119, "Graham to Abert," Nov. 16, 1851, 333-335.

40. Ibid., "Stuart to Gray," Oct. 31, 1851, 118.

41. Ibid., "Stuart to Gray," & "Stuart to Emory," Nov. 4, 1851, 121.

4. Seeing Inez Home

1. In Sonora, Carrasco had the rank of general, but in the regular army, he was a colonel. Francisco Almada, *Diccionario de Historia, Geografía y Biografía Sonorenses*, 146, and *Diccionario de Historia, Geografía y Biografía Chihuahuenses*, 89.

2. Bartlett, *Narrative*, 270.

3. Ibid., 226.

4. Paige W. Christiansen, *The Story of Mining in New Mexico*, 19-20.

5. John C. Cremony, *Life Among the Apaches*, 52.

6. *New York Times*, Sept. 30, 1851, quoting a letter from Bartlett.

7. SED 119, "Bartlett to Conde," June 28, July 2, 1851, 159-261, "Bartlett to Peter Blacklaws," June 30, 1851, 260.

8. Ibid., "Bartlett to Conde," July 2, 1851, 260-261; Cremony, *Life*, 59-72; Bartlett, *Narrative*, 310-318.

9. Bartlett, *Narrative*, 376.

10. Ibid., 402-405.

11. "Webb to Graham," *Correspondence File* (July-Sept), Bartlett Papers.

12. SED 119, "Bartlett to Stuart," Nov. 12, 1851, 463; Bartlett, *Narrative*, 455-456.

13. Cremony, *Life Among the Apaches*, 98-117.

14. SED 119, "Stuart to Whipple," Feb. 21, 1852, 126.

15. "Emory to Capt. R. E. Clary," Sept. 28, 1851, Emory Papers.

16. Ibid., "Emory to James R. Pierce," Jan. 1852.

17. Ibid., "Emory to Stuart," Dec. 8, 1851, "Hardcastle to Emory," Dec. 8, 1851, "Emory to Col. E. V. Sumner," Jan. 2, 1852.

18. Ibid., "Tillinghast to Emory," May 11, 1852.

19. Ibid., "M. V. Hippel to Emory," May 15, 1852, "Emory to George Whiting," Oct. 15, 1852.

20. Ibid., "Emory to José Salazar," *Minutes of Official Minutes at Presidio del Norte*, Aug. 26, 1852.

21. Ronnie C. Tyler, *The Big Bend: A History of the Last Texas Frontier*, 75-97.

22. "Miles To Emory," March 21, 1852, Emory Papers.

5. A Curse and a Counter Curse

1. *San Diego Herald*, Feb. 4, 1852, Bartlett Papers.

2. Clo Edgington, "The Death of Lt. Col. Craig near Alamo Mucho, June 5, 1852," *The Wrangler*, 6-8; Bartlett, *Narrative*, 137-138.

3. John C. Cremony, *Life Among the Apaches*, 56-58.

4. Bartlett, *Narrative* (Vol. 2), 412-414.

5. Ibid., 429.

6. Ibid., 517.

7. SED 119, "Report of the Sec. of Interior in Relation to the Mexican Boundary Commission," July 1, 1852, 1.

8. SED 60, 1,628-1,660; SED 89, "Stuart to William R. King," June 22, 1852, 1-2; CG, XXV, 1,650-1,700.

9. *Appendix to CG*, XXV, "Speeches of the Honorable V. E. Howard of Texas to the House of Reps.," July 6, 1852, 776-781.

10. SED 345, "The Mason Report," Aug. 20, 1852, 1-7; CG, "An Act Making Appropriations for the Civil and Diplomatic Expenses of Gov.," XXIV, Part 3, XViii.

11. SED 1. Stuart, smarting from the Senate attack upon his integrity, also called attention to the unfairness of Congress for "refusing to pay the employees of the U.S. commission for the arduous and laborious services which they, in good faith, had rendered in obedience to the orders of their superior." Oct. 11, 1852, 50-55.

12. SED 41, "The Bartlett Report," 1-32; SED 55, "The Gray Report," 1-50; Hine, *Bartlett's West*, 82-83.

13. Misc. newspaper clippings, n.d., Bartlett Papers; also see Bartlett, *Narrative* (Vol. 2), 429-430.

6. Bad Roads and Flags of Contention

1. Read Kenneth Franklin Neighbours, *Robert Simpson Neighbors and the Texas Frontier, 1836-1859*, and William Turrentine Jackson's, *Wagon Roads West*.

2. Gov. George T. Wood appointed Spruce M. Baird as the 11th Judicial District Judge with headquarters in Santa Fe. Upon his arrival on Nov. 10, 1848, Baird presented his credentials to Lt. Col. John Washington, the New Mexico military

governor, and informed him that U.S. legal jurisdiction was over. Washington declined to accept Baird's authority, and Baird returned to Austin.

3. "Neighbors to Bell," April 14, 1850, Santa Fe Papers, part 2.

4. *Northern Standard*, Sept. 7, 1850; Neighbours, *Robert Simpson Neighbors*, 87-102.

5. F. S. Donnell, "When Texas Owned New Mexico to the Rio Grande," *NMHR*, 65-75; J. J. Bowden, "The Texas-New Mexico Boundary Dispute Along the Rio Grande," *SHQ*, 221-227; W. J. Spillman, "Adjustment of the Texas Boundary in 1850," *Quarterly of the Texas State Historical Association*, 177-195; P. M. Baldwin, "A Historical Note on the Boundaries of New Mexico," *NMHR*, 117-137.

6. SED 879, "Report No. 940 – New Mexico Boundary Line," 1-9; Mark E. Nackman, *A Nation Within A Nation*, 110-133.

7. José Cordero was born Dec. 27, 1798 in Valle de Allende near Parral, and became one of northern Mexico's wealthiest men. He welcomed the French invaders into Chihuahua, a fact not politically damaging to him after the French left. Cordero died on Dec. 18, 1867. See Francisco R. Almada, *Historia . . . Chihuahuenses*, 116-118.

8. Ibid. Col. Emilio Langberg was born in Switzerland in 1815 and achieved European fame as a violinist. After arriving in Mexico in 1838, he entered the army and by 1845 held the rank of lt. colonel. During the Mexican War he rose to full colonel while fighting American forces at Angostura and in Mexico City. Langberg died in Sonora on Sept. 4, 1886, while fighting with French occupation forces against Mexican regulars during the Battle of Guadalupe.

9. Father Ramón Ortiz, better known as *Cura* Ortiz, arrived in El Paso del Norte in 1836. He opposed the Treaty of Guadalupe Hidalgo, and helped organize the Mexican border villages of Mesilla, Guadalupe and San Ignacio for the refugees of American harrassment. For over a half century he was the most prominent priest in northern Mexico. He died in Juarez on March 9, 1886.

10. *New York Times*, March 16, 1853.

11. Robert W. Larson, *New Mexico's Quest for Statehood, 1846-1912*, 76; Calvin Horn, *New Mexico's Troubled Years*, 40.

12. Larson, *New Mexico's Quest*, 78.

13. I b i d .

14. George Griggs, *History of the Mesilla Valley*, 39. Griggs quotes a letter from Lane to D. Antonio Jáquez and Tomás Zuloaga (which probably should read "Luis" Zuloaga), March 23, 1853. According to this statement, Louis W.

Geck, an American citizen, lost over $10,000 in Mesilla property when he was forced out by the Trías proclamation.

15. William G. B. Carson (ed.), "Gov. William Carr Lane Diary," *NMHR*, 191.

16. HR 81, "William Carr Lane to J. L. Taylor," Jan. 23, 1854, 1-2.

17. *Periódico Oficial* (month and day missing), 1853.

18. Mansfield Papers, "Lane to Col. D. S. Miles," March 19, 1853, Library of Congress.

19. *New York Herald*, July 1, 1853.

7. Sell the Land or We Will Take It

1. Gray's efforts fell into disrepute beause of his association with Robert J. Walker, owner of the railroad. A tiny man in size, Walker was a respected as well as a hated financial wizard. Although he possessed little money, he spent a lifetime cultivating and influencing those who had plenty. He served as a U.S. Senator from Mississippi and lasted through a single appointment as sec. of the treasury during the Polk administration. His record for shady and controversial dealings was not helped by an involvement in the Dancing Rabbit land scandals and the Mississippi bond repudiation.

2. Paul Neff Garber, *The Gadsden Treaty*, 89; J. Fred Rippy, "The Negotiation of the Gadsden Treaty," *SHQ*, 1-26.

3. J. Fred Rippy, "A Ray of Light on the Gadsden Purchase," *SHQ*, 238; Henry P. Walker and Don Bufkin, *Historical Atlas of Arizona*, 19-22.

4. David Hunter Miller (ed.), *Treaties and Other International Agreements of the USA*, Vol. 1, 342-347.

5. *New York Herald*, Jan.-June, 1854; *New York Times*, Jan.-July 1854.

6. J. Fred Rippy, *The United States and Mexico*, 148-167.

7. Garber, *The Gadsden Treaty*, 140-143; Dean Smith, "General Gadsden's Purchase," *AH*, 2-7, 16-17.

8. David Meriwether, *My Life in the Mountains and on the Plains*, 234-35.

9. Robert M. Utley, *International Boundary*, 24.

8. A Complete Line at Last

1. Emory, *Report*, 15.

2. Ibid., 58.

3. Ibid., 61; W. J. Hughes, *Rebellious Ranger*, 100-246; Ernest Shearer, "The Carvajal Disturbances," *SHQ*, 201-230.

4. Emory, *Report*, 16, 75-80; Ronnie C. Tyler, *The Big Bend*, 80-100.

5. "C. Radziminski to Emory," Nov. 28, 1853, Emory Papers; Emory, *Report*, 58.
6. IBWC commissioners Joseph Friedkin for the U.S. and David Herrera Jordán for Mexico, paid tribute to Emory and Salazar on Dec. 8, 1972, by unveiling historic plaques at Boundary Marker No. 1 and designating the site as "Boundary Monument No. 1 Park."
7. "Emory to McClelland," Aug. 9, 1855, Emory Papers; William H. Goetzmann, *Army Exploration in the American West, 1803-1863*, 196; Robert M. Utley, *The International Boundary: U.S. and Mexico*, 42-43; Joseph Richard Werne, "Major Emory and Captain Jiménez: Running the Gadsden Line," *JS*, 209.
8. SED 57, 1-75. This entire document is taken up with the controversy of paying Mexico the $3 million.
9. Emory, *Report*, 113; Marshall Trimble, "The Gadsden Purchase Survey," *AH*, 8-15; Werne, "Major Emory and Captain Jiménez," 211-214;. Werne was able to locate the reports and correspondence of Captain Jiménez, and these records have presented a different view of Mexican participation in the Gadsden surveys.
10. Emory, *Report*, 115; Warren A. Beck and Ynez D. Haase, *Historical Atlas of New Mexico*, 27-28; Werne, "Major Emory and Captain Jiménez," 215-220.
11. Francisco Almada, *Diccionario Chihuahuenses*, 476; Almada, *Diccionario Sonorenses*, 708.
12. "Emory to McClelland," Nov. 4, 1855, Emory Papers; Goetzmann, *Army Exploration*, 197.
13. "Emory to George Engelmann," April 8, 1856, Emory Papers.

9. Teeth of Iron

1. After making the border reconnaissance, Symons aided in the construction of the Washington aqueduct, took charge of the important river and harbor works in Portland, Oregon, began notable engineering projects on the Great Lakes, and constructed the Buffalo breakwater, which was the world's largest. Possibly his greatest achievement was the New York Barge Canal. While an impressive example of engineering skill, it unfortunately had little economic value, a fact diminishing Symons' otherwise notable accomplishments.
2. George Look MS.
3. Regulations regarding prostitution are spelled out in weekly accounts of the El Paso City Council minutes.
4. Lt. Thomas W. Symons, Corps of Engineers, *Preliminary Reconnaissance of the Boundary Line Between the U.S. and Mexico from the Rio Grande at El Paso to the Pacific Ocean*, Nov. 14, 1893. Since the entire account of the Symons expedition is taken from this journal, no further notes will be cited about the survey.
5. FRUS 1887, 692-743; and FRUS 1888, 1187-1188.
6. Ibid., 1887, 872-883, and 1888, 1,298-1,300.
7. "R. S. Souler, Comptroller, Treasury Dept., to Sec. of State," Oct. 20, 1893, "Barlow to Gresham," Sept. 11, 1893, and "Miscellaneous typewritten material copies, 1894-1896," RG 76, NA.
8. Only one serious accident marred the boundary commission prior to leaving El Paso. Leonard Lee, a teamster, drove his mule-drawn wagon past Fort Bliss, and a nearby train engineer amused himself by blowing the steam whistle. The mules bolted, overturned the wagon and crushed the right leg of Lee. The accident happened within a few yards of the military hospital, and Dr. D. M. Appel, the post physician, amputated the limb. A court of inquiry found the engineer guilty of maliciously blowing the whistle, and assessed a fine of four months salary. "Barlow to James Blaine," May 24 1892, in "Letters Sent from U.S. Commissioners, 1891-1896." *El Paso Times*, Feb. 25, 1892.
9. *Report of the International Boundary Commission: U.S. and Mexico*, 14; *Memoria de la Sección Mexicana de la Comisión Internacional de Límites Entre Mexico y Los Estados Unidos Que Restableció Los Monumentos de El Paso al Pacífico*, 14.
10. The American commission hired approximately sixty persons, including administrative personnel, carpenters, wagonmasters, packers, teamsters, cooks and helpers. To feed the crew and animals, the commissary stocked 30 pounds of "good" oatmeal at 5 cents a pound, 20,000 pounds of whole barley at $1.35 a hundred pounds, 8 boxes of "good" raisins at 65 cents per container, 15 cases of canned corn at $2 per case, 20 pounds of Oolong tea at 30 cents per pound, 3,000 pounds of Irish potatoes at $2.19 per 100 pounds, 150 pounds of smoked bologna sausage at 11 cents per pound, 300 pounds of Arbuckles roasted coffee at 25 cents per pound, and 20 pounds of chewing tobacco plus 10 pounds of smoking tobacco, all at 45 cents per pound. While the supply list never mentioned distilled spirits, when teamster John Kenny fell off a wagon and broke his ankle, Gaillard described the

mishap as "due to bad roads and equally bad whiskey." Ibid., 120, 182.

11. "Memorandum Prepared for the Committee on Claims With Reference to S. 15," 1-13.

12. *Report of International Boundary Commission, U.S. and Mexico,* 177-179.

13. SED 591-598, April 15, 1912.

14. "Memorandum Prepared by Committee on Claims," 11.

15. Ibid., 4-6.

16. Ibid., 5; SED 591-598.

17. SB 15, Jan. 4, 1939.

18. Interview with Edwin E. Hamlyn, Chief (Retired), Boundary Section, U.S. IBWC, El Paso, Tex., Oct. 2, 1976.

19. "Joint Reports of the Principal Engineers on the Placement of Markers on the Land Boundary between the U.S. and Mexico," IBWC, June 17, 1975; and "Minute No. 249, Placement of Markers on the Land Boundary," July 14, 1975.

20. "Barlow to Blanco," Sept. 21, 1894, *Letters Sent to U.S. Commissioners, 1891-1896,* RG 76, NA.

21. *Report of the IBC, U.S. and Mexico,* 23-25, 41-47; *Western Land Boundary Monument Data,* n.d., no pagination.

22. FRUS 1897, 398-403.

10. Filibusters and Slavers

1. C. A. Bridges, "The Knights of the Golden Circle: A Filibustering Fantasy," *SHQ,* 287-302.; Earl W. Fornell, "Texans and Filibusters in the 1850s," *SHQ,* 411-428.

2. Nash Smith, *Virgin Land,* 40.

3. Rodolfo F. Acuña, *Sonoran Strongman: Ignacio Pesqueira and His Times,* 28.

4. Michael Paul Rogin, *Fathers & Children: Andrew Jackson and the Subjugation of the American Indian,* 309.

5. Acuña, *Sonoran Strongman,* 28.

6. *El Siglo XIX,* Oct. 21, 28, 1850; *El Universal,* July 9, 1850.

7. Sec. of War Mariano Arista, *Colonias Militares, Proyecto para su Establecimiento en las Fronteras de Oriente y Occident;* Odie B. Faulk, "Projected Mexican Military Colonies for the Borderlands, 1848," *JAH,* 39-47.

8. Mariano Paredes, *Proyectos de leyes sobra colonización y comercio en el estado de Sonora, presentados a la Cámara de Diputados por el representante de aquel estado, en la sesión extraordinaria del día 1850,* published in Odie B. Faulk's, "A Colonization Plan for Northern Sonora, 1850," *NMHR,* 293-314.

9. Juan N. Almonte, *Proyectos de Leyes sobre colonización.*

10. Paul Horgan, *Great River* (Vol. 2), 559-570; Milton Lindheim, *The Republic of the Rio Grande;* Jerry Thompson, *Sabers on the Rio Grande,* 88-96; Jerry Don Thompson, *The Republic of the Rio Grande,* 1-5; J. B. Wilkinson, *Laredo on the Rio Grande Frontier,* 165-174; David M. Vigness, "Relations of the Republic of Texas and the Republic of the Rio Grande," *SHQ,* 312-321.

11. Joseph Allen Stout, Jr. *The Liberators: Filibustering Expeditions into Mexico, 1848-1862, and the Last Thrust of Manifest Destiny,* 143-168; Jay J. Wagoner, *Early Arizona,* 373-382; Robert H. Forbes, *Crabb's Filibustering Expedition into Sonora, 1857,* 35; Fred J. Rippy, "Anglo American Filibusters and the Gadsden Treaty," *HAHR,* 155-180.

12. Ernest Shearer, "The Carvajal Disturbances," *SHQ,* 201-230; W. J. Hughes, *Rebellious Ranger: Rip Ford and the Old Southwest,* 100-105.

13. Rosalie Schwartz, *Across the Rio to Freedom,* 10-17.

14. Kenneth W. Porter, "The Seminole in Mexico, 1850-1861," *HAHR,* 6; Earl W. Fornell, "The Abduction of Free Negroes and Slaves In Texas," *SHQ,* 369-380.

15. Ronnie C. Tyler, "The Callahan Expedition of 1855: Indians or Negroes?," *SHQ,* 574-585; Ernest C. Shearer, "The Callahan Expedition, 1855," *SHQ,* 430-451.

16. *Houston Telegraph,* July 31, 1860.

17. William W. White, "The Texas Slave Insurrection of 1860," *SHQ,* 262-263; *State Gazette,* Aug. 25, 1860, quoting from the *Galveston News,* Aug. 4, 1860.

18. *Bastrop Advertiser,* Aug. 11, 1860.

19. *Colorado Citizen,* Sept. 5, 1860.

20. Schwartz, *Across the Rio to Freedom,* 46-50.

11. Blue & Gray at the Border

1. Jerry Don Thompson, *Vaqueros in Blue & Gray,* 77-79.

2. Nannie M. Tilly (ed.), *Federals on the Frontier: The Diary of Benjamin F. McIntyre, 1862-1864,* 245-390. Unless otherwise noted, all references to McIntyre come from this source.

3. S. S. Brown to Lew Wallace, Jan. 13, 1865, *OR,* Series 1, Vol. XLVIII, Pt. I, 512-513.

4. Robert W. Delaney, "Matamoros: Port for Texas During the Civil War," *SHQ,* 473-487; Ronnie C. Tyler, "Cotton on the Border, 1861-1865," Ibid., 456-477; Marilyn McAdams Sibley, "Charles Stillman: A Case Study of Entrepreneurship on the Rio Grande, 1861-1865," Ibid., 227-240; *New Orleans Times,* Nov. 12, 30, Dec. 1, 2, 1864.

5. James A. Irby, *Backdoor at Bagdad: The Civil War on the Rio Grande*, 7-11.
6. *OR*, Ser. 1, Vol. XXVI, Pt. I, 439-442 and Part II, 350, 415.
7. Thompson, *Vaqueros in Blue & Gray*, 43-48; *Sabers on the Rio Grande*, 206.
8. Jerry D. Thompson, *Mexican Texans in the Union Army*, 1-7.
9. "W. W. Mills to His Father," Oct. 25, 1861, Mills Collection, U.T. El Paso Archives. The letters have been published as "Letters Home: W. W. Mills Writes to His Family," edited by Eugene O. Porter, *Password*, 1972.
10. A. F. H. Armstrong, "The Case of Major Isaac Lynde," *NMHR*, 1-35; Kenneth A. Goldblatt, "The Defeat of Major I. Lynde, U.S.A.," *Password*, 16-21; William I. Waldrip, "New Mexico During the Civil War," *NMHR*, 251-290; George Wythe Baylor, *John Robert Baylor: Confederate Governor of Arizona*; William A. Keleher, *Turmoil in New Mexico, 1846-1868*, 323-330; Robert A. Lawson, *New Mexico's Quest for Statehood*, 84-85.
11. Martin Harwick Hall, "Colonel James Riley's Diplomatic Mission to Chihuahua and Sonora," *NMHR*, 232-242; Martin Harwick Hall, *The Confederate Army of New Mexico*, 50-56.
12. Don E. Alberts (ed.), *Rebels on the Rio Grande: The Civil War Journal of A. B. Peticolas*, 99-140; David Westphall, "The Battle of Glorieta Pass," *NMHR*, 137-151.
13. Ernest Wallace, *The Howling of the Coyotes*, 49-55.
14. C. L. Sonnichsen, "Major McMullen's Invasion of Mexico," *Password*, 38-43.
15. Ibid.
16. Gilbert J. Pedersen, "A Yankee in Arizona," *JAH*, 136.
17. Ibid., Francis P. Brady, "Portrait of A Pioneer: Peter R. Brady, 1825-1902," 171-194; Ibid.; Boyd Finch, "Sherod Hunter and the Confederates in Arizona," 137-206.
18. Clarence C. Clendenen, "General James Henry Carleton," *NMHR*, 23-24; Hall, "Col. James Reily's Diplomatic Mission to Chihuahua and Sonora," *NMHR*, 233-242; Acuña, *Sonoran Strongman*, 79-80.
19. Residents met in Tucson and Mesilla to protest the inadequate representation in far off Santa Fe. They demanded a territory south of 34° 20' (roughly, the Gadsden Purchase), as a Territory (or state) of Arizona. The issue died in Congress because of the slavery question.
20. Bert Fireman, "What Comprises Treason," *Arizonian*, 5-11; B. Sacks, "Sylvester Mowry," *AM*, 14-24; Constance Wynn Altshuler, "The Case of Sylvester Mowry," *A&W*, 63-82, 149-174.
21. Many soldiers, such as Shelby, offered to fight for Juárez. However, most sold their talents to the French in the mistaken belief that Maximilian was a winner. Read Andrew F. Rolle, *The Lost Cause: The Confederate Exodus to Mexico*, and Lawrence F. Hill, *The Confederate Exodus to Latin America*.
22. C. L. Sonnichsen, *Pass of the North*, 164-65.
23. Ibid., 162-67.
24. Carland Elaine Crook, "Benjamin Theron and French Designs in Texas During the Civil War," *SHQ*, 432-454; Steward Alexander MacCorkle, *American Policy of Recognition Towards Mexico*, 55-56; J. Fred Rippy, *The United States and Mexico*, 252-74.

12. Cowhides and Rangers

1. HED 39, *Report of the United States Comisioners*, Dec. 16, 1872, 18-19.
2. Ibid., 19-21.
3. HED 701, *Report and Accompanying Documents of the Committee of Foreign Relations on the Relations of the U.S. and Mexico*, "Lt. Col. A. M. McCook to Thomas F. Wilson," Aug. 2, 1871, Appendix B, 85-86.
4. Samuel Edwin Bell and James M. Smallwood, "The Mexican Zona Libre, 1858-1905," (Thesis in History: Texas Western Press, Dec., 1969), 25-48.
5. HED 39, 39-41.
6. Walter Prescott Webb, *The Texas Rangers*, 241-245. Webb cites a letter from William Callicott.
7. HED 701, 171.
8. "Wilson to Hamilton Fish," Oct. 14, 1875, "Dispatches from Consuls in Matamoros," Roll 7, Microcopy 18. A narrative can be found in Michael G. Webster's, "Intrigue on the Rio Grande: The Rio Bravo Affair, 1875," *SHQ*, 149-164.
9. John L. Davis, *The Texas Rangers: Their First 150 Years*, 55.
10. HED 701. According to E. O. C. Ord, McNelly brought back only a portion of the stolen cattle, ones that "were too crippled or bruised" to be driven deeper into Mexico. p. 173.
11. Ibid.
12. Ibid., 173-180.
13. Ignacio Galindo, Antonio Garc52a Carrillo, and Agusts2n Siliceo, *Reports of the Committee of Investigation*, 127-153.
14. Ibid., iii, 27-33, 61-65, 107-111, 169-177, 206-213.
15. Ibid., 442.

13. Marauders, Soldiers and Salt

1. FRUS 1877, "John W. Foster to Evarts," April 24, 1877, 400-407.
2. Charles W. Goldfinch, *Juan Cortina: Two Interpretations*, 34.
3. Américo Parades, *A Texas-Mexican Cancionero: Folksongs of the Lower Border*, 47-48.
4. HED 81, "Official Report of Major Heintzelman," 1-14; HED 52, "Difficulties of the Southwestern Frontier," 1-147; Webb, *Texas Rangers*, 175-193; Hughes, *Rebellious Ranger*, 160-178.
5. HR 701, "The Corpus Christi Raid," Appendix B, 164-167; Leopold Morris, "The Mexican Raid of 1875 on Corpus Christi," *SHQ*, 128-139.
6. Ibid.
7. Ernest Wallace (ed.), *Ranald S. Mackenzie's Official Correspondence Relating to Texas, 1871-1873*, 159-190. For a broad account of the Red River War, see Robert M. Utley's *Frontier Regulars: The United States Army and the Indian, 1866-1890*, 219-235.
8. SED 39, "Report of the United States Commissioners to Texas," 22-25; HR 701, "Relations of the United States With Mexico," XII-XIX.
9. Robert G. Carter, *On the Border with Mackenzie*, 422-23.
10. A. M. Gibson, *The Kickapoos: Lords of the Middle Border*, 236-252; Ernest Wallace and Adrian S. Anderson, "R. S. Mackenzie and the Kickapoos: The Raid into Mexico in 1863," *A&W*, 105-126.
11. Kenneth Wiggins Porter, "The Seminole-Negro Indian Scouts, 1870-1881," *SHQ*, 358-377.
12. Edward W. Wallace, "General John Lapham Bullis: Thunderbolt of the Texas Frontier," *SHQ*, 77-85; HP 701, "Texas Frontier Problems," the testimony of Col. William R. Shafter, Jan. 11, 1878, 21-31.
13. HED 13, 4-5, 14-15, 57-61, 70-71, 139-150; HR 701, "Texas Frontier Troubles," the testimony of General William Steele, 50.
14. HED 13, 76-98.
15. FRUS 1878, 527-532.
16. Kelly lavished his affection on Gavina Ramírez Favór, wife of Juan Favór, who lived in Presidio del Norte, Mexico. The husband suspected he was being cuckolded, so he pretended to leave on a trip, then circled back to the house. He caught the two lovers in an embrace, and killed Mose Kelly. After he escaped to the American side of the border, his father, Milton Favór, criticized him for not shooting the wife too. He then surrendered to Mexican authorities and was released. Leavitt Corning, Jr., *Baronial Forts of the Big Bend*, 58-59.
17. Letters Received by the Office of the Adjutant General, "Gov. Samaniego to Mose Kelly," Dec. 3, 1876, Main Series, NA.
18. Ibid., "Col. George L. Andrews to Asst. Adj. Gen.," Dec. 21, 1876. "Kelly to Andrews," Dec. 5, 1876, "Kelly to Capt. Lawson," Dec. 24, 1876.
19. HED 13, 157.
20. Ibid.
21. Eugene O. Porter (ed.), *Letters of Ernst Kohlberg, 1875-1877*, 30.
22. Ibid., 52; C. L. Sonnichsen, *Pass of the North*, 174, 203-204.
23. HED 13, 167-168; Porter, *Letters*, 52, 56-57.
24. HED 93, "El Paso Troubles in Texas;" HR 701, "Report of the Committee of Foreign Affairs," Appendix B, 277-286; *Annual Report of the Sec. of War, 1878*, 51; C. L. Sonnichsen, *The El Paso Salt War*, 1-68; C. L. Sonnichsen, *Pass of the North*, 173-210.
25. *Las Vegas Daily Optic* (New Mexico), Dec. 27-31, 1880, Feb. 28, 1881; *Daily New Mexican*, Dec. 29, 1880.
26. Kenneth A. Goldblatt and Leon C. Metz, "The Baca-Gillett Incident," *TMH*, 271-282.
27. Marshall Hail, *Knight in the Sun*, 19-28; James B. Gillett, *Six Years With the Texas Rangers*, 211-239.

14. The Order of June 1, 1877

1. HED 39, "Report of the United States Commissioners to Texas," 1-40.
2. HED 13, 14-15. This lengthy document of 244 pages discusses the background and reasons for the Order of June 1.
3. Robert D. Gregg, *The Influence of Border Troubles on Relations Between the United States and Mexico, 1876-1910*, 58-68.
4. A side benefit of this cooperation came when Ord's daughter, a strikingly beautiful blonde named Roberta Augusta, married General Treviño and bore him several children. She died in Mexico at a young age. See Daniel Cosío Villegas, *The United States vs Porfirio Díaz*, 185-186.
5. J. Fred Rippy, *The United States and Mexico*, 310.
6. FRUS 1880, 759-760.
7. Eve Ball, *In the Days of Victorio*, 98-102; Dan L. Trapp, *Victorio and the Mimbres Apaches*, 301-308.
8. Charles I. Bevans (compiler), *Treaties and Other International Agreements of the USA, 1776-1949*, 847-849.
9. Dan L. Trapp, *The Conquest of Apacheria*, 275-276; Donald E. Worcester, *The Apaches: Eagles of the Southwest*, 259-264.

10. FRUS 1886, 585-592.
11. Ibid.
12. Bruno J. Rolak, "General Miles' Mirrors," *JAH*, 145-160.
13. Lynda A. Sánchez, "The Lost Apaches of the Sierra Madre," *AH* (Sept. 1986), 25-26; Jay J. Wagoner, "Geronimo," Ibid., 12-23. This same issue of *Arizona Highways* has an interesting article by C. L. Sonnichsen, "The Remodeling of Geronimo," 4-11. Sonnichsen describes how in modern literature, Geronimo has been changed from the "worst Indian" into one of God's noblest children.

15. The Struggle Begins

1. David F. Myrick, *Railroads of Arizona: the southern roads*, Vol. 1, 69-122.
2. FRUS 1905, 638-649; Ibid., 1906, 136-1488, 1114-1121; Ibid., 1907, 833-851; *Mexican Herald*, Dec. 21, 1905; Evelyn HuDehart, "Development and Rural Rebellion: Pacification of the Yaquis in the Late Porfiriato," *HAHR*, 72-93; and Edward H. Spicer, *Cycles of Conquest*, 67-73, 81-882, 404-405.
3. John Coatsworth, "Railroads, Landholdings and Agrarian Protest in the Early Porfiriato," *HAHR*, 67-68.
4. David M. Pletcher, "The Development of Railroads in Sonora," *IAEA*, 5-40.
5. John H. McNeely, *The Railways in Mexico: A Study in Naturalization*, 1-56.
6. Victor S. Clark, "Mexican Labor in the United States," *BBL*, 469-474; Fred Wilbur Powell, *The Railroads of Mexico*, 127-129.
7. Marvin D. Bernstein, *The Mexican Mining Industry, 1890-1950*, 47-99; George Griggs, *Mines of Chihuahua*, 10-55; Charles S. Dahlgren, *Historic Mines of Mexico*, 3-23.
8. Mary Antoine Lee, "A Historical Survey of the American Smelting and Refining Company in El Paso, 1877-1950." (Master's Thesis, Texas Western College, 1950), 3-17.
9. Allen H. Rogers, "Character and Habits of the Mexican Miner," *EMJ*, 700-702; Evan Fraser-Campbell, "The Management of Mexican Labor," Ibid., 1104-1105; Hugh G. Elwes, "Points About Mexican Labor," Ibid., 662; Edward H. Davison, "Labor in Mexican Mines," *MSP*, 260.
10. George Griggs, *Mines of Mexico*, 32. Griggs is reciting a quote from *Modern Mexico*, Nov. 1906, 14.
11. Ira B. Joralemon, *Copper*, 143; Mike Casillas, "The Cananea Strike of 1906," *SEC*, 19; Antonio G. Rivera, *La Revolución en Sonora*, 20, 140-142.
12. C. L. Sonnichsen, *Colonel Greene and the Copper Skyrocket*, 19-34.

13. Dwight E. Woodbridge, "La Cananea Mining Camp," *EMJ*, 624-627; Morris J. Elsing, "Mining Methods Employed at Cananea, Mexico," Ibid., 914-918.
14. Allen H. Rogers, "Character and Habits," *EMJ*, 702.
15. See James E. Hyslop Collection, U.T. El Paso Archives.
16. Rodney D. Anderson, "Mexican Workers and the Politics of Revolution," *HAHR*, 94-113; Manuel J. Aguirre, *Cananea: las garras del Imperialismo en las entrañas de Mexico*, 50-63.
17. Sonnichsen, *Colonel Greene*, 184-185.
18. James Morton Callahan, *American Foreign Policy in Mexican Relations*, 523.
19. Herbert O. Brayer, "The Cananea Incident," *NMHR*, 399-404; *Bisbee Daily Review*, June 2, 3, 1906; Carl Rathbun, "Keeping the Peace Along the Mexican Border," *HW*, 1632-1634; Captain Thomas H. Rynning, *Gun Notches*, 290-315.
20. Cornelius C. Smith, Jr., *Emilio Kosterlitzky: Eagle of Sonora and the Southwest Border*, 127-176.

16. The First Battle of Juarez

1. James D. Crockcroft, *Intellectual Precursors of the Mexican Revolution, 1900-1913*, 124.
2. Myra Ellen Jenkins, "Ricardo Flores Magón and the Mexican Liberal Party" (Dissertation, U. of New Mexico, 1953), v-vii; W. Dick Raat, *Revoltosos: Mexico's Rebels in the United States, 1903-1923*, 149-171.
3. *Regeneración*, Sept. 3, 1910.
4. Myra Ellen Jenkins, "Ricardo Flores Magón," 91.
5. Stanley R. Ross, *Francisco I. Madero: Apostle of Mexican Democracy*, 120-127; Ramón Eduardo Ruíz, *The Great Rebellion: Mexico 1905-1924*, 139-152.
6. *El Paso la Reforma Social*, Dec. 6, 1910. Only scattered issues of this paper exist, and this one is in the possession of LCM.
7. Ward Sloan Albro, III, "Ricardo Flores Magón: An Inquiry into the Orgins of the Mexican Revolution of 1910" (Dissertation, U. of Arizona, 1967), 99-107; *El Paso Daily Times*, Oct. 20-21, 1906; *El Paso Herald*, Oct. 23, 1906.
8. FRUS 1909, "President of the United States to the President of Mexico," June 5, 1909, 425.
9. Charlotte Crawford, "The Border Meeting of Presidents Taft and Díaz," *Password*, 92.
10. Ibid.; Benjamin Herrera Varga, *Aqui Chihuahua! Cuna y Chispa de la Revolución Mexicana*, 126-147.
11. *Galveston Daily News*, Oct. 17, 1909.

12. Michael C. Meyer, *Mexican Rebel: Pascual Orozco and the Mexican Revolution, 1910-1915*, 21.
13. Alberto Calzadíaz Barrera, *Hechos Reales de la Revolución*, 43.
14. Mardee Belding de Wetter, "Revolutionary El Paso, 1910-1917," *Password*, 53-55.
15. Photos of Yaqui insurgents can be found in *Photographs from the Border: The Otis A. Aultman Collection*, by Mary A. Sarber, 72-73.
16. I. J. Bush, *Gringo Doctor*, 199-211.
17. Timothy G. Turner, *Bullets, Bottles and Gardenias*, 23.
18. Michael Dennis Carman, *United States Customs and the Madero Revolution*, 1-87; Stephen E. Akers, "The United States and the Madero-Díaz Struggle" (Master's Thesis, U.T. El Paso, 1976), 29-34.
19. Richard Medina Estrada, "Border Revolution: The Mexican Revolution in the Ciudad Juarez-El Paso Area, 1906-1915" (Master's Thesis, U.T. El Paso, 1975), 84-89.
20. Joseph U. Sweeney, "Judge Sweeney Watches A Revolution," (edited by Mildred Torok), *Password*, 70.
21. *El Paso Morning Times*, May 8-11, *El Paso Herald*, May 8-12, 1911; Giuseppe Garibaldi, *A Toast to Rebellion*, 96-110.
22. Florence Cathcart Melby, interview with LCM, Dec. 10, 1978, El Paso Texas.
23. FRUS 1911, "Taft to Sec. of the Treasury," May 12, 1911, 482-483.

17. The Border in Flames

1. Conrey Bryson, *Down Went McGinty*, 58-63; C. L. Sonnichsen, *Pass of the North*, 393-394; I. J. Bush, *Gringo Doctor*, 181-188.
2. Bush, *Gringo Doctor*, 181-188.
3. W. T. Millington to W. W. Follett, Dec. 27, 1910, Presidio, Texas.
4. Ibid., Jan. 2, 1911.
5. Dennis Carman Michael, *United States Customs and the Madero Revolution*, 47.
6. Ibid., 40-44.
7. "Millington to Follett," Feb. 13, 1911.
8. Ibid., May 2, 1911; Ronnie C. Tyler, *The Big Bend*, 159-162.
9. *Tucson Citizen*, Feb. 1, 9, 27, March 25, 1911.
10. Anne Pace, "Mexican Refugees in Arizona, 1910-1911," *A&W*, 5-18.
11. The question of how many Americans and other foreigners fought in the Mexican Revolution will always be controversial. Lowell L. Blaisdell, *The Desert Revolution*, 99-112, furnishes some perspective. Also see Brig. Gen. Tasker
H. Bliss to War Dept., April 30, 1911 (Records of the USA Commands, Dept. of Calif. & Texas, RG 98, NA); Consul George B. Schmucker to State Dept., April 24, 1911 (Records of Foreign Service Posts, RG 84, NA).
12. *Industrial Worker*, June 8, 1911, & May 16, 1912.
13. Blaisdell, *Desert Revolution*, 99-100, 118-126; *San Diego Sun*, May 9, 1911; *Los Angeles Express*, June 5, Sept. 26, 1911; *San Diego Union*, Sept. 27, 1911.
14. Richard Estrada, "Border Revolution," 103-104.
15. FRUS 1912, "Consul Edwards in Juarez to Sec. of State," May 4, 1912, 809; Mardee de Wetter, "Revolutionary El Paso," 107-120.
16. Dale Walker, "Tracy Richardson: Machine Gun for Hire," *Kaleidoscope: El Paso Magazine*, 4-7, 15.
17. B. Carmen Hardy, "The Trek South: How the Mormons Went to Mexico," *SHQ*, 1-17; Estelle Webb Thomas, *Uncertain Sanctuary: A Story of Mormon Pioneering in Mexico*, 80-110.
18. Karl Young, "Brief Sanctuary," *AW*, 66-67; Oscar Martínez, *Fragments of the Mexican Revolution*, 263-269.
19. Some accounts have González being thrown beneath the wheels of a train, but most have him executed alongside a train. See William H. Breezley's, *Insurgent Governor: Abraham González and the Mexican Revolution in Chihuahua*, 159-160.
20. Susan M. Deeds, "José María Maytorena and the Mexican Revolution in Sonora," *A&W*, 21-40.
21. Charles C. Cumberland, *Mexican Revolution: The Constitutionalist Years*, 222-269; Silvestre Terrazas, *El Verdadero Pancho Villa*, 210-214.
22. Cornelius C. Smith, Jr., *Don't Settle for Second: Life and Times of Cornelius C. Smith*, 113-117; Cornelius C. Smith, Jr., *Emilio Kosterlitzky*, 177-213.
23. Ruth M. Reinhold, *Sky Pioneering: Arizona in Aviation History*, 31-38, 46-51.
24. Florence C. and Robert H. Lister, *Chihuahua: Storehouse of Storms*, 229-232; C. L. Sonnichsen, *Pass of the North*, 389-400.
25. *New York Times*, Jan. 3, 14, 1916; *El Paso Morning Times* and the *El Paso Herald* are filled with news of these camps and their prisoners.
26. Alvaro Obregón, *Ocho mil kilómetros en campaña*, 30-39; *New York Times*, Sept. 27, 28, 1914.
27. *Bisbee Daily Review*, Aug. 29, 30, 31, 1914; Luís Aguirre Benavides, *Las grandes batallas de la División del Norte*, 196-201; Francisco R. Almada, *Diccionario Sonorenses*, 347.

28. Michael C. Meyer, *Huerta: A Political Portrait,* 227-231.
29. *El Paso Morning Times,* Sept. 1, 1915, Spanish edition of the *Times,* Sept. 2, 191; Michael C. Meyer, *Mexican Rebel,* 131-135; Interview with E. A. "Dogie" Wright, July 16, 20, 1968.
30. *Bisbee Daily Review,* Oct. 4, 6, 7, 1914, *New York Times,* Sept. 27, 1914.
31. *Dallas Morning News,* Oct. 19, 1914; *Arizona Daily Star,* Oct. 18, 1914.
32. FRUS 1914, "Sec. of State to Brazilian Minister," Dec. 26, 1914, 653.
33. Larry D. Christiansen, "Bullets Across the Border" (Part III), *CQ,* 6-7; Hugh L. Scott, *Some Memories of A Soldier,* 507-512; Frank E. Vandiver, *Black Jack: The Life and Times of John J. Pershing,* I, 589-590.
34. *Douglas Daily Dispatch,* Oct. 22, 1915.

18. The Punitive Expedition

1. C. F. Leonard, "Villa Invasion of Sonora, Mexico, Oct.-Nov.-Dec. 1915," Feb. 11, 1916, Adjutant General's File, NA.
2. *Douglas Daily Dispatch,* Oct. 31, 1915.
3. Ibid., Nov. 4, 5, 6, 10, 1915.
4. Antonio G. Rivera, *La Revolución en Sonora,* 469.
5. FRUS 1915, "Special Agent Cobb to Sec. of State," Oct. 16, 1915, 769.
6. Thomas H. Naylor, "Massacre at San Pedro de las Cueva: The Significance of Pancho Villa's Sonora Campaign," *WHQ,* 125-150.
7. *Arizona Daily Star,* Jan. 4, 1916; *Bisbee Daily Review,* Jan. 4, 1916; *Douglas Daily Dispatch,* Jan. 4, 1916; *Tucson Daily Citizen,* Jan. 4, 1916; Alberto Calzadíaz Barrera, *Hechos reales de la revolución,* 162.
8. "Villa to Zapata," San Geronimo, Jan. 8, 1916, NA.
9. FRUS 1916, 478-482.
10. Docket No. 651-654, 664-666 (1916), State of New Mexico vs Renterina, et al., New Mexico State Archives; *Columbus Courier,* June 9, 1916; *Deming Democrat,* June 29, 1916; María Elena Evans, "Mass Hangings in Deming, NM," (Research Paper, Western NM University, n.d.)
11. FRUS 1916, "The Adjutant General to General Funston," March 10, 13, 1916, 489; Col. Frank Tompkins, *Chasing Villa,* 70-77.
12. Haldeen Braddy, *Pershing's Mission in Mexico,* 24-26; Clarence C. Clendenen, *Blood on the Border: The United States Army and the Mexican Irregulars,* 259-264; Herbert Malloy Mason, Jr., *The Great Pursuit,* 133-138.
13. FRUS 1916, "Generals Scott and Funston to the Sec. of War," April 30, 1916, 533-534; Clarence C. Clendenen, *The United States and Pancho Villa: A Study in Unconventional Diplomacy,* 270-285; Robert Bruce Johnson, "The Punitive Expedition: A Military, Diplomatic, and Political History of Pershing's Chase After Pancho Villa, 1916-1917" (Dissertation, U. of Southern California, 1964), 512-518; P. Edward Haley, *Revolution and Intervention: The Diplomacy of Taft and Wilson with Mexico, 1910-1917,* 204-210.
14. FAUS 1916, "Gen. Funston to Sec. of War," June 17, 1916, 577.
15. Moses N. Thisted, *With the Wisconsin National Guard on the Mexican Border in 1916-1917,* 49.
16. Capt. C. D. Wood, "The Glen Springs Raid," *Sul Ross State College Bulletin,* 65-71.
17. Fall Committee *Report,* Vol. I, Testimony of O. G. Compton," 1060-1063; FRUS 1916, "Vice Consul Blocker to Sec. of State," May 8, 1916, 544-546.
18. Robert Bruce Johnson, "Punitive Expedition" (Dissertation for Ph. D. in History at University of S. Cal., 1964), 756-758.
19. Raymond Reed, "The Mormons in Chihuahua: Their Relations with Villa and the Pershing Expedition, 1916-1917" (Master's Thesis, U. of New Mexico, 1938), 30-35.
20. Edward Eugene Briscoe, "Pershing's Chinese Refugees: An Odyssey of the Southwest" (Master's Thesis, St. Mary's U., 1974), 28.

19. Politics and Peace

1. FRUS 1919, "The Consul at Ciudad Juarez (Dow) to the Acting Sec. of State," June 15, 1919, 557-558 and "The Mexican Ambassador (Bonillas) to the Acting Sec. of State — Memorandum," March 20, 1919, 555-556.
2. Ibid., 556-585; *El Paso Times,* June 10-20, 1919; *El Paso Herald,* June 13-19, 1919.
3. John M. Carroll, *Col. Tommy Tompkins: A Military Heritage and Tradition,* 17-21, 101-106.
4. Stacy C. Hinkle, *Wings Over the Border,* 6-9.
5. Stacy C. Hinkle, *Wings and Saddles: The Air and Cavalry Punitive Expedition of 1919,* 38-42; *San Antonio Express,* June 15-23, 1920.
6. *El Paso Times* and *El Paso Herald,* Aug. 20, 1919.
7. FRUS 1919, 561-562, 564-565.
8. Kenneth Baxter Ragsdale, *Wings Over the Border: Pioneer Military Aviation in the Big Bend,* 10-85.
9. John W. F. Dulles, *Yesterday in Mexico,* 280-320; Brigaido Caro, *Plutarco Elias Calles, Dictador Bolsheviqui de Mexico,* 94-107.

10. Dulles, *Yesterday in Mexico*, 333-354.
11. René A. Valenzuela, "Chihuahua, Calles and the Escobar Revolt in 1929" (Master's Thesis, U.T. El Paso, 1975), 35.
12. FRUS 1929, "The Sec. of State to the Ambassador in Mexico," March 8, 1929, 353.
13. Francisco R. Almada, *Gubernadores del Estado de Chihuahua*, 566-569; Valenzuela, "Chihuahua, Calles," 36.
14. "A Ringside Seat for Mexican Revolutions," *Literary Digest*, 11.
15. FRUS 1929, "The Sec. of State to the Ambassador in Mexico," March 12, 1929, 360-61; *El Paso Herald-Post*, March 8, 1929.
16. Duncan Aikman, "$50,000 Cannon Balls," *HM*, July 1929.
17. FRUS 1929, "Sec. of State to the Sec. of War," April 13, 1929, 393-394.
18. Ibid., "The Consul at Nogales to the Sec. of State," April 26, 1929, 404.
19. Ibid., "The Vice Consul at Agua Prieta to the Sec. of State," April 4, 1929, 384; Tom Mahoney, "Into the Clouds for A Lost Cause, Being the Story of the American Aviators Who Flew for the Escobar Revolutionaries in Mexico," *Air Travel News*, Dec. 1929; C. O. Peterson, "Naco, Arizona: Accidental Place in History," *AW*, 44-47.
20. FRUS 1929, "The Ambassador in Mexico to the Sec. of State," May 21, 1929, 425.
21. Ibid., "The Consul at Agua Prieta to the Sec. of State," May 2, 1929, 410-411.
22. Carlos Alvear Acevedo, *Lázaro Cárdenas, El Hombre y El Mito*, 33.
23. Linda B. Hall, *Alvaro Obregón: Power and Revolution in Mexico, 1911-1920*, 249-259.

20. To Chain a River

1. A few of the Colorado's best published histories are: Frank Waters, *The Colorado*; Richard Yates and Mary Marshall, *The Lower Colorado: A Bibliography*; John Wesley Powell, *The Exploration of the Colorado River*, Robert Brewster Stanton, *Down the Colorado*; Philip L. Fradkin, *A River No More*; John Upton Terrell, *War for the Colorado*; and David Lavender, *Colorado River Country*.
2. Alton Duke, *When the Colorado River Quit the Ocean*, 3-19; and *Historic Salton Sea* (no author), edited and published by the Imperial Irrigation District, 2-3.
3. Dr. W. T. Heffernan, *Personal Recollections of the Imperial Valley*, 9-22.
4. J. A. Alexander, *The Life of George Chaffey*, 92.
5. Robert G. Schonfeld, *The Early Development of California's Imperial Valley*, 289; Otis B. Tout, *The First Thirty Years, 1901-*

1931: History of Imperial Valley and Southern California, USA, 9; William O. Hendricks, "Developing San Diego's Desert Empire," *JSDH*, 3-10; Hugo de Vries (edited by Peter W. van der Pas), "The Imperial Valley in 1904," *JSDH*, 26-40.
6. Helen Hosmer, "Imperial Valley," *AM*, 40.
7. "H. M. Hoyt, Act. Attorney General to Sec. of State John Hay," June 14, 1902, and "John Hay to Anson Mills," June 16, 1902, *Proceedings of the IBC*, Vol. 2, 427.
8. Ibid., 427-430.
9. Ibid.
10. Ibid.
11. SD 142, "Problems of Imperial Valley and Vicinity," Vol. II, 1922, 1-325.
12. "Hearings Before the Committee on Irrigation of Arid Lands," *All American Canal in Imperial County, California*, 107-107; SD 4193, Feb. 8, 1904, 1,700.
13. *All American Canal*, 209-213.
14. Robert L. Sperry, "When the Imperial Valley Fought for Its Life," *JSDH*, 1-25; Harry T. Cory, *Imperial Valley and the Salton Sink*, 1-72; Remi A. Nadeau, *The Water Seekers*, 139-166; David F. Myrick, *Railroads of Arizona*, Vol. 1, 124-126; SD 212, "Message From the President of the U.S. Relative to the Threatened Destruction by the Overflow of the Colorado River in the Sink or Depression Known as the Imperial Valley or Salton Sink Region," Jan. 12, 1907; SD 846, "Flood Waters of the Colorado River," 1912.
15. Norris Hundley, Jr., *Water and the West*, 32-35; Lowell L. Blaisdell, *The Desert Revolution*, 26-40; Eugene K. Chamberlin, "Mexican Colonization Versus American Interests in Lower California," *PHR*, 43-55.
16. Norris Hundley, Jr., *Dividing the Waters*, 37-39.
17. FRUS 1911, 543-544.
18. Blaisdell, *The Desert Revolution*, 38-50; *Los Angeles Record*, Feb. 17, 1911; *New York Times*, Jan. 30, 1911.
19. FRUS 1911, 556-557.
20. Ibid., 557-565; Blaisdell, *The Desert Revolution*, 50-52.
21. FRUS 1911, "Wilson to Sec. of State," Feb. 17, 1911, 559.
22. Ibid., "Knox to the American Chargé d'Affaires," March 2, 1911.
23. Ibid., "Knox to American Ambassador," June 1, 1911 and "J. A. Ockerson, to the Commander of Mexican Troops," May 10, 1911, 564-565.
24. George Sibley, "The Desert Empire," *H*, 54; HED 73, "J. W. Powell, Report on the Lands of the Arid Region of the U.S.," 75; John Wesley Powell, *The Exploration of the Colorado River*, xix.

25. "Problems of the Imperial Valley and Vicinity," 62-71; Hundley, *Dividing the Waters*, 34.
26. HR 2903, "Hearings on Protection and Development of Lower Colorado River Basin," House Committee on Irrigation and Reclamation, 1,649-1,666.
27. HR 6044, "Hearings on All-American Canal in Imperial and Coachella Valleys, Ca.," House Committee on Irrigation of Arid Lands, 48-50, 94, 142, 287.
28. "Hearings Before the Committee of Foreign Relations, U.S. Senate, Treaty With Mexico Relating to the Utilization of the Waters of Certain Rivers," *Water Treaty With Mexico*, Jan. 22-26, 1945, Part 1, 75.
29. Hundley, *Water and the West*, 138-281; T. H. Watkins, "Conquest of the Colorado," *AW*, 61.
30. Erwin Cooper, *Aqueduct Empire: A Guide to Water in California*, 559-68, 89-101.
31. *U.S. Statutes at Large*, XLV, 1,057-1,066; *Cong. Rec*, 1928, 560-561.
32. Hundley, *Water and the West*, 302-303.

21. A Call for Partnership

1. *Secretaría de Fomento, Colonización y Industria, Dirección General de Estadística, Territorio de la Baja California*, 21; *Secretaría de la Economia Nacional, Dirección General de Estadística*, May 15, 1930, 11-14.
2. *San Diego Union*, Dec. 4, 1914; *Los Angeles Times*, Dec. 1-12, 1914; Blaisdell, Lowell L., "Harry Chandler and the Mexican Border Intrigue, 1914-1917," *PHR*, 386.
3. Senate Resolution 16, *Cong. Record*, May 20, 1919, 63; *Tucson Citizen*, Jan. 29, June 12, 1919.
4. *New York Times*, Sept. 21, 1930, Jan. 11, 1931.
5. Gabino Vázquez, *The Agrarian Reform in Lower California*, 3-13; Chamberlain, "Mexican Colonization Versus," *PHR*, 53-54.
6. Hundley, *Dividing the Waters*, 68-69.
7. House Document 359, "Report of the American Section," 32.
8. HR 6091, "Hearings on Control of Flood Waters on the American Side of the Rio Grande in the State of Texas," 4ff.
9. Ibid.
10. Arizona Colorado River Commission, *Colorado River: International Problem*, 5-11, 30-36; Colorado River Basin Committee of Fourteen, *Proceedings*, June 22-23, 1938, 15-19; Interview with former Am. Boundry Commissioner Joseph Friedkin, April 1, 1988.
11. U.S. Dept. of the Interior, *Surplus Waters of the Colorado River System*, 37-44.

12. Cline, *The United States and Mexico*, 267; Norris Hundley, Jr., "The West Against Itself: The Colorado River — An Institutional History," *New Courses for the Colorado River: Major Issues for the Next Century*, (edited by Gary D. Weatherford and F. Lee Brown), 25-35.
13. Committee of Fourteen and Sixteen, Subcommittee of Eight, *Proceedings*, Oct. 26-27, 1942, 2-6, 14-16; FRUS 1942, 548-552; "Hearings on Water Treaty With Mexico," *Senate Committee on Foreign Affairs*, 683-712.
14. Committees of Fourteen and Sixteen, *Proceedings*, April 14, 16, 1943, 30-72.
15. Ibid.
16. Ibid.

22. Salty River, Thirsty Land

1. "Hearings on Water Treaty With Mexico," 1,217, 1,335-1,337; *El Tratado de Aguas Internacionales*, 46-47.
2. FRUS 1943, "Memorandum by the Legal Adviser (Hackworth) to the Sec. of State and the Under Sec. of State (Wells)," April 23, 1943; *El Universal*, Aug. 1, 1945; SD 98, "Water Treaty of the Colorado River and Rio Grande Favors Mexico," 17.
3. *Los Angeles Times*, Feb. 17, 1944; *Oakland Tribune*, Feb. 19, 20, 1944; *Sacramento Bee*, Dec. 1, 1944; *San Francisco Chronicle*, Feb. 19, 1944; "Roosevelt to Downey," *Roosevelt Papers*, Feb. 7, 12, 1944, File 482-A.
4. "Hearings on Water Treaty With Mexico," 230, 322; FAUS 1944, "The American Commissioner, IBC (Lawson), to Mr. Charles A. Timm of the Division of American Affairs," March 23, 1944, 1,362-1,363.
5. David A. Gantz, "United States Approaches to the Salinity Problem on the Colorado River," *NRJ*, 498.
6. "Hearings by Committee of Foreign Relations, U.S. Senate," *Water Treaty With Mexico*, Part I, 107.
7. Ibid., Part V, 1,761.
8. Hundley, *Dividing the Waters*, 163.
9. *El Universal*, Aug. 1, 1945.
10. *Joint Projects of the U.S. and Mexico Through the IBWC*, 27.
11. Ibid., 28.
12. *Wellton-Mohawk Irrigation and Drainage District*, n.p.; Norris Hundley, Jr., "The Colorado River Dispute," *Foreign Affairs*, 499-500; "Eleventh Mexico-United States Interparliamentary Conference," (Background Materials for U.S. Delegation Use Only), Confidential Joint Committee Print, 138-139; Myron B. Holburt, *International Problems of the Colorado River*, paper presented to the "American

Association for the Advancement of Science," San Francisco meeting, March 1, 1974.

13. David A. Gantz, "United States Approaches to the Salinity Problem on the Colorado River," *NRJ*, 496-509.

14. Edward Weinberg, "Salt Talks: U.S. and Mexico Style," *Colorado River Salinity Problem*, Vol. III, 9-10; Henry C. Dethloff and Irvin M. May, Jr. *SA*, 245-270.

15. Hundley, *Dividing the Waters*, 176.

16. "Joint Communique Issued Between President John F. Kennedy and President López Mateos Following Discussions in Mexico City," June 29-30, 1962, *Colorado River Salinity Problem*, Vol. I, 1-4.

17. Minute No. 218, IBWC.

18. *Cong. Record*, "Address by the President of the United Mexican States to the Joint Meeting of the House and Senate," June 5, 15, 1972; *Wall Street Journal*, June 22, 1972; *The Christian Science Monitor*, June 10, 1973.

19. *Louisville Courier-Journal*, June 24, 1972; *Denver Post*, June 14, 1972.

20. *Colorado Salinity Problem*, "Joint Communique of President Nixon and President Écheverria Following their Meeting in Washington," Vol. 2, June 16, 1972.

21. "Herbert Brownell Report," Dec. 28, 1972, *Colorado River Basin Salinity Control Act*, Public Law 93 – 320, June 24, 1974, 139-175; Myron B. Holburt, "International Problems of the Colorado River," 12-13; Herbert Brownell and Samuel D. Eaton, "The Colorado River Salinity Problem With Mexico," *AJIL*, 263-274.

22. Fradkin, *A River No More*, 312-313.

23. Minute 242, IBWC.

24. S 496, "Hearings Before the Sub-Committee on Energy Research and Development of the Committee on Energy and Natural Resources, U.S. Senate," *Amending Title I of the Colorado River Basin Salinity Control Act*, April 12, 1979, 36; *Fact Sheet*, Bureau of Reclamation.

25. HR 96-177, *Increasing the Appropriations Ceiling for Title I of the Colorado River Basin Salinity Control Act . . . and for Other Purposes*, May 15, 1979, 4.

26. Ibid., 4-16; SR 96-181, Calendar No. 192, *Amending Title I of the Colorado River Basin Salinity Control Act*, May 15, 1979, 7-27.

27. SR 96-181, 3-4, 9-10, 20.

28. S. 494, 73-74, 76.

29. Ibid., *Fact Sheet*, Bureau of Reclamation; Serial No. 97-L, "Hearings Before the Sub-Committee on Dept. Operations, Research, and Foreign Agriculture of the Committee on Agriculture, House of Reps.," June 10, 1981.

30. *Aqueduct*, Fall, 1976, 7.

31. Ibid., 9.

32. George Sibley, "The Desert Empire," *H*, 67.

33. Truman Temple, "The Colorado: America's Hardest Working River," *E. P. A. Journal*, 46-48; Daniel B. Luten, "The Use and Misuse of A River," *AW*, 47-53, 73; T. H. Watkins, "Conquest of the Colorado," *AW*, 5-9, 48.

34. William Douglas Back and Jeffery S. Taylor, "Navajo Water Rights: Pulling the Plug on the Colorado River," *NRJ*, 74; David Sheridan, "The Colorado: an engineering wonder without enough water," *Smithsonian*, 50-52; Terrell, *War for the Colorado River*, 23-24, 297; Marshal Trimble, *Arizona*, 364-366; Fradkin, *A River No More*, 250-260; David H. Getches and Charles J. Meyers, "The River of Controversy: Persistent Issues," *New Courses for the Colorado River*, 62-66.

35. *Joint Projects of the U.S. and Mexico*, IBWC, 35-36.

36. Sheridan, "The Colorado," *Smithsonian*, 47-52; Ellwyn R. Stoddard, "Anticipating Transboundary Resource Needs and Issues in the U.S.-Mexico Border Region to the Year 2000," Summary Report paper read before working group on U.S.-Mexico Transboundary resources needs and issues, South Padre Island, Texas, April 23-25, 1981.

37. Allen V. Kneese and Gilbert Bonem, "Hypothetical Shocks to Water Allocation Institutions in the Colorado Basin," *New Courses for the Colorado River*, 87-108.

23. Great River, Great Problems

1. There are numerous books that touch on the Rio Grande, but only three will be cited: Paul Horgan, *Great River*, Jerry E. Mueller, *Restless River*, and Pat Kelley, *River of Lost Dreams*.

2. Pat Kelley, *River of Lost Dreams: Navigation on the Rio Grande*, 1-4; "Hearings Before the Committee on Foreign Relations, U.S. Senate, on Treaty With Mexico Relating to the Utilization of Certain Rivers," Part 1, 25.

3. HR 701, "Testimony of General E. O. C. Ord," Appendix B, 176-181; SED 34, 18.

4. Ibid., "Testimony of General William Steele," 47-52.

5. FRUS 1893, 64.

6. *Chamizal Arbitration: Counter Case of the USA*, 212.

7. SED 34, Part 2, 15.

8. *Chamizal Arbitration: Appendix*, "Cushing to McClelland," Nov. 11, 1856, 559.

9. Ibid., 593-699.

10. "Boundary Waters: Rio Grande and Colorado," *Treaties and Other International Agreements of the USA*, Vol. 9 (March 1972), 865-867.
11. J. J. Wagoner, *Early Arizona*, 158-241.
12. Donald M. Powell, *The Peralta Grant: James Addison Reavis and the Barony of Arizona*, 98-129.
13. George W. Julian, "Land Stealing in New Mexico," *NAR*, 20-23; Howard Roberts Lamar, *The Far Southwest, 1846-1912*, 49-52; William W. Morrow, "Spanish and Mexican Private Land Grants," *MM*, 1-27.
14. V. C. Hefferan, "Thomas B. Catron" (Master's thesis, U. of NM, 1940), 156; Victor Westphall, *Thomas Benton Catron and His Era*, 71-72.
15. Howard R. Lamar, "Land Policy in the Spanish Southwest, 1846-1891," *JEH*, 514.
16. Richard Wells Bradfute, *The Court of Private Land Claims: The Adjudication of Spanish and Mexican Land Grant Titles, 1891-1904*, 1-25.
17. J. J. Bowden, *Spanish and Mexican Land Grants in the Chihuahua Acquisition*, 104-110; J. J. Bowden, *The Ponce de Leon Grant*, 1-56.
18. The Emory map had not been signed, although it bore previous traces of having been signed and erased. Apparently after several discussions, the Salazar map was accepted by both parties as official. *Proceedings of the IBC*, Vol. 1, sheet 29, p. 46.
19. W. L. Diffenderfer Survey No. 40, Section 1, El Paso County Clerk's Office; *Deed Records*, Vol. A, 472, El Paso County Clerk's Office; *Proceedings*, Vol. 1, 62.
20. Anson Mills Survey No. 145, Vol. A-1, *Deed Records*, El Paso County Clerk's Office; Anson Mills, *My Story*, 51-63.
21. "J. M. Dean to His Excellency, L. S. Ross," Jan. 30, 1888, *Chamizal Arbitration: Appendix*, 691-692, 701-702, 714-718.
22. Kenneth Duane Yeilding, "The Chamizal Dispute: An Exercise in Arbitration, 1845-1945," (Dissertation, Texas Tech University, 1973), 38-40.
23. "Maj. Ernst to Mr. Bayard," Dec. 12, 1888, *Chamizal Arbitration: Appendix*, 758-769; "Report of Ingeniero Garfias," 769-781, 796-806. Also see FRUS 1889, 621-637; Ira G. Clark, *Water in New Mexico: A History of Its Management and Use*, 90-91.
24. "Convention Between the USA and the U.S. of Mexico to Facilitate the Carrying Out of the Principles Contained in the Treaty of Nov. 12, 1884," Proclaimed Dec. 26, 1890. Text in Malloy, *Treaties*, 1.

25. *Proceedings*, Vol. 1, 101-116.
26. Eugene O. Porter, "The Great Flood of 1897," *Password*, 95-103; *El Paso Times*, April 29, May 11-29, 1897.
27. *Proceedings*, Vol. 1, 14.
28. Ibid., 149-171; *Chamizal Arbitration: Counter Case*, 69-112.
29. *Proceedings*, Vol. 1, 50.
30. Ibid., 51.
31. Ibid., 60.
32. Ibid., 53-62.
33. Ibid., 55.
34. Ibid., 65-67.
35. Ibid., 83.
36. "Creel to Root," March 21, 23, 25, 1907, *Appendix to the Case of the USA*, 450-452.
37. Yeilding, "The Chamizal Dispute," 38-62.
38. J. F. Hulse, *Texas Lawyer: The Life of William H. Burges*, 169-162.
39. *Chamizal Arbitration, Minutes of the IBC: Dissenting Opinions, Protest of the Agent of the U.S.*, 3-5.
40. Salvador Mendoza, *El Chamizal, Un Drama Jurídico y Histórico*, 21; Gladys Gregory, *The Chamizal Settlement*, 33.
41. *El Paso Times*, June 17, 1911.

24. A Banco Here, a Banco There

1. *Chamizal Arbitration: Appendix*, 694. Cocke is occasionally spelled "Cooke" in these reports.
2. *Proceedings*, Vol. 1, 173-174.
3. Ibid., 175-190; Anson Mills, *International Boundary Commission Press Books*, Vol. 4, no pagination; Jerry E. Mueller, *Restless River*, 49-64; Charles A. Timm, *The International Boundary Commission*, 71-114.
4. Robert M. Utley, *International Boundary: U.S. & Mexico*, 95-96; "Convention Between the U.S. and Mexico for the Elimination of Bancos in the Rio Grande," proclaimed June 5, 1907.
5. George Curry, *An Autobiography, 1861-1947*, 295-300.
6. Information furnished by IBWC.

25. Dams for the River

1. HED 93, "El Paso Troubles in Texas," 11-12.
2. HED 125, "Mills to Sec. of State," Dec. 10, 1888, 22; Timm, *International Boundary Commission*, 179-180; Mills, *My Story*, 259-260; Huntley, *Dividing the Waters*, 22-31; *El Paso Times*, March 29, April 30, 1890; *Proceedings*, 281.
3. SED 229, "Equitable Distribution of Waters of the Rio Grande," 179-180.
4. SED 154, "Equitable Distribution of Waters of the Rio Grande," 190.

5. SED 928, "Report of the Special Committee of the U.S. Senate on the Irrigation and Reclamation of Arid Lands," 24-25.
6. SED 229, "Equitable Distribution of Waters of the Rio Grande," Vol. 2, 280-332.
7. *Proceedings*, 333.
8. Ibid., 338, 374.
9. Ibid., 338-339.
10. Ira G. Clark, "The Elephant Butte Controversy Over the Waters of the Upper Rio Grande," *Journal of American History*, 1,021.
11. P. L. Haney, "The International Controversy over the Waters of the Upper Rio Grande" (Thesis, College of Mines and Metallurgy, 1948), 67.
12. *Proceedings*, 343.
13. Ibid.
14. Ibid., 413; Kelley, *River of Lost Dreams*, 98-101.
15. *The Rio Grande Claim: Appendix to the Answer of the U.S.*, 1-759, especially 463-483. This item is the most complete source regarding Boyd's charges and countercharges. Also see, *In Re The Elephant Butte Dam Affair*, by Dr. Nathan Boyd, 166 pages, copy in office of IBWC, El Paso; Kelley, *River of Lost Dreams*, 96-97.
16. Hundley, *Dividing the Waters*, 27-28; SED 104, "History of the Rio Grande Dam and Irrigation Company and the Elephant Butte Dam Case," Jan. 1901.
17. *The Rio Grande Claim: American and British Claims Arbitration* (Washington, D.C., 1923), 29.
18. John T. Ganoe, "The Origin of A National Reclamation Policy," *MVHR*, 40-47; Ira Clark, *Water in New Mexico*, 95; Kelley, *River of Lost Dreams*, 98-101.
19. *El Paso Times*, Nov.20, 1904.
20. Ibid.
21. HED 359, "Joaquin Casasús to Sec. of State," March 28, 1906, and "Report of the American Section," 410-411.
22. "Convention for Equitable Distribution of Waters of the Rio Grande," *U.S. Statutes at Large*, XXXIV, 2,953.

26. The Upper River Becomes a Ditch

1. Information furnished by the El Paso Division of the Bureau of Reclamation, Aug. 25, 1983.
2. J. C. Day, "Urban Water Management of An International River: The Case of El Paso-Juarez," *NRJ*, 457-458; Conrey Bryson, "El Paso's Water Supply: Problems and Solutions, 1921-1959," (Master's Thesis, Texas Western College, 1959), 33.; *El Paso Herald*, Aug. 29, 1914; Christopher M. Wallace, *Water Out of the Desert*, 20-21; Interview with David

Overbold and Dan Page, Bureau of Reclamation, El Paso, March 19, 1988.
3. Alice M. White, "History of Development of Irrigation in the El Paso Valley" (Master's Thesis, Texas Western College, 1950), 105-153.
4. Ibid., 125-131; *Project History, 1917*, 2 (IBWC office, El Paso).
5. *Cong. Record*, March 23-24, 1914, 5,279-5,289; "Hearings of Committee of Foreign Affairs Relating to International (Water) Boundary Commission, U.S. and Mexico," Feb. 5, 11, 1914.
6. George Warton James, *Reclaiming the Arid West*, 18-21; Helen Orndorff, "A Brief History of the Origin of Elephant Butte Dam," *Password*, 43-44; Chris P. Fox, "The Dream: Elephant Butte Dam," Ibid., 21-26; Patrick Rand, "An Early Trip to Elephant Butte," Ibid., 111-116.
7. James Willis Kirby, "Water Resources — El Paso County, Texas: Past, Present, Future" (Master's Thesis, U.T. El Paso, 1968), 68-77; Raymond A. Hill, "Development of the Rio Grande Compact of 1938," *NRJ*, 163-199; *El Paso Times*, Dec. 20, 1928; Ira Clark, *Water in New Mexico*, 218-221.
8. S. E. Reynolds and Philip B. Mutz, "Water Deliveries Under the Rio Grande Compact," *NRJ*, 210; J. C. Day, "International Management of the Rio Grande Basin: the United States and Mexico," *WRB*, 939.
9. Conrey Bryson, "Biographical Sketch of Lawrence M. Lawson," *Password*, 13-15.
10. U.S. Section, IBWC, *Technical Summaries of Projects Along the International Boundary Between the U.S. and Mexico*, 1977, Tab. 1, 2, 6; *El Paso Herald-Post*, Aug. through Dec. 1934-1935.
11. David Herrera Jordán and Joseph F. Friedkin, "The IBWC: U.S. and Mexico," *International Conference on Water for Peace*, 7; Robert M. Utley, *International Boundary: U.S. and Mexico*, 102-103; "Rio Grande Rectification Project," U.S. Section IBWC, *History and Development of the International Boundary and Water Commission: U.S. and Mexico*, n.p.; Ira Clark, *Water in New Mexico*, 222-223.
12. "Rio Grande Canalization Project," (U.S. Section IBWC), n.p.; HR 20, "IBC: U.S. and Mexico," Jan. 23, 1935, 6; Clark, *Water in New Mexico*, 220-225; interview with former American Boundary Commissioner Joseph F. Friedkin, El Paso, April 1, 1988.
13. HD 359, "Report of the American Section," 266; Charles A. Timm, *International Boundary*, 186-188; Alice M. White, "History of the Development," 144-146.

14. U.S. Section, IBC, *Preliminary Report: Control and Canalization of the Rio Grande Caballo Dam, N.M. to El Paso, Texas*, Aug. 1, 1935, 12.
15. White, "History of the Development," 138-139.
16. Timm, *International Boundary*, 187; *San Antonio Express*, Aug. 1, 1934; Friedkin interview, April 1, 1988.
17. U.S. Section, IBWC, *Technical Summaries of Projects*, Tab 3.
18. Interview with Manuel R. Ybarra, Sec., American Section, IBWC, Oct. 24, 1983.
19. Figures furnished by the IBWC: also see IBWC water bulletins, *Flow of the Rio Grande and Related Data*, Vol. 1 through 53.

27. The Lower Rio Grande Valley

1. Lawrence Francis Hill, *José de Escandon and the Founding of Nuevo Santander*, 15.
2. J. B. Wilkinson, *Laredo and the Rio Grande Frontier*, 25.
3. Florence Johnson Scott, *Historical Heritage of the Lower Rio Grande Valley*, 64.
4. Ibid.
5. W. H. Bourland and James R. Miller, *A Report of the Commissioners to Investigate Land Titles West of the Nueces*, 27.
6. HD 359, "Report of the American Section," 365-366.
7. Ibid., 28; Hundley, *Dividing the Waters*, 57.
8. Timm, *International Boundary*, 196-199.
9. HD 359, "Report of the American Section," 85-244.
10. Ibid., "Treaty With Mexico Relating to the Utilization of the Waters of Certain Rivers," *Hearings Before the Senate Committee on Foreign Relations*, Jan. 1945, 5 parts; Timm, 212-213; Hundley, 95.
11. IBWC, *Joint Projects*, 2-3; *Treaty for Utilization of the Waters of the Colorado and Tijuana Rivers and of the Rio Grande*, (59 Stat. 1219), copy at IBWC, El Paso; *El Universal*, Aug. 1, 1945.
12. FRUS 1944, 1,361-1,383.
13. "Treaty With Mexico Relating to the Utilization of the Waters of Certain Rivers," *Hearings Before the Senate Committee on Foreign Relations*, Part I, 25, testimony of Commissioner Lawson.
14. IBWC, *Technical Summaries of Projects Along the International Boundary*, Tabs 9, 13, 14.
15. J. C. Day, "International Management of the Rio Grande Basin: The U.S. and Mexico," *WRB*, 943.
16. IBWC, *Technical Summaries*, Tab 11.
17. Day, "International Management," 941-945.
18. Friedkin interview, April 1, 1988.
19. IBWC, *Joint Projects of the U.S. and Mexico*, 15-16.
20. Friedkin Interview, April 1, 1988.

28. The Kennedy Give-Away and Other Oddities

1. *Executive N*, "Hearings Before the Committee on Foreign Relations, U.S. Senate," Dec. 1963, 12-14; J. Sam Moore, Jr. and Cesar Sepulveda, "The United States and Mexico — Sources of Conflict," *Southwestern Law Journal*, 86-109.
2. Gladys Gregory, *The Chamizal Settlement*, 39; James E. Hill, Jr. "El Chamizal: A Century Old Boundary Dispute," *Geographical Review*, 510-522.
3. *Executive N*, Dec. 12 & 13, 1963, 54-64, 71-72.
4. *El Paso Times*, July 19, 1963.
5. *Executive N*, 12; *The Chamizal: International Border Improvement Project*, 1964, 1-7.
6. "Testimony of Commissioner Friedkin," Hearings Before the Committee on Foreign Relations, *The Chamizal: International Border*, Jan. 21, 1956, 8-16.
7. *Executive N*, "Testimony of Ambassador Mann," 6-9. Mann said that to have given Mexico all 437 acres from the Chamizal would have meant drawing the line even farther north into more heavily populated areas. "The cost of the settlement would have gone up enormously," he stated, "and the number of people that would have had to move would also have gone up enormously." Also see *Hands Across the Border: The Story of Chamizal* (no author), 11.
8. "Boundary Solution to the Problem of the Chamizal," *Treaties and Other International Acts*, series 5,515, 3-7.
9. *Programa Nacional Fronterizo*, Boletín Pronaf, Oct. 1967, 1-22.
10. U.S. Public Law 92-36, 85 STAT., 88; El Paso City Ordinance 4838 Changing the Zoning of the Chamizal Treaty Property, April 27, 1972.
11. Frank Smith, Supt. of Chamizal National Memorial to LCM, Jan. 9, 1987.
12. Chris P. Fox to Sen. Lloyd Bentsen, June 4, 1979. L. Lorraine Mintzmyer, National Park Service, to Sen. Lloyd Bentsen, July 27, 1979. Letter copies in possession of author; "Hearings Before the Subcommittee on Inter-American Affairs of the Committee of Foreign Affairs," Feb. 1964, 88-300.
13. Jon Cunningham, Dir. of Planning, City of El Paso, to E. A. Loughran, Bureau of Immigration and Naturalization, Feb. 10, 1964. Copy in possession of author. Cun-

ningham offered the Bureau of Immigration six possible city areas available for detention facilities. He blistered the bureau for even considering Cordova Island, and said Robert M. Utley, Historian for the National Park Service, "would refuse to recommend the development of a park on Cordova Island if the Alien Detention facility and the Sector Headquarters were placed there."

14. Fact Sheet provided by the IBWC.
15. Senate Executive B, "Treaty With Mexico Resolving Boundary Differences – Message From the President of the U.S.," 1971.
16. Ibid., vii.
17. Ibid., vi & vii.
18. *Proceeding of the IBC in Relation to the Diversion of the Rio Grande by the American Rio Grande Land and Irrigation Company near Horcón Ranch, Tamaulipas, Mexico.*
19. James E. Hill, Jr., "El Horcón: A United States-Mexican Boundary Anomaly," *The Rocky Mountain Social Science Journal*, 49-61.
20. *Senate Executive B*, vii.
21. Minute No. 251, April 28, 1976, IBWC.
22. *El Paso Herald-Post*, Nov. 30, 1976; Pete Magaro, Chief Legal Officer, U.S. Dept. of Justice, to author, July 11, 1977.
23. *Administrative Decision Under Immigration and Nationality Laws*, (17 I&N Dec.), Vol. 17, 190; Pete Magaro to author, Aug. 18, 1983; *San Antonio Express-News*, Aug. 23, 1980.
24. John Reed, *Insurgent Mexico*, 74.
25. HR 10623, 10624, 14573, entitled "American-Mexican Boundary Commission," Hearings Before the Subcommittee on Inter-American Affairs, testimony of Richard C. White, May 1, 1972.
26. Compere and Compere, *Preliminary Economic Study of Presidio-Ojinaga Area*, Sept. 1970, 3-15.
27. Tom Miller, *On the Border*, 104; Alan Weisman, *La Frontera*, 72-75.
28. FRUS 1934, 477-484; IBWC Minutes No. 72, 120, 237, 239.
29. *El Paso Herald-Post*, Feb. 3, 1977; IBWC Minutes No. 246, 247; *Joint Projects of the U.S. and Mexico*, 13-14.

29. I Lift My Lamp

1. 1986 Immigration Control and Reform Act, P.L. 99-603.
2. William H. McNeill and Ruth S. Adams, *Human Migration: Patterns and Policies*, 3-20.
3. Stan Steiner, *Fusang: The Chinese Who Built America*, 124.
4. H.R. 2915, *Hearings on Chinese Exclusion*, 1891, 54; Delber L. McKee, *Chinese*

Exclusion Versus the Open Door Policy, 1900-1906, 1-30.
5. H.R. 4048, House Subcommittee on Immigration & Naturalization, "Investigation of Chinese Immigration, with Testimony, 1891," 22.
6. Marion T. Bennett, *American Immigration Policies: A History*, 36; Maldwyn A. Jones, *Destination America*, 1-21.
7. Ibid., P. 1-10, 540-580; H.R. 2915, "Preventing Immigration of Chinese Labor from Canada & Mexico, 1891."
8. Sunset Heights sits on a granite shelf at the south end of the Rocky Mountains. To dig a tunnel through nearly solid rock would have been a near impossibility for the time. Furthermore, keeping Rio Grande water from entering the tunnel would have taxed even today's engineering skills. As for tunnels and ditches between the houses, that information came from an interview with Mrs. Helen Keleher, June 15, 1981, El Paso, Texas.
9. H. D. 758, Report of Commissioner of Immigration, 70.
10. S.D. 663, "Immigrants in Industries," Part 2, Vol. 3, 13-30, hereafter referred to as "Dillingham Report."
11. *Bulletin of the Bureau of Labor*, Vol. 78, 470.
12. Carey McWilliams, *North From Mexico*, 167-69.
13. Ibid.; *Dillingham*, 26.
14. *Bureau of Labor Bulletin*, 468, 475. *El Paso Times*, Sept. 14, 1908.
16. *Dillingham*, 26; Mario T. Garcia, *Desert Immigrants: The Mexicans of El Paso, 1880-1920*, 54.
17. *Bureau of Labor Bulletin*, 468, 472-473. "Peon Country" was so named because the plantation labor there resembled peonage.
18. *Desert Immigrants*, 45; *Bulletin of the Bureau of Labor*, 472.
19. Mark Reisler, *By the Sweat of Their Brow: Mexican Immigrant Labor in the United States, 1900-1940*, 16.
20. *Bulletin of the Bureau of Labor*, 482.
21. *Desert Immigrants*, 46-49. The baths were located under the bridge.
22. *By the Sweat of their Brow*, 33-34.
23. Hearings Before Committee of Immigration and Naturalization *Relating to the Temporary Admission of Illiterate Mexican Laborers* (Jan. 26-Feb. 2, 1920), 6, 12-25.
24. *By the Sweat of Their Brow*, 50.
25. Ibid., 57-59.
26. Roy Garis, *Immigration Restriction: A study of the Opposition to and Regulation of Immigration into the United States*, 146, 170.
27. Sidney Kansas, *U.S. Immigration, Exclusions and Deportations*, 25-26, 68-69;

Lawrence A. Cardoso, *Mexican Emigration to the United States, 1897-1931*, 94.
28. Dept of Labor, Annual Report of the Commission-General of Immigration (1924), 23, and (1927), 17.
29. *By the Sweat of their Brow*, 61-65; California *Bureau of Labor Statistics*, 22nd Biennial Report, 1925-26, 117-119.
30. *By the Sweat of Their Brow*, 63-70; *Los Angeles Times*, June 7, 1926.

30. The Deportations

1. Kenneth L. Roberts, "Mexicans or Ruin," *Saturday Evening Post*, Feb. 18, 1928, 14-15. The *Post* ran an evocative three part series by Roberts.
2. Ibid., Feb. 4, 1928; S. J. Holmes, "Perils of the Mexican Invasion," *North American Review*, May, 1929, 615; Remsen Crawford, "The Menace of Mexican Immigration," *Current History*, 902-907.
3. *Seasonal Agricultural Workers From Mexico*, House Committee of Immigration & Naturalization, Jan. 28, 1926, 15; *Restrictions on Western Hemisphere Immigration*, Sen. Committee on Immigration, Feb. 1, 1928, 25.
4. *Seasonal Agricultural*, 5-10.
5. Charles Wollenberg, "Huelga, 1928 Style: The Imperial Valley Cantaloupe Workers' Strike," *PHR*, Feb. 1969, 45-58.
6. Abraham Hoffman, *Unwanted Mexican Americans in the Great Depression*, 32. Hoffman did a lot of work on the repatriations from Los Angeles, but he also tied those activities in with national deportation trends.
7. Howard Fields, "Where Shall the Alien Work," *Social Forces*, Dec. 1933, 213-221.
8. "Mexican Exodus," *Newsweek*, July 31, 1939, 11.
9. Hoffman, *Unwanted-MexicanAmericans*, 124-127.
10. Reuben Oppenheimer, "The Deportation Terror," *New Republic*, Jan. 13, 1932; "Barring Aliens to Aid Our Jobless," *The Literary Digest*, April 25, 1931, 10.
11. Reynolds McKay, "Texas Mexican Repatriation During the Great Depression" (Dissertation, U. of Oklahoma, 1982), 141-149.

31. The Braceros

1. Ernesto Galarza, *Merchants of Labor*, 22-45; James C. Foster (ed.), *American Labor in the Southwest*, 180-186; Otey M. Scruggs, "The United States, Mexico, and the Wetbacks," *Selected Readings on U.S. Immigration Policy and Law*, Oct. 1980.

2. U. S. Stat., (1942), Vol. LVI, Part 2, pp. 1759-1769.
3. Otey M. Scruggs, "Texas and the Bracero Program," 1942-1947, *PHR*, 251-264.
4. Letter from Robert A. Lovett (Act. Sec. of State) to Don Rafael de la Colina (Minister Plenipotentiary, Chargé d'Affaires ad interim of Mexico), Oct. 22, 1948, and letter from Rafael de la Colina to Robert A. Lovett, Oct. 23, 1948. Letters republished in *Mexican Workers in the United States*, edited by George C. and Martha Woody Kiser, p. 153-155. Also see *El Paso Times* and *El Paso Herald-Post* for this period.
5. Galarza, *Merchants of Labor*, 51-52, 56, 80-83.
6. Ibid., 58-71; U. S. Dept. of Justice, INS Reporter. July 1956, 4-6.
7. *Imperial Valley Press*, Jan. 15, 18, 23, 1954; *Brawley News*, Jan. 30, 1954; *San Diego Union*, Jan. 25, 1954.
8. Galarza, *Merchants of Labor*, 67-70.
9. Juan Ramón García, *Operation Wetback: The Mass Deportation of Mexican Undocumented Workers in 1954*. Garcia gives a balanced evaluation of Operation Wetback, citing hundreds of pertinent sources.
10. Matt S. Meier & Feliciano Rivera, *The Chicanos: A History of Mexican Americans*, 224-226.
11. Galarza, *Merchants of Labor*, 84.

32. A Place to Work

1. "Surge of Illegal Immigrants Across American Borders," *U.S. News & World Report*, Jan. 17, 1972, 36.
2. One of the better attempts to make sense of border events was "One River, One Country: The U.S.-Mexico Border," CBS REPORTS, Sept. 3, 1986.
3. David Halberstam, *The Reckoning*, is a brilliant evaluation of the American and Japanese auto industry, and why America decided to compete from overseas (and Mexico) plants.
4. Don Shuffstall manuscript. Shuffstall was a Senior Vice President of MBank El Paso, and director of the International Department. He is one of the world's recognized authorities on *Maquilas*, and now has a private consulting service. Also see Oscar J. Martinez, *Border Boom Town*, 130-37; Raul A. Fernandez, *The United States-Mexico Border: A Politico-Economic Profile*, 131-148; Niles Hansen, *The Border Economy: Regional Development in the Southwest*, 97-102.
5. Interview with William Mitchell, March 2, 1988.
6. Ellwyn R. Stoddard, *Maquila: Assembly Plants in Northern Mexico*, 16-22.

7. Shuffstall MS.; "United States-Mexico Economic Relations," Senate Hearings Before the Committee on Appropriations, Dec. 7, 1984, 70-73.
8. Interview with Don Shuffstall, May 9, 1987; Mitchell interview, March 2, 1988.
9. Stoddard, *Maquila*, 56-66.
10. *Commerce Department's Promotion of Mexico's Twin Plant Program*, Hearing before the Subcommittee on Economic Stabilization, Nov. 25, 1986; Serial No. 99-105, p.17-31; Rep. Jim Kolbe, "Maquiladoras: A Foundation for U.S.-Mexico Relations," *Twin Plant News*, 14.
11. Interview with Don Shuffstall, May 2, 1987; Stoddard, *Maquila*, 16-26, 44-46.

33. The Art of Pulling Together

1. Howard G. Applegate, *Air Quality Issues: El Paso/Juarez*, 1-7.
2. "Dead Cats and Toxins," *Time Magazine*, April 20, 1987, 68-69.
3. Lawrence A. Herzog (ed.), *Planning the International Border Metropolis: Trans-Boundary Policy Options for the San Diego-Tijuana Region*, 1-105; Kiki Skagen, (ed.), "San Diego/Tijuana: The International Border in Community Relations: Gateway or Barriers," *Fronteras 1976*, California Council for the Humanities in Public Policy, San Diego, 1976, 19.
4. *Situation in Mexico*. Hearings Before the Subcommittee on Western Hemisphere Affairs for the Committee on Foreign Relations, U.S. Senate. May 13, June 17 & 26, 1986, 115-143; Office of Technology Assessment, *The Border War on Drugs*, 19.
5. *Situation in Mexico*, 163-172.

BIBLIOGRAPHY

(see abbreviation code prior to Notes)

GOVERNMENT DOCUMENTS
U.S. Congress

SED 52, *The Treaty Between the United States and Mexico* (Treaty of Guadalupe Hidalgo). 30th Cong., lst Sess., 1848.

SED 32, *Report of the Sec. of the Interior in Answer to a Resolution of the Senate Calling for Information in Relation to the Operation of the Commission Appointed to Run and Mark the Boundary Between the United States and Mexico.* 32nd Cong., lst Sess., parts 1 and 2. 1851-52.

SED 89, *Information on steps taken to investigate charges against commissioner appointed to run and mark the boundary with Mexico.* 32nd Cong., 1st Sess., 1851-1852.

SED 60, *Copy of charges preferred against commissioner appointed to run and mark the Mexican Boundary.* 32nd Cong., lst Sess., 1851-1852.

SED 1., 32nd Cong., 2d Sess. 1852-53.

SED 345, *The Mason Report.* 32nd Cong., 1st Sess., 345, 1852-53.

SED 41, *Report of commissioner appointed to run and mark the boundary line with Mexico.* 32nd Cong., 2d Sess., 1852-53.

HR 81, "Governor William Carr Lane to J. L. Taylor." 33rd Cong., 1st Sess., Jan. 23, 1854.

SED 55, *Report, with map, on Mexican boundary.* 33rd Cong., 2d Sess., 1854-55.

HED 135, *Report on the United States and Mexican Boundary Survey,* by William H. Emory. 34th Cong., lst Sess., 1855-56.

HED 81, *Troubles on the Texas Frontier,* "Official Report of Major Heintzelman." 36 Cong., 1st Sess., 1860

HED 52, *Difficulties on the Southwestern Frontier.* 36th Cong., 1st Sess., 1860.

HED 39, *Report of the United States Commissioners to Texas.* 42nd Cong., 3d Sess., Dec. 16, 1872.

HED 13, *Mexican Border Troubles.* 45th Cong., 1st Sess., 1877.

HED 701, *Report and Accompanying Documents of the Committee on Foreign Relations.* 45th Cong., 2d Sess., 1878.

HED 93, *El Paso Troubles in Texas.* 45th Cong., 2d Sess., May 1878.

HED 73, J. W. Powell's *Report on the Lands of the Arid Region of the United States.* 45th Cong., 2d Sess., 1878.

Annual Report of the Secretary of War, 1878.

SR 928, *Report of the Special Committee of the U.S. Senate on the Irrigation and Reclamation of Arid Lands.* 51st Cong., 1st Sess., 1891.

HR 4048, House Subcommittee on Immigration & Naturalization. *Investigation of Chinese Immigration, with Testimony.* 51st Cong., lst Sess., 1891.

HR 2915, House Hearings on *Preventing Immigration of Chinese Labor from Canada & Mexico.* 51st Cong., 1st Sess., 1891.

HR 2915, House Hearings on *Chinese Exclusion.* 51st Cong., 1st Sess., 1891.

HED 125, *International Dam in Rio Grande River, near El Paso, Tex.: Letter from Col. Anson Mills.* 54th Cong., 1st Sess., Jan. 1896.

SED 229, *Equitable Distribution of Waters of the Rio Grande.* 55th Cong., 2d Sess., April 1898.

SED 104, *History of the Rio Grande Dam and Irrigation Company and the Elephant Butte Dam Case.* 56th Cong., 2d Sess., Jan. 1901.

SED 154, *Equitable Distribution of Waters of the Rio Grande,* 57th Cong., 2d Sess., 1902.

HD 758, Report of Commissioner of Immigration, 58th Cong., 2d Sess., 1903.

SD 4193, *An Appeal of Water from the Colorado for Irrigation Purposes.* 58th Cong., 2d Sess., Feb. 8, 1904.

SD 212, *Imperial Valley or Salton Sink Region.* 59th Cong., 2d Sess., Jan. 1907.

SD 633, "Immigrants in Industries," called the *Dillingham Report,* 61st Cong., 2d Sess., 1911.

SED 879, *Report No. 940 — New Mexico Boundary Line.* 61st Cong., 3d Sess., 1911.

SD 591-598, *Finding of Court of Claims: Edward Gaynor, Theodore Gebler, Lee W. Mix, Arthur L. Peck, Thomas D. Casanega, Joseph de Lusignan, Joseph H. Berger, John T. Brickwood.* 61st Cong., 2d Sess., April 15, 1912.

SD 846, *Flood Waters of the Colorado River.* 62nd Cong., 2d Sess., 1912.

HR 39, *Orders and Regulations of the Interior Department Touching Upon Use, Appropriation, or Disposition of the Waters of the Rio Grande and Its Tributaries.* 62nd Cong., 1st Sess., 1912.

Congressional Record

Congressional Globe

HR 6044, House Hearings by Committee on Irrigation of Arid Lands. *All-American Canal in Imperial and Coachella Valleys, Calif.* 66th Cong., 1st Sess., July 1919.

SR 106, Senate Committee on Foreign Relations, better known as "Fall Committee." *Investigation of Mexican Affairs.* 66th Cong., 2d Sess. (vols. 9 & 10), 1920.

House Committee of Immigration and Naturalization. *Temporary Admission of Illiterate Mexican Laborers.* 66th Cong., 2d Sess., Joint Resolution 271. (Jan. 26-Feb. 2, 1920).

SD 142, *Problems of Imperial Valley and Vicinity.* 67th Cong., 2d Sess., 1922.

HR 2903, House Hearings by Committee on Irrigation and Reclamation. *Protection and Development of Lower Colorado River Basin.* 68th Cong., 1st Sess., 1924.

Dept. of Labor. *Annual Report of the Commissioner-General of Immigration.* 1924-27.

House Committee of Immigration and Naturalization. *Seasonal Agricultural Workers From Mexico.* Jan. 28, 1926.

Senate Committee on Immigration. *Restrictions on Western Hemisphere Immigration.* Feb. 1, 1928.

HD 359, International Water Commission, U.S. and Mexico. *Report of the American Section.* 71st Cong., 2d Sess., April 1930.

SD 44, *Flood Control at Nogales, Arizona-Mexico.* 72nd Cong., 1st Sess., Jan. 7, 1932.

HR 20. *International Boundary Commission: U.S. & Mexico.* 74th Cong., 1st Sess., Jan. 23, 1935.

HR 6091, House Hearings by Committee on Flood Control. *Control of Flood Waters on the American Side of the Rio Grande in the State of Texas.* 74th Cong., 1st Sess., 1935.

U.S. Statutes: 77th Cong., 2d Sess. Vol. LVN, Part 2, 1942.

Hearings Before the Senate Committee on Foreign Relations. *Treaty With Mexico Relating to the Utilization of the Waters of Certain Rivers.* 79th Cong., 1st Sess., (5 parts). Jan. 1945.

Senate Committee on Foreign Affairs. *Hearings on Water Treaty With Mexico.* 79th Cong., 1st Sess. 1945.

SED 39, *Water Supply Below Boulder Dam.* 79th Cong., 1st Sess., 1945.

SED 98, *Water Treaty of the Colorado River and Rio Grande Favors Mexico.* 79th Cong., 1st Sess., 1945.

Executive N, Hearings Before the Senate Committee on Foreign Relations. *Convention With Mexico for Solution of the Problems of Chamizal.* 88th Cong., 1st Sess., 1963.

S 2394, Senate Committee on Foreign Relations. *Compliance With Convention on Jan. 21, 1964 (Chamizal).* 88th Cong., 2d Sess., 1964.

Treaty to Resolve Pending Boundary Differences and Maintain the Rio Grande and Colorado River as the International Boundary. *Treaties and Other International Acts Series 7313,* signed at Mexico, Nov. 23, 1970.

PL 93-320, Colorado River Basin Salinity Control Act. *Herbert Brownell Report.* 93rd Cong., 2d Sess., Dec. 28, 1972.

HR 10623, 10624, 14573, Hearings Before Subcommittee on Inter-American Affairs. *American-Mexican Boundary Cooperation.* 93rd Cong., 2d Sess., May 1, 1972.

S 496, Senate Hearings Before the Subcommittee on Energy and Natural Resources. *Amending Title 1 of the Colorado River Basin Salinity Control Act.* 96th Cong., 1st Sess., April 12, 1979.

SR 96-181, *Amending Title 1 of the Colorado River Basin Salinity Control Act.* 96th Cong., 1st Sess., Calendar No. 192. May 15, 1979.

HR 96-177, *Increasing the Appropriations Ceiling for Title 1 of the Colorado River Basin Salinity Control Act (Act of June 24, 1974: 88 Stat. 266), and for Other Purposes.* 96th Cong., 1st Sess., May 15, 1979.

Selected Readings On U.S. Immigration Policy and Law. A Compendium prepared at the request of Senator Edward M. Kennedy, Chairman of the Committee on the Judiciary, for the use of the Select Commission on Immigration and Refugee Policy. 96th Cong., 2d Sess. October 1980.

House Hearings Before the Subcommittee on Department Operations, Research, and Foreign Agriculture of the Committee on Agriculture. *Salinity Control in Colorado River Basin.* 97th Cong., 1st Sess., June 10, 1981.

Senate Committee on Appropriations for United States-Mexico Economic Relations, Dec. 7, 1984.

Oversight Hearings Before the Subcommittee on Immigration, Refugees, and International Law of the Committee of the Judiciary, House of Representatives. *Immigration and Naturalization Service.* 99th Cong., 2d Sess. March 13, 1986. Serial No. 92.

Hearings Before the Subcommittee on Western Hemisphere Affairs of the Committee on Foreign Relations, U.S. Senate. *Situation in Mexico.* 99th Cong., 2d Sess. May 13, June 17 & 26, 1986.

Hearings Before the Subcommittee on Crime of the Committee of the Judiciary, House of Rep. *Current Law Enforcement Problems on U.S. Land Borders.* 99th Cong., 2d Sess. May 22, 1986. Serial No. 86.

Hearings Before the Subcommittee on Immigration, Refugees, and International Law of the Committee on the Judiciary, House of Rep. *Administration of the Immigration and Nationality Laws.* H.R. 4823, H.R. 4444, and H.R. 2184. 99th Cong., 2d Sess. July 22, 1986. Serial No. 95.

Hearings Before the Subcommittee on Immigration, Refugees, and International Law of the Committee on the Judiciary, House of Rep. *Legal Immigration.* 99th Cong., 2d Sess. July 30, 1986. Serial No. 75.

House Subcommittee on Economic Stabilization of the Committee on Banking, Finance and Urban Affairs. *Commerce Department's Promotion of Mexican Twin Plant Program,* 99th Cong., 2d Sess. Nov. 25, 1986.

PL 99-603, *Immigration Control and Reform Act.* 1986.

NATIONAL ARCHIVES AND LIBRARY OF CONGRESS

Records of the Office of Judge Advocate General (Army), RG 153 and 94. NA.

Letters Received by the Office of Adjutant General. Main Series.

Records of Foreign Service Posts at Matamoros, Juarez, Tijuana and other Mexican border communities. GP 84. NA.

Letters from United States commissioners. RG 96, NA.

Records of the U.S.A. commands, Department of California and Texas. RG 98, NA.

Mansfield papers. Library of Congress.

Roosevelt papers. File 482-A. Roosevelt Library. Hyde Park, New York.

Taft, William Howard. Papers. Library of Congress, Ser. 8, 7:460-461.

PRINTED PUBLIC DOCUMENTS

Bartlett, John R. *Report of the Secretary of Interior, communicating, in compliance with a resolution of the Senate, a report from Mr. Bartlett on the subject of the Boundary line between the United States and Mexico.* 32nd Cong., 2d Sess. SED 41.

Bevans, Charles I. *Treaties and Other International Agreements of the United States of America, 1776-1949.* Department of State. 1972.

The Border War on Drugs. Office of Technology Assessment. Washington, D.C.: U.S. Gov. Printing Office, March 1987.

Boundary Solution to the Problem of Chamizal: Convention Between the U.S. and Mexico. *Treaties and Other International Acts,* series 5515. Washington: 1964.

Bulletin of the Bureau of Labor, No. 78. Sept. 1908.

California Bureau of Labor Statistics, 22nd biennial report, 1925-26.

The Chamizal: Internationnal Border Improvement Project. Dept. of Planning. City of El Paso. 1964.

Colorado River: International Problem (no author). Arizona Colorado River Commission: Phoenix, 1938.

Convention With Mexico for Solution of Problem of Chamizal. Executive N. Washington: 1963.

HED 135, Emory, William H. *Report of the United States and Mexican Boundary Survey.* 44th Cong., 1st Sess., (2 volumes).

Executive Agreement Series 351. Department of State. Washington: 1943.

Fall, Albert B. *Investigation of Mexican Affairs* (volumes 9 and 10). 1919-1920.

Galindo, Ignacio & Antonio García Carrillo and Agustín Siliceo. *Reports of the Committee of Investigation.* Baker & Baker, Printers: New York, 1875.

Hearings Before the Committee on Foreign Relations. *Compliance with Chamizal Convention.* Washington: 1964.

HR 10623, 10624, 14573, Hearings Before Subcommittee on Inter-American Affairs. *American-Mexican Boundary Cooperation,* Washington: 1972.

Historic Salton Sea and Imperial Irrigation District. Imperial Irrigation District: El Centro, Ca., 1965.

PL 99-603, *Immigration Control and Reform Act,* 1986.

Malloy, W. M. *Treaties, Conventions, International Acts, Protocols and Agreements between the USA and Other Powers.* 1923. (3 volumes).

Memorandum Prepared for the Committee on Claims with Reference to S. 15. 76th Cong., 1st Sess. Washington: 1939.

Memoria de la Sección Mexicana de la Comisión Internacional de Límites Entre Mexico y Los Estados Unidos Que Restableció Los Monumentos de El Paso al Pacífico. Imprenta de John Polhemus: New York, 1901.

Miller, David Hunter. *Treaties and Other International Agreements of the United States of America.* Washington.

Mills, Anson. *Proceedings of the International Boundary Commission.* Washington: 1903. (2 volumes)

The Rio Grande Claim: American and British Claims Arbitration. Washington: 1923.

The Rio Grande Claim: Appendix to the Answer of the United States. Washington: 1923.

Salazar Ylarregui, José. *Datos de los Trabajos Astrónomicos y Topográficos, Dispuestos en Forma de Diario. Practicadós Durante el Año de 1849 y Principios de*

1850 por la Comision de Límites Mexicana en la Línea que Divide Esta Republica de Los Estados Unidos. Mexico, D.F., 1850.

Secretaría de Fomento, Colonización y Industria, Dirección General de Estadística, Territorio de la Baja California. Mexico 1913.

Secretaria de la Economia Nacional, Direccion General de Estadistica, Quinto, Censo de poblacion, 15 de Mayo 1930: Baja California. Distrito Norte, Vol. 1, tomo 11 (Mexico 1933).

SED 119. 32nd Cong., 1st Sess. 1851-52.

SED 92, Treaty With Mexico Resolving Boundary Differences. *Message from the President of the United States.* 92nd Cong., 1st Sess. 1971.

El Tratado de Aguas Internacionales Celebrado entre Mexico y los Estados Unidos el 3 de Febrero de 1944. Antecedentes, Consideraciones y Resoluciones del Problema de los Aguas Internacionales. Mexico, D.F. 1947.

Utilization of Waters of the Colorado and Tijuana Rivers and of the Rio Grande. Treaty Between the U.S. and Mexico. Washington: 1946.

War of the Rebellion. A Compilation of the Official Records of the Union and Confederate Armies, seventy volumes. Washington: 1880-1901.

Wellton-Mohawk Irrigation and Drainage District, Wellton, Arizona. Board of Directors, Wellton-Mohawk Irrigation and Drainage District. 1962.

Whom Shall We Welcome: Report of the President's Commission on Immigration and Naturalization. (U.S. Gov. Printing Off., Washington, D.C.: 1953).

PAPERS OF THE AMERICAN SECTION OF THE IBWC

Boyd, Dr. Nathan. *In Re the Elephant Butte Affair.* 166 pp., undated.

Colorado River Salinity Problems, five volumes of papers and communiques filed by American Section of IBWC.

Flow of the Rio Grande and Related Data. Annual Water Bulletins published by the IBWC.

Graham, Col. J. D. *Correspondence Book,* USBC, 1851-52.

History and Development of the International Boundary and Water Commission: U.S. and Mexico, published by U.S. Section, April 1952. (Revised, April 1954).

Joint Projects of United States and Mexico through the IBWC. Published by the U.S. Section, 1981.

Joint Report of the Principal Engineers on the Placement of Markers on the Land Boundary of the United States and Mexico. July 7, 1975.

Millington Papers (Letters to W. W. Follett).

Mills, Anson. *International Boundary Commission Press Books.* 4 vols. No pagination, no date.

Minutes

News Releases

Preliminary Economic Impact Study of Presidio-Ojinaga Area for IBWC as of September 1970. By Compere & Compere.

Preliminary Report: Control and Canalization of the Rio Grande Caballo Dam, New Mexico to El Paso, Texas. Published by IBC. Aug. 1, 1935.

Programa Nacional Fronterizo. Boletín Pronaf. Vol. 7, No. 77. Mexico, 1967.

Project Histories of the Bureau of Reclamation. Compiled on a year by year basis by the Bureau of Reclamation.

Study of Presidio-Ojinaga Area, 1971. Compere & Compere, Preliminary Economic Impact.

Symons, Lt. Thomas W. *Preliminary Reconnaissance of the Boundary Line Between the U.S. and Mexico from the Rio Grande at El Paso to the Pacific Ocean.* Typescript.

Technical Summaries of Projects Along the International Boundary Between the United States and Mexico. Published by U.S. Section. Sept. 1977. (Revised, Jan. 1981).

Western Land Boundary Monument Data. Compiled by the U.S. Section of the IBWC., no pagination, no date.

Hands Across the Border: The Story of Chamizal. U.S. Dept. of State: Dec. 13, 1968.

MANUSCRIPT COLLECTIONS

Arista, Mariano (Mexican Sec. of War). *Colonias Militares, Proyecto para Su Establecimiento en las Fronteras de Oriente y Occident.* Imprenta de 1, Complido, 1848, Mexico City. Holliday Collection, Arizona Historical Society, Tucson.

Bartlett, John Russell. Boundary Commission papers (1850-1853) in John Carter Brown Library, Brown University, Providence.

Committees of Fourteen and Sixteen. Subcommittee of Eight. *Proceedings Relating to Colorado River Basin.* California Colorado River Board, Los Angeles.

Deed Records, El Paso County. County Clerk's office, County courthouse.

Effinger, R. P. Personal papers in San Diego Historical Society.

El Paso City Council Minutes (typescript), El Paso Public Library.

Emory, William H. Personal papers in Beinecke Library, Yale University.

Frémont, Jesse Benton. Manuscript. Bancroft Library.

Holt Collection, New Mexico State University Archives, Las Cruces.

Horburt, Myron B., "International Problems of the Colorado River," paper presented to the "American Association for the Advancement of Science," San Francisco, March 1, 1974.

Hyslop, James E. Personal papers. Library Archives, U.T. El Paso.

Look, George. Manuscript in El Paso Public Library.

Mills, Anson. Personal letters to family. Library Archives, U.T. El Paso.

One Country: The U.S.-Mexico Border (typescript). CBS Reports. Sept. 3, 1986.

Parrish, Joe. Papers relating to Chamizal, plus unrelated manuscripts. Library Archives, U.T. El Paso.

Santa Fe Expedition Papers. Texas State Archives. Austin, Texas.

State of New Mexico vs. Renteria, et al. Docket Nos. 651-654, 664-666. New Mexico State Archives, Santa Fe.

Shuffstall, Don. Manuscript relating to Maquilas. 1987. Copy in possession of author.

Stoddard, Ellwyn R. "Anticipating Transboundary Resource Needs and Issues in the U.S.-Mexican Border Region to the Year 2000." Summary report paper read before Working Group of U.S.-Mexico Transboundary Resource Needs and Issues. South Padre Island, Texas, April 23-25, 1981.

THESES AND DISSERTATIONS

Akers, Stephen E. "The United States and the Madero-Díaz Struggle (Master's Thesis, U.T. El Paso, 1976).

Albro, Ward Sloan, 111. "Ricardo Flores Magón: An Inquiry into the Origins of the Mexican Revolution of 1919." (Dissertation, U. of Arizona, Tucson, 1967).

Allen, Kenneth J. "The Rio Grande Valley Farm Workers Strike and March: A Descriptive Study." (Master's Thesis, U.T. Austin, 1967).

Bell, Samuel Edwin. "The Mexican Zona Libre, 1858-1905." (Master's Thesis, Texas Tech University, Lubbock, 1969).

Briscoe, Edward Eugene. "Pershing's Chinese Refugees: An Odyssey of the Southwest." (Master's Thesis, St. Mary's University, San Antonio, 1947).

Bryson, Conrey. "El Paso Water Supply: Problems and Solutions, 1921-1959." (Master's Thesis, Texas Western College, El Paso, 1959).

Carlson, Paul. "William R. Shafter: Military Commander in the American West." (Ph.D., Texas Tech University, Lubbock, 1973).

Dillman, C. Daniel. "The Functions of Brownsville, Texas, and Matamoros, Tamaulipas: Twin Cities of the Lower Rio Grande." (Ph.D., University of Michigan, 1968).

Estrada, Richard Medina. "Border Revolution: The Mexican Revolution in the Ciudad Juarez-El Paso Area." (Master's Thesis, U.T. El Paso, 1975).

Evans, Marie Elena. "Mass Hangings in Deming, New Mexico." (Research Paper, New Mexico University, Albuquerque, 1916).

Garibay, Lorenzo, Jr. "The Border Industrial Program of Mexico: A Case Study of the Matamoros, Tamaulipas Experience." (Master's Thesis, U.T. Austin, 1977).

Haney, P. L. "The International Controversy Over the Waters of the Upper Rio Grande." (Master's Thesis, College of Mines and Metallurgy, El Paso, 1948).

Hefferan, V. C. "Thomas B. Catron." (Master's Thesis, University of New Mexico, Albuquerque, 1940).

Jenkins, Myra Ellen. "Ricardo Flores Magón and the Mexican Liberal Party." (Dissertation, University of New Mexico, Albuquerque, 1953).

Johnson, Robert Bruce. "The Punitive Expedition: A Military, Diplomatic, and Political History of Pershing's Chase After Pancho Villa, 1916-1917." (Dissertation, University of Southern California, Los Angeles, 1964).

Kirby, James Willis. "Water Resources – El Paso County, Texas: Past, Present and Future." (Master's Thesis, U.T. El Paso, 1968).

Lee, Mary Antoine. "A Historical Survey of the American Smelting and Refining Company in El Paso, 1887-1950." (Master's Thesis, Texas Western College, El Paso, 1950).

McCain, Jonnie Mae. "Contract Labor as A Factor in the United States-Mexican Relations, 1942-1947." (Ph.D., U.T. Austin, 1964).

McKay, R. Reynolds. "Texas Mexican Repatriation During the Great Depression." (Dissertation, University of Oklahoma, Norman, 1982).

Mitchell, Jacquelyn A. "The Southwest Border Regional Commission. Issues and Challenges. A Case Study of the In-Bond Industry." (Master's Thesis, Princeton University, Princeton, 1978).

Reed, Raymond. "The Mormons in Chihuahua: Their Relations with Villa and the Pershing Punitive Expedition, 1916-1917." (Master's Thesis, University of New Mexico, Albuquerque, 1938).

Smith, Melvin T. "The Colorado River: Its History in the Lower Canyon Area." (Dissertation, Brigham Young University, 1972).

Valenzuela, Rene A. "Chihuahua, Calles and the Escobar Revolt of 1929." (Master's Thesis, U.T. El Paso, 1975).

Vassbert, David Erland. "The Use of Mexicans and Mexican-Americans as an Agricultural Work Force in the Lower Rio Grande Valley of Texas." (Master's Thesis, U.T. Austin, 1966).

White, Alice M. "History of the Development of Irrigation in the El Paso Valley." (Master's Thesis, Texas Western College, El Paso, 1950).

Yeilding, Kenneth Duane. "The Chamizal Dispute: An Exercise in Arbitration, 1845-1945." (Dissertation, Texas Tech University, Lubbock, 1973).

INTERVIEWS:

Ira Clark
Paul Copenbarger
Ray Daguerre
James Day
Richard Estrada
T. R. Fehrenbach
Edd Fifer
Joseph Friedkin
Al H. Giugni
Peggy Goiner
Joanne L. Gouge
Edwin E. Hamlyn
Marta Durón Hernández
Narendra Gunaji
Pat Kelley
Helen Keleher
Carmen Leal
Florence Cathcart Melby
Bill Mitchell
Art Moreno
David Overbold
Don Shuffstall
Franklin Smith
C. L. Sonnichsen
Robert Steele
Ellwyn R. Stoddard
W. H. Timmons
Dale L. Walker
Judson Williams
E. A. "Doggie" Wright
Manuel R. Ybarra
Myrna Zanetell

NEWSPAPERS

Arizona Daily Star
Bastrop Advertiser
Bisbee Daily Review
Brawley News
Christian Science Monitor
Colorado Citizen
Columbus Courier
El Continental
The Daily New Mexican
Dallas Morning News
Deming Headlight
Denver Post
Douglas Daily Dispatch
El Faro
The Galveston Daily News
Galveston News
Houston Telegraph
Imperial Valley Press
Industrial Worker
Las Vegas Daily Optic
Los Angeles Express
Los Angeles Record
Louisville Courier-Journal
Mexican Herald
New Orleans Picayune
New Orleans Times
New York Herald
New York Times
Northern Standard
Oakland Tribune
El Paso Herald
El Paso Herald-Post
El Paso Morning Times
El Paso Times
Periódico Oficial
Providence Journal
La Reforma Social
Regeneración
Sacramento Bee
San Antonio Express
San Diego Herald
San Diego Sun
San Diego Union
San Francisco Chronicle
El Siglo
Tucson Citizen
Tucson Daily Citizen
El Universal
Wall Street Journal

BOOKS

Acuña, Rodolfo F. *Sonoran Strongman: Ignacio Pesqueira and His Times.* (University of Arizona: Tucson, 1974).

Aguirre, Manuel J. *Cananea: las garras del Imperialismo en las entrañas de Mexico.* (Editorial B. Coast-Amic: Mexico, 1958).

Alberts, Don E. (editor). *Rebels on the Rio Grande: The Civil War Journal of A. B. Peticolas.* (University of New Mexico: Albuquerque, 1984).

Alexander, J. A. *The Life of George Chaffey.* (Melbourne, 1928).

Almada, Francisco. *Diccionario de Historia, Geografia y Biografia Sonorenses.* (Published by author: Chihuahua City, 1952).

_____, Francisco R. *Gobernadores del Estado de Chihuahua.* (Mexico City, 1950).

_____. *Diccionario de Historia, Geografia y Biografia Chihuahuenses.* (Juarez, Chihuahua, 1968).

Applegate, Howard. *Air Quality Issues: El Paso/Ciudad Juarez.* (Center for Inter-American Studies, U.T. El Paso: El Paso, 1982).

_____, Howard. *Environmental Problems of the Borderlands.* (Texas Western Press: El Paso, 1979).

Ball, Eve. *In the Days of Victorio.* (University of Arizona: Tucson, 1970).

Barrera, Alberto Calzadíaz. *Hechos reales de la revolución.* (Mexico, 1072).

Bartlett, John Russell. *Personal Narrative of Exploration and Incidents.* (Rio Grande Press: Chicago, 1965).

Batchelder, Roger. *Watching and Waiting on the Border.* (Houghton Mifflin: Cambridge, 1917).

Baylor, George Wythe. *John Robert Baylor: Confederate Governor of Arizona.* (Arizona Pioneers Historical Society: Tucson, 1966).

Beck, Warren A. and Ynez D. Haase. *Historic Atlas of New Mexico.* (University of Oklahoma: Norman, 1969).

Bell, Samuel E. & James M. Smallwood. *The Zona Libre 1858-1905: A Problem in American Diplomacy.* (Texas Western Press: El Paso, 1982).

Benavides, Luis Aguirre. *Las grandes batallas de la División del Norte.* (Editorial Diana: Mexico, 1964).

Bennett, Marion T. *American Immigration Policies: A History.* (Public Affairs Press: 1963).

Bernstein, Marvin D. *The Mexican Mining Industry, 1890-1950.* (State University of New York: Albany, 1964).

Bigelow, John. *Memoir of the Life and Public Services of John Charles Frémont.* (Derby & Jackson: New York, 1856).

Blaisdell, Lowell L. *The Desert Revolution: Baja California, 1911.* (University of Wisconsin: Madison, 1962).

Bowden, Charles. *Killing the Hidden Waters.* (University of Texas: Austin, 1977).

Bowden, J. J. *The Ponce de Leon Grant.* (Texas Western Press: El Paso, 1969).

_____. *Spanish and Mexican Land Grants in the Chihuahua Acquisition.* (Texas Western Press: El Paso, 1971).

Braddy, Haldeen. *Pershing's Mission in Mexico.* (Texas Western Press: El Paso, 1966).

Bradfute, Richard Wells. *The Court of Private Land Claims: The Adjudication of Spanish and Mexican Land Grant Titles, 1891-1904.* (University of New Mexico: Albuquerque, 1975).

Breezley, William H. *Insurgent Governor: Abraham González and the Mexican Revolution in Chihuahua.* (University of Nebraska: Lincoln, 1973).

Bryson, Conrey. *Down Went McGinty. El Paso in the Wonderful Nineties.* (Texas Western Press: El Paso, 1977).

Bush, I. J. *Gringo Doctor.* (Caxton: Caldwell, 1939).

Byrkit, James W. *Forging the Copper Collar: Arizona's Labor-Management War, 1901-1921.* (University of Arizona: Tucson, 1982).

Callahan, James Morton. *American Foreign Policy in Mexican Relations.* (Macmillan: New York, 1932).

Campa, Arthur L. *Hispanic Culture in the Southwest.* (University of Oklahoma: Norman, 1979).

Cardoso, Lawrence A. *Mexican Emigration to the United States, 1897-1931.* (University of Arizona: Tucson, 1980).

Carman, Michael Dennis. *United States Customs and the Madero Revolution.* (Texas Western Press: El Paso, 1976).

Caro, Brigido. *Plutarco Elías Calles: Dictador Bolsheviqui de Mexico.* (Los Angeles, 1924).

Carroll, John M. *Colonel Tommy Tomkins: A Military Heritage and Tradition.* (J. M. Carroll & Co.: New York, 1984).

Carter, Robert G. *On the Border With Mackenzie.* (Antiquariana: New York, 1961).

Christiansen, Paige W. *The Story of Mining in New Mexico.* (New Mexico Bureau of Mines and Mineral Resources: Socorro, 1974).

Clark, Ira G. *Water in New Mexico: A History of its Management and Use.* (University of New Mexico: Albuquerque, 1987).

Cleland, Robert Glass. *A History of Phelps Dodge, 1834-1950.* (Knopf: New York, 1952).

Clendenen, Clarence C. *The United States and Pancho Villa: A Study in Unconventional Diplomacy.* (Cornell University: Ithaca, 1961).

_____. *Blood on the Border: The United States Army and the Mexican Irregulars.* (Macmillan: New York, 1969).

Cline, Howard F. *The United States and Mexico.* (Atheneum: New York, 1969).

Coalson, George O. *The Development of the Migratory Farm Labor System in Texas, 1900-1954.* (R & E Research Associates: San Francisco, 1977).

Cockcroft, James D. *Intellectual Precursors of the Mexican Revolution, 1900-1913.* (University of Texas: Austin, 1968).

Coerver, Don M. and Linda B. Hall. *Texas and the Mexican Revolution: A Study in State and National Border Policy, 1910-1920.* (Trinity University Press: San Antonio, 1984).

Confederate Victories in the Southwest: Prelude to Defeat. (Horn and Wallace: Albuquerque, 1961).

Cooper, Erwin. *Aqueduct Empire: A Guide to Water in California.* (Arthur H. Clark: Glendale, 1968).

Copp, Nelson G. *Wetbacks and Braceros: 1930-1960.* (R. & E. Associates: San Francisco, 1971).

Corle, Edwin. *The Gila: River of the Southwest.* (Bison: Lincoln, 1951).

Corning, Leavitt. *Baronial Forts of the Big Bend.* (Trinity University Press: San Antonio, 1967).

Cory, Harry T. *Imperial Valley and the Salton Sink.* (Dodd Mead: San Francisco, 1915).

Couts, Cave J. (Edited by Henry F. Dobyns). *The Journal of Cave J. Couts.* (Arizona Pioneers' Historical Society: Tucson, 1961).

Crowe, Rosalie & Sidney B. Brinckerhoff (editors). *Early Yuma.* (Northland: Flagstaff, 1976).

Cremony, John C. *Life Among the Apaches.* (Arizona Silhouettes: Tucson, 1954).

Cumberland, Charles C. *Mexican Revolution: The Constitutionalist Years.* (University of Texas: Austin, 1972).

Curry, George. *George Curry: An Autobiography, 1861-1947.* (University of New Mexico: Albuquerque, 1958).

Dahlgren, Charles B. *Historic Mines in Mexico.* (New York, 1883).

D'Antonio, William V. & William H. Form. *Influentials in Two Border Cities: A Study in Community Decision-Making.* (University of Notre Dame: Notre Dame, 1965).

Davis, John L. *The Texas Rangers: Their First 150 Years.* (Institute of Texan Cultures: San Antonio, 1975).

Debo, Angie. *Geronimo: The Man, His Time, His Place.* (University of Oklahoma: Norman, 1976).

Dethloff, Henry C. & Irvin M. May, Jr. (editors). *Southwestern Agriculture: Pre-Columbian to Modern.* (Texas A&M University: College Station, 1982).

Duke, Alton. *When the Colorado River Quit the Ocean.* (Southwest Printers: Yuma, 1974).

Dulles, John W. F. *Yesterday in Mexico: A Chronicle of the Revolution, 1919-1936.* (University of Texas: Austin, 1972).

Faulk, Odie B. *Too Far North, Too Far South.* (Westernlore: Los Angeles, 1967).

Fehrenbach, T. R. *Lone Star: A History of Texas and Texans.* (Macmillan: New York, 1968).

_____. *Fire and Blood: A History of Mexico.* (Macmillan, New York, 1973).

Fergusson, Harvey. *The Rio Grande.* (Tudor: New York, 1945).

Fernandez, Raul A. *The United States-Mexico Border: A Politico-Economic Profile.* (University of Notre Dame: Notre Dame, 1977).

Forbes, Robert H. *Crabb's Filibustering Expedition into Sonora, 1857.* (Arizona Silhouettes: Tucson, 1952).

Foster, James C. (ed.). *American Labor in the Southwest: The First One Hundred Years.* (University of Arizona: Tucson, 1982).

Fradkin, Philip L. *A River No More: The Colorado River and the West.* (Knopf: New York, 1981).

Frost, Elsa Cecilia, Michael C. Meyer y Josefina Zoraida Vazquez. *El trabajo y los trabajadores en la historia de Mexico.* (El Colegio de Mexico: Mexico, 1979).

Galarza, Ernesto. *Merchants of Labor: The Mexican Bracero Story.* (McNally & Lofton: Santa Barbara, 1978).

Gamio, Manuel. *Mexican Immigration to the United States.* (University of Chicago: Chicago, 1930).

Garber, Paul Neff. *The Gadsden Treaty.* (Peter Smith: Gloucester, 1959).

García, Juan Ramon. *Operation Wetback: The Mass Deportation of Mexican Undocumented Workers in 1954.* (Greenwood: Westport, 1980).

García, Mario T. *Desert Immigrants: The Mexicans of El Paso, 1880-1920.* (Yale: New Haven, 1981).

Garis, Roy. *Immigration Restriction: A Study of the Opposition to and Regulation of Immigration into the United States.* (Macmillan: New York, 1927).

Gehlbach, Frederick R. *Mountain Islands and Desert Seas: A Natural History of the U.S.-Mexican Borderlands.* (Texas A&M: College Station, 1981).

Gibson, A. M. *The Kickapoos: Lords of the Middle Border.* (University of Oklahoma: Norman, 1975).

Gillett, James B. *Six Years With the Texas Rangers.* (Yale: New Haven, 1925).

Goetzmann, William H. *Army Exploration in the American West, 1803-1863.* (Yale: New Haven, 1959).

Goldfinch, Charles W. *Juan Cortina: Two Interpretations.* (Arno: New York, 1974).

Gregg, Robert D. *The Influence of Border Troubles on Relations Between the United States and Mexico, 1876-1910.* (John Hopkins: Baltimore, 1937).

Gregory, Gladys. *The Chamizal Settlement: A View From El Paso.* (Texas Western Press: El Paso, 1963).

Grieb, Kenneth J. *The United States and Huerta* (University of Nebraska: Lincoln, 1969).

Griggs, George. *Mines of Chihuahua.* (Chihuahua, 1911).

_____. *History of the Mesilla Valley.* (Bronson Printing: Las Cruces, 1930).

Guzmán, Martin Luis. *Memoirs of Pancho Villa.* (University of Texas: Austin, 1965).

Hail, Marshall. *Knight in the Sun.* (Little Brown; New York, 1962).

Halberstam, David. *The Reckoning.* (Morrow: New York: 1986).

Haley, P. Edward. *Revolution and Intervention: The Diplomacy of Taft and Wilson with Mexico, 1910-1917.* (MIT Press: Cambridge, 1970).

Hall, Linda B. *Alvaro Obregón: Power and Revolution in Mexico, 1911-1920.* (Texas A&M: College Station, 1981).

Hall, Martin Harwick. *The Confederate Army in New Mexico.* (Presidial: Austin, 1978).

_____. *Sibley's New Mexico Campaign.* (University of Texas: Austin, 1960).

Halsell, Grace. *The Illegals.* (Stein & Day: New York, 1978).

Hansen, Niles. *The Border Economy: Regional Development in the Southwest.* (University of Texas: Austin, 1981).

Harris, Charles H. & Louis R. Sadler, editors. *The Border and the Revolution.* (Center for Latin American Studies: NMSU: Las Cruces, NM, 1988).

Heffernan, W. T. *Personal Recollections of the Imperial Valley.* Bound, with Charles R. Rockwood's account, *Born of the Desert.* (Calexico, 1930).

Herzog, Lawrence A. (editor). *Planning the International Border Metropolis: Trans Boundary Policy Options for the San Diego — Tijuana region.* (Center for U.S. Mexican Studies, Monograph Series 19, University of California: San Diego, 1986).

Hill, Lawrence F. *The Confederate Exodus to Latin America.* (Columbus: 1936).

Hill, Lawrence Francis. *José de Escandon and the Founding of Nuevo Santander.* (Ohio State University Studies. Contributions in History and Political Science, No. 9. Columbus, 1926).

Hine, Robert V. *Bartlett's West.* (Yale: New Haven, 1968).

Hinkle, Stacy C. *Wings Over the Border: The Army Air Service Armed Patrol of the U.S.-Mexico Border.* (Texas Western Press: El Paso, 1970).

_____. *Wings and Saddles: The Air and Cavalry Punitive Expedition of 1919.* (Texas Western Press: El Paso, 1967).

Hoffman, Abraham. *Unwanted Mexican Americans in the Great Depression: Reparation Pressures, 1929-1939.* (University of Arizona: Tucson, 1974).

Horgan, Paul. *Great River: The Rio Grande in North American History.* (Rinehart: New York, 1954).

Horn, Calvin. *New Mexico's Troubled Years: The Story of the Early Territorial Governors.* (Horn & Wallace: Albuquerque, 1963).

Hughes, W. J. *Rebellious Ranger: Rip Ford and the Old Southwest.* (University of Oklahoma: Norman, 1964).

Humphrey, Robert R. *90 Years and 535 Miles: Vegetation Changes Along the Mexican Border.* (University of New Mexico: Albuquerque, 1987).

Hundley, Norris, Jr. *Dividing the Waters: A Century of Controversy Between the*

United States and Mexico. (University of California: Berkeley, 1966).

_____. *Water and the West: The Colorado River Compact and the Politics of Water in the American West.* (University of California: Berkeley, 1975).

Hulse, J. F. *Texas Lawyer: The Life of William F. Burges.* (Mangan Books: El Paso, 1982).

Irby, James A. *Backdoor to Bagdad: The Civil War on the Rio Grande.* (Texas Western Press: El Paso, 1977).

Jackson, William Turrentine. *Wagon Roads West: A Study of Federal Road Surveys and Construction of the Trans-Mississippi West, 1846-1969.* (University of California: Berkeley, 1952).

Jamail, Milton H. & Scott J. Ullery. *International Water Use Relations along the Sonoran Desert Borderlands.* (Office of Arid Lands Studies: U. of Arizona: Tucson, 1979).

James, George Warton. *Reclaiming the Arid West.* (Dodd Mead: New York, 1917).

Jones, Maldwyn A. *Destination America.* (Holt Rinehart Winston: New York, 1976).

Jones, Oakah L. *Los Paisaños: Spanish Settlers on the Northern Frontier of New Spain.* (University of Oklahoma: Norman, 1979).

Joralemon, Ira B. *Copper.* (Howell-North: Berkeley, 1973).

Keleher, William A. *Turmoil in New Mexico.* (Rydal: Santa Fe, 1952).

Kelley, Pat. *River of Lost Dreams: Navigation on the Rio Grande.* (University of Nebraska: Lincoln, 1986).

Kiser, George C. & Martha Woody (editors). *Mexican Workers in the United States: Historical and Political Perspectives.* (University of New Mexico: Albuquerque, 1979).

Kjonegaard, Vernon. (ed.). *Border Perspectives on the U.S./Mexico Relationship.* (New Scholar: U. of California: Santa Barbara, 1984).

Knowlton, Clark S. (ed.) *International Water Law Along the Mexican-American Border.* (Committee on Desert and Arid Zones Research: The University of Texas at El Paso, 1968).

Kruszewski, Z. Anthony, Richard L. Hough & Jacob Ornstein-Galicia. *Politics and Society in the Southwest: Ethnicity and Chicano Pluralism.* (Westview Press: Boulder, 1982).

Lamar, Howard Roberts. *The Far Southwest, 1846-1912.* (Norton: New York, 1970).

Larson, Robert W. *New Mexico's Quest for Statehood, 1846-1912.* (University of New Mexico: Albuquerque, 1968).

Lavender, David. *Colorado River Country.* (Dutton: New York, 1982).

Lewis, Tracy Hammond. *Along the Rio Grande.* (Lewis Publishing: New York, 1916).

Lindheim, Milton. *Republic of the Rio Grande*. (W. W. Morrison: Waco, 1964).

Lister, Florence C. & Robert H. *Chihuahua: Storehouse of Storms*. (University of New Mexico: Albuquerque, 1966).

MacCorkle, Steward Alexander. *American Policy of Recognition Towards Mexico*. (Johns Hopkins: Baltimore, 1933).

Mangan, Frank. *El Paso in Pictures*. (Mangan Books: El Paso, 1971).

Martin, Douglas D. *Yuma Crossing*. (University of New Mexico: Albuquerque, 1954).

Martínez, Oscar J. *Border Boom Town: Ciudad Juarez Since 1848*. (University of Texas: Austin, 1975).

_____. *Fragments of the Mexican Revolution: Personal Accounts From the Border*. (University of New Mexico: Albuquerque, 1983).

_____. *Troublesome Border*. (University of Arizona: Tucson, 1988).

Mason, Herbert Malloy, Jr. *The Great Pursuit: General John J. Pershing's Punitive Expedition Across the Rio Grande to Destroy the Mexican Bandit Pancho Villa*. (Random House: New York, 1970).

Mavis, Frederic T. (consulting editor). *Reclamation in the United States*. (McGraw Hill: New York, 1952).

McKee, Delber L. *Chinese Exclusion Versus the Open Door Policy, 1900-1906*. (Wayne State University: Detroit, 1977).

McNeely, John H. *The Railways of Mexico: A Study in Nationalization*. (Texas Western Press: El Paso, 1964).

McNeill, William H. & Ruth S. Adams. *Human Migration: Patterns and Policies*. (University of Indiana: Bloomington, 1978).

McWilliams, Carey. *North From Mexico*. (Greenwood: Westport, 1968).

Meier, Matt S. & Feliciano Rivera. *The Chicanos: A History of Mexican Americans*. (Wang & Wang: New York, 1972).

Mendoza, Salavador. *El Chamizal, Un Drama Jurídico y Histórico*.

Meriwether, David. *My Life in the Mountains and on the Plains*. (University of Oklahoma: Norman, 1965).

Meyer, Eugenia. *Museo Historico de la Revolución en el Estado de Chihuahua*. (Secretaría de la Defensa Nacional: Mexico, 1982).

Meyer, Michael C. *Mexican Rebel: Pascual Orozco and the Mexican Revolution, 1910-1915*. (University of Nebraska: Lincoln, 1967).

_____. *Huerta: A Political Portrait*. (University of Nebraska: Lincoln, 1972).

_____. *Water in the Hispanic Southwest: A Social and Legal History*. (University of Arizona: Tucson, 1984).

Miller, Tom. *On the Border*. (Harper & Row: New York, 1981).

Mills, Anson. *My Story*. (Press of Byron S. Adams: Washington, 1918).

Mills, W. W. *Forty Years in El Paso*. (Edited by Rex Strickland) (Carl Hertzog: El Paso, 1962).

Morris, Milton D. *Immigration: the Beleaguered Bureaucracy*. (The Brookings Institution: Washington, D.C., 1985).

Mueller, Jerry E. *Restless River*. (Texas Western Press: El Paso, 1975).

Muller, Thomas, Thomas J. Espenshade, and others. *The Fourth Wave: California's Newest Immigrants*. (Urban Institute Press: Washington, 1985).

Myrick, David F. *Railroads of Arizona: the southern roads*. (Howell-North: Berkeley, 1975).

Nackman, Mark E. *A Nation Within A Nation: The Rise of Texas Nationalism*. (Kennikat: Port Washington, 1975).

Nadeau, Remi A. *The Water Seekers*. (Peregrine Smith: Santa Barbara, 1974).

Neighbours, Kenneth Franklin. *Robert Simpson Neighbors and the Texas Frontier, 1836-1859*. (Texian Press: Waco, 1975).

Obregón, Alvaro. *Ocho mil kilómetros en campaña*. (Fundo de Cultura Economica: Mexico, 1959).

Paredes, Américo. *A Texas-Mexican Cancionero: Folksongs of the Lower Border*. (University of Illinois: Urbana, 1976).

Porter, Eugene O. (ed.). *Letters of Ernst Kohlberg* (Texas Western Press: El Paso, 1973).

Pourade, Richard F. *The History of San Diego: The Explorers*. (Union Tribune: San Diego, 1960).

Powell, Donald M. *The Peralta Grant: James Addison Reavis and the Barony of Arizona*. (University of Oklahoma: Norman, 1960).

Powell, Fred Wilbur. *The Railroads of Mexico*. (Stratford: Boston, 1921).

Powell, John Wesley. *The Exploration of the Colorado River*. (University of Chicago: Chicago, 1957).

Price, John A. *Tijuana: Urbanization in A Border Culture*. (University of Notre Dame: Notre Dame, 1973).

Price, Thomas J. *Standoff at the Border: A Failure of Microdiplomacy*. (Texas Western Press: El Paso, 1989).

Raat, W. Dirk. *Revoltosos: Mexico's Rebels in the United States, 1903-1923*. (Texas A&M: College Station, 1981).

Ragsdale, Kenneth Baxter. *Wings Over the Mexican Border: Pioneer Military Aviation in the Big Bend*. (University of Texas: Austin, 1984).

Reich, Peter L. *Statistical Abstract of the United States-Mexico Borderlands*. (UCLA Latin American Center Publications: Los Angeles, 1984).

Reinhold, Ruth M. *Sky Pioneering: Arizona in Aviation History*. (University of Arizona: Tucson, 1982).

Reisler, Mark. *By the Sweat of Their Brow: Mexican Immigrant Labor in the United States, 1900-1940.* (Greenwood: Westport, 1976).

Reisner, Marc. *Cadillac Desert: The American West and Its Disappearing Water.* (Viking: New York, 1986).

Riding, Alan. *Distant Neighbors.* (Knopf: New York, 1985).

Rippy, J. Fred. *The United States and Mexico.* (Knopf: New York, 1926).

Rittenhouse, Jack D. *Disturnell's Treaty Map.* (Stagecoach Press: Albuquerque, 1965).

Rivera, Antonio G. *La Revolución en Sonora.* (Imprenta Arana: Mexico, 1969).

Rogin, Michael Paul. *Fathers & Children: Andrew Jackson and the Subjugation of the American Indian.* (Knopf: New York, 1975).

Rolle, Andrew F. *The Lost Cause: The Confederate Exodus to Mexico.* (University of Oklahoma: Norman, 1966).

Ross, Stanley R. *Francisco R. Madero: Apostle of Mexican Democracy.* (AMS Press: New York, 1955).

Ruíz, Ramón Eduardo. *The Great Rebellion: Mexico, 1905-1924.* (Norton: New York, 1980).

_____, Vicki L. & Susan Tiano. (editors). *Women on the U.S.-Mexico Border: Responses to Change.* (Allen & Unwin: Winchester, 1987).

Rynning, Captain Thomas H. *Gun Notches.* (Frederick A. Stokes: New York, 1931).

Samora, Julian. *Los Mojados: The Wetback Story.* (University of Notre Dame: Notre Dame, 1971).

Sarber, Mary A. *Photographs From the Border: The Otis A. Aultman Collection.* (El Paso Public Library Assn.: El Paso, 1977).

Schonfeld, Robert G. *The Early Development of California's Imperial Valley.* Parts 1 & 2. (Historical Society of Southern California: Los Angeles, 1969).

Schwartz, Rosalie. *Across the Rio to Freedom: U. S. Negroes in Mexico.* (Texas Western Press: El Paso, 1975).

Scott, Florence Johnson. *Historical Heritage of the Lower Rio Grande.* Revised Edition. (La Retama Press: Waco, 1966).

Scott, Hugh L. *Some Memoirs of A Soldier.* (The Century Co.: New York, 1928).

Smith, Cornelius C., Jr. *Emilio Kosterlitzky: Eagle of Sonora and the Southwest Border.* (Arthur Clark: Glendale, 1970).

_____. *Don't Settle for Second: Life and Times of Cornelius C. Smith.* (Presidio: San Rafael, 1977).

Smith, Nash. *Virgin Land: The American West as Symbol and Myth.* (Howard University: Cambridge, 1950).

Sonnichsen, C. L. *The El Paso Salt War.* (Texas Western Press: El Paso, 1961).

_____. *Pass of the North: Four Centuries on the Rio Grande.* (Texas Western Press: El Paso, 1968).

_____. *Colonel Greene and the Copper Skyrocket.* (University of Arizona Press: Tucson, 1974).

Spicer, Edward H. *Cycles of Conquest.* (University of Arizona: Tucson, 1962).

Stambaugh, J. Lee and Lillian J. *The Lower Rio Grande Valley of Texas.* (Naylor: San Antonio, 1954).

Stanton, Robert Brewster. *Down the Colorado.* (University of Oklahoma: Norman, 1965).

Steiner, Stan. *Fusang: The Chinese Who Built America.* (Harper & Row: New York, 1979).

Stoddard, Ellwyn R. *Mexican Americans.* (Random House: New York, 1973).

_____. *Maquila: Assembly Plants in Northern Mexico.* (Texas Western Press: El Paso, 1987).

_____. Richard L. Nostrand and Jonathan P. West (editors). *Borderlands Sourcebook: A Guide to Literature on Northern Mexico and the American Southwest.* (University of Oklahoma: Norman, 1983).

Stout, Joseph Allen, Jr. *The Liberators: Filibustering Expeditions Into Mexico, 1848-1862, and the Last Thrust of Manifest Destiny.* (Westernlore: Los Angeles, 1973).

Strickland, Rex. *Six Who Came to El Paso.* (Texas Western Press: El Paso, 1969).

_____. *El Sabio Sembrador.* (Texas Western Press: El Paso, 1969).

Terrazas, Silvestre. *El Veradero Pancho Villa.* (Margarita Terrazas: Chihuahua City, 1984).

Terrell, John Upton. *War for the Colorado River.* Two volumes. (Arthur H. Clark: Glendale, 1965).

Thisted, Lt. Col. Moses N. *With the Wisconsin National Guard on the Mexican Border, 1916-1917.* (Helmet, Ca., 1984).

Thomas, Estelle Webb. *Uncertain Sanctuary: A Story of Mormon Pioneering in Mexico.* (Westwater Press: Salt Lake City, 1980).

Thompson, Cecilia. *History of Marfa and Presidio County, Texas, 1535-1946.* (Nortex Press: Austin, 1985).

Thompson, Jerry. *Sabers on the Rio Grande.* (Presidial: Austin, 1974).

_____. *Vaqueros in Blue & Gray.* (Presidial: Austin, 1976).

_____. *The Republic of the Rio Grande.* (Nuevo Santander Museum Complex: Laredo, 1985).

_____. *Mexican Texans in the Union Army.* (Texas Western Press: El Paso, 1986).

Thrapp, Dan L. *The Conquest of Apacheria.* (University of Oklahoma: Norman, 1967).

_____. *Victorio and the Mimbres Apaches*. (University of Oklahoma: Norman, 1974).

Tilly, Nannie M. (ed.). *Federals on the Frontier: The Diary of Benjamin F. McIntyre, 1862-1864*. (University of Texas: Austin, 1963).

Timm, Charles A. *The International Boundary Commission, United States and Mexico*. (University of Texas: Austin, 1941).

Tompkins, Col. Frank. *Chasing Villa*. (Military Service Publishing Company: Harrisburg, 1934).

Tout, Otis B. *The First Thirty Years — 1901-1931: History of Imperial Valley, Southern California, U.S.A.* (Otis B. Tout: San Diego, 1932).

Trafzer, Clifford E. *The Yuma Crossing: A Short History*. (Yuma County Historical Society: Yuma, 1974).

Trimble, Marshall. *Arizona: A Panoramic History of A Frontier State*. (Doubleday: New York, 1977).

Turner, Timothy G. *Bullets, Bottles & Gardenias*. (South-West Press: Dallas, 1935).

Tyler, Ronnie C. *The Big Bend: A History of the Last Texas Frontier*. (National Park Service: Washington, 1975).

Utley, Robert M. *International Boundary: U.S. and Mexico*. (U.S. Department of Interior: Santa Fe, 1964).

_____. *Frontier Regulars: The United States Army and the Indian*. (Macmillan: New York, 1973).

Vanderwood, Paul J. and Frank N. Samponaro. *Border Fury: A Picture Postcard Record of Mexico's Revolution and U.S. War Preparedness, 1910-1917*. (University of New Mexico Press: Albuquerque, 1988).

Vandiver, Frank E. *Black Jack: The Life and Times of John J. Pershing*, 2 volumes. (Texas A&M: College Station, 1977).

Varga, Benjamin Herrera. *¡Aqui Chihuahua! Guna y Chispa de la Revolucion Mexicana*. (Chihuahua: no date).

Vázquez, Gabino. *The Agrarian Reform in Lower California*. (Mexico, 1937).

Von Schack, Alexander. *Experiences on the Mexican Border*. (Published by author, n.d.).

Villegas, Daniel Cosío. *The United States vs Porfirio Díaz*. (University of Nebraska: Lincoln, 1963).

Wagoner, Jay J. *Early Arizona: Prehistory to Civil War*. (University of Arizona: Tucson, 1975).

Walker, Henry P. & Don Bufkin. *Historical Atlas of Arizona*. (University of Oklahoma: Norman, 1979).

Wallace, Christopher M. *Water Out of the Desert*. (Texas Western Press: El Paso, 1969).

Wallace Ernest (ed.) *Ranald S. Mackenzie's Official Correspondence Relating to Texas, 1871-1873*. (West Texas Museum Assn: Lubbock, 1967).

_____. *The Howling of Coyotes: Reconstruction Efforts to Divide Texas*. (Texas A&M: College Station, 1979).

Washington, Thomas P. (publications chairman). *Selections from the Collected Papers of the Lower Rio Grande Valley Historical Society, 1949-1979*. (Lon C. Hill Memorial Library: Harlingen, 1983).

Waters, Frank. *The Colorado*. (Rinehart: New York, 1946).

Weatherford, Gary D. & F. Lee Brown (editors). *New Courses for the Colorado River: Major Issues for the Next Century*. University of New Mexico, Albuquerque, 1986).

Weaver, Thomas & Theodore Downing. *The Douglas Report: The Community Context of Housing and Social Problems*. (Bureau of Ethnic Research, University of Arizona: Tucson, 1975).

Webb, Walter Prescott. *The Texas Rangers: A Century of Frontier Defense*. (Houghton Mifflin: New York, 1935).

Weisman, Alan. *La Frontera: The United States Border With Mexico*. (Harcourt Brace Jovanovich: New York, 1986).

Westphall, Victor. *Thomas Benton Catron and His Era*. (University of Arizona: Tucson, 1973).

Wilkinson, J. B. *Laredo and the Rio Grande Frontier*. (Jenkins: Austin, 1975).

Woodard, Arthur. *Feud On the Colorado*. (Westernlore: Los Angeles, 1955).

Wooldridge, Ruby A. and Robert B. Vezzetti. *Brownsville: A Pictorial History*. (Donning: Norfolk, 1982).

Worcester, Donald E. *The Apaches: Eagles of the Southwest*, (University of Oklahoma: Norman, 1979).

Worster, Donald. *Rivers of Empire: Water, Aridity and the Growth of the American West*. (Pantheon: New York, 1985).

Yates, Richard & Mary Marshall. *The Lower Colorado River: A Bibliography*. (Arizona Western College Press: Yuma, 1974).

ARTICLES

(no author) "A Ringside Seat for Mexican Revolutions." *Literary Digest*, April 13, 1929.

(no author) "Barring Aliens to Aid Our Jobless." *Literary Digest*, CIX. April 25, 1931.

(no author) "Mexican Exodus." *Newsweek*, Vol. XIV, 45, July 31, 1939.

Aikman, Duncan. "$50,000 Cannon Balls." *H*, July 1929.

Alisky, Marvin. "United States-Mexico Border Conflicts and Compromises." *Southeastern Latin Americanist*, Sept. 1973.

Altshuler, Constance Wynn. "The Case of Sylvester Mowry." *A&W*, Vol. 15, No. 1-2 (Spring and Summer, 1973).

Anderson, Rodney D. "Mexican Workers and the Politics of Revolution." *HAHR*, Vol. 54, No. 1 (Feb. 1974).

Archbold, John C. "The Mexicali Valley Water Problem." *California Geographer*, 1966.

Armstrong, A. F. H. "The Case of Major Isaac Lynde." *NMHR*, Vol. XXXV1, No. 1 (Jan. 1961).

Back, William Douglas and Jeffery S. Taylor. "Navajo Water Rights: Pulling the Plug on the Colorado River." *NRJ*, Vol. 20, No. 1 (Jan. 1980).

Baerresen, Donald W. "Unemployment and Mexico's Border Industrial Program." *IAEA*, Vol. 29, No. 2, 1975.

Baldwin, P. M. "A Historical Note on the Boundaries of New Mexico." *NMHR*, Vol. V, No. 2 (April 1930).

Blaisdell, Lowell L. "Harry Chandler and Mexican Border Intrigue, 1914-1917." *Pacific Historical Quarterly*, ,XXXX, No. 4 (Nov. 1966).

Bowden, J. J. "The Texas-New Mexico Boundary Dispute Along the Rio Grande." *SHQ*, LXIII, No. 2 (Oct. 1959).

Brady, Francis P. "Portrait of a Pioneer: Peter R. Brady, 1825-1902." *JAH*, 16, No. 2 (Summer 1975).

Brawner, Marlyn R. "Migration and Educational Achievement of Mexican Americans." *Social Studies Quarterly*, 53 (March 1973).

Brayer, Herbert O. "The Cananea Incident." *NMHR*, 13, No. 3 (Oct. 1938).

Bridges, C. A. "The Knights of the Golden Circle: A Filibustering Fantasy." *SHQ*, XLIV, No. 3 (Jan. 1941).

Briggs, Vernon M., Jr. "Illegal Aliens: A Need for a More Restrictive Border Policy." *SHQ*, 56 (Dec. 1975).

_____, "Mexican Workers in the United States Labor Market." *International Labor Review* (Nov. 1975).

Brownell, Herbert and Samuel D. Eaton. "The Colorado River Salinity Problem with Mexico." *AJIL*, vol. 69. (April 1975)

Bryson, Conrey. "Biographical Sketch of Lawrence M. Lawson." *Password*, VII, No. 1 (Winter 1962).

Burman, Barbara G. and others. "Needed: A Ground Water Treaty Between the United States and Mexico." *NRJ*, (April 1975).

Bustamante, Jorge A. "The Historical Context of the Undocumented Immigration From Mexico to the United States." *Aztlan* (Fall 1972).

Carson, William G. B. (ed). "William Carr Lane Diary." *NMHR*, XXXIX, No. 3 (July 1964).

Casillas, Mike. "The Cananea Strike of 1906." *SES*, 3, No. 2 (Winter, 1977&1978).

Chamberlin, Eugene K. "Mexican Colonization versus American Interests in Lower California." *PHR*, XX, No. 1 (Feb. 1951).

Christiansen, Larry D. "Bullets Across the Border." *CQ*, 5, Nos. 1,2,3,4 (Winter 1975).

Clark, Ira G. "The Elephant Butte Controversy Over the Upper Waters of the Rio Grande." *Journal of American History*, LXI, No. 4 (March 1975).

Clark, Victor S. "Mexican Labor in the United States." *BBL*, Vol. 78 (Sept. 1908).

Clendenen, Clarence C. "General James Henry Carleton." *NMHR*, XXX, No. 1 (Jan. 1955).

_____, "Mexican Unionists: A Forgotten Incident in the War Between the States." *NMHR*, XXXIX, No. 1 (Jan. 1964).

Coatsworth, John. "Railroads, Landholding, and Agrarian Protest in the Early Porfiriato." *NAHR*, 54, No. 1 (Feb. 1974).

Crawford, Charlotte. "The Border Meeting of Presidents Taft and Díaz." *Password*, III, No. 3 (July 1958).

Crawford, Remsen. "The Menace of Mexican Immigration." *Current History*, XXXI, Feb. 1930.

Crook, Carland Elaine. "Benjamin Theron and French Designs in Texas During the Civil War." *SHQ*, LXVIII, No. 4 (April 1965).

Davidson, Edward H. "Labor in the Mexican Mines." *MSP*, 92, April 14, 1906.

Day, J. C. "International Management of the Rio Grande Basin: The United States and Mexico." *WRB*, 8, No. 5 (Oct. 1972).

_____. "Urban Water Management of an International River: The Case of El Paso-Juarez." *NRJ*, 15, No. 15 (July 1975).

Deeds, Susan M. "José María Maytorean and the Mexican Revolution in Sonora," part 1 & 2. *A&W*, 18, 1976.

Delaney, Robert W. "Matamoros: Port for Texas During the Civil War." *SHQ*, LVII, No. 4 (April 1955).

Deverell, William F. "To Loosen the Safety Valve: Eastern Workers and Western Lands," *WHQ*, XIX, No.3 (Aug. 1988).

Donnell, F. S. "When Texas Owned New Mexico to the Rio Grande." *NMHR*, VII, No. 2 (April 1933).

Elsing, Morris J. "Mining Methods Employed by Cananea, Mexico." *EMJ*, Vol. 64, Nov. 5, 1910.

Edgington, Clo. "The Death of Lt. Col. Craig Near Alamo Mucho, June 5, 1852." *The Wrangler*, San Diego Westerners Corral, Vol. 2, No. 4 (Sept. 1969).

Elwes, Hugh G. "Points About Mexican Labor." *EMJ*, Vol. 85, April 4, 1908.

Ericson, Anna-Stina. "The Impact of Commuters on the Mexican-American Border Area." *Monthly Labor Review* (Aug. 1970).

Faulk, Odie B. "A Colonization Plan for Northern Sonora, 1850." *NMHR*, XLIV, No. 4 (Oct. 1969).

_____. "Projected Mexican Military Colonies for the Borderlands, 1848." *Journal of Arizona History*, IX, No. 1 (Spring 1968).

Fields, Harold. "Where Shall the Alien Work." *Social Forces*, 12, No. 2 (Dec. 1933).

Finch, Boyd. "Sherod Hunter and the Confederates in Arizona." *JAH*, 10, No. 3 (Autumn 1969).

Fireman, Bert. "What Comprises Treason?" *Arizonian*, 1, No. 4 (Winter 1960).

Fornell, Earl W. "Texans and Filibusters in the 1850s." *SHQ*, LIX, No. 4 (April 1956).

_____, "Agitation in Texas for Reopening the Slave Trade." *SHQ*, LX, No. 2 (Oct. 1956).

_____, "The Abduction of Free Negros and Slaves in Texas." *SHQ*, LX, No. 3 (Jan. 1957).

Fox, Chris P. "The Dream: Elephant Butte Dam." *Password*, XXI, No. 1 (Spring 1976).

Fraser-Campbell, Evan. "The Management of Mexican Labor." *EMJ*, 85, April 4, 1908.

Frazier, Robert W. "Military Posts in San Diego." *JSDH*, XX, No. 3 (Summer 1974).

Ganoe, John T. The Origin of A National Reclamation Policy." *MVHR*, XVIII (June 1931)".

Gantz, David A. "United States Approaches to the Salinity Problem on the Colorado River." *NRJ*, 12, No. 4 (Oct. 1972).

García, Mario T. "Merchants and Dons: San Diego's Attempt at Modernization, 1850-1860." *JSDH*, XXI, No. 1 (Winter 1975).

Goldblatt, Kenneth A. "The Defeat of Major I. Lynde, U.S.A." *Password*, XI, No. 1 (Spring 1970).

_____ & Leon C. Metz. "The Baca-Gillet Incident." *TMH*, 6, No. 44 (Winter 1967).

Griswold del Castillo, Richard. "The Discredited Revolution: Magonista Capture of Tijuana in 1911." *JAH*, XXVI, No. 4 (Fall 1980).

Hall, Martin Harwick. "Colonel James Reily's Diplomatic Mission to Chihuahua and Sonora." *NMHR*, XXXI, No. 3 (July 1956).

Hardy, B. Carmen. "The Trek South: How the Mormons Went to Mexico." *SHQ*, LXXIII, No. 1 (July 1969).

Hendricks, William O. "Developing San Diego's Desert Empire." *JSDH*, XVII, No. 3 (Summer 1971).

Herrera Jordán, David & Joseph F. Friedkin. "The IBWC: United States and Mexico." *International Conference on Water for Peace* (paper). Washington: May 23-31, 1967.

Hill, James E., Jr. "El Horcón: A United States-Mexican Boundary Anomaly." *Rocky Mountain Social Science Journal.* 1967.

_____. "El Chamizal: A Century Old Boundary Dispute." *GR*, 55. No. 4 (Oct. 1955).

Hill, Raymond A. "Development of the Rio Grande Compact of 1938." *NRJ*, 14, No. 2 (April 1974).

Holmes, S. J. "Perils of the Mexican Invasion." *NAR*, 227, No. 5 (May 1929).

Hxu-Dehart, Evelyn. "Development and Rural Rebellion: Pacification of the Yaquis in the Late Porfiriato." *HAHR*, 54, No. 1 (Feb. 1974).

Kolbe, Rep. Jim. "Maquiladoras: A Foundation for U.S.-Mexico Relations." *Twin Plant News*, 3, No. 3 (Oct. 1987).

Hosmer, Helen. "Imperial Valley." *AW* III, No. 1 (Winter 1966).

Kajencki, Francis C., "Charles Radziminski and the United States-Mexican Boundary Survey," *NMHR*, 63, No. 3 (July 1988).

Lamar, Howard R. "Land Policy in the Spanish Southwest, 1846-1891." *JEH*, XXII, No. 4 (Dec. 1962).

Lesley, Lewis B. "The International Boundary Survey From San Diego to the Gila River, 1849-1850." *CHSQ*, IX, No. 1 (March 1930).

Luten, Daniel B. "The Use and Misuse of a River." *AW*, IV, No. 2 (May 1967).

Mahoney, Tom. "Into the Clouds for a Lost Cause, Being the Story of the American Aviators Who Flew for the Escobar Revolutionists in Mexico." *Air Travel News*, Dec. 1929.

Moore, J. Sam, Jr. & Cesar Sepulveda. "The United States and Mexico: Sources of Conflict." *SLJ*.

Morris, Leopold, "The Mexican Raid of 1875 on Corpus Christi." *Texas Historical Assn. Quarterly*, IV (Oct. 1900).

Naylor, Thomas H. "Massacre at San Pedro de la Cueva: The Significance of Pancho Villa's Disasterous Sonora Campaign." *WHQ*, 8, No 2 (April 1977).

Oppenheimer, Reuben. "The Deportation Terror." *New Republic*, LXIX, No. 893 (Jan. 13, 1932).

Orndorff, Helen. "A Brief History of the Origin of Elephant Butte Dam." *Password*, XII, No. 2 (Summer, 1967).

Pace, Anne. "Mexican Refugees in Arizona, 1910-1911." *A&W*, 16, No. 1 (Spring 1974).

Pedersen, Gilbert J. "A Yankee in Arizona." *JAH*, 16, No. 2 (Summer 1975).

Peterson, C. O. "Naco, Arizona: Accidental Place in History." *AW*, XX, No. 1 (Jan.-Feb. 1983).

Pletcher, David M. "The Development of Railroads in Sonora." *IAEA*, 1, No. 4 (March 1948).

Porter, Eugene O. (ed.). "Letters Home: W. W. Mills Writes to His Family." *Password*, XVII, No. 1-4 (Spring through Winter, 1972).

_____ ."The Great Flood of 1897." *Password*, XVIII, No. 3 (Fall 1973).

Porter, Kenneth W. "The Seminole in Mexico, 1850-1861." *HAHR*, XXXI, No. 1 (Feb. 1951).

_____ ."The Seminole-Negro Indian Scouts, 1870-1881." *SHQ*, LV, No. 3 (Jan. 1952).

Radzyminski, Charles F. "Charles F. Radzyminski: Patriot, Exile, Pioneer." *Chronicles of Oklahoma*, XXXVII, No. 4 (Winter 1960).

Rand, Patrick. "An Early Trip to Elephant Butte." *Password*, XX; No. 3 (Fall 1975).

Rathbun, Carl. "Keeping the Peace Along the Mexican Border." *HW*, 50 (Nov. 1906).

Reynolds, S. E. "The Water Quality Problem of the Colorado River." *NRJ*, 12, No. 4 (Oct. 1972).

Reynolds, S. E. and Philip B. Mutz. "Water Deliveries Under the Rio Grande Compact." *NRJ*, 14, No. 2 (April 1974).

Riley, Michael. "Dead Cats and Toxins." *Time*, 129, No. 16 (April 20, 1987).

Rippy, J. Fred. "A Ray of Light on the Gadsden Purchase." *SHQ*, XXIV, No. 3 (Jan. 1921).

_____ . "The Negotiations of the Gadsden Treaty." *SHQ*, XXVII, No. 1 (July 1923).

_____ . "Anglo American Filibusters and the Gadsden Treaty." *HAHR*, 2, No. 2 (Oct. 1922).

Roberts, Kenneth L. "Wet and Other Mexicans." *Saturday Evening Post*, 200, No. 32 (Feb. 4, 1928).

_____ . "Mexicans or Ruin." *Saturday Evening Post*, 200, No. 34, (Feb. 18, 1928).

Rodríguez, Richard. "Across the Borders of History: Tijuana and San Diego Exchange Futures." *H*, 274, No. 1642 (March 1987).

Rogers, Allen H. "Character and Habits of the Mexican Miner." *EMJ*, 85 (April 4, 1908).

Rolak, Bruno J. "General Miles' Mirrors." *JAH*, 16, No. 2 (Summer 1975).

Sacks, B. "Sylvester Mowry." *AW*, 1, No. 3 (Summer 1964).

Sánchez, Lynda A. "The Lost Apaches of the Sierra Madre." *AH*, 62, No. 9 (Sept. 1986).

Scruggs, Otey M. "The United States, Mexico, and the Wetbacks, 1942-1947." *PHR*, 30, No. 2 (May 1961).

_____ . "Texas and the Bracero Program, 1942-1947." *PHR*, 32, No. 3 (Aug. 1963).

Sepulveda, Cesar. "Mexican American International Water Quality Problems: Prospects and Perspectives." *NRJ*, 12, No. 4 (Oct. 1972).

Shearer, Ernest. "The Carvajal Disturbances." *SHQ*, LV, No. 2 (Oct. 1951).

_____ . "The Callahan Expedition, 1855." *SHQ*, LIV, No. 4 (April 1951).

Sheridan, David. "The Colorado: an engineering wonder without enough water." *Smithsonian*, 13, No. 1 (Feb. 1983).

Sibley, George. "The Desert Empire." *H*, 225, No. 1529 (Oct. 1977).

Sibley, Marilyn McAdams. "Charles Stillman: A Case Study of Entrepreneurship on the Rio Grande, 1861-1865." *SHQ*, LXXVII, No. 2 (Oct. 1973).

Skagen, Kit (ed.). "San Diego/Tijuana — The International Border in Community Relations: Gateway or Barrier." Proceedings of a Conference, Nov. 1976, in California. Council for the Humanities in Public Policy, San Diego. *Fronteras*, 1976.

Smith, Dean. "General Gadsden's Purchase." *AH*, 59, No. 4 (April 1983).

Sobarzo, Alejandro. "Salinity on the Colorado: An Interpretation of the Mexican-American Treaty of 1944," *NRJ*, 12, No. 4 (Oct. 1963).

Sonnichsen, C. L. "Major McMullen's Invasion of Mexico." *Password*, II, No. 2 (May 1957).

_____ . "The Remodeling of Geronimo." *AH*, 62, No. 9 (Sept. 1986).

Sperry, Robert L. "When the Imperial Valley Fought For Its Life." *JSDH*, XXI, No. 1 (Winter 1975).

Spillman, W. J. "Adjustment of the Texas Boundary in 1850." *Quarterly of the Texas St. Historical Assn.*), VII, No. 3 (Jan. 1904).

Stocker, Joseph "The Arizona Rangers." *AH*, 58, No. 8 (Aug. 1982).

Strickland, Rex. "W. W. Mills: El Paso Politician." *Password*, VII, No. 3 (Summer 1962).

Sweeney, Joseph U. "Judge Sweeney Watches A Revolution." (edited by Mildred Torak). *Password*, XVII, No. 2 (Summer 1972).

Temple, Truman. "The Colorado: America's Hardest Working River." *E. P. A. Journal*, 6, No. 4 (April 1980).

Trimble, Marshall. "The Gadsden Purchase Survey — From Los Nogales to Fort Yuma, Along El Camino del Diablo." *AH*, 59, No. 4 (April 1983).

Tyler, Ronnie C. "The Callahan Expedition of 1855: Indians or Negros?" *SHQ*, LXX, No. 4 (April 1967).

_____ . "Cotton on the Border, 1861-1865." *SHQ*, LXXIII, No. 4 (April 1970).

Vigness, David M. "Relations of the Republic of Texas and the Republic of the Rio Grande." *SHQ*, LVII, No. 3 (Jan. 1954).

deVries, Hugo (edited by Peter W. van der Pas). "The Imperial Valley in 1904." *JSDH*, XXII, No. 1 (Winter 1976).

Wagoner, Jay J. "Geronimo: Guerrilla Fighter." *AW*, 62, No. 9 (Sept 1986).

Waldrip, William I. "New Mexico During the Civil War." *NMHR*, XXVIII, No. 3 (July 1953).

Walker, Dale L. "Tracy Richardson: Machine Gun for Hire." *Kaleidoscope: El Paso Magazine*, 4, No. 3 (Dec. 1973).

Wallace, Edward S. "General John Lapham Bullis: Thunderbolt of the Texas Frontier." *SHQ*, LV, No. 1 (July 1951).

Wallace, Ernest and Adrian S. Anderson. "R. S. Mackenzie and the Kickapoos." *A&W*, 7, No. 2 (Summer 1956).

Watkins, T. H. "Conquest of the Colorado." *AW*, VI, No. 4 (July 1969)

Weber, David J. "From Hell Itself: The Americanization of Mexico's Northern Frontier, 1821-1846." *CQ*, 16, No. 2 (Summer 1986).

Webster, Michael G. "Intrigue on the Rio Grande: The Rio Bravo Affair, 1875." *SHQ*, LXXIV, No. 2 (Oct. 1970).

Werne, Joseph Richard. "Partisan Politics and the Mexican Boundary Survey, 1848-1853." *SHQ*, XC, No. 4 (April 1987).

_____. "Major Emory and Captain Jiménez: Running the Gadsden Line." *JS*, 29, No. 2 (Summer 1987).

Westphall, David. "The Battle of Glorieta Pass." *NMHR*, XLIV, No. 2 (April 1969).

de Wetter, Mardee. "Revolutionary El Paso: 1910-1917." *Password*, Vol. 3 & 4 (July and Sept. 1958).

White, William W. "The Texas Slave Insurrection of 1860." *SHQ*, 2, No. 3 (Jan. 1949).

Wollenberg, Charles. "Huelga, 1928 Style: The Imperial Valley Cantaloupe Workers' Strike." *PHR*, XXXVIII, No. 1 (Feb. 1969).

Wood, Captain C. D. "The Glen Springs Raid." *Sul Ross College Bulletin*, XLIII, No. 3 (Sept. 1963).

Woodbridge, Dwight E. "La Cananea Mining Camp." *EMJ*, LXXXII (Oct. 6, 1906).

Young, Carl. "Brief Sanctuary." *AW*, IV, No. 2 (May 1967).

INDEX

About the Author

LEON METZ was born and educated in Parkersburg, West Virginia, and has resided in El Paso, Texas, since 1952. He is past president of Western Writers of America and was honored by that organization in 1985 with the prestigious Saddleman Award for his overall contributions to interest in western writing. Besides being a prolific writer, he has worked in the West Texas oil fields and law enforcement, as a university archivist, an aide to a large city mayor and as public affairs officer for a bank. Author of nine books and numerous articles in magazines, newspapers and historical journals, Metz is now a popular, much sought-after lecturer on gunfighters, military lore and the borderlands.

Border: The U.S.-Mexico Line

ISBN 978-0-87565-364-8

$29.95

ISBN 978-0-87565-364-8

9 780875 653648

52995